An Introduction to the Philosophy of Language

This book is a critical introduction to the central issues of the philosophy of language. Each chapter focuses on one or two texts that have had a seminal influence on work in the subject, and uses these as a way of approaching both the central topics and the various traditions of dealing with them. Texts include classic writings by Frege, Russell, Kripke, Quine, Davidson, Austin, Grice, and Wittgenstein. Theoretical jargon is kept to a minimum and is fully explained whenever it is introduced. The range of topics covered includes sense and reference, definite descriptions, proper names, natural-kind terms, *de re* and *de dicto* necessity, propositional attitudes, truth-theoretical approaches to meaning, radical interpretation, indeterminacy of translation, speech acts, intentional theories of meaning, and scepticism about meaning. The book will be invaluable to students and to all readers who are interested in the nature of linguistic meaning.

MICHAEL MORRIS is Professor of Philosophy at the University of Sussex. He is author of *The Good and the True* (1992) and numerous articles.

An Introduction to the Philosophy of Language

MICHAEL MORRIS
University of Sussex

CAMBRIDGE UNIVERSITY PRESS
Cambridge, New York, Melbourne, Madrid, Cape Town, Singapore, São Paulo

Cambridge University Press
The Edinburgh Building, Cambridge CB2 2RU, UK

Published in the United States of America by Cambridge University Press, New York

www.cambridge.org
Information on this title: www.cambridge.org/9780521603119

First published 2007

Printed in the United Kingdom at the University Press, Cambridge

A catalogue record for this publication is available from the British Library

ISBN-13 978-0-521-84215-0 hardback
ISBN-13 978-0-521-60311-9 paperback

Contents

Acknowledgements

A number of people have read and commented on drafts of individual chapters of this book: Michael Ireland, Marie McGinn, Adrian Moore, Murali Ramachandran, David Smith. I am very grateful to them. I am also particularly grateful to an anonymous reader, who read the whole book in draft and produced a large number of detailed and helpful comments and suggestions. Finally, I would like to thank Hilary Gaskin, the philosophy editor at Cambridge University Press, for her supportive guidance through the various stages of writing the book.

Introduction

What is language? What is it for words to have meaning? What is the meaning of words? These are the basic questions of the philosophy of language. And here's a natural-seeming way of answering them. Language is a system of signs which we use to communicate with each other. Communication is a matter of letting other people know what we think. The signs which make up language get their meaning from our associating them with the thoughts we want to express. The meaning of words of common languages, such as English or French or Japanese, is a matter of a convention among speakers to use them with agreed associations.

Something very much in the spirit of that natural-seeming way of answering these basic questions was proposed by John Locke at the end of the seventeenth century. Recent philosophy of language is most simply understood by considering where it stands in relation to Locke's view. The most decisive shift came with the judgement – associated most obviously with John Stuart Mill and Gottlob Frege – that our words concern things in the world, rather than things in our minds. So complete has this transformation been that it is now accepted as simply obvious that one of the central things which has to be understood in the philosophy of language is how language relates to the world. That major change apart, however, there are significant points of overlap between Locke's view and the standard assumptions of contemporary philosophers of language. It continues to be assumed that words are signs, and that the basic business of language is communication. And it is generally accepted – even if it is sometimes questioned – that the meaning of words in common languages is a matter of convention.

The task of this book is to expose the issues here to serious scrutiny. This is done by considering carefully the arguments of the best minds to have dealt with them. Each chapter takes as its focus one or two articles, or a few chapters of a book, and uses these texts to provide a critical introduction to the issues. I hope that the individual chapters will enable readers to understand the texts (which are sometimes quite difficult), and to raise serious questions about them. The accuracy of my presentation of the issues of the texts, and the fairness of my criticisms, can be checked against the texts themselves. This should encourage an understanding of the issues which is deeper because of being reached through a double perspective – the texts themselves, and the chapters of this book.

The book begins with an examination of the short passage in Locke where his famous view is presented. I present a fairly orthodox interpretation of Locke's view, and try to draw out what is significant about it. After that the book jumps historically, to the work of Frege at the end of the nineteenth century. The rest of the book examines works which are, by common consent, among the jewels of the analytic tradition of philosophy.

Chapters 2 to 9 deal with the ramifications of the judgement that our words are associated with things in the world, rather than things in our minds. This seems to suggest that if two linguistic expressions are linked to the same item in the world, they have the same meaning, and if an expression is linked to no item in the world it has no meaning. There are contexts which make this hard to swallow, most notably those in which we use words in a 'that'-clause to say what someone thinks or feels. We might call this the *Basic Worry* for views which follow Mill and Frege in linking words to the world. In response to this worry, Frege suggested that there is a *cognitive* aspect of meaning, which he called *Sense*: this suggestion is the topic of chapter 2. Bertrand Russell did not acknowledge the existence of such a thing as Fregean Sense: chapter 3 deals with his attempt to deal with the same problems by means of a different sort of analysis of a certain basic kind of expression, so-called *definite descriptions* (mostly singular noun phrases beginning with the definite article).

Russell's account only succeeds in dealing with the Basic Worry by treating a wide variety of terms as equivalent in meaning to descriptive phrases. Saul Kripke argued that this kind of account fails to deal adequately with proper names, and he and Hilary Putnam applied similar reasoning to the case of natural-kind terms. These are the topics of chapters 4 and 5, respectively. One particularly striking argument they offer is that views like Russell's belong with, and force us into, an unacceptable conception of necessity. Among other things, then, their arguments aim to make us revise our view of what can be necessary and what contingent.

The leading advocate of the view of necessity which Kripke and Putnam were keen to overturn was Willard Van Orman Quine. His position on this topic is dealt with in chapter 6. Contexts of necessity have a lot in common with contexts in which we say what people think and feel: we use a 'that'-clause to say what is necessary, and it seems, on the face of it, that these clauses exploit something more in the meaning of linguistic expressions than just which items in the world they're correlated with. Unsurprisingly, then, there's a close parallel between Quine's treatment of contexts of necessity and his treatment of contexts in which we say what people think and feel, which is the topic of chapter 7. Chapter 8 generalizes the problem of trying to explain what words are doing when we use them to describe people's thoughts and feelings, focusing on famous articles by Kripke and Donald Davidson. Chapter 9 deals with Davidson's approach to an even more general problem: how to explain what words are doing whenever they occur. The most obvious difficulty for his proposal is a version of the Basic Worry which Frege introduced his notion of Sense to solve.

Chapters 2 to 9 are concerned with the question what kind of meaning linguistic expressions have. From chapter 10 we're concerned with the question what kind of thing, in general, linguistic meaning is. Chapter 10 introduces the idea, advocated by Quine and Davidson, that linguistic meaning is something which is always, in principle, open to being learned by someone who approaches a language as an outsider, and constructs a kind of scientific theory of what speakers of the language are up to. This can be seen as an elaboration of the Lockean – and everyday – assumption that words are signs. Quine takes this to have the consequence that beyond certain clear limits, there is no fact of the matter about what words mean: two theoretical accounts of the meaning of a language might differ in their interpretation of the words of that language, and yet both be correct, in the only sense in which interpretation can be correct. This view is examined in chapter 11.

If chapters 10 and 11 consider the idea of languages as objects of scientific interpretation, chapters 12 and 13 are concerned with trying to understand more deeply the place of language in our lives. Chapter 12 considers J. L. Austin's theory of speech acts, according to which the basic thing which needs to be understood about any linguistic item is what a speaker is doing in uttering it. Chapter 13 deals with what seems to be an even more basic issue: what is it for a linguistic expression to mean anything at all? H. P. Grice attempted to explain the meaning of linguistic expressions in terms of what speakers mean by them; and he tried to explain what speakers mean by the expressions they use in terms of what they are trying to communicate.

The nature of linguistic meaning is put radically in question by a sceptical challenge which Saul Kripke thought he found in the later work of Ludwig Wittgenstein. What is it about me which establishes that I mean one thing rather than another when I use a particular expression? If we can't find anything, then it's hard to see how I can mean anything at all. Chapter 14 is concerned with this problem, and with various proposed solutions to it.

Chapter 15 deals with a short extract from the work of Wittgenstein's which led Kripke to consider that problem. Wittgenstein remains an awkward figure in the analytic tradition: the ultimate inspiration for much of its best work, but also rejected by many who work in the analytic mainstream. His work is difficult to interpret, but it seems cowardly to ignore it. Chapter 15 presents two different kinds of interpretation of this work, neither of which is likely to be entirely acceptable to any Wittgensteinian, but both of which capture something of the text. These two interpretations present Wittgenstein as an opponent of the analytic mainstream, in order to allow questions to be raised about some of the tradition's deepest assumptions.

The philosophy of language – and its treatment by the analytic tradition, in particular – has a formidable reputation for difficulty. The aim of this book is to make the issues and texts at the heart of analytic philosophy of language accessible even to those with a minimal philosophical background. (I have included a glossary to help here.) I also hope to have said something of interest to scholars in the field (and even the glossary is not entirely uncontroversial).

1   Locke and the nature of language

Key text

John Locke, *An Essay Concerning Human Understanding*, book III, chs. 1 and 2.

1.1   Introduction

This book is an introduction to philosophy of language in the analytic tradition. Analytic philosophy begins with Gottlob Frege, who wrote at the end of the nineteenth and the beginning of the twentieth centuries. So why begin this book with John Locke, whose principal work was written at the end of the seventeenth century? Briefly: because Locke presents in a clear and simple way the background to <u>analytic</u> philosophy of language.

[handwritten note: breaking up anything complex into simple elements.]

    In the first place, Locke's general theory of language initially strikes many of us as extremely natural. His views about what words are and what language is for are shared with almost the whole analytic tradition. But he is also a clear representative of a line of thinking about language which has been the main target of much of the analytic tradition. Frege's philosophy of language can be said to begin with a rejection of what seem to be central features of Locke's view. And much recent work on proper names and natural-kind terms (the topics of chapters 4 and 5) is defined by its opposition to a broadly Lockean kind of view.

[handwritten note: highly original & influential. Central to the understanding of a topic.]

1.2   What Locke says

One of the four books of John Locke's vast and seminal work, *An Essay concerning Human Understanding*, is dedicated to language. The core of his conception of language is laid out in one paragraph; here it is:

> Man, though he have great variety of thoughts, and such, from which
> others, as well as himself, might receive profit and delight; yet they are all
> within his own breast, invisible, and hidden from others, nor can of
> themselves be made appear. The comfort and advantage of society not being
> to be had without communication of thoughts, it was necessary, that man
> should find out some external sensible signs, whereby those invisible *ideas*,
> which his thoughts are made up of, might be made known to others. For
> this purpose, nothing was so fit, either for plenty or quickness, as those
> articulate sounds, which with so much ease and variety he found himself
> able to make. Thus we may conceive how *words*, which were by nature so
> well adapted to that purpose, come to be made use of by men, as *the signs of*
> their *ideas*; not by any natural connexion, that there is between particular
> articulate sounds and certain *ideas*, for then there would be but one
> language amongst all men; but by a voluntary imposition, whereby such a
> word is made arbitrarily the mark of such an *idea*. The use then of words, is
> to be sensible marks of *ideas*; and the *ideas* they stand for, are their proper
> and immediate signification.[1]

This general conception of language is not original to Locke: much of it
can be found in Hobbes, and elements of it can be traced back to Aristotle.[2]
Some such conception remained dominant in western philosophy for two
centuries after Locke wrote, and significant parts of it continue to be
accepted now. Much of it may indeed seem to you to be so obvious that it
hardly needs a great philosopher to state it. Locke's achievement is to state
it so succinctly that some of the problems it faces become immediately
evident.

What exactly does Locke commit himself to in this short passage? First,
he thinks of language as some kind of artefact, whose nature is therefore
defined by the job it does – that is, by its function. Let's isolate that, to
begin with, as a significant assumption:

(L1) The nature of language is defined by its function.

---

[1] J. Locke, *An Essay concerning Human Understanding*, ed. P. Nidditch (Oxford: Oxford
  University Press, 1975), III, ii, 1; I have retained Locke's punctuation and italicization,
  but have not followed his practice of capitalizing almost all nouns.

[2] T. Hobbes, *Leviathan*, ed. J. Plamenatz (Glasgow: Collins, 1962), part 1, ch. 4; Aristotle, *De
  Interpretatione*, ch. 1.

Locke is clear in this passage about what that function is:

(L2) The function of language is to communicate.

(But he does allow elsewhere that language can be used 'for the recording of our own thoughts'.)[3]

He is equally clear (in this passage, at least) about what is communicated in language:

(L3) What language is meant to communicate is *thought*.

Without communication of thought there can be no society, and without society human beings miss out on significant 'comfort and advantage'; according to another writer, their life without society is 'solitary, poor, nasty, brutish, and short'.[4] The ultimate good furnished by language is the security and prosperity provided by society; and language promotes that by making communication possible.

This functional conception of language seems to be used by Locke to give a general account of what words mean. The basic idea seems to be that if language communicates thought, then words, being the components of language, must communicate the components of thought. We might put the fundamental assumption here like this:

(L4) Words signify or mean the components of what language is meant to communicate.

(L4), however, is a bit of a fudge. Locke certainly thinks that words are *signs of*, and therefore *signify*, the components of thought; and he occasionally uses the notion of *meaning* instead;[5] but it is not quite obvious that his notion of *signification* is the same as we might ordinarily think was involved in the notion of *meaning*. Having raised that question, I'll leave it aside for now and return to it in the next section.

It is certainly clear enough that Locke thinks that words are signs of the components of thought. What are the components of thought? Here is Locke's answer:

(L5) The components of thought are *Ideas*.

---

[3] Locke, *Essay*, III, ix, 1.   [4] T. Hobbes, *Leviathan*, p. 143.
[5] For example, at *Essay*, III, iv, 6: 'the meaning of words, being only the *ideas* they are made to stand for by him that uses them'.

The word 'Idea', as it is used here, is a technical term, and Locke registers the fact that it's a technical term by scrupulously italicizing it whenever he uses it. I'll register the same fact by capitalizing the word. Because it's a technical term, it is hard to be sure what it means without going deep into Locke's philosophy, and this is not the place to do that. What do we think thoughts are composed of? This may not strike us as an obvious or natural question: ideas, perhaps we might say (using the word in an everyday sense), or concepts – though we are unlikely to be clear what ideas or concepts are. Casually speaking, we can think of Locke's *Ideas* as like ideas, in the modern sense, or concepts – whatever, precisely, those are – but we probably get closer to Locke if we think of a Lockean Idea as a kind of mental image.[6] Whatever their nature, Locke was clear about one thing: Ideas are 'invisible and hidden from others'; that is to say:

(L6) One person's Ideas cannot be perceived by another.

In addition to all of these assumptions, Locke endorses what seems no more than common sense when he insists that there is no natural connection between sounds and Ideas: the relation between words and Ideas is arbitrary, he says. We can separate two distinct assumptions here. The first is this:

(L7) The relation between words and what they signify or mean is arbitrary.

The second is involved in the fact that Locke seems clearly to think of words as just sounds. In particular, they are sounds which people find themselves able to make. What this suggests is that words are not *intrinsically* meaningful: they only come to be meaningful by being set up as 'sensible marks of *ideas*'. Let's record this final assumption, then:

(L8) Words are not intrinsically meaningful.

These are eight significant assumptions involved in that short paragraph of Locke's. Now we need to understand what would be involved in questioning them.

Margin note: to be decided by ones liking, opinion or prejudice → uncertain / varying.

---

[6] For the view that Locke's Ideas are images, see M. Ayers, *Locke: Epistemology and Ontology* (London: Routledge, 1991), ch. 5.

1.3 Meaning and signification

On a quick reading of Locke, it's natural to think that his view is simply that words mean Ideas. Defenders of Locke, however, have claimed that this is unfair. In the first place, it's not clear that 'signify' means the same as 'mean'. And in any case, what Locke says is just that the Ideas they stand for are the 'proper and immediate' signification of words.[7]

Let's take that second point first. According to Locke's general theory, Ideas are representations of other things. So my Idea of gold represents the metal, gold; perhaps it is an *image* of the metal. If the word 'gold', as I use it, is in the first instance a sign of my Idea of gold, then it seems that it must be possible in principle for the word to be a sign in some way – indirectly or 'mediately' – of the metal. If we ignore for the moment the worry about whether 'signify' is equivalent to 'mean', it seems that there has to be some sense in which the word 'gold' *means* the metal, gold, on Locke's view. We might say that a word *first* – directly or immediately – means an Idea in the mind of its user, and *secondly* – indirectly or mediately – means the thing which that Idea represents.[8]

The same point could be made about any theory which supposes that words are signs, in the first instance, of things like concepts (even if we're not quite sure what concepts are). For a concept is always a concept *of* something: the concept of gold is the concept *of* gold. It doesn't matter whether we think (rather as Locke seems to have done) that concepts are *representations* of the things they are concepts of (as if they were pictures of them); they have to be concepts of something to be concepts at all. If we think that a word is in the first instance a sign of a concept, this means that we can always say that it is *also* some kind of sign of whatever it is that the concept is a concept *of*.

Is it fair to attribute to Locke the view that words *mean* Ideas? We might think that this is so unnatural a view that we should hesitate in ascribing it to Locke: surely the word 'gold' means *gold*, the metal, and not any Idea or concept of it? Speaking for ourselves, we may say that the word 'gold' *means* the metal, but, as we use it, *expresses* our concept of the metal. And it might be tempting to attribute such a view to Locke too. The notion of

---

[7] *Essay*, III, ii, 1.

[8] This point is made by N. Kretzmann, 'The Main Thesis of Locke's Semantic Theory', *Philosophical Review*, 77 (1968), pp. 175–96.

signification, we may say, is loose enough to allow that the word 'gold' in some way *signifies* – for example, by *expressing* – a concept or Idea of gold. But it doesn't follow from that the word 'gold' *means* the concept or Idea.[9]

My own view is that it's hard to deny that Locke thought that words *mean* Ideas – at least in the first instance. This is because he doesn't just say that words signify Ideas: he says that words are *meant* to signify Ideas – that's what words are for. If the nature of language is to be understood by its function, and a word is *meant* to signify something, it's hard to see how that thing could not be what the word means. But even if you disagree about this, it seems clear enough that Locke is committed to the view that it is *part* of the meaning of words that they signify Ideas, and that is enough to raise some of the most obvious objections to his theory.

1.4 Problems about communication

The most obvious difficulty with Locke's conception of language is that it makes it impossible for language to do what it thinks that language is supposed to do: it makes communication impossible. To see this, we need to think about what genuine communication between two people requires. It's not enough for one person to transfer something (a thought, say) to another, as if the second were catching a disease from the first. Genuine communication involves one person *understanding* another, and this requires that she should *know* what the other person means. This is just what is impossible, on Locke's picture.[10]

On Locke's account, knowing what someone means when she speaks is (at least in part) a matter of knowing which Ideas are signified by her words. Words themselves are not intrinsically meaningful, according to (L8): they're just sounds, which might mean anything or nothing. So the only way we can know which Ideas they signify is by knowing something

---

[9] Defences of Locke, on broadly these lines, are proposed by I. Hacking, *Why Does Language Matter to Philosophy?* (Cambridge: Cambridge University Press, 1975), ch. 5, E. J. Ashworth, 'Locke on Language', *Canadian Journal of Philosophy*, 14 (1984), pp. 45–73, and E. J. Lowe, *Locke on Human Understanding* (London: Routledge, 1995), ch. 7.

[10] The argument which follows is a version of one of the simpler strands of argument which make up what is known as Wittgenstein's 'Private Language Argument': for a vivid excerpt see, e.g., L. Wittgenstein, *Philosophical Investigations*, 3rd edn (Oxford: Blackwell, 2001), § 293.

about the relation between these sounds and a person's Ideas. But the Ideas themselves cannot be perceived by another person, according to (L6). So we could only know which Ideas were signified by a person's words if there were some dependable, reliable relation between particular words and particular Ideas: that would give us the right to make an inference from the presence of a particular word to the presence in a person's mind of a particular Idea. But the relation between words and what they signify or mean is arbitrary, according to (L7). That means that we have no right to make any assumptions about the Ideas signified by particular words. That means that we can never know what someone means when she speaks, on Locke's account of the meaning of words. And that means that genuine communication is impossible.

↓ Argument

Some people might be tempted to accept this conclusion: perhaps communication really is impossible. You may think it's just true that no one else can really know what you mean by your words. But this doesn't look like a very stable position to hold. In the first place, it cannot sensibly be accepted by a Lockean, or anyone else who thinks that the nature of language is defined by its function ((L1)) and that the function of language is to communicate ((L2)). Think for a moment about the reasons for holding that the nature of language is defined by its function. The idea here is to try to explain what language is by seeing what job it does. If you think the job is communication, and you think that communication is impossible, you're trying to explain what language is in terms of the job you think it does, even though you accept that it doesn't actually do that job at all. If you think that communication is impossible, it seems silly to try to explain the nature of language in terms of the function of communicating in the first place.

↓ counter!

And in fact it's hard to see how you could really believe that nobody else knows the meaning of the words you use. Ask yourself: why do you use the particular words you do use, rather than some others? You'll be bound to answer: because of the meaning of these words, which is appropriate for what you want to say, whereas the meaning of those other words is not. And how do you know the meaning of these words? Because you learned them from your parents and other people who speak the language. And, of course, that shows that you're already assuming that it's possible for one person to know the meaning of the words another person uses: you have come to know the meaning of the words used by other people who speak the same language.

Perhaps you think that there is still something about the meaning of the words you use which no one else *can* know. Perhaps no one else can know the particular associations which the words you use have for you. But it's not obvious that no one else *can* know the particular associations which the words you use have for you: why can't you just tell other people? It's certainly true that other people do not in fact know all the particular associations which words have for you, but this seems just to show that these associations have got nothing to do with meaning. After all, you seem to assume that other people do know what the words you use mean, even though they don't know all the associations these words have for you.

This seems to show something quite significant: the psychological associations which a word might have for particular people are irrelevant to the meaning of the word. Whatever meaning is, it can't be just a matter of what people happen to think of when they hear or read or use a word. We might put the same point in another way by saying that meaning is connected with understanding. Meaning is what you know when you understand a word; and understanding a word does not involve knowing the psychological associations which a word might have.

What is clear is that Locke's theory as a whole, which accepts all of the assumptions (L1)–(L8), needs revision. The slightest revision might be to change this:

(L6) One person's Ideas cannot be perceived by another.

But if we think of Ideas as being a kind of mental image, revising (L6) will not be an attractive option, because it will not seem very plausible that one person could perceive another's mental images.

The next slightest revision would be to change this:

(L5) The components of thought are Ideas.

What else might they be? You might take refuge in the word 'concept' – whatever exactly that means – and suggest *this* instead of (L5):

(L5*) The components of thought are *concepts*.

The reason for suggesting this change is that it might seem – on an everyday understanding of the word 'concept' – that you could tell from someone's behaviour what concepts she has. After all, you might think that you can tell that a dog has the concept of her master or mistress, the concept of dinner time, and the concept of a walk; and you can tell that a dog does not have the concept of impressionism as a painting style or the concept of the square root of three. One major tradition in recent philosophy of language can be seen as differing from Locke's theory in accepting something (L5*) instead of (L5): the great German philosopher and mathematician, Gottlob Frege, can be understood as belonging to this tradition, though in a slightly complicated way (see chapter 2).

You would get a more radical alternative to Locke's theory if you questioned *this* assumption:

③

Big change!

(L3) What language is meant to communicate is *thought*.

(L3) – at least as it is understood within the context of a Lockean theory – arises from a peculiarity of Locke's general conception of communication. Locke's conception of communication (like Hobbes's, from which it, in part, derives) is fundamentally *individualist*. Each person is thought of as an autonomous individual, whose basic relationships with the world and with other people are independent of society and social institutions. The individual person has to understand the world and other people for herself, and make sense of them all in her own terms. Other people figure in this picture, not in the first instance as other members of a society to which each person originally belongs, but as potential rivals for a common resource, as potential aids in projects which might lead to mutual benefit, and as potential objects of affection and concern. If each person starts off as an autonomous individual among other autonomous individuals, the fundamental goal of communication is clear: each individual needs to find out what the other individuals are thinking. Only in this way can we anticipate the actions of our rivals, plan with our colleagues, and understand how things are with the people we feel for. Speaking a language will then be part of a general process of giving up our independence, by revealing our thoughts, in the hope of the larger or safer benefits of co-operation.

But this isn't the only possible conception of communication. We might instead have a fundamentally *collaborative* view. On such a view, the basic purpose of communication will not be to find out what other people are thinking, but to inform one another of how things are in the world. If we take this collaborative view, then we may propose *this* as an alternative to (L3):

(L3*) What language is meant to communicate are *facts*.

If (L3*) is meant to be a genuine alternative to (L3), it will change the orientation of language radically. Whereas on Locke's conception language is concerned first with what is in people's minds, on this alternative view language is fundamentally concerned with things in the world. How might this view be developed? Suppose we still accept the following assumption:

(L4) Words signify or mean the components of what language is meant to communicate.

What might the components of facts be? Perhaps they will include *objects*, such as tables and chairs; we could count people as objects for this purpose too. Perhaps they will include *qualities* or *properties*, like whiteness or waspishness. If we accept that suggestion, we will propose this instead of (L5):

(L5**) The components of facts are *objects* and *properties*.

If we accept this world-oriented conception of language, then the meaning – even in the first instance – of a name, like 'Socrates', will just be a particular person, Socrates the philosopher himself, instead of an image of that person (as it would have been on the Lockean view) or a concept of that person (as it would have been on an individualist view which accepts (L3) and (L5*)). And the meaning – even in the first instance – of an adjective, like 'waspish', will be a particular quality, waspishness, instead of an image of waspishness (as it would have been on the Lockean view) or the concept of waspishness (as it would have been on an individualist view which accepts (L3) and (L5*)). This world-oriented view of language is also represented in a major tradition in recent philosophy of language: Bertrand Russell was one of its pioneers (see chapter 3).

1.5 Words and sentences

We should look again at an assumption we've just rushed past:

(L4) Words signify or mean the components of what language is meant to communicate.

The idea behind this was that words are the basic components of language, so the meanings of words must be the basic components of what is meant by language. But what does it mean to say that words are the basic components of language? And what could it be for something to be a basic component of what is meant by language?

It's tempting to think that the sense (whatever it is) in which words are components of language is the same as the sense (whatever it is) in which words are components of sentences. Sentences are made up of words, and whatever is spoken or written is constructed in sentences – or at least is meant to be constructed in sentences. But why should we think that words are the *basic* components of sentences? What about letters (if the sentences are written) or sounds (if they are spoken)?

The answer is that words are thought to be the basic components of sentences as far as *meaning* is concerned. The meaning of sentences depends systematically on the meaning of the words of which they are composed; but the meaning of words does not depend systematically on the meaning of the parts of words. There's no systematic dependence of the meaning of words on the letters which are used in writing them, or on the sounds which are used in speaking them. The idea here is that words are, so to speak, *atomic* in an account of meaning. An atom, etymologically speaking, is something which cannot be divided. If we think of breaking down the meaning of a bit of text by looking at the meaning of the sentences of which it's composed, and then of breaking down the meaning of sentences by looking at the meaning of their parts, we have to stop at the level of words: the idea is that words are meaningful, but parts of words are not.

This assumption could be doubted in one of two obvious ways. First, you might think that there are compound words (like 'ice-pack' or 'ice-pick'), or words with standard prefixes (like 'un-' in 'unhappy', 'pre-' in 'premarital', or 'sub' in 'subnormal') or suffixes (like '-ness' in 'idleness', or '-ly' in 'stupidly'), whose meaning does depend systematically on the meaning of their component parts. One simple solution to this kind of problem might be to change our conception of what counts as a single word: so we might say that 'ice-pack' is two words, and prefixes and suffixes are words themselves.

The other way of doubting the assumption that words are atomic as far as meaning is concerned is to question whether the letters and sounds from which a word is made really are irrelevant to its meaning. This is to doubt whether words are arbitrary signs: if words are arbitrary signs, then, whatever word you think of, a quite different word (one spelled or pronounced quite differently) could have had the same meaning; and that makes it look as if the meaning itself doesn't depend at all on the letters and sounds from which a word is made. I'll come back to this issue briefly in section 1.6.

So much for the way in which words might be thought to be the *basic* components of sentences, taking for granted that in some sense words are components of sentences. But in what sense are words *components* of sentences at all? How are words put together to make sentences? In the first place, it's crucial to notice that sentences are not just lists of words. Compare a sentence with a list:

(i)   Socrates is waspish;
(i*) Socrates, being, waspishness.

The basic difference between the sentence (i) and the list (i*) is that (i) is complete in a way that (i*) is not. We could have stopped (i*) after 'being' and we would still have had a list; we could have added any word after 'waspishness' and we would still have had a list. But if we had stopped (i) anywhere earlier than its end, we would not have had something which would ordinarily be counted as a whole sentence. (Only in a pretentious mood can we hear 'Socrates is' as a sentence – unless it's an abbreviated answer to a question, such as 'Who's the one talking to Protagoras?') And we cannot add just any word after 'waspish' and still have a sentence. This feature which sentences have and mere lists do not is sometimes called the *unity of the proposition*: in one of its senses 'proposition' means *sentence*.[11]

The unity of the sentence turns out to be very hard to explain, or even acknowledge, unless you think of words as already being suited for particular roles in sentences – that is, unless you think of words as already having built into them, as it were, a grammar which dictates how they can combine to form sentences. If, for example, you think of all words as being names, grammatically speaking, it's hard to see how you can avoid treating a sentence as just a list.

---

[11] For a consideration of the treatment of the problem in the early analytic tradition, see M. Gibson, *From Naming to Saying: The Unity of the Proposition* (Oxford: Blackwell, 2004).

The use of the word "need" n "wants" (handwritten)

Locke seems bound to find it difficult to explain the unity of the sentence, because he seems to treat words as names of Ideas. In fact, though, he makes an exception for some words – precisely to deal with this problem. This is what he says:

> The mind, in communicating its thought to others, does not only need signs of the *ideas* it has then before it, but others also, to shew or intimate some particular action of its own, at that time, relating to those *ideas*. This it does several ways; as, *Is*, and *Is not*, are the general marks of the mind, affirming or denying. [12]

The "Is" and the "is not" AFFIRM OR Deny (handwritten margin)

The suggestion seems to be this. If I say, 'Socrates is waspish', then I am *affirming* waspishness *of* Socrates; if I say, 'Socrates is not waspish', then I am *denying* waspishness *of* Socrates. What happens, according to Locke, is that the various Ideas are joined together in an action of the mind. The unity of the sentence, then, is created by the mind.

Does this really solve the problem? I think the problem is just transferred. A unity is created by an action of the mind – of affirming or denying, for example – but the nature of the unity which is created is left mysterious. What exactly does the mind do in affirming waspishness of Socrates? How does this create a unity? At best it seems that the unity of the proposition is explained in terms of the [unity of something in the mind] – a *judgement* or a *thought*, perhaps. But it is left mysterious in what sense a judgement or a thought is a unity, and not just a collection of Ideas.

unity of something in the mind (handwritten margin)

The Proposition (handwritten margin)

What we have here is an indication of the real difficulty of understanding the sense in which words are *components* of sentences. [13] This difficulty is just as significant for a world-oriented kind of theory as it is for a mind-oriented theory like Locke's. On a theory like Locke's the unity of sentences is explained in terms of an apparently more basic unity of something mental – judgements or thoughts. On a world-oriented theory it is likely to be explained in terms of an apparently more basic unity of something out there in the world – *facts*, for example. But in both cases the nature of the apparently more basic unity is left mysterious.

---

[12] *An Essay concerning Human Understanding*, III, viii, 1.
[13] We will return to this difficulty in chs. 2 and 9.

why do you have a monopoly on whore and when like Bostion who gave you such insight. (handwritten note)

1.6 Locke's less disputed assumptions

I've concentrated here on the assumptions Locke makes which have been at the centre of debate in recent philosophy of language. But we should not forget the other assumptions which form part of Locke's picture, even if they are generally shared by modern philosophers.

Locke's whole account is built on these two basic assumptions:

(L1) The nature of language is defined by its function;
(L2) The function of language is to communicate.

It's worth pausing a moment to consider whether we should accept them. (L1) and (L2) both assume that language has a single function. Is that obvious? Aren't there many things which we can do with language? It is not immediately clear that any one of these is basic.[14]

Perhaps, though, it might seem obvious that all the different things which we can do with language depend at least on the possibility of using language to communicate. This may be true, but it is not so clear that this is enough to make communication the basic *point* of language. If we think that the function of language is to communicate, we will focus on the role of language in certain everyday dealings. We use language to warn people of danger, to inform them of various things, to ask for information, to get them to do things for us, and so on. In this way, language is part of the business of everyday living. But there are other uses of language which are not – or, at least, are not *obviously* – concerned with communication in the same way. The clearest cases are provided by literature. It's not at all obvious that it is the business of a poem, a play, or a novel to *communicate* something – at least, if communication is the kind of thing which is important in ordinary workaday dealings. It is mostly rather odd to think of a poem or a novel as something like a contribution to a conversation. It seems generally to be part of the point of a work of literature that it should transcend its immediate context, and have a meaning which is not just a matter of its contribution to a particular historical situation.

---

[14] This kind of point is emphasized by Ludwig Wittgenstein, e.g. in his *Philosophical Investigations*. See ch. 15 below.

The other Lockean assumptions which are commonly accepted are these two:

(L7) The relation between words and what they signify or mean is arbitrary;
(L8) Words are not intrinsically meaningful.

(L7) is the claim that is familiarly known as the thesis that words are arbitrary signs. Its basic point can be expressed like this: whatever one word means could have been meant by a different word; so it's arbitrary that we use this word – rather than that other one – to mean it. What would make that other word different from the one we started with? Presumably, the way it is pronounced and spelled. So it seems that (L7) requires us to say that anything which depends on the pronunciation and spelling of a word is irrelevant to its meaning. To see what might be controversial about this, consider again the use of words in a poem. It seems that all kinds of things about a word are relevant to what we might intuitively call the meaning of a poem: the sound of its vowels and consonants, its rhythm, its etymology, its spelling. These are just the features which someone who accepts (L7) will count as *irrelevant* to meaning.

Why should anyone think they are irrelevant? I suspect that this view depends, in the end, on some assumptions like (L1) and (L2). If we think that the function of language is to communicate, we may think that all these features which depend on pronunciation and spelling make no difference to *what* is communicated – only to the *way* in which it is communicated. So we might think they can safely be ignored in an account of meaning. If this diagnosis is correct, then we ought to worry about (L7) if we start to question (L1) and (L2).

Finally, we should note that (L8) goes beyond what is required for (L7). (L8) is commonly expressed by saying that words are just types of sound or mark, which are meaningless in themselves, but are given meaning by their role in something we do with them. This is a very natural assumption – and, indeed, it is shared by many philosophers in the analytic tradition – but it is hard to see why it should seem so compelling. The fact that we can speak and write words does not mean that they are nothing but sounds or marks. It looks as if Locke is motivated by a general philosophical theory of the kinds of things there are in the world. If we begin with a very general conception of the things we might expect to encounter – in science, for example – and ask which of *these* are words, then it does seem natural to think that words are just types of sound or mark.

In fact, if we try to respect our ordinary, pre-theoretical conception of the nature of words, it becomes very difficult to say what they are. To begin with, it seems that the same word could be pronounced differently (by people who speak the same language in different places, for example), or spelled differently (by people who speak the same language at different times, for example): so it's hard to see how we can define what counts as the same word just in terms of sound and shape. This makes the Lockean conception of words rather unnatural. But it's not clear that it will help just to include the *meaning* of words as part of their identity: after all, we usually think that the same word can *change* its meaning over time. ('Nice' originally meant *ignorant* or *foolish*, for example – it comes from the Latin 'nescius'.) The issue of what words are has largely been ignored in the philosophy of language.

The four assumptions we've just been considering – (L1), (L2), (L7), and (L8) – have generally been accepted without question in the analytic tradition. And nothing we'll consider in the rest of the book will cast them into serious doubt. For all that, it's worth reflecting on whether they really have to be accepted.

Further reading

For a general introduction to Locke, see E.J. Lowe, *Locke on Human Understanding* (London: Routledge, 1995): chapter 7 deals with Locke's account of language. For papers specifically on Locke's philosophy of language, see N. Kretzmann, 'The Main Thesis of Locke's Semantic Theory', *Philosophical Review*, 77 (1968), pp. 175–96, and E.J. Ashworth, 'Locke on Language', *Canadian Journal of Philosophy*, 14 (1984), pp. 45–73.

2   Frege on Sense and reference

Key text

Gottlob Frege, 'Über Sinn und Bedeutung', *Zeitung für Philosophie und philosophische Kritik*, 100 (1892), pp. 25–50; translated (for example) as 'On Sense and Meaning' in G. Frege, *Collected Papers on Mathematics, Logic, and Philosophy*, ed. B. McGuinness (Oxford: Blackwell, 1984); this paper appears in many anthologies in various translations.[1]

2.1 Introduction

The German mathematician and philosopher, Gottlob Frege, is widely regarded as the father of analytic philosophy. His work has shaped everything which has been written in the philosophy of language in the analytic tradition. I think there are two principal reasons for this. First, his philosophy of language presents a way of accepting what seems most natural and intuitive about the kind of approach to language found in Locke, while decisively rejecting what seems most questionable about it. And, secondly, his work offers the prospect of a thoroughly systematic approach to meaning.

Frege shares with Locke these three crucial assumptions which we identified in chapter 1:

(L1) The nature of language is defined by its function;
(L2) The function of language is to communicate;
(L3) What language is meant to communicate is *thought*.

---

[1] In page references to this work, I'll use the page numbers of the original, which appear (in the margins, or in brackets) in some translations.

But his clearest disagreement with the Lockean tradition comes in his treatment of these two assumptions:

(L4) Words signify or mean the components of what language is meant to communicate;

(L5) The components of thought are *Ideas*.

Frege accepts some version of (L4), but understands it in a non-Lockean way. Locke had the following conception of how words are components of sentences. Individual words – or most of them, at least – stand for self-standing Ideas in the mind of the speaker, and these are combined into something sentential by an action of the speaker's mind. Frege rejects this: sentences are, in some sense, basic, and individual words only make sense in the context of sentences. Frege holds that the Lockean conception of the relation between words and sentences has to be rejected if we are to avoid accepting that words mean Ideas (in a broadly Lockean sense of the term), and he is adamant that words cannot mean Ideas. Since Frege accepts (L3) and (L4), he has to deny (L5).

The other striking innovation of Frege's philosophy of language is his use of the materials of formal logic to characterize the meaning of words. He was peculiarly well-placed to make such an innovation. His first great work was the invention of a new system of formal logic. This new system forms the basis of what is studied as elementary logic today: it has completely superseded the Aristotelian logic which was dominant before, and is taken for granted in all analytic philosophy. Almost all analytic philosophy of language works with some variant of this Fregean logical system.

2.2   Psychologism and the Context Principle

Frege's first philosophical (as opposed to mathematical or logical) work was *The Foundations of Arithmetic*. The Preface to this work contains two principles which are central to Frege's philosophy of language.

The main preoccupation of the Preface is with an attack on something which is often known as *psychologism*. Frege is concerned with more than one thing here,[2] but the claim of his which is most important for our purposes is this:

---

[2] He is also concerned to argue that psychology (like history) is irrelevant to philosophy. This makes him opposed to psychologism in the same way as Edmund Husserl was (in

(F1) It is not true that all words mean or refer to Ideas.[3]

Frege seems to offer two arguments for (F1). The first is that different people, who presumably all understand a given word, associate different ideas with it. The guiding assumption here seems to be this:

(F2) The meaning of a word is what is known by someone who understands the word.

And the argument from that assumption seems to be this. All these people understand a given word in the same meaning, although they associate different Ideas with the word; so the Ideas must be irrelevant to the meaning. This argument might be countered by someone denying that all these people understand the word in the same meaning (precisely because they associate different Ideas with the word). But that counter-argument in turn can be countered by saying that if we do not understand words in the same meaning, then communication is impossible; so if we want to continue to assume that the function of language is to communicate, we will have to distinguish between the meaning of a word and its associated Ideas.[4]

The other argument which Frege presents for (F1) is much simpler and more direct. It is just that mathematics (to take the example closest to his immediate concerns) has nothing to do with Ideas: in arithmetic, we are concerned with *numbers*, not Ideas of any kind – whether they be Ideas of numbers or anything else.[5] The same point would, perhaps, be even clearer in other fields: the aeronautical engineer is concerned with aeroplanes, not with Ideas of aeroplanes; the gardener with plants, not with Ideas of plants. If this is to form the basis of an argument for (F1), two further assumptions are needed. First, we need to assume that words belong to fields of human concern, so that the character of the relevant human concern determines the meaning of a word: the number words might, then, be thought to belong to mathematics, and plant words to gardening. And secondly, we need to assume that the basic objects of

[handwritten margin note: how come we all have the same idea of money but different ideas of love]

---

fact, Husserl was influenced in this by Frege): see, e.g., E. Husserl, *Logical Investigations*, trans. J. N. Findlay (London: Routledge, 2001), vol. 1, ch. 3.

[3] Frege used the German word 'Vorstellung' rather than the English word 'idea', but it seems clear that his target is something very like the Lockean view, on a natural reading of that view. So it seems fair to characterize Frege's view by means of the technical term 'Idea'.

[4] G. Frege, *Foundations of Arithmetic*, vi.   [5] Ibid., v.

human concern are not, in general, Ideas: mathematicians will be concerned with numbers, gardeners with plants – only certain kinds of psychologist will be concerned with Ideas.[6]

What's interesting about this is that it gives us a fundamentally *world-oriented* conception of meaning: words will mean things which are the object of our concern, and those are the things which make up the world. In considering Locke's account of language, I drew a crude initial contrast between theories which think of language as being designed to communicate *thoughts* and those which think of language as being designed to communicate *facts*. The former think of communication as being concerned with the contents of people's minds, whereas the latter think of it as being concerned with the state of the world. As we will see, Frege thinks that language is concerned with the communication of thoughts, and yet here we find that he clearly has some kind of world-oriented conception of language. This suggests that the contrast between the two conceptions is not as simple as it might initially have seemed.

So much for (F1). The other famous commitment of the Preface has had a subtler kind of influence. This is to a principle known as the *Context Principle*. Here is its first formulation:

> [N]ever to ask for the meaning of a word in isolation, but only in the context of a sentence.[7]

And here's another version:

> [It] is only in the context of a sentence that words have any meaning.[8]

It's not entirely clear what this principle amounts to, but Frege seems to want to insist on this:

> (CP) There is no more to the meaning of a word than its contribution to the meaning of sentences in which it may occur.

Why should we accept (CP)? Frege's principal reason was that unless we insist on (CP), we'll be driven to think that words mean Ideas. Here's the

---

[6] This kind of reasoning can be found in 'Über Sinn und Bedeutung'; see. e.g., pp. 28 and 31–2.

[7] G. Frege, *The Foundations of Arithmetic*, trans. J. L. Austin (Oxford: Blackwell, 1980), x. Note that I have used 'sentence' in place of Austin's 'proposition'.

[8] *Foundations of Arithmetic*, p. 73, with the same alteration.

reasoning. If we don't insist on (CP), we'll think that a word has meaning in virtue of some isolable correlation between it and something which could be encountered outside language. And if we're looking for something extra-linguistic to be correlated with every word, we'll be driven to look inside the mind. If we insist on (CP), on the other hand, we'll think that, in some sense, the basic thing is the meaning of sentences, and this will remove the temptation to think that words have meaning in virtue of the kind of correlation which seems to be involved in the Lockean theory.

There's also another reason for accepting (CP): it gives us at least the beginning of a response to the problem of the unity of the sentence.[9] The problem of the unity of the sentence is this: what is it that distinguishes a sentence (which cannot have words added or removed arbitrarily while still remaining a sentence) and a list (whose being a list is not affected by arbitrary additions and subtractions)? The problem seems to be created by thinking of words as working as Locke thinks they do: by being correlated with independently recognizable extra-linguistic items. We then have a puzzle explaining how we might reach something which has the special grammatical completeness of a sentence. The response suggested by (CP) is this: we don't try to explain the unity of a sentence as something generated from independently meaningful parts; instead we take the unity of the sentence as basic, and the meaning of its parts as in some way derivative from the meaning of sentences.

But there is a difficulty in understanding how (CP) can be true. This arises because Frege seems also to have implicitly endorsed a kind of converse principle, which we can call the *Principle of Compositionality*:

(PC) There is no more to the meaning of a sentence than what is
        determined by the meanings of the words of which it is composed and
        the way in which they are arranged.

(PC) is a statement of one of the most basic facts about language: that the meaning of sentences depends on the meaning of their component words. (PC) is the core principle in the study of *semantics*, of which Frege was perhaps the founding father. Semantics is the systematic explanation of how the meaning of words determines the meaning of sentences composed from them.[10]

---

[9] This problem is also considered briefly in ch. 1, § 1.5.

[10] I will always use the term 'semantics' in this precise sense, which is, I think, faithful to the central point of semantics in analytic philosophy of language. Other people,

Here is the problem. (CP) says that sentences are basic; (PC) says that words are basic. How can they both be true? The solution has to be to find some difference in the kinds of basicness involved. One suggestion might be this.[11] The sentence is basic in our understanding of the relation between language and what is outside language: it is only in whole sentences that we get language to engage with the world. But the word is basic in our understanding of the relation between each sentence and the rest of the language to which it belongs. Each sentence means what it does in virtue of its connections with all of the other sentences which can be constructed in the same language; and those connections are embodied in the words which are found in those sentences.

2.3   Frege and logic

Frege's whole approach to language was shaped by his work on logic. With his early work *Begriffschrift* (literally, 'concept-script' or 'concept-notation'),[12] Frege invented the logical system which is now studied as elementary logic.

Logic is the study of *validity*. The basic understanding of validity is this: an argument is *valid* if its conclusion really *follows* from its premises. For this it doesn't matter whether the premises are true: all that matters is whether the conclusion follows from them. The general task of logic is to understand what makes an argument valid, how the premises and conclusion of an argument have to be related for the conclusion really to follow from the premises.

Formal logic advances the study of validity by studying formal logical systems. A formal logical system begins with a clearly (even if implicitly) defined conception of validity, and then introduces special logical symbols whose meaning is defined to suit that notion of validity. Frege's whole

---

however, think that semantics is centrally concerned with the relation between language and the world.

[11] This suggestion is in line with what it is natural to find in the work of Donald Davidson: see chs. 9, 10, and 11. An alternative is offered by Michael Dummett, *Frege: Philosophy of Language* (London: Duckworth, 1973), ch. 1.

[12] G. Frege, *Begriffschrift, eine der arithmetischen nachgebildete Formalsprache des reinen Denkens* (Halle, 1879); trans. in full in J. van Heijenoort, ed., *From Frege to Gödel: A Source Book in Mathematical Logic, 1879–1931* (Cambridge, MA: Harvard University Press, 1967).

philosophy of language – and that of much philosophy of language in the analytic tradition – is shaped by the conception of validity which is implicit in his system. In Frege's system, validity can be defined roughly as follows:

(v) An argument is valid if and only if it is impossible for all of its premises to be true and its conclusion false.[13]

If you adopt (v) as your definition of validity, you can see that what really matters about the premises and conclusions of arguments is something very simple: whether they are true or false.

Frege's logic (modern elementary logic) is built in two layers, and the first depends on just this fact. The basic layer of Frege's logic is *sentence logic*.[14] This is concerned with arguments which depend on relations between whole sentences. Since Fregean logic uses the conception of validity expressed by (v), what really matters about the sentences which appear as whole sentences in arguments is just whether they are true or false. The next layer – known as *predicate* logic or *predicate calculus* – is concerned with arguments which depend on relations between *parts* of sentences. At its heart is a view of how sentences divide into parts. At bottom, Frege recognizes two basic kinds of parts of sentences. One kind consists of words or phrases which refer to particular individual objects – words like 'Protagoras', and phrases like 'this biscuit' or 'that iguana'. These are known as singular terms; Frege called them *proper names*. The other kind of basic part of sentences is the *predicate*.

What is a predicate? Suppose you begin with a sentence containing one or more singular terms. Here are two examples:

(S1) Vlad was cruel;
(S2) Vlad was at least as cruel as Tamerlane.

Now suppose you knock out the singular terms, and mark the places where they were with variables ('x', 'y', 'z', etc.).[15] You'll get these two

---

[13] Strictly, this is not quite precise: the impossibility has to be due to the *form* of the argument.

[14] Sometimes also called sentential *calculus* or *propositional calculus*.

[15] I'm assuming a simple, but not entirely uncontroversial philosophical account of variables here: on this account, (singular) variables simply mark the gaps where singular terms can go. The common alternative is to treat the variable as a kind of blank name: it can be used as a name of anything in an appropriate context.

linguistic strings:

(P1) *x* was cruel;

(P2) *x* was at least as cruel as *y*.

These are *predicates*. A predicate is just the result of removing one or more singular terms from a sentence. (P1) is a *one*-place ('monadic') predicate (with one place where a singular term can go); (P2) is a *two*-place ('dyadic') predicate. (Obviously there can be predicates with any number of singular-term gaps – predicates of any 'adicity'.)

These, then, are the basic units of language found by Frege's logical analysis – not counting special logical words. There are whole sentences; there are singular terms; and there are predicates. Since Frege's logical system depends on the simple definition of validity given by (V), we can specify quite simply what matters about the meaning of each of these three kinds of linguistic unit:

For sentences – whether they are true or false;

For singular terms – which objects they refer to;

For predicates – what difference they make to the truth and falsity of sentences, given any particular choice of singular terms in place of the variables.

Frege's whole philosophy of language is shaped by the fact that these very basic aspects of meaning are what's important for his logical system.

2.4   Frege's mature system (i): reference

So far we've looked at the commitments of relatively early work in Frege's career. During this period, he used almost interchangeably two German words which have to do with meaning. One is 'Bedeutung' (a noun from the verb 'bedeuten'): this might naturally be translated by 'significance' or 'signification', as well as 'meaning'. The other is 'Sinn', which is naturally translated by 'sense'. By the 1890s, however, he had come to see that he needed to distinguish two aspects of meaning, and he used these two words to mark them.

The basis of Frege's mature account of language is his theory of *Bedeutung*. There are two striking things about this. First, he takes *Bedeutung* to account for what matters about meaning for the purposes of logic, and perhaps for science in general. And, secondly, he understands *Bedeutung* in a way which the German word makes natural, but would seem odd to us if we took it to be simply equivalent to 'meaning'. The German word is sometimes used to speak of meaning a *thing* by a word, or even of the *thing meant* by a word. In his account of the *Bedeutung* of expressions, Frege seems to follow this suggestion, and to look for a kind of thing which might be assigned to a word as its *Bedeutung*.

This makes it natural to translate the word 'Bedeutung', as it is used in Frege's mature philosophy, as *reference*; and that is what I'll do too. Frege aims to account for the basic operation of the fundamental categories of linguistic expression by assigning them things which they refer to, or (as the jargon has it) *referents*.

This is reasonable enough in the case of singular terms. It's natural to say that singular terms *refer* to objects, and this is what Frege says. The cases of predicates and sentences are harder, though. It's not obviously natural to regard predicates and sentences as having referents at all. Consider predicates, first. Given what matters about predicates in Frege's logic, if we want something to be what a predicate refers to, what we want is a thing which will yield the truth or falsity of sentences, given a particular choice of objects as the referents of the singular terms which can take the place of the variables in the predicate. Such a thing is known as a *function*, in virtue of an analogy Frege made with mathematical functions. A function is said to have a *value* for particular *arguments*: once the 'arguments' are supplied, the 'value' is yielded. So, for example, $x + y$ has the value 5 for the arguments 2 and 3: that is, if you put '2' and '3' in place of 'x' and 'y' in the expression '$x + y$', you get what looks like a way of describing the number 5. Frege therefore proposed that predicates should be said to refer to functions of a particular kind. These are functions from objects (whose names might replace the variables) to truth and falsity. The objects whose names might replace the variables are the possible *arguments* of the function referred to by a predicate. The possible *values* of this function are just truth and falsity. Frege (rather confusingly) called functions of this kind *concepts*, and predicates *concept-words*. I'll treat this as a technical use, and speak of *Concepts* (with a capital 'C') when I follow Frege's terminology.

It's not clear that Frege's decision to explain the meaning of predicates by assigning them referents – things which they refer to – is well-judged.

On the face of it, it seems to throw away much of the point of the Context Principle. It seems to be doing the very thing which the Context Principle seemed to warn us against: insisting on treating the meaning of sub-sentential expressions as a matter of their being correlated with some thing which they signify. And it leads Frege into a peculiar problem.

Frege hopes to hold onto the grammatical difference between singular terms and predicates, while treating both as kinds of expression which have referents, by insisting on a fundamental difference between the referents of these types of expression. The referents of singular terms Frege calls *objects*, and he holds that they are complete or saturated. The referents of predicates, on the other hand – Concepts, in Frege's sense – are incomplete or unsaturated. (A one-place Concept, for example, will have space in it for one object, just as a one-place predicate has a space for one singular term.) But it's not clear that this is a stable position. The problem is that the very idea of the referent of a predicate seems to force us into treating it as some kind of object. (So far I have carefully described the referents of predicates merely as *things* of a certain kind; but that looks like an evasion.) Consider for example – it's Frege's example[16] – the Concept *horse*, the referent of the predicate 'x is a horse'. Frege is adamant that the Concept *horse* is not an object: it's the referent of a predicate, not of a singular term. Unfortunately, he seems bound to treat the phrase 'the Concept *horse*' as a singular term, in which case it is bound to refer to an object. And this, in turn, threatens the distinction between Concepts and objects. Consider, for example, the following sentence:

(*) The Concept *horse* is not an object.

If the phrase 'The Concept *horse*' is a singular term (as Frege seems to think it is), then what it refers to must be an object. But that means that (*) must be false. And that makes it look as if Frege won't ever be able to say truly that Concepts are not objects.[17]

Frege also claims that sentences have referents too. What are they? Clearly what matters about sentences for Frege's logic is their truth or

---

[16] Frege, 'On Concept and Object', in G. Frege, *Collected Papers on Mathematics, Logic, and Philosophy*, ed. B. McGuinness (Oxford: Blackwell, 1984).

[17] For more on this issue, see M. Dummett, *Frege: Philosophy of Language*, ch. 7, and M. Furth, 'Two Types of Denotation', in N. Rescher, ed., *Studies in Logical Theory* (Oxford: Blackwell, 1968), pp. 9–45.

falsity. Frege, in effect, turned truth and falsity into things and named them *the True* and *the False*. The True and the False are the *values* of the functions referred to by predicates, so they're known as *truth-values*. These two truth-values are the referents of sentences, on Frege's theory. Once again, this move seems in danger of collapsing the difference between singular terms and sentences, and so of losing much of the point of the Context Principle.

Apart from the oddity of treating the True and the False as things, there's a question about why truth and falsity should really be what matters about the meaning of sentences. Frege seems to offer two arguments for his view. The word 'Bedeutung', which is sometimes translated as *meaning* and sometimes as *reference*, may also mean *significance* in a sense which is close to that of 'importance'. So if we think of the Context Principle as being concerned with *Bedeutung*, we might understand it as having to do with what matters about words and sentences. This is what Frege seems, in effect to do.[18] He asks: why should it be *important* to us that a singular term has reference, that there is a real object to which it refers? After all, it doesn't seem to matter in fiction. His answer is that it matters to us that there is a real object to which a singular term refers when, and only when, it matters to us whether what is said in whole sentences is really true or false. So the real truth or falsity of sentences is important in just the same way as the real existence of the referents of singular terms is. And this makes it natural to think of the truth or falsity of sentences as the referents of sentences.

The other argument Frege uses in support of this claim relies on the Principle of Compositionality, (PC). If we accept (PC), then the meaning of a sentence must be whatever remains unchanged if we swap the words within it for other words whose meaning is the same. Frege applies this principle to *reference* as well as meaning in a more ordinary sense. He claims that it is only the truth-values of sentences which remain unchanged if you exchange their component words with other words whose reference is the same, and concludes that sentences refer to their truth-values.[19]

---

[18] I am here offering an interpretation of the passage of argument of 'Über Sinn und Bedeutung', pp. 32–4.

[19] 'Über Sinn und Bedeutung', p. 35. This argument is the precursor of an argument now known as the 'Slingshot', which aims to show that if sentences refer to anything, they

Neither of these arguments is conclusive. Take the first argument first, and recall the kind of world-oriented conception of language which I considered in section 1.4 of chapter 1. That view might take singular terms to refer to objects (such as Socrates or Protagoras), predicates to refer to qualities or properties (such as waspishness or ugliness), and true sentences to refer to facts (such as the fact that Socrates is waspish). If we took that view, we might think that it matters to us whether our names refer to real objects in just the circumstances in which it matters to us whether our sentences refer to real facts. That would give us an argument for thinking that true sentences refer to *facts* which is just as good as Frege's first argument for thinking that they refer to the True.

And we can offer an argument in favour of thinking that true sentences refer to facts which is as good as Frege's *second* argument as well. Suppose we say that we have the same fact if we have the same objects combined in the same way with the same qualities or properties, and take names to refer to objects and predicates to refer to qualities or properties – such as the quality of being a horse, or of waspishness – rather than to Fregean Concepts. Then one thing which remains the same if names or predicates with the same reference are swapped within a true sentence is the fact which corresponds to the sentence; so we can take that fact as the reference of the sentence just as easily as the value True.

2.5   Frege's mature system (ii): Sense

Frege's theory of reference leaves a huge gap between the reference of expressions and what might ordinarily be called their meaning. All true sentences have the same reference: to the True. So do all false sentences: to the False. But it's absurd to think that all true sentences, or all false sentences, have the same meaning. Similarly, on Frege's theory, two predicates will have the same reference if they are true of the same things. It seems that exactly the same creatures have hearts as have kidneys. So the predicates 'x has a heart' and 'x has a kidney' are true of just the same things. This means they will have the same reference, on Frege's theory. But, again, it's absurd to think that they have the same meaning: after all,

---

refer to truth-values. For a thorough discussion of the Slingshot, see S. Neale, *Facing Facts* (Oxford: Oxford University Press, 2001).

one has something to do with hearts, and the other has something to do with kidneys.

Given this, Frege had to find another aspect to the meaning of linguisic expressions if his theory was to have any general plausibility as an account of meaning. He used the word 'Sinn' to refer to this extra dimension of meaning. The word is standardly translated *sense*. I'll follow that practice here, but it's important to recognize that Frege's use of the word is a technical one: we have no right to assume that 'Sinn', as Frege uses it, means the same as our ordinary word 'sense'. So I'll capitalize the word and speak of *Sense* when discussing the Fregean notion.

Frege uses mathematical equations to introduce his notion of Sense. Compare these two:[20]

(1) $(2 \times 2^3) + 2 = 18$;
(2) $18 = 18$.

Equation (2) is obvious: we can see that it's true without thinking. Equation (1) is quite different: we need to do a bit of arithmetic to work out that it's true; if we are told that it is true, we are told something that could be news to us. Equation (1) can give us new knowledge, but equation (2) cannot; (1) is informative, while (2) is not.

But if we consider just the *reference* of these two equations, there seems no difference between them. The expressions '$(2 \times 2^3) + 2$' and '18' both count as singular terms on Frege's view; they're in the same category as proper names. Since equation (1) is true, they both have the same referent: the number 18. The other expression, '=', refers to a Concept, in Frege's technical sense. And obviously it refers to the same Concept in both (1) and (2). So all of the crucial component parts of (1) and (2) have the same reference. Moreover, (1) and (2) are both true, so the sentences as wholes also have the same referent – what Frege called *the True*.

This may seem absurd: surely '$(2 \times 2^3) + 2$' is semantically complex – it has meaningful parts – and surely that explains the difference between (1) and (2)? It is a significant feature of Frege's theory that he can recognize

---

[20] Frege's own examples in 'Über Sinn und Bedeutung' are the rather schematic equations '$a = a$' and '$a = b$'. I think equations like (1) and (2) (his own examples in 'Function and Concept') are the kind of thing he generally has in mind in thinking the notion of Sense; but his choice of the more schematic equations perhaps belongs with his assimilation of complex to simple singular terms.

the semantic complexity of '$(2 \times 2^3) + 2$' in terms of his notion of reference, but cannot use it to distinguish the referents of (1) and (2). For Frege, a large number of arithmetical expressions are functional expressions. In general, functional expressions have gaps for singular terms to go in, and themselves form singular terms once the gaps have been filled. So '$x \times y$', for example, has two gaps for singular terms (marked by 'x' and 'y'); if you put names of numbers in those gaps, the result is an expression which, in effect, counts as the name of a number. So if you put the number words '2' and '3' in the gaps, you end up, in effect, with a name of the number 6. That means that what matters in the end about the whole expression '2×3' is just that it names the number 6: the number 6 is its referent.

What this means is that although the reference of the parts of expressions formed from functions is important for deciding which object is referred to by the expression as a whole, once that has been decided the contribution of the parts has been used up. All that the whole expression contributes to *sentences* in which it occurs is the object it refers to. So although '$(2 \times 2^3) + 2$' and '18' get to refer to the number 18 in different ways, all that matters about their contribution to the reference of sentences is just the brute fact that they both refer to the number 18.

The result is that there's no significant difference in reference between (1) and (2), although there does seem to be an important difference of some kind between them: after all, (1) is informative while (2) is not. In *Begriffschrift*, his early logical work, Frege had supposed that identity statements were really about the words involved: they said just that the words on the left had the same content (what he would now call *reference*) as the words on the right.[21] In the famous paper 'Über Sinn und Bedeutung', he now thinks that this won't do. An equation like (1) conveys substantial knowledge about its topic (in this case arithmetic), but since he thinks that words and mathematical symbols are arbitrary signs, nothing very significant about the topic could be conveyed simply by saying that the words on the left have the same reference as the words on the right. Saying that the words have the same reference conveys relatively superficial *linguistic* knowledge, on Frege's view, but an equation like (1) tells us something substantial about *arithmetic*.

Accordingly, Frege proposes that there's a further aspect of what we would ordinarily call the *meaning* of words – in addition to their reference. This

---

[21] G. Frege, *Begriffschrift* (Halle, 1879), section 8.

further aspect he calls *Sinn*, Sense. Frege then claims that although '$(2 \times 2^3) + 2$' and '18' (for example) have the same reference, they differ in Sense.

But what is Sense? Frege says that it 'contains' the way in which the object (in the case of singular terms) is given; Sense contains the *mode of presentation* of the referent. This seems clear enough in the case of complex expressions like '$(2 \times 2^3) + 2$'. In this case, for example, the number 18 is given to us as the result of finding the cube of 2, doubling it, and adding 2 to the product. Frege, however, thought that the same point could be made even for expressions which don't have meaningful parts. Thus 'Aphla' and 'Ateb' could be two names for the same mountain – one associated with its appearance from the south, the other with its appearance from the north.[22] The southern aspect provides one way in which the mountain may be given; the northern aspect provides another. This association of these two names with different ways of having knowledge of the same mountain ensures that the two names differ in Sense, according to Frege. Consequently, there can be a difference in informativeness between the following two sentences:

(3) Aphla is the same mountain as Ateb;
(4) Aphla is the same mountain as Aphla.

(3) could be news to a traveller, but (4) is no news at all.

We might wonder whether the phrase 'mode of presentation' could mean the same thing in the case of both complex singular terms (like '$(2 \times 2^3) + 2$') and simple singular terms (like ordinary proper names). After all, in the case of a complex singular term the way in which the object is given is visibly present in the singular term itself: the object is given in that way *by* the complex phrase. But in the case of a simple singular term, the way in which the object is given is something which can only be *associated* with the singular term. It is a way in which the object is given *to someone* in certain circumstances. It is, in effect, a way in which the object

---

[22] This example is from a draft letter from Frege to Philip Jourdain, in G. Frege, *Philosophical and Mathematical Correspondence*, eds. G. Gabriel, H. Hermes, F. Kambartel, C. Thiel, and A. Veraart, abridged for the English edition by B. McGunness (Oxford: Blackwell, 1980), p. 80. For an actual example, consider the names 'Sagarmatha' and 'Chomolungma', which are the Nepali and Tibetan names, respectively, for the mountain most of us know as Everest.

can be known. This seems to leave some indeterminacy in the notion of Sense itself: I'll return to that point in section 2.7.

Frege thought that all kinds of linguistic expression could have Sense as well as reference. In particular, he thought that sentences as wholes had Sense, and he thought that the Senses of sentences were what we ordinarily think of as *thoughts*: the Sense expressed by a sentence is the *thought*. Again, it would be wise at this stage to treat the notion as a technical one, and speak of Fregean *Thoughts* (capital 'T').

Frege's distinction between reference and Sense offers a way of resolving an awkwardness that is felt in an account of language like Locke's. In section 1.3 of chapter 1, I noted that it feels unnatural to say that the word 'gold', for example, *means* an Idea or concept of gold. Don't we want to say that 'gold' means *gold*, the metal, though it may *express* our Idea or concept of the metal? Frege's distinction between reference and Sense allows us to say something very like this. On Frege's account, 'gold' *refers to* ('bedeutet') gold, the metal, but it *expresses* the Sense of 'gold', a certain way in which the metal is presented to us. The sentence 'Gold is a metal' *refers to* the True, but it *expresses* the Thought that gold is a metal.[23] Of course, Fregean Senses are very different from Lockean Ideas, as we'll see, but it seems that Frege's distinction between Sense and reference has allowed us to say something that was crying out to be said, and to resolve an ambiguity which we were always uneasily aware of in the everyday notion of meaning.

2.6   Two further uses of the notion of Sense

As he introduces it, Frege's notion of Sense is defined in terms of informativeness.[24] This forms the basis of what Gareth Evans has characterized as the *Intuitive Criterion of Difference*, which he formulates as follows:

> [T]he thought associated with one sentence S as its sense must be different from the thought associated with another sentence S' as *its* sense, if it is possible for someone to understand both sentences at a given time while coherently taking different attitudes towards them, i.e., accepting

---

[23] Thus Frege: 'We say a sentence *expresses* a thought' ('Thoughts', in his *Collected Papers*, p. 354).

[24] 'Über Sinn und Bedeutung', p. 32.

(rejecting) one while rejecting (accepting), or being agnostic about, the other.[25]

If the notion of Sense is what is needed to solve Frege's puzzle about informative identity statements, it must be characterized by means of Evans's Intuitive Criterion of Difference. A true sentence is informative if you can understand it without thinking that it's true. Two sentences differ in informativeness if you can understand both without thinking that they have the same truth-value.

Having introduced the notion of Sense to deal with the problem of informative identity statements, Frege used it in a way that offers solutions to two further problems.

The first is what to do about sentences containing singular terms which don't refer to any real thing. There are two kinds of case here. The first is that of sentences involving singular terms which are semantically complex (which have meaningful parts). One of Frege's examples of such a complex singular term is 'the least rapidly converging series': it can be demonstrated that there is no such thing, but Frege takes it to be obvious that the phrase has a Sense. A different kind of case is that of sentences in fiction. Frege (obviously regarding the *Odyssey* as a work of pure fiction) takes as his example the following sentence:

(5) Odysseus was set ashore at Ithaca while sound asleep.

If the name 'Odysseus' doesn't refer to any real thing, then, according to Frege, it has no reference. And if the name has no reference, the sentence as a whole can have no reference either. But it seems that it is meaningful in some way: after all, reading the *Odyssey* is not a wholly empty exercise. Frege suggests a solution to this problem by proposing that the name 'Odysseus' has Sense, but no reference, and the sentence (5) as a whole expresses a Thought, even though it has no truth-value.

We might wonder how this is intelligible, given Frege's original account of the notion of Sense. Sense, we were told, goes with 'mode of presentation' – the way in which the referent is given. How can this make sense if there is no referent? Strictly, of course, we cannot talk about a way in which *the* referent is given if there is no referent. But we can make sense of a way of specifying *a* referent – or *the* referent *if there is one*. This

---

[25] G. Evans, *The Varieties of Reference* (Oxford: Oxford University Press, 1982), p. 19.

would be done by providing a condition which something would have to meet to count as the referent. This is quite a natural way of understanding the notion of 'mode of presentation' in connection with a phrase like 'the least rapidly converging series': something could only be referred to by that phrase if it is the least rapidly converging series.[26] It is perhaps less natural in connection with proper names, like Frege's two names for the same mountain, 'Aphla' and 'Ateb'. This is a point I'll return to in section 2.7.

The other problem Frege uses the notion of Sense to solve is one that arises in offering a semantics for ordinary languages. A semantics or semantic theory for a language is a systematic account of how the meaning of sentences in that language depends on the meaning of their parts. Much of the latter part of 'Über Sinn und Bedeutung' can be understood as being concerned with providing the outline of a semantics for ordinary languages.[27] Such languages contain devices for reporting speech indirectly ('Galileo said that ... '), and for describing the thoughts and feelings of people ('Amy believes that ... ', 'Arthur hoped that ... ', 'Agnes knew that ... ', 'Alan fears that ... ', and so on). Let us call all of these forms of words devices for introducing *indirect contexts*, in which sentences are used to report sayings, thoughts, and feelings indirectly, as opposed to by means of direct quotation.

Consider the case of Carol, a classicist, who comes across some references in Latin poems to a heavenly body which sometimes appears in the morning: it's known as *the morning star*. She also comes across references to a heavenly body which sometimes appears in the evening: this (naturally enough) is known as *the evening star*. It never occurs to her

---

[26] This interpretation is suggested by David Bell, 'How "Russellian" was Frege?', *Mind*, 99 (1990), p. 275.

[27] It may be more accurate historically to think of Frege himself as being concerned with the slightly different task of explaining how arguments involving a wide variety of ordinary-language constructions work – doing what's known as *philosophical logic*, rather than philosophy of language. (This is the view, e.g., of David Bell in 'How "Russellian" was Frege?') But the significance of the notion of Sense for later philosophy of language depends on understanding what Frege is offering here as a proposal in ordinary-language semantics. And there are certainly features of 'Über Sinn und Bedeutung' – for example, the grounds of the original introduction of the notion of Sense – which suggest a more general interest in the philosophy of language.

that the two heavenly bodies are one and the same. The following sentence involving an indirect context is true:

(6) Carol thinks that the evening star appears in the evening.

It seems that the sentence 'the evening star appears in the evening' is *part* of the larger sentence, (6).[28] And it seems as if the phrase 'the evening star' is part of that contained sentence, and hence also part of the whole sentence (6). Moreover it is also *true* that the morning star is the same thing as the evening star; so the phrases 'the morning star' and 'the evening star', which are regarded by Frege as singular terms, refer to the same thing (the planet Venus). It might seem, then, that the following sentence must be true:

(7) Carol thinks that the morning star appears in the evening.

But if it has never occurred to her that the two heavenly bodies are one and the same, surely she thinks no such thing

Again, if the reference of (6) as a whole depended on the normal reference of the contained sentence 'the evening star appears in the evening', then any other sentence with the same reference could be put in its place within (6). But that contained sentence is true, so any other true sentence should have the same reference, on Frege's theory. The sentence 'The atomic number of gold is 79' is true. So if the reference of (6) depended on the normal reference of the contained sentence, then *this* should also be true:

(8) Carol thinks that the atomic number of gold is 79.

But suppose Carol knows no chemistry: then (8) will surely be false, even though (6) is true.

Frege's response to this problem is, in effect, to accept that the contained sentence 'the evening star appears in the evening' is part of the whole sentence (6), and to maintain that the reference of the whole sentence (6) depends on the reference of its parts – but to deny that in this context the parts have their *normal* reference. In contexts like this, Frege claimed, contained sentences and their parts have as their reference not

---

[28] This assumption is natural but questionable: it is questioned by Davidson, in his 'On Saying That', in his *Inquiries into Truth and Interpretation* (Oxford: Oxford University Press, 1984), pp. 93–108. This view is discussed in ch. 8, below.

their normal *reference* but their normal *Sense*. This means that you can only swap expressions contained in these contexts if they have the same *Sense*. Frege has already claimed that the phrase 'the morning star' differs in Sense from the phrase 'the evening star', so those two phrases cannot be swapped to license the move from (6) to (7). And it's obvious that the sentences 'the evening star appears in the evening' and 'the atomic number of gold is 79' differ in Sense, so they can't be swapped to license the move from (6) to (8).

It may seem odd to suppose that in these contexts ordinary words might suddenly refer to their normal Senses instead of their normal referents, but it does bring a side-benefit. It reinforces Frege's view that Sense is an aspect of what we might ordinarily think of as the *meaning* of linguistic units. If we accept that these contained sentences are really part of the sentences which contain them, we'll want to understand how the meaning of the containing sentences depends on the meaning of the contained sentences, just as we want to understand in general how the meaning of sentences depends on the meaning of their parts. But it does seem that it is differences of informativeness which are relevant to the role played by contained sentences; so it does seem that something like Frege's notion of Sense is what matters there. And if that's right, it seems that Sense is at least an aspect of meaning, since it is the feature of the contained sentences which the meaning of the containing sentences depends on.

2.7   Questions about Sense

Frege agrees with Locke on this point:

(L3) What language is meant to communicate is *thought*.

But he disagrees with him over the nature of thought.

The core of Frege's account of communication is that what is communicated are Thoughts, the Senses of sentences. How can Frege claim that Thoughts in this sense are anything like what is ordinarily meant by 'thought', and therefore are plausible candidates for being what is communicated? The crucial point is that a Thought, in Frege's sense, is *what* is thought when someone thinks, rather than the thinking of it. And he can claim that *what* is thought is the Sense of a sentence, if he is right in his account of the meaning of indirect contexts – those contexts with some kind of psychological verb ('think', 'wish', 'hope', 'feel', and so on) combined with a 'that'-clause. This is because he claims that what is referred to by such a 'that'-clause – assuming, as Frege does, that it refers to something – is the Sense of the words which follow; and the 'that'-clause tells us *what* is thought (or wished, or hoped, and so on).

The claim that Frege offers a fundamentally different account of communication from Locke's depends on making it clear that Fregean Thoughts are fundamentally different from Lockean Ideas. Although Frege means the difference to be vast, there are several respects in which one might doubt whether it is as large as it initially seems.

At first sight, the difference could hardly be greater. Locke's Ideas are private things, perceptible only to the person whose Ideas they are, and dependent on that person's psychology. The Lockean conception of communication accordingly presents a speaker as attempting to reveal to an audience the workings of her own mind. Frege's view seems wholly different. Fregean Thoughts are objective in two respects: the same Thought can be grasped by different people, and Thoughts can exist independently of human beings.[29] If I think that the morning star is a body illuminated by the sun, and you think that the morning star is a body illuminated by the sun, you and I think the same Thought. And that Thought was there to be thought before anyone actually thought it. According to Frege, this is what made it possible for it to be a discovery that the so-called morning star is actually a planet: that Thought was there already, and true already, before anyone ever considered it. One day that Thought occurred to people: they wondered whether it was true. Later it was confirmed: that Thought, which had always existed, and had always *been* true, was *found* to be true.

The first respect in which the difference between Lockean Ideas and Fregean Thoughts ends up looking less than it might initially seem is that Fregean thoughts seem more personal than his official account might suggest. If different people have different ways of picking out the same object, it seems that they will associate a different Sense with any name of that object.[30] What this means is that in many cases it will be

---

[29] These points are emphasized in Frege's late paper, 'Thoughts', in his *Collected Papers*, pp. 351–72.

[30] Frege himself acknowledges this: see 'Über Sinn und Bedeutung', n. 4.

unlikely – and might even be impossible – that two people will think the same Thought.

This leads to another difficulty. If *different* people can associate different Senses with the *same* word, it seems obvious that it will always be possible for the *same* person to associate different Senses with *different* words. The problem arises because we are usually quite liberal in what we count as understanding: different people are counted as understanding the same word, even if they think of the referent of the word in quite different ways. This liberal conception of understanding seems to guarantee it will be possible for a single person to understand almost any two words which refer to the same thing without realizing that they refer to the same thing. As a result, any two words seem bound to differ in Sense. That, in turn, undermines another contrast which Frege wants to draw between Sense and Lockean Ideas.

Frege makes a distinction between Sense and 'colouring' (which later scholars have called *tone*).[31] He holds that two words may have the same Sense, while differing in colouring. Good translation should preserve Sense, but cannot be expected to preserve colouring. Colouring is a matter of the Ideas associated with words, and is the concern of poetry rather than science. 'Colouring and shading', Frege says, 'are not objective, and must be evoked by each hearer or reader according to the hints of the poet or the speaker.'[32] The difficulty is that as long as anything like Evans's 'Intuitive Criterion of Difference' characterizes the notion of Sense, it seems that a difference of colouring or shading between two words is likely to be enough for a difference of Sense, since it is likely to be enough to allow someone to understand both words without realizing that they have the same reference.

The final respect in which it seems harder than it might have been thought to maintain a firm contrast between Fregean Sense and Lockean Ideas concerns the relation between Sense and reference. Insofar as Locke's theory allows room for reference at all, words refer to things in the real world only *indirectly*: they stand, in the first place, directly, for Ideas, and then, only indirectly, do they refer to things in the world. This indirectness is particularly significant if we adopt, as Locke perhaps did, a

---

[31] E.g., Dummett, *Frege: Philosophy of Language*, p. 2.
[32] 'Über Sinn und Bedeutung', p. 31.

traditional empiricist approach to Lockean Ideas. On this view, an Idea is an image which is before our mind when we perceive something. What we directly perceive are Ideas; that there is something real in the world which is the cause of these Ideas in our mind is something we can only infer. We could be viewing the same Idea even if we were hallucinating.

Frege's use of the notion of Sense to explain the meaningfulness of sentences containing names of things which don't really exist might seem to give him a view which is not altogether unlike Locke's in making the link between word and object indirect. This seems to follow from an orthodox interpretation of Frege, but there are difficulties in making it consistent with all of Frege's views, and it is possible to develop a conception of Sense which does not have this consequence.

At the core of the difficulty with understanding Frege's views is a certain crudeness in his analysis of grammar. Frege treats a wide variety of expressions as singular terms, on a par with ordinary proper names. In particular, he treats the complex expression 'the least rapidly converging series' and the simple proper name 'Odysseus' in the same way. The first of these is what is known as a *definite description*. It is a *description* because it says something about what it purports to be concerned with (in this case, that it's a least rapidly converging series); and it is *definite* in the same way as the definite article 'the' (which, of course, it contains) is definite: it is somehow implied that there is one and only one thing which the description applies to. Other definite descriptions include 'the man who invented bifocals', 'the woman who murdered her husband to take the Russian crown', 'the King of France'. There are definite descriptions without the definite article, of course: 'whoever discovered the elliptic form of the planetary orbits' is one.

Frege holds the following things about these expressions:

(F3) Ordinary proper names and definite descriptions are *singular terms*;
(F4) Ordinary proper names and definite descriptions all have Sense (as well, perhaps, as reference).

What is meant by the notion of a 'singular term' in (F3)? The core idea is this:

(ST1) The business of a singular term is to refer to an object.

And that seems to mean that at least *this* must be true:

(ST2) A sentence containing a singular term has no truth-value if there is no object corresponding to that singular term.

The significance of (ST2) can be seen by looking at one of Frege's examples:

(9) Whoever discovered the elliptic form of the planetary orbits died in misery.[33]

What Frege thinks is that the assertion of (9) *presupposes* the truth of the following:

(10) There was someone who discovered the elliptic form of the planetary orbits.

But he does not think that someone who asserts (9) is also *asserting* that (10) is true. This is a characteristic feature of sentences which contain singular terms: their assertion will *presuppose* but not *assert* the existence of an object corresponding to the singular term.

If we count both definite descriptions and proper names as terms of the same type, and focus on definite descriptions, it's natural to think that Frege offers an indirect account of reference, which might be thought to have some affinity with Locke's. If we begin with definite descriptions, it will be natural to think that a 'mode of presentation' is a way of specifying an object. This will suggest that a term refers to an object in the following way. The term offers us a condition which something has to meet in order to count as the referent of the term, and an object is then the term's referent in virtue of meeting that condition. This provides a kind of indirectness in the way that reference might be thought to work. The term has to be understood as *first* introducing a condition of some kind, and only *then* picking out an object, in virtue of the object's meeting that condition. This view fits easily with Frege's suggestion that a linguistic expression can have Sense without reference, which looks like a kind of counterpart to the Lockean view that you can perceive the same Idea, whether or not you are hallucinating. The Sense of an expression contains the mode of presentation – that is, it contains the condition which an object has to meet to count as the referent of the expression. The condition can exist, even if no object actually meets it.

---

[33] Considered at 'Über Sinn und Bedeutung', pp. 39–40.

How would we deal with ordinary proper names, on this conception? A natural thought is that the Sense of an ordinary proper name is given by a definite description. Indeed, Frege suggests as much himself: he supposes that the Sense of the name 'Aristotle' might be *the pupil of Plato and teacher of Alexander the Great*.[34] In that case, we will suppose that proper names refer to their objects in just the same way as definite descriptions: in virtue of the objects meeting some condition which is associated with the names as their Senses. And it will seem natural to think that a proper name could continue to have Sense, even if it has no referent, because, again, the condition for being its referent can continue to exist, even if nothing meets it.

This is probably the orthodox account of Frege, and it certainly fits with much of what Frege says. But it leads to some awkwardness when we take proper account of (F3), the claim that definite descriptions and proper names are singular terms. This awkwardness makes it natural to suggest an alternative, but still broadly Fregean, account of Sense.

The problem which arises over (F3) can be explained as follows. If definite descriptions are singular terms, then sentences containing them will have no truth-value if the descriptions refer to no objects. Consider an example:

(11) Earth's second moon is made of cheese.

Earth has only one moon, so the phrase 'Earth's second moon' refers to no object. It follows, by (ST2), that (11) has no truth-value. Nevertheless, according to the doctrine which Frege endorses, (11) is supposed to have Sense. So someone who utters (11) is still saying something (that Earth's second moon is made of cheese, to be specific). But it's hard to make sense of something actually having been said, if it's neither true nor false.

The difficulty is already clear in Frege's account of sentences involving definite descriptions. According to him, someone who uses them *presupposes*, but does not assert, the existence of an object referred to by the description. But what happens if someone uses a sentence presupposing something, and the presupposition is false? The natural suggestion is that she doesn't succeed in saying anything at all. Frege, however, because he holds (F3), (F4), and that it is possible for an expression to have Sense without reference, seems forced to say that she does say something – only

---

[34] 'Über Sinn und Bedeutung', n. 4.

it is something that cannot be true or false. This is just what is difficult to understand.

We can construct an alternative, but still broadly Fregean, conception of Sense, if we begin from the other side of the assimilation of names and definite descriptions, by focusing on proper names, which are *unstructured* singular terms. What might it be for an unstructured singular term to have Sense? It seems that it cannot itself *contain* a specification of a condition which something must meet to count as its referent. It's tempting at this point to turn to Frege's example of the two names for the same mountain: 'Aphla' and 'Ateb'. These names don't seem to be equivalent to definite descriptions: they're just used in different communities with different modes of access to the mountain in question. That difference is enough to ensure that the names will have a difference in Sense, according to the informativeness criterion with which the notion of Sense was first introduced: one could be familiar with both names in both communities without realizing that they were both names of the same mountain. This suggests a different conception of what a 'mode of presentation' is: it's a way in which a particular object is made available to us. It does not seem intelligible that we could have such a mode of presentation without the object being there. That means that reference will be a pre-condition of Sense. On this conception of Sense – in contrast with the more orthodox conception considered before – Sense is not something which mediates between a word and its referent. We will not suppose that words refer to their referents only *indirectly*, in virtue of the referents meeting some condition associated with the words, and we will be able to draw a stronger contrast between a Fregean approach to language and a Lockean one.

How would we deal with fictional names (like 'Odysseus', on Frege's view of *The Odyssey*) on this account? After all, fictional names have no real referents; on this account, they cannot have any real Sense. There may be other possibilities, but one is this. We suppose that fictional names have fictional Senses as well as fictional referents. Frege has sometimes been understood to have flirted with something like this line in material he was developing for a book on logic which he never published, probably written a few years after 'Über Sinn und Bedeutung'.[35]

---

[35] See G. Frege, *Posthumous Writings*, eds. J. Hermes, F. Kambartel, and F. Kaulbach (Oxford: Blackwell, 1979), p. 130. Evans takes this to be the core of Frege's view of

We end up with some uncertainty about what we should think about the notion of Sense. One model makes Sense independent of reference; the other makes it impossible to have Sense without reference. This uncertainty can be traced to the indeterminacy which we noticed when the idea of a 'mode of presentation' was first introduced.

2.8   Sense and the Basic Worry

Frege introduced the notion of Sense in order to deal with what may be described as the *Basic Worry* with the view that the meaning of words concerns things in the world, rather than things in the mind.[36] In its most general form, the Basic Worry is this. If what matters about the meaning of words is which things in the world are associated with them, we might expect two words which are associated with the same thing in the world to have the same meaning, and a word which is associated with no thing in the world to have no meaning. But it's natural to think that this is wrong: two words can be associated with the same things in the world, and yet have different meanings. And we may think that a word could be associated with no thing in the world, and still be meaningful. The notion of Sense is introduced precisely in order to deal with this Basic Worry. We've seen that there are some difficulties with the notion of Sense: might we do without it?

The Basic Worry is very clear for Frege, because he took such an austere view of the reference of predicates and sentences: two predicates which are true of the same things have the same reference, according to Frege, and so do two sentences which have the same truth-value. Might we avoid at least some aspects of Basic Worry if we took a less austere view of the reference of predicates and sentences? This is, in effect, the response of Russell, the subject of chapter 3.

Sense without reference in his 'Understanding Demonstratives', in his *Collected Papers* (Oxford: Oxford University Press, 1985), pp. 291–321. David Bell argues that Evans's reading depends on a mistranslation of the original German: see D. Bell, 'How "Russellian" was Frege?', p. 273.

[36] With the exception of mental words, of course, for which things in the mind form part of the relevant world.

Further reading

Those wanting to pursue Frege's philosophy of language further should read at least the Introduction to his early philosophical work, *The Foundations of Arithmetic*, trans. J. L. Austin (Oxford: Blackwell, 1980), and his late article, 'Der Gedanke', translated as 'Thoughts' in G. Frege, *Collected Papers on Mathematics, Logic, and Philosophy*, ed. B. McGuinness (Oxford: Blackwell, 1984). Next after that should be the papers 'Function and Concept' and 'On Concept and Object', which are roughly contemporaneous with 'Über Sinn und Bedeutung': they are also translated in the *Collected Papers*. A useful volume is M. Beaney, ed., *The Frege Reader* (Oxford: Blackwell, 1997), which contains all four of the articles just cited, as well as selections from both *Begriffshrift* and *The Foundations of Arithmetic*.

Frege's work has been the subject of an enormous secondary literature. There are two helpful introductory works: H. Noonan, *Frege: A Critical Introduction* (Cambridge: Polity Press, 2000); and A. Kenny, *Frege* (London: Penguin, 1995). The most influential work on Frege is M. Dummett, *Frege: Philosophy of Language* (London: Duckworth, 1973); all later scholars owe some kind of debt to this book. For an advanced and sustained attempt to develop a non-orthodox conception of Sense, see G. Evans, *The Varieties of Reference* (Oxford: Oxford University Press, 1982).

3 Russell on definite descriptions

Key text

Bertrand Russell, 'On Denoting', *Mind*, 14 (1905), pp. 479–93.

3.1 Introduction

'Alexandra', 'Rasputin', and 'Felix Youssoupoff' are all proper names: they're names of the wife of the last Tsar of Russia, the monk she admired, and the man who shot that monk, respectively. We use these names to refer to those people: that seems to be what the names are for.

But what about those other phrases I've just used: the phrases 'the wife of the last Tsar', 'the monk she admired', and 'the man who shot that monk'? Phrases like these are known as *definite descriptions*. What do *they* do? How do they work? Do they refer to the people in question? Do they work like names? It might seem just common sense to suppose they do work like names; that's certainly what Frege seems to have thought. This chapter focuses on a famous article by Bertrand Russell which argued that definite descriptions work quite differently, despite initial appearances. Although it's apparently concerned with something very minor – the meaning of the word 'the' – Russell's article was part of a revolution in the philosophy of language.

What is Frege's view, precisely? As we saw in chapter 2, he's committed to these two claims:

(F3) Ordinary proper names and definite descriptions are *singular terms*;

(F4) Ordinary proper names and definite descriptions all have Sense (as well, perhaps, as reference).

And the crucial things about the notion of a 'singular term' used in (F3) are these:

(ST1) The business of a singular term is to refer to an object;

(ST2) A sentence containing a singular term has no truth-value if there is no object corresponding to that singular term.

Russell was generally suspicious of the notion of Sense. (Note that in 'On Denoting', Russell refers to Fregean Sense as *meaning*, and Fregean reference is included within his use of the term 'denotation'.) He initially thought that there was only an argument for it in a special case: that of 'complexes whose referent is an object'.[1] Such 'complexes' are definite descriptions, treated as singular terms. The dramatic proposal of Russell's great paper of 1905, 'On Denoting', is that these complex expressions do not in fact refer to objects. That is, Russell denies (F3), at least for the case of definite descriptions. And this, he thinks, will enable him to deny (F4), and avoid appealing to the notion of Sense altogether. (We'll see how his approach can be extended to ordinary proper names in section 3.8 below.)

3.2   The problems

Russell treats Frege's notion of Sense as a theoretical notion designed to deal with certain problems. His claim is that these problems are dealt with better by his alternative theory, which denies both (F3) and (F4).

We've already seen that Frege uses the notion of Sense to deal with the following problems:

(P1) How identity statements can be both true and informative;

(P2) How there can be a difficulty in swapping within psychological or epistemic contexts (such as 'believes that … ', 'discovered that … ') words which have the same ordinary reference;

(P3) How something meaningful can be said using ordinary proper names and definite descriptions which refer to no existing objects.

These problems can all be thought of as aspects of what I've called the *Basic Worry* with the view that the meaning of words relates to things in the

---

[1] Letter from Russell to Frege, 12 December 1904, in G. Frege, *Philosophical and Mathematical Correspondence*, G. Gabriel, H. Hermes, F. Kambartel, C. Thiel, and A. Veraart, eds., abridged by B. McGuinness, trans. H. Kaal (Oxford: Blackwell, 1980), p. 169. I have replaced 'meaning', which Kaal uses to translate 'Bedeutung' (Russell wrote to Frege in German) with 'referent', in line with the policy of ch. 2.

world, rather than things in our minds.[2] The worry is that in certain contexts, there is something more – or something different – in the meaning of words than which objects in the world are referred to. Frege solves (P1) by introducing the notion of Sense to mark the fact that expressions which have the same reference can differ in informativeness. He solves (P2) by claiming that sameness of Sense, rather than sameness of ordinary reference, is what's needed to allow words to be swapped within psychological or epistemic contexts. And he solves (P3) by claiming that singular terms can have Sense, even if they have no real reference.

Russell's theory is designed to solve all of these problems, and two more besides:

(P4) How the Law of Excluded Middle applies to sentences including such phrases as 'the present King of France' (given that there is now no King of France);

(P5) How there can be true denials of existence of the (apparent) form 'N does not exist'.

These two problems need a little explanation. The Law of Excluded Middle, as Russell uses that phrase,[3] says that, for every meaningful sentence, either it or its negation is true. Consider Russell's sentence 'The King of France is bald'. By Russell's Law of Excluded Middle, either that sentence is true, or its negation – 'It is not the case that the King of France is bald' – is true. But if 'the King of France' is a singular term, then – according to (ST2) above – neither sentence can be really true, since there is now no King of France. Russell thinks that logic demands that the Law of Excluded Middle be upheld, so there's a problem with thinking of phrases like 'the King of France' as singular terms.

---

[2] See ch. 2, § 2.8, above.

[3] It is now customary to distinguish between the *Principle of Bivalence* – which says that every meaningful sentence has exactly one of the two truth-values – and the *Law of Excluded Middle* – according to which every instance of the schema '*p* or not-*p*' is true. The Principle of Bivalence is a general principle about truth; the Law of Excluded Middle (as it is now generally understood) is the claim that a certain logical formula is a tautology (this claim holds good in some logical systems, but not in others). It turns out to be possible to deny the Principle of Bivalence while accepting the Law of Excluded Middle as it is now understood. Russell did not distinguish between the two, and it is arguable that his real concern was closer to what we now know as the Principle of Bivalence.

As for (P5), consider this sentence:

(1) Santa Claus does not exist.

If 'Santa Claus' is a singular term, and we accept (ST2), it's hard to see how (1) could be true. For if (1) were true, then there would be no entity corresponding to the name 'Santa Claus'. But if there were no object corresponding to the name 'Santa Claus' and 'Santa Claus' were a singular term, then, according to (ST2), (1) could have no truth-value.

Problems (P4) and (P5) cannot be solved by introducing the notion of Sense, if (ST2) is still maintained. And it's clear that Frege himself accepted (ST2). But could we, in fact, modify (ST2)? What if we distinguished between existent and non-existent objects, and allowed that singular terms might refer to non-existent objects?[4] If we did that, then we could say that there are sentences containing singular terms which are really true or false, even though there are no real objects corresponding to the singular terms.

How would this help with our problems? It seems that it would help with (P5) and (P3): (1) for example, would simply be saying that Santa Claus, though an object of some kind, is not a *real* object. And as long as there is *some* object referred to by an ordinary proper name or definite description, there seems no obvious problem with thinking that sentences involving them can be meaningful, even if the object in question does not really exist. Furthermore, it seems – initially, at least – that dropping (ST2) might help with (P4). Consider the non-existent object supposedly referred to by the phrase 'the King of France'. If we were to drop (ST2), couldn't we say that this unreal object either was, or was not bald? And this would then let us preserve the Law of Excluded Middle.

But this treatment of (P4) isn't really satisfactory. It might be that we could say of any – even imaginary – object which we had in mind that it was either bald or not bald,[5] but the problem with the phrase 'the King of

---

[4] This view is associated with Alexius Meinong, 'Über Gegenstandstheorie', in Meinong (ed.) *Untersuchungen zur Gegenstandtheorie und Psychologie* (Leipzig: Barth, 1904); translated as 'On the Theory of Objects', in R. Chisholm, ed., *Realism and the Background of Phenomenology* (Glencoe, II: Free Press, 1960), pp. 76–117.

[5] As it happens, baldness provides a tricky example. If someone is balding, is he bald, or not bald? It is tempting to think that he is neither precisely bald, nor precisely not bald. In that case, we might think that the claim, 'He is bald', is not precisely true or false in this case.

France' is that it's hard to see that there is even any particular non-existent object it refers to. We don't think, 'That man, the King of France, does not exist'; we think simply, 'There's no *such* person as the King of France.' Moreover, dropping (ST2) seems to offer no solution at all to problems (P1) and (P2).

Russell himself was impatient with any suggestion that there might be objects which don't really exist. In 'On Denoting', he seems to have regarded any theory which supposed that there could be such things as committed to obvious contradictions: he thought it would need to say both that such things exist and that they don't exist. In the chapter on descriptions in his later work, *Introduction to Mathematical Philosophy*, he is more cautious, but almost as dismissive. In such theories, he says, 'there is a failure of that feeling for reality which ought to be preserved even in the most abstract studies'.[6]

3.3 Russell's solution in outline

At the core of Russell's solution to the problems he sets himself is a revolutionary approach to the structure of language: superficial similarities between types of sentence should not be taken as evidence for thinking the sentences really work in the same way. Traditionally – and in this respect Frege follows tradition – definite descriptions had been assimilated to the class of proper names, because they seemed to play a similar role in sentences. Russell begins by assimilating them instead to a quite different class of expressions: what he calls 'denoting phrases'.

Russell gives no very clear definition of this term: he introduces it by means of a range of examples. What is interesting is what he chooses to put in that range; apart from definite descriptions, the examples are these: 'a man', 'some man', 'any man', 'every man', 'all men'. These phrases all receive a particular kind of analysis in the (then new) logical system invented by Frege and developed (semi-independently) by Russell himself.

All these phrases involve *quantifiers*. A quantifier is an expression which specifies some quantity of a given group (people, eggs, dishwashers, or whatever). Frege's logic – which was Russell's logic too – deals with

---

[6] B. Russell, *Introduction to Mathematical Philosophy*, 2nd edn (London: George Allen and Unwin, 1920), p. 169.

quantifiers that are represented in English by 'all', 'every', 'any' and 'some'. The Fregean representation of quantifiers is rooted in the Fregean conception of the basic sentence: a sentence involving one or more names and a predicate. Consider this sentence:

(2) Youssoupoff shot someone.

The Fregean analysis sees this as involving a one-place predicate – which Russell seems in 'On Denoting' to call a *propositional function*:[7]

(3) Youssoupoff shot x.

The Fregean system represents (2) by attaching the quantifier 'There is at least one x such that' to the front of (3), to get this:

(4) There is at least one x such that Youssoupoff shot x.

In 'On Denoting', Russell attempted to explain what this kind of expression means. In his terms, (4f) means this:

(4r) The propositional function (i.e., predicate) 'Youssoupoff shot x' is sometimes true.

A bit more colloquially, we might represent (4) like this:

(4e) There is at least one object which Youssoupoff shot.

When Russell counts definite descriptions as 'denoting phrases', the prime examples of which involve quantifiers, he is claiming, in effect, that definite descriptions are quantifier phrases. The difference between 'some' and 'the' (at least when 'the' is coupled with a *singular* noun phrase) is

---

[7] This interpretation of Russell's term 'propositional function' is perhaps controversial: it might be understood to be what a predicate refers to. Russell introduces the term, alongside the word 'proposition', at 'On Denoting', p. 480 (n. 2). The crucial sentence of the text is this: 'I use "c(x)" to mean a proposition [footnote: "More exactly, a propositional function"] in which x is a constituent, where x, the variable, is essentially and wholly undetermined'. This sentence is a mess, because of the odd use of 'mean', but I think it's clear that Russell here is using 'proposition' to mean *(declarative) sentence*, and therefore the term 'propositional function' must be being used to refer to a part of a declarative sentence. 'On Denoting' as a whole (and indeed, much of Russell's work in this period), is shot through with this kind of confusion between words and what they refer to.

simple. 'Some' means: *there is at least one object which* ... 'The' (coupled with a singular noun phrase) means: *there is exactly one object which* ...

Russell is concerned with this sentence:

(5) The present King of France is bald.

According to him, (5) means this:

(5r) There is exactly one object which is now King of France, and that object is bald.

Russell sometimes expresses this in a slightly more complicated way, as being equivalent to the following combination of sentences:

(5r*) (i) There is at least one object which is now King of France;
      (ii) There is at most one object which is now King of France; and
      (iii) Whatever is now King of France is bald.

Russell draws two morals from his analysis of phrases like 'some man', which apply to his analysis of definite descriptions too. On his analysis, the phrase 'the present King of France' is not a name of the present King of France, any more than 'some man' is a name of some man. And the phrase has no meaning on its own, although it's meaningful enough in the context of a sentence. What the phrase 'the present King of France' contributes to any sentence in which it occurs is - speaking a little loosely - a quantifier ('there is exactly one object which ... ') and a predicate ('*x* is now King of France'). But on its own the phrase 'the present King of France' does not mean *there is exactly one present King of France*, since it's not a sentence. These two points are themselves developments of Russell's deep thought that the superficial appearance of a sentence is not a reliable guide to its real structure.

3.4 Russell's solution in detail

How does Russell's approach deal with problems (P1)–(P5)? Let's begin with (P1). Here's an identity statement involving definite descriptions:

(6) The morning star is the evening star.

The problem arises from treating the definite descriptions as singular terms. Since (by (ST1)) it's the business of a singular term to refer to an object, two singular terms which refer to the same object seem to do the same job. The difficulty then is to explain how they could differ in meaning.

Russell's analysis of (6) makes it equivalent to something like this:

(6r) (i) There's exactly one object which is a morning star;
(ii) There's exactly one object which is an evening star;
(iii) Whatever is a morning star is an evening star, and vice versa.

On this account, what appeared initially as the informativeness of an identity statement is now understood as the informativeness of an equivalence at step (iii). The crucial part of the claim effectively says that the *predicates* '*x* is a morning star' and '*x* is an evening star' are equivalent, in the sense that they apply to the same thing. And since these predicates are naturally thought to have different meanings, it is not surprising that the equivalence is informative.[8]

The second problem, (P2), concerned substitution in psychological contexts. Recall the case of Carol, the classicist who has heard of both the evening star and the morning star, but doesn't know that they are one and the same. This is true:

(7) Carol thinks that the evening star appears in the evening.

It seems that the phrases 'the morning star' and 'the evening star' have the same normal reference, but that still doesn't mean that the following sentence is true:

(8) Carol thinks that the morning star appears in the evening.

Russell's official response to this is that we should only expect (8) to be derivable from (7) if we supposed that definite descriptions are singular terms which have an isolable meaning of their own – which is what his theory denies.[9] According to Russell, these definite descriptions cannot be analysed outside their contribution to whole sentences. In this respect Russell insists more firmly than Frege himself on Frege's Context

---

[8] It's arguable, however, that this solution is vulnerable to the same difficulty as Russell's official solution to (P2), and, like that, needs Russell's new theory of the reference of predicates to make it finally plausible.

[9] Russell, 'On Denoting', pp. 488–9.

Principle.[10] If we insist on treating them as expressions which are distinct from singular terms, and which can only be understood in terms of their contribution to whole sentences, we cannot say that they have the same reference, and the idea of swapping them for each other does not even arise.

In fact, this is a superficial response. For we might expect (8) to be derivable from (7), even within Russell's theory, if the *predicates* '*x* is a morning star' and '*x* is an evening star' have the same meaning. And according to Frege's theory, these two predicates have the same *reference*, because they are true of exactly the same things (one thing, in fact). To deal with this difficulty, we will need to give an account of the reference of predicates which is different from Frege's, if we're not to end up appealing to Sense after all. In fact, Russell did do that, so he can respond to this criticism: we will return to the issue in section 3.8.

Russell protects his treatment of (P2) with a further observation. This is that there are two readings of sentences like (7), which are brought out clearly in his analysis. Notice the position of the phrase 'there is exactly one object which is an evening star' in the following two sentences:

(7rn) Carol thinks that there is exactly one object which is an evening star and that object appears in the evening;

(7rw) There is exactly one object which is an evening star and Carol thinks that that object appears in the evening.

In (7rn) we say that one of the things which Carol thinks is that there's exactly one thing which is an evening star. We don't say that in (7rw): in (7rw) we simply say for ourselves that there's exactly one thing which is an evening star before reporting what Carol thinks about it.

The difference between (7rn) and (7rw) is a difference of what is known as *scope*. In (7rn) the phrase 'there is exactly one object which is an evening star' occurs *within* the context created by the phrase 'Carol thinks that': we say that it falls *within its scope*. This means that the scope of the phrase 'Carol thinks that' is *wider* than that of the phrase 'there is exactly one object which is an evening star'. In (7rw) the situation is reversed: the phrase 'there is exactly one object which is an evening star' does *not* occur

---

[10] For which see ch. 2, § 2.2, above.

within the scope of the phrase 'Carol thinks that'. We may then say that *it* has wider scope than the phrase 'Carol thinks that'.

According to Russell – though he used a different terminology[11] – there are *narrow-scope* and *wide-scope* readings of the definite description in (7): we can take the description 'the evening star' to occur within the scope of 'Carol thinks that', or outside it. We might make the *wide*-scope reading – the one where the description is *outside* the 'that'-clause – clear in more-or-less everyday terms by rephrasing it like this:

(7ew) Concerning the evening star: Carol thinks that it appears in the evening.

Russell thinks that, even though definite descriptions are not isolable semantic units, there is no harm in swapping 'the morning star' for 'the evening star' in its position in the *wide*-scope reading – in (7ew), for example.

Russell's application of scope distinctions to sentences involving definite descriptions and psychological contexts (such as (7)) is not altogether a happy move. It draws attention to two awkward features of his theory. First, we might think that it's not at all obvious that (7rn) is equivalent to any natural reading of the English (7) – even if we suppose that the definite description 'the evening star' occurs *within* the scope of 'Carol thinks that'. Russell supposes, of course, that the sentence 'The evening star appears in the evening' is properly analysed by means of the sentence 'There is exactly one object which is an evening star and that object appears in the evening.' But even if he's right, it's not clear that this means that the two sentences can be swapped in psychological contexts. Secondly, we might wonder *why* swapping definite descriptions which occur *inside* the scope of psychological verbs is problematic, if swapping them is unproblematic when they occur *outside* the scope of such contexts.

Be that as it may, having once made the distinction between wide-scope and narrow-scope readings of sentences involving definite descriptions, Russell uses it again to deal with problem (P4). Recall Russell's

---

[11] Russell talks of 'primary' and 'secondary' occurrences of definite descriptions. Roughly speaking, 'primary' occurrences are *wide*-scope occurrences (as in (7rw) and (7ew)) and 'secondary' occurrences are *narrow*-scope occurrences (as in (7rn)).

problem sentence:

(5) The present King of France is bald.

According to what Russell calls the Law of Excluded Middle, either (5) or the following sentence must be true:

(5*) It is not the case that the present King of France is bald.

The difficulty is that if 'the present King of France' is a singular term, and (ST2) is true, then neither (5) nor (5*) can be true.

According to Russell, (5) is false, because it's equivalent to this:

(5r) There is exactly one object which is now King of France, and that object is bald.

So if the Law of Excluded Middle holds, (5*) must be true. But, according to Russell, (5*) only seems untrue if we read the description as having wider scope than 'it is not the case that', making (5*) equivalent to this:

(5*w) There is exactly one object which is now King of France, and it is not the case that that object is bald.

But we can read the description as having *narrow* scope, which will then make (5*) equivalent to *this*:

(5*n) It is not the case that there is exactly one object which is now King of France and that object is bald.

And (5*n) is true. So if we read (5*) in the manner of (5*n), the Law of Excluded Middle can be seen to hold.

Now let's move to (P5), the problem of denying existence. Here's a sentence of the relevant form:

(9) The present King of France does not exist.

Bearing in mind Russell's standard analysis of definite descriptions, it might be tempting to analyse (9) as follows:

(9*) There is exactly one object which is a present King of France, and that object does not exist.

But (9*) is exactly the kind of thing Russell wants to avoid, since it involves thinking that there are things which don't exist. The solution a Russellian needs involves a different application of the general thought that in understanding language superficial appearance is no guide to real structure. On a Russellian view, the problem with (9) arises from being uncritical about the word 'exists'. This seems to be part of a predicate, '*x* exists'. But if this is really a predicate, the variable must mark a place where a singular term could go. But if we put a singular term in place of the variable, and keep accepting (ST2) as Russell does, we end up with something which cannot intelligibly be denied. Since it's natural to think that nothing can intelligibly be said by a sentence which cannot intelligibly be denied, this means that there cannot really be a predicate '*x* exists'.

So what does 'exists' mean? The Russellian view is that it's a part of a quantifier: 'there is an object … '. In that case, since there's already such a quantifier involved in sentences using definite descriptions, there must be something malformed about (9). This is a natural thought anyway. Instead of (9) we would surely prefer to say something like this:

(9**) There is no present King of France.

Russell could have insisted that (9) is malformed, and refused to go further than (9**), and it may be that this is the best Russellian response. It's not entirely clear what Russell himself actually suggests. He may be taken to suggest this as an analysis of (9):

(9r) It is not the case that there is exactly one object which is now King of France.

But (9r) doesn't mean the exactly the same as (9). (9r) is true if *either* there is no King of France *or* there's more than one.

Finally, let's turn to the last remaining problem, (P3), about the meaningfulness of names and descriptions which refer to no existing objects. Here's a sentence using such a term (assuming the Greek gods don't really exist):

(10) Apollo is jealous.

If the name 'Apollo' is a singular term, it seems we're in trouble here. But what else could it be? If we look up the name 'Apollo' in a classical dictionary, we're likely to find that Apollo is the sun-god. Russell's proposal is simple: we take the name 'Apollo' to be equivalent in meaning to some definite description, like 'the sun-god', and that definite description is then analysed in Russell's usual way. (10) then becomes equivalent to this:

(10r) There is exactly one object which is a sun-god, and that object is jealous.

(10r) is certainly meaningful – though presumably it's false.

3.5 Strawson on definite descriptions

Does Russell give a correct account of the meaning of sentences involving definite descriptions? In his famous paper, 'On Referring', P. F. Strawson argues that he does not.[12]

To begin with, Strawson claims that certain crucial semantic terms are not properly applied to sentences, words and phrases (expressions) at all: they are only properly applied to *uses* of expressions. So we cannot properly say that a *sentence* is true or false, or that a word or phrase *refers* to an object: it is only *uses* of sentences which can be true or false, and only *uses* of words or phrases which are referring. What is this distinction? The word 'I' may be used by anyone to refer to herself. Its use by me to refer to myself is one use; its use by you to refer to yourself is another. But both these uses are uses of the same word; the word 'I' itself cannot be said to refer to anyone. Similarly, the sentence 'I am typing at a keyboard' may be used by me to say something true, or it may be used by you to say something false. These are different uses of the same sentence: the sentence itself cannot be said to be true or false.

Sentences, on the other hand, can be said to be *meaningful*, according to Strawson. For a sentence to be meaningful, it must be *possible* to use it to say something true or false. That is to say, there must be established proper uses of it which are true or false. A sentence can be meaningful even if, on a particular occasion, nothing would be said by uttering it. Consider the sentence, 'You have won the lottery'. It's easy enough to imagine circumstances in which this sentence could be used to say something true or false; so it's meaningful by Strawson's test. But what if I were to speak that sentence with no one in particular in mind – as a mad announcement on a show, perhaps? Then it seems that I would have said

---

[12] P. F. Strawson, 'On Referring', *Mind*, 59 (1950), pp. 320–44.

nothing; since I didn't say anything about any particular person, it is hard to see how there could be anything there to be true or false.

Strawson uses the distinction between the kinds of thing that can properly be said of linguistic expressions, on the one hand, and the kinds of thing that can properly be said of *uses* of expressions, on the other, to remove some of the motivation for Russell's theory. In particular, we cannot insist that either a sentence or its negation must be true if it's meaningful. It is not even obvious that we should insist that if a sentence is meaningful, any *use* either of it or of its negation must be true: if I have no one in particular in mind whom I am referring to by 'you', it's not clear that either 'You have won the lottery' or 'You have not won the lottery' need be true. If there's no particular person in question, Strawson would want to say, the question of truth or falsity doesn't even arise. This does not in the least threaten the meaningfulness of the sentence itself.

Strawson makes precisely this point in connection with definite descriptions, in at least one important range of uses of such phrases. Recall Russell's famous example (5). Russell's analysis makes it simply false, because there is no present King of France. Strawson, however, claims that if there is no present King of France, a non-fictional use of (5) is not false; rather, the question of its truth or falsity does not even arise.

Strawson takes the same line with uniqueness as he does with existence. Consider the following sentence:

(11) The table is covered with books.

Suppose that someone uttered (11) in the presence of several tables, without having any particular table in mind.[13] Then, on the Strawsonian view, the question of truth and falsity would not even arise. It would not be that the person who uttered (11) in these circumstances had said something which was false: rather, she wouldn't have said anything at all.[14]

---

[13] This form of the problem is not in fact Strawson's own, though it is one which naturally follows from some of Strawson's considerations, and it uses one of Strawson's examples. It is due to M. Ramachandran, 'A Strawsonian Objection to Russell's Theory of Descriptions', *Analysis*, 53 (1993), pp. 209–12.

[14] Strawson's overall point can be expressed in terms of Russell's use of the notion of denotation. On Russell's use, a description of the form 'The *F*' *denotes* a certain particular object if and only if that object, and that object alone, is *F*. Strawson claims

Strawson's overall claim can be put like this. There are certain central uses of definite descriptions which are *referring uses*. If a use of a description is a referring use, then the person who uses the description does not *assert* the unique existence of an object which satisfies the description, as Russell thought.[15] Instead, the unique existence of an object which satisfies the description is *presupposed*.[16] In this, Strawson follows Frege. It was Frege's view that someone who said 'Whoever discovered the elliptic form of the planetary orbits died in misery' presupposed but did not assert that there was exactly one person who discovered the elliptic form of the planetary orbits.[17] But there's a crucial difference. Frege thought that sentences could have Sense without being true or false, and names and descriptions could have Sense without referring to anything. If we put this point in Strawson's terms, Frege's view is that something can still be said by a use of a name or referringly-used description which refers to no real object, and by the use of a sentence which has no real truth value. On Strawson's view, by contrast, nothing can be said – no statement can be made – by such uses.[18]

3.6 Donnellan on referential and attributive uses of descriptions

So far we have a fairly simple picture. Frege thought of definite descriptions, in all uses, as singular terms, and hence as referring expressions.

---

that, for certain central uses of sentences involving definite descriptions, if nothing is denoted by the description, nothing is said by that use of the relevant sentence.

[15] Lycan claims that Russell never said that someone who uses a description *asserts* the unique existence of something which satisfies the description: W. Lycan, *Philosophy of Language* (London: Routledge, 2000), p. 23. But this is false. Russell says, 'Thus when we say "x was the father of Charles ɪɪ" we not only assert that x had a certain relation to Charles ɪɪ, but also that nothing else had this relation': 'On Denoting', pp. 481–2.

[16] In his original paper, Strawson says, 'To say, "The King of France is wise" is, in some sense of "imply" to *imply* that there is a King of France: 'On Referring', p. 330.

[17] G. Frege, 'On Sense and Meaning', in his *Collected Papers on Mathematics, Logic, and Philosophy*, ed. B. McGuinness (Oxford: Blackwell, 1984), p. 168.

[18] Note, however, that Strawson doesn't think that these referring uses of definite descriptions are the only intelligible ones: he acknowledges that there might be a variety of uses; he says nothing about natural uses of descriptions like 'the least rapidly converging series'; and he explicitly puts fictional uses on one side, as a different kind of case: see 'On Referring', p. 331.

Russell claimed that they were never referring expressions. Strawson adopts something close to Frege's view for some uses. In 'Reference and Definite Descriptions', Keith Donnellan complicates this simple picture.[19] He claims that there are both referential and non-referential uses of definite descriptions: in this he disagrees with both Frege and Russell. But he claims that the referential uses do not rest on the presupposition that there is exactly one thing which satisfies the description: in this he disagrees with Frege and Strawson. Moreover, whether a use is referential does not depend on the general form of the sentence in which it occurs, or on what we would ordinarily say if we heard it, but on the intentions of the speaker who uses it.

Donnellan's distinction is most vividly explained by means of a single sentence:

(12) Smith's murderer is insane.

Suppose I utter this sentence knowing merely that Smith has been murdered and that Smith was the most lovable person in the world. It is hard to think that there is a particular person I have in mind, and hence that there is a particular person I am referring to here. Donnellan says that in such a case I am using the description, not referentially, but *attributively*. We might give the character of such a use of (12) by means of a paraphrase:

(12a) Whoever murdered Smith is (must be) insane.

But now imagine a different scenario. A particular person – I forget his name – has been charged with Smith's murder and is widely believed to be guilty. He has been behaving oddly in his trial, and I want to comment on that. I might now utter (12), using the description 'Smith's murderer' simply as a convenient way of making clear who I'm talking about (given that I've forgotten his name). In such a case, Donnellan says, the description is being used *referentially*. We might give the character of this kind of use of (12) by means of a different paraphrase:

(12r) That man (you know – Smith's murderer) is insane.

---

[19] K. Donnellan, 'Reference and Definite Descriptions', *Philosophical Review*, 75 (1966), pp. 281–304.

According to Donnellan, in the attributive use the definite description is essential to what I want to say: in our case, I want to make a specific connection between being Smith's murderer and being insane. In the referential use, on the other hand, the description is not essential to what I want to say: I simply want to say something about *that person*, and using the description is just one of a number of possible ways of making it clear which person is involved. This is the crucial connection with the speaker's intentions: whether the use is attributive or referential depends on whether or not the description is essential to what *I want to say*. Note that this means that I can still use a description attributively, even if I think I know which person is meant. I can still mean to say what (12a) says when I utter (12), even if I think I know who killed Smith; so I can still be using the description attributively, even if I have a particular person in mind.

It might be tempting to propose a friendly compromise at this point. We might be tempted to accept Donnellan's distinction, and give a Russellian account of the attributive uses and a Strawsonian account of the referential uses. But this is exactly what Donnellan does not want to do: he thinks that Russell's account is wrong for the attributive uses, and Strawson's is wrong for the referential uses.

Consider the referential uses first. If I use (12) in the way indicated by (12r), then, according to Donnellan, all I really want to say is that *that man is insane*. Donnellan claims, in effect, that this is all I really *do* say: the phrase 'Smith's murderer' is simply part of an extrinsic device to help me to say just that. If that's what I do say, then what I say is true if the man in question is insane – even if he's not actually Smith's murderer. And this is the crucial difference with Strawson. On Strawson's account, a referential use of (12) would involve presupposing that there is exactly one thing which murdered Smith; and if that presupposition were false, then nothing – either true or false – would be said in an utterance of (12). But according to Donnellan's account, the truth or falsity of what Strawson takes to be presupposed is strictly speaking irrelevant to the truth or falsity of (12), in the referential use. It may help if either the speaker or the audience *believe* that exactly one person murdered Smith, but even that is not strictly necessary.

On the other hand, Donnellan seems to think that the Russellian account is wrong about attributive uses. Donnellan thinks that someone who utters (12) attributively – that is, meaning roughly what is expressed by (12a) – does presuppose the unique existence of a murderer of Smith. This would mean that if either no one or more than one person murdered Smith, then nothing – either true or false – would be said by someone who uttered (12), in the attributive use. So it's precisely in the *non*-referential uses, according to Donnellan, that there's a Strawsonian presupposition.[20]

3.7 Russellian defences

Can a Russellian find anything to say in response to Strawson's and Donnellan's criticisms? Yes: plenty.

In the first place, Strawson's distinction between what can properly be said of *expressions* and what can properly be said only of *uses* of expressions is easily neutralized. Russell's theory of descriptions is designed to solve a number of specific problems. Most of my formulations of those problems are already suited to Strawson's distinction, and the others are easily adapted by inserting some reference to *uses*.[21] Russell's theory likewise can be adapted in very minor ways to deal with the problems in their revised formulations.

The Russellian will attempt to meet the remaining criticisms brought by Strawson and Donnellan by making two distinctions:

(i) Between what is strictly true or false and what is helpful or unhelpful in a conversational context;
(ii) Between what is *strictly and literally said* in a use of a sentence, and what a *speaker means* in uttering it.[22]

Consider, to begin with, Strawson's objection that someone who utters, 'The present King of France is bald' is not asserting that there is exactly one present King of France. Why does Strawson say this? Because, he says,

---

[20] Donnellan's view can be put in terms of Russell's notion of denotation (see footnote 11 above). In some uses (the attributive ones), nothing is said if nothing is denoted by the description; and in others (the referential ones) something is said even when nothing is denoted by the description, but the truth of what is said does not depend on there being something which the description denotes.

[21] For example, (P4) is easily amended using the phrase 'contemporary uses of sentences' instead of just 'sentences'.

[22] For an elaborate defence of Russell's theory by means of such distinctions, see S. Neale, Descriptions (Cambridge, MA: MIT Press, 1990), ch. 3.

no normal speaker would respond to an utterance of such a sentence by saying 'That's untrue'.

The Russellian will not find this evidence convincing. Let's grant that the reactions of normal speakers will be as Strawson claims:[23] does that show that a contemporary use of the sentence 'The present King of France is bald' is not, in fact, false? It's not so clear. The Russellian will think that the everyday reaction can be explained in another way. In general, in ordinary conversation, when we use definite descriptions there is no doubt about the existence of something to which the description applies. We talk about the moon and the sun: they are visibly there. We wonder whether we have locked the front door: of course the front door exists! In these circumstances, if someone says that a use of a sentence involving a definite description is false, we don't even consider the possibility of the falsehood being due to there being nothing which satisfies the description. If I say, 'The front door is locked', and you, having checked, say, 'That's untrue', you mean that the front door, whose existence you do not question, is not locked.

Against this background, we will naturally understand the response 'That's untrue' to a contemporary use of the sentence 'The present King of France is bald' as suggesting acceptance of the existence of a present King of France, and to be asserting, in effect, that the person so described is, in fact, not bald. When we know that there's no present King of France, we will regard such a response as unhelpful and misleading. According to the Russellian, our reluctance to say that 'The present King of France is bald' is false arises from a reluctance to say something misleading, rather than a reluctance to say something false. Taking the evidence in Strawson's way, the Russellian will claim, is failing to make distinction (i).[24]

What about Strawson's other objection, involving a case where there's *more than* one thing which satisfies the description? The Russellian is aware, of course, that most definite descriptions do not say enough explicitly to ensure uniqueness. Suppose I utter the following sentence in some ordinary, easily imaginable situation:

---

[23] In fact, there are cases where the Strawsonian reaction is much less natural: 'This morning my father had breakfast with the King of France', for example, might seem to be obviously false. (The example is due to S. Neale, Descriptions, p. 27.)

[24] This response can be found in M. Sainsbury, *Russell* (London: Routledge and Kegan Paul, 1979), pp. 120–1.

(13)   The door is locked.

No Russellian imagines that I'm asserting that there is only one door in the world. Instead, the Russellian will suppose that the context normally restricts our attention sufficiently to ensure that only one door could be relevant. One way of explaining this is to treat (13) as if it were elliptical for something like this:

(13*) The door which … is locked.

And we'll imagine that the context will implicitly fill in the gaps.[25] Now suppose I utter the following sentence, in the presence of lots of tables and with no particular table in mind:

(11) The table is covered with books.

According to the Russellian, this will be like asserting the following, with nothing at all filling the gaps:

(11*) The table which … is covered with books.

But if there's nothing at all filling the gaps in (11*), (11*) is not a complete sentence; and that's why we naturally feel that when (11) is uttered in the imagined circumstances, nothing true or false has been said.

The Russellian deals with Donnellan's alternative conception by insisting on distinction (ii). Donnellan's distinction between referential and attributive uses depends on a distinction in what the speaker wants to say. He assumes that what the speaker says is just what the speaker wants to say, and this is what the Russellian will deny.[26] The Russellian will say that the meaning of words is independent of what any particular person may mean by them, and will claim that the strict and literal meaning of sentences containing definite descriptions is given by the Russellian

---

[25] An alternative (or at least: *apparently* alternative) approach supposes that the context fixes the domain of quantification. In ordinary language, we don't just quantify unrestrictedly over all of the objects in the universe: instead, we fix the area of our interest before we begin, and then quantify over objects within that area or domain. In English, this is sometimes done by using nouns after quantifier expressions like 'all', 'every', and 'some'. 'All whales are mammals' might be understood as saying something like this: consider just whales – well, they're all mammals. It's not clear that in the end the two ways of appealing to context are significantly different.

[26] This issue will return again in ch. 13: see especially, § 13.6.

analysis in terms of quantifiers. Of course, a particular speaker may use such sentences to convey different particular things in particular circumstances; but what the speaker conveys, or means to convey, is not the same as what she strictly and literally says.[27]

There's room for doubt about how effective these defences are. A Strawsonian will want to claim, for example, that her unwillingness to say that a contemporary use of 'The present King of France is bald' is false is not due simply to a desire to avoid being misleading. And it's natural to think that there is more to Donnellan's distinction between referential and attributive uses than a difference merely in speakers' intentions.

The differences between the Russellian view and its critics are manifestations of a deeper difference between their approaches to the philosophy of language. Russell himself was impatient with appeals to our ordinary understanding of ordinary language, because he thought that it was the business of philosophy to refine ordinary language for its own particular philosophical purposes, just as the sciences refine ordinary language for their purposes.[28] But even if we don't follow Russell in his ambition to improve ordinary language, there's still room for large differences of approach. On the one hand, we can think of human languages as like very complicated machines: the task of the philosopher is then to understand how they tick. We might call this the *mechanical* conception of language. If we take this view, we will think that the operation of human languages is governed by laws which are similar in status to the laws of physics. Our inclination will be to look for uniform explanations of a variety of phenomena, with particular variations being due to variations in local circumstances.

The Russellian approach to definite descriptions broadly fits this model. It offers a uniform account of the strict and literal meaning of *all* uses of sentences containing definite descriptions. Within the mechanical conception, the uniformity of the basic approach is itself a virtue. Particular variations and surprising intuitions are then explained, as they would be within a scientific theory of a relevantly similar range of

---

[27] For a developed form of this kind of response, see S. Kripke, 'Speaker's Reference and Semantic Reference', in P. French, T. Uehling, and H. Wettstein, eds., *Contemporary Perspectives in the Philosophy of Language* (Minneapolis: University of Minnesota Press, 1977), pp. 6–27.

[28] See, e.g., B. Russell, 'Mr Strawson on Referring', *Mind*, 66 (1957), pp. 387–8.

phenomena, as the result of other factors which affect the operation of the system in particular situations. We explain counter-intuitions, like those which Strawson appeals to, by understanding what would inevitably happen to such a system in the ordinary circumstances of everyday life.

Strawson and Donnellan, however, take a different kind of view. They do not suppose that there is a system which can in any way be compared to a machine whose operation we need to understand. They expect to find nothing deeper than the complications of everyday life: their concern is just to be true to those complications. There is no virtue for them in uniformity of explanation, just as such: they are reluctant to generalize too quickly; they expect there to be exceptions to every rule. For them, in the end, the philosophy of language is not concerned with understanding how language ticks, but with what people are doing when they speak.[29]

This opposition is easily caricatured, and the differences should not be overstated. Those who adopt the mechanical conception of language are prolific in producing accounts of what people are doing when they speak – in order to account for the fact that the way in which we normally take various uses of language differs considerably from what any systematizing approach would lead one initially to expect. And those who adopt the other approach are happy to adopt makeshift rules and discern general tendencies insofar as that is helpful. But the general difference of emphasis is clear enough.

3.8   Russell beyond descriptions

One of Russell's principal motives in producing his theory was a distrust of Frege's notion of Sense. Has he managed to do without it? Russell has some solution of the problems which Sense was introduced to solve in the case of definite descriptions and proper names of fictional entities, but at the time of 'On Denoting' he seems to have regarded most ordinary proper names as singular terms. This leads to an obvious intuitive difficulty.

'Alice Cooper' is the name taken by a rock musician who was previously called *Vincent Furnier*. My friend Frankie knows nothing of rock music,

---

[29] This approach to language was inspired by the later work of Wittgenstein: see ch. 15 below.

which explains why the following is true:

(14) Frankie thinks that Alice Cooper is a woman.

But Frankie knows that 'Vincent' is a man's name, so it seems that the following is *false*:

(15) Frankie thinks that Vincent Furnier is a woman.

This seems to show that we cannot swap proper names which refer to the same thing within psychological contexts.

This is an aspect of what I've called the Basic Worry with the view that the meaning of words concerns things in the world, rather than things in our minds. In its general form, this aspect of the worry is that if two words are associated with the same thing in the world, we might expect them to have the same meaning, but this seems unnatural. How can we deal with this without introducing the notion of Sense? One way would be to tough it out: we might insist that (15) is true after all. We might, for example, try to explain the counter-intuitiveness of (15) as being due to its being *misleading* rather than false. This robust option has indeed been pursued recently.[30] But it might seem more natural to extend Russell's treatment of fictional names to cover all ordinary proper names as well. We would then regard ordinary proper names as equivalent to definite descriptions.[31] The name 'Alice Cooper' might be equivalent to some description like 'the leader of that famous rock band', and the name 'Vincent Furnier' to some such description as 'the male child of the Furniers'. These descriptions might then be given a Russellian analysis, to make (14) and (15) equivalent to these two sentences:

(14r) Frankie thinks that there is exactly one object which is a leader of that famous rock band, and that object is a woman;

(15r) Frankie thinks that there is exactly one object which is a male child of the Furniers, and that object is a man.

---

[30] This kind of line is advocated in N. Salmon, *Frege's Puzzle* (Cambridge, MA: MIT Press, 1986), and, in a different way, in S. Soames, *Beyond Rigidity: The Unfinished Semantic Agenda of* Naming and Necessity (Oxford: Oxford University Press, 2002). The issues raised here are dealt with in ch. 8, below.

[31] Russell himself suggested that ordinary names are 'a sort of truncated or telescoped description': Russell, 'The Philosophy of Logical Atomism', in B. Russell, *Logic and Knowledge*, ed. R. Marsh (London: George Allen and Unwin, 1956), p. 243.

We might question the naturalness of these analyses, but we can now deploy Russell's standard explanation of the illegitimacy of swapping definite descriptions which denote the same object: definite descriptions have no isolable meaning, so the issue of swapping them doesn't arise.

As we saw before, this isn't a finally satisfying solution. We need to understand why the two *predicates* – '*x* is a leader of that famous rock band' and '*x* is a male child of the Furniers' – cannot be swapped, even though they're both true of the same thing. After all, being true of the same thing is enough for both predicates to have the same reference, according to Frege. In response to this, it's natural to revise Frege's conception of the reference of predicates, and suggest that predicates refer to *qualities* and *relations*. Qualities correspond to one-place predicates (wisdom corresponds to '*x* is wise', for example), and relations to predicates with two or more places (*being-to-the-left-of* corresponds to '*x* is to the left of *y*', for example). The *quality* of being a leader of that famous rock band is different from the *quality* of being a male child of the Furniers, even if the corresponding predicates are true of the same thing.

How might this affect the general shape of our semantic theory? We can still hold that singular terms refer to objects, though there will be relatively few genuine singular terms, if ordinary proper names are treated as being equivalent to definite descriptions, and definite descriptions are analysed in Russell's way. In the end Russell thought that the only genuine singular terms – what he called 'logically proper names' – were demonstratives (such as 'this' and 'that') which refer to features of momentary sense experience (ironically, something very like Lockean Ideas).[32]

What about sentences? If singular terms refer to objects, and predicates refer to qualities or relations, it's natural to take sentences to refer to things we might call *situations* or *states of affairs*.[33] This seems easy enough when the sentences are true: we can say that a true sentence refers to a *fact*. So the sentence 'Vincent Furnier is a rock musician' refers to the fact *that Vincent Furnier is a rock musician*. But what if the sentence is false? We can't say that the sentence 'Alice Cooper is a woman' refers to a fact, because there is no such

---

[32] See Russell, 'The Philosophy of Logical Atomism', p. 201.

[33] In his early period, Russell himself took sentences to refer to what he called 'propositions' – combinations of objects and qualities or relations: see, e.g., *Principles of Mathematics*, 2nd edn (London: George Allen and Unwin, 1937), § 51, p. 47. He then identified facts with true propositions.

fact: the fact is that Alice Cooper is *not* a woman. It seems that we have to say that a false sentence refers to a merely *possible* situation or state of affairs.

Russell was tempted by a semantic theory of this general style from relatively early in his career (around the time of 'On Denoting'). He inaugurated a tradition which provides a genuine alternative to Fregean theories.[34] Frege used a very austere notion of reference – sentences refer to truth-values, predicates to functions from objects to truth-values – and supplemented that with the notion of Sense to deal with the Basic Worry which that seems to make so acute. The Russellian alternative begins with a richer notion of reference – sentences refer to facts or situations,[35] and predicates to qualities or relations – and makes no appeal to Sense at all. It aims to deal with the Basic Worry by means of this richer notion of reference, combined with the policy of treating ordinary proper names as definite descriptions, and definite descriptions as quantifier expressions.

Further reading

The most famous objections to Russell's theory are those provided by Strawson and Donnellan: see P. F. Strawson, 'On Referring', *Mind*, 59 (1950), pp. 320–44, and K. Donnellan, 'Reference and Definite Descriptions', *Philosophical Review*, 75 (1966), pp. 281–304. A sustained defence of Russell's theory in the face of these and related objections is provided by S. Neale, *Descriptions* (Cambridge, MA: MIT Press, 1990).

An alternative presentation of Russell's theory – neater in some ways, but without the helpful orientation towards the problems which led Frege to introduce the notion of Sense – is to be found in Russell's *Introduction to Mathematical Philosophy* (London: George Allen and Unwin, 1919), ch. 16. Russell's mature philosophy of language is to be found in his 'The Philosophy of Logical Atomism', *Monist*, 28 (1918) and 29 (1919), reprinted in B. Russell, *Logic and Knowledge*, ed. R. Marsh (London: George Allen and Unwin, 1956), pp. 177–281. A general book on Russell, dealing with the theory of descriptions and much else besides, is M. Sainsbury, *Russell* (London: Routledge and Kegan Paul, 1979).

---

[34] Recent work in this Russellian tradition includes J. Barwise and J. Perry, *Situations and Attitudes* (Cambridge, MA: MIT Press, 1983), and N. Salmon, *Frege's Puzzle*.

[35] Or, in Russell's version, 'propositions', which are understood as combinations of objects and qualities or relations.

4   Kripke on proper names

Key text

Saul Kripke, *Naming and Necessity*, 2nd edn (Oxford: Blackwell, 1980), lectures I and II.

4.1   Introduction

'Alice Cooper' is a proper name; 'the famous shock-rock musician' is a definite description which tells you something about the person whose name it is. Frege thought that both names and descriptions were singular terms – expressions whose business is to refer to objects. Russell thought that neither ordinary proper names nor definite descriptions were singular terms. But Russell and Frege were agreed in this: they both thought that names and descriptions work in the same way. Indeed, they both seem to have thought that ordinary proper names were equivalent in meaning to definite descriptions.

In this they were opposed to an older and simpler view held by J. S. Mill, that proper names 'do not indicate or imply any attributes as belonging to those individuals' which they refer to.[1] A simple amplification of Mill's view – let's call this the *Millian* view – holds that there is no more to the meaning of a name than the fact that it refers to the object it does refer to. The most obvious difficulty for the Millian view is provided by the kind of case which led Frege to introduce the notion of Sense in the first place. The kind of difficulty involved here is an aspect of what I've called the Basic Worry for the view that the meaning of words is concerned with things in the world, rather than things in the mind.[2] Consider Art, a native of

---

[1] J. S. Mill, *A System of Logic* (London: Longmans, Green, Reader, and Dyer, 1875), I, ii, 5, 5

[2] See ch. 2, § 2.8, above.

Detroit, born in the late 1940s. He remembers Vincent Furnier with some affection as a child he knew slightly at school. Art's children are fans of Alice Cooper: much to Art's disgust – he hates this kind of music. Art is unaware that 'Alice Cooper' is now Vincent Furnier's name. *This* is true:

(1) Art thinks that Alice Cooper is a rock musician.

But it's natural to think that *this* is false:

(2) Art thinks that Vincent Furnier is a rock musician.

Frege and Russell adopted the same solution to the puzzle this kind of case creates. On their view, the name 'Alice Cooper' means the same (for Art, at least) as some such description as 'the famous shock-rock musican', and the name 'Vincent Furnier' means the same (for Art, at least) as 'the child at school'.

This is the simple version of what is known as the *description* theory of names. The obvious problem with it was acknowledged by Frege (and is visible in the cautious formulations I've just used). The same name will seem to be equivalent to *different* descriptions for different people. Some people will think of Alice Cooper as a rock musician; others will think of him as a Little League baseball coach; others again as a restaurateur. No one description can be thought to give *the* meaning of the name 'Alice Cooper'.

John Searle proposed a simple solution to this difficulty.[3] We do not take a name as it stands in a linguistic community to be equivalent to a *single* identifying description: we take it to be associated with a (slightly indeterminate) *cluster* of descriptions. To put the point a little more precisely, the claim is this. In a given community, a single name will be associated with a number of identifying descriptions. To count as understanding a name, someone must associate it with a suitable (even if vaguely specified) proportion of these descriptions. If you and I both understand the name 'Aristotle', we will each understand a suitable proportion of the identifying descriptions associated with the name in our community. And even if we don't associate precisely the same descriptions with the name, we will still understand each other in our uses of the name if the descriptions we associate with it overlap. A given proper name may

---

[3] John R. Searle, 'Proper Names', *Mind*, 67 (1958), pp. 166–73.

be said to be equivalent in meaning to one set of descriptions for one person, and to another set of descriptions for another person, so the meaning of a name *for a person* (or for a person at a time) can be specified. But there's no set of descriptions which is equivalent to the name *for the whole community* (or for any very extended period of time), so the meaning of the name for the community, or in the language, cannot be informatively specified. People count as belonging to a linguistic community in virtue of there being sufficient overlap in the meaning (for each of them) of the words they use.

In one form or another, the description theory of names held sway with little question for about half a century. This chapter focuses on the work which upset that domination. In January 1970 Saul Kripke gave three lectures at Princeton, which were published soon afterwards in a collection of articles,[4] and eventually as a book. They have established a new orthodoxy on the topics of their title, naming and necessity. The first two lectures are concerned to argue that ordinary proper names work quite differently from definite descriptions. They also go some way towards re-instating something like Mill's view of names.

4.2 Kripke's target

Kripke's attack on the description theory of names takes Searle's version as the theory's best representative. Kripke aims to undermine the most fundamental commitments of the description theory. Since the theory is concerned at base with the meaning a proper name has *for an individual*, the theory's fundamental commitments concern what has to be true for a name to have meaning for an individual. These commitments are supposed to apply for any name; so in what follows '0' could be any name. And they're supposed to apply for the meaning of a name for any speaker; so S could be any speaker. To show that any one of these basic commitments is wrong, we only need to show that there could be some name, or some individual speaker, that they don't apply to.

---

[4] In D. Davidson and G. Harman, eds., *Semantics of Natural Language* (Dordrecht: Reidel, 1972), pp. 253–355.

Kripke identifies a range of basic commitments of the description theory. We can formulate them as follows:[5]

(DN1) If 'O' is a name which is meaningful for a speaker, S, there is a family of things which S believes to be true of O:

(DN2) If 'O' is a name which is meaningful for S, S must believe that some of the things which she believes to be true of O are true of only one thing;

(DN3) If 'O' is a name which is meaningful for S, then if most of the things (or most of the important things) which S believes to be true of O are in fact true of just one particular thing, then that particular thing is the referent of the name 'O' as S understands it;

(DN4) If 'O' is a name which is meaningful for S, then if there is not exactly one thing to which most of the things which S believes to be true of O in fact apply, then 'O', as S understands it, does not refer:

(DN5) If 'O' is a name which is meaningful for S, then S knows *a priori* that, if O exists, most of what she believes to be true of O is in fact true of O (as S understands 'O');

(DN6) If 'O' is a meaningful name for S, then it is necessarily true that, if O exists, most of what S believes to be true of O is indeed true of O (as S understands 'O').

(DN1) and (DN2) are commitments which are needed to make sense of what follows: they have no independent rationale. (DN3) and (DN4) encapsulate a certain conception of how proper names manage to refer to objects. The conception is this: a proper name refers to an object in virtue of that object's satisfying the condition specified in the description which gives the meaning of the name for a particular speaker. In our example, the conditions would be *being the famous shock-rock musician* for the name 'Alice Cooper' and *being the child at school* for the name 'Vincent Furnier' – as these names are understood by Art.

---

[5] The formulation of these commitments differs from Kripke's own in two crucial respects. First, Kripke's formulations are not always well formed: the grammatical relationship between the different theses is obscure, for example. And secondly, in order to avoid certain possible misinterpretations, Kripke introduces some technicalities in his formulations which I have preferred to avoid. I have tried to straighten out the relationship between the different theses, and have offered informal formulations, trusting to the naturalness of the intended interpretation, rather than trying to remove the possibility of misinterpretation.

Commitments (DN5) and (DN6) are meant to follow from the idea that definite descriptions (or families of them) give the *meaning* of proper names. It seems to be part of the meaning of the word 'bachelor' – to use a hackneyed parallel – that bachelors are unmarried men. So it can be known *a priori* (without observation) that if someone is a bachelor he's unmarried, and nobody *could* be a bachelor and be married.

Kripke associates one final commitment with the description theory of names, which is really a conception of how the other commitments are to be understood. It's a non-circularity condition:

> (NC) The things referred to in (DN1)–(DN6) as being believed by *S* to be true of *O* must not themselves involve the notion of reference in an ineliminable way.

What kind of circularity is Kripke trying to avoid? Here is a clear example:

> (*) Alice Cooper is *the person referred to by the name 'Alice Cooper' in this very sentence*.

On Kripke's view, the italicized phrase here cannot be the description which a description theory supposes gives the meaning of the name 'Alice Cooper' whenever it occurs in someone's use (with the phrase 'this sentence' referring to whichever sentence it occurs in, on each occasion), since the description itself depends on the independent meaningfulness of the name.

Is this characterization of the description theory fair? I think it's clearly close enough to at least one conception of the point of the description theory. Tinkering with the odd commitment here and there won't protect the theory from Kripke's criticisms. He argues that *all* of the basic commitments, apart from (DN1), are wrong, if we keep the non-circularity condition in place.

4.3 Kripke's objections (i): simple considerations

To begin with, let's ask what most of us know (or think we know) about various famous people (not counting such things as their being called what they are, which seem to violate the non-circularity condition). Who was Cicero? A Roman orator. Who was Afra Behn? A seventeenth-century poet. Who was Gödel? The man who discovered the incompleteness of arithmetic. Who was Marie Curie? A scientist who died of cancer. Most of us know almost nothing about these (and most other) famous people, and yet we seem able to use their names, apparently with understanding. Kripke's first objections depend upon these informal descriptions being the best which we can, in general, produce for people whose names we think we understand. If we demand any more complete descriptions than these, it will turn out that most of us don't understand most of the names we use.

(DN2)–(DN4) are very quickly vulnerable, if we confine our attention to such descriptions as these. Consider first (DN4), which states that if there is not exactly one thing which meets the conditions associated with the name, the name does not refer. Surely there have been more than one Roman orator, more than one seventeenth-century poet, and more than one scientist who has died of cancer? In that case, the ordinary names 'Cicero', 'Afra Behn', and 'Marie Curie', as most of us understand them, fail to refer: there are no such people as Cicero, Afra Behn, and Marie Curie, as we understand the names. Which is absurd.

(DN2) is, if anything, even worse. Which of us *believes* that there have been only one Roman orator, seventeenth-century poet, or scientist who has died of cancer? None of us: so (DN2), it seems, is simply false.

What of (DN3), which says that if something is the one thing which meets the condition associated with a name, it's what the name refers to? Consider the case of the name 'Gödel'. This is one (rare) case, when what we know of the person named seems, in fact, to be enough to pick out a single individual uniquely. But, says Kripke, suppose we're wrong: suppose that in fact the incompleteness of arithmetic was proved not by Gödel, but by an obscure Austrian named Schmidt. Would that mean that the unheard-of Schmidt was Gödel? Would that mean that when we use the name 'Gödel' we would suddenly be referring, not to Gödel, whom some people we know have known, but to Schmidt? Of course not: the story is properly characterized as I have characterized it; in the imagined scenario, there are two men, Gödel and Schmidt, and Schmidt, remaining merely Schmidt, discovered the incompleteness of arithmetic, and Gödel, remaining Gödel, did not. The name 'Gödel' continues to refer to the same man, whom some people we know have known.

4.4   Kripke's objections (ii): epistemic and modal considerations

So much for the simpler points which Kripke makes against the description theory. But the objections which have had the most impact on later philosophy have been those against (DN5) and (DN6). Of particular importance is the fact that Kripke argues that they need to be dealt with by *different* objections. Consider the following sentence:

(3) Vincent Furnier is Vincent Furnier.

This seems obviously true (given that there is such a person as Vincent Furnier). It couldn't but have been true; we know it's true without observation or experiment, that is, *a priori*. Compare that with this sentence:

(4) Vincent Furnier is Alice Cooper.

It doesn't seem possible to know this *a priori*: we need to know a little of the history of English literature to find it out. So it might seem that it isn't necessary: on the face of it, it seems that we can imagine it being false.

One of Kripke's fundamental points is that this reasoning is mistaken. There are two basic distinctions among types of truths. There is the distinction between *contingent* and *necessary* truths: between statements which, though true, *might not* have been, and those which *could not but* have been true. And there is the distinction between *a posteriori* and *a priori* truths: between those which can only be known by observation and experience, and those which can be known without observation or experience. The first distinction is concerned with how things could have been, objectively: Kripke calls it a *metaphysical* distinction. (Others have used the word 'ontological' to make the same point.) The second distinction is concerned with how things can be *known*: it is an *epistemic* distinction (concerned with knowledge, rather than how things are).

These two distinctions were thought to coincide: all *a priori* truths were thought to be necessary, and vice versa; all *a posteriori* truths were thought to be contingent, and vice versa. But Kripke points out that since the distinctions are made in quite different ways, it shouldn't be *obvious* that they coincide. If we're to address (DN5) and (DN6) properly, we need to understand what each distinction involves, and keep the two distinctions separate in our minds.

Consider, then, (DN5), the claim that someone must be able to know *a priori* that if the object referred to by a name exists, it meets the condition associated with the name. And recall what most of us know about many of the names we think we can meaningfully use. Do I know *a priori* that Cicero was a Roman orator? Surely not: I read it in a book. Do I know *a priori* that Marie Curie died of cancer? Surely not: I heard it from someone. The crucial point is that the meaningfulness of these names, as I understand them, does not depend on the truth of what I believe about the people concerned.

Kripke's most famous objection to the description theory of names is his objection to (DN6), the claim that it's necessarily true that if the object referred to by a name exists, it meets the condition associated with the name. Now consider one of those names of famous people, and suppose that all I know about the person is contained in the brief characterization I offered before. Suppose, then, that this is all I know about Gödel:

(5) Gödel discovered the incompleteness of arithmetic.

According to (DN6), the following is necessarily true:

(6) If Gödel existed, Gödel discovered the incompleteness of arithmetic.

But that is absurd: surely Gödel could have followed a different career, or died before he discovered the proof, and if either of those things had happened, (6) would have been false. It doesn't matter for this point that only one, rather brief, description is involved: even if you add the fullest range of descriptions which it's plausible to imagine an ordinary speaker might associate with the name, you will still have only contingent truths. These descriptions will concern things Gödel did, people he met, places he was seen in, and so on: in every such case, Gödel could have done something different, met other people, gone to different places, while remaining the same person.

According to Kripke, the contingency of (6) marks a point of contrast between proper names and definite descriptions. If the name 'Gödel' were equivalent in meaning to the description 'the discoverer of the incompleteness of arithmetic', then the following sentence would be equivalent to (6):

(7) If anyone discovered the incompleteness of arithmetic, the discoverer of the incompleteness of arithmetic discovered the in-completeness of arithmetic.

But although (6) seems to be contingent, (7) is necessary. Using descriptions instead of names seems to be enough to make a modal difference – a difference concerning possibility and necessity.

How is this to be explained? Let's first introduce the term 'designator': a designator is an expression which is used to pick out an individual. Designators then include proper names and definite descriptions, even if descriptions are understood in Russell's way, as expressions which introduce quantifiers. Kripke claims that proper names are designators of quite a different kind from definite descriptions.

To explain this difference, Kripke introduces some terminology which is useful in explaining the validity of arguments involving possibility and necessity.[6] This involves the notion of a *possible world*. A possible world, roughly speaking, is a *way the world might have been*. So if something *could* have happened, there's a possible world in which it *does* happen. If Gödel could have become a banker, there's a possible world in which he *is* a banker. In general, something is *possible* if there is some possible world in which it is the case. Something is *necessarily* true if it *could not but* be true. In terms of possible worlds, that means that something is necessarily true if there's *no* possible world in which it is *not* true; that is, if it's true in *every* possible world. A *contingent* truth is one which is true in the *actual* world, but not *all* possible worlds.

Look again at (6) and (7). According to Kripke's view, (7) is true in every possible world. But (6) is contingent: it's true in the actual world, but not all possible worlds. The following, however, is true in all possible worlds in which Gödel exists:

(8) Gödel was Gödel.

Here's how we can make sense of such claims, according to Kripke. We can imagine that different people, people other than Gödel, might have discovered the incompleteness of arithmetic. Perhaps the Austrian, Schmidt, might have done. Or perhaps the Bavarian, Braun, might have done. Suppose (bizarrely, but for the sake of argument) that only one of

---

[6] To put the point very simply, it allows us to explain the validity of arguments involving possibility and necessity using fundamentally the same apparatus as is used to explain the validity of arguments using quantifiers such as 'all' and 'some'.

these three – Gödel, Schmidt, and Braun – could possibly have discovered the incompleteness of arithmetic. We can imagine a situation in which Schmidt found the proof: call this *possible world A*. And we can imagine a situation in which Braun found the proof: call this *possible world B*. And, of course, there's a possible world in which Gödel found the proof: the *actual* world. Now let's ask: is (7) true in all of these worlds? On Kripke's view, to find out the answer, what we need to do is first consider who found the proof in each world, and then ask: did that person, whoever it was, discover the incompleteness of arithmetic in that world? The answer in each case is obviously *Yes*. So (7) is true in all of the possible worlds in which anyone discovered the incompleteness of arithmetic.

But consider (6) and (8). According to Kripke's view, to find out whether (6) is true in each world, you first find *Gödel*, and then ask whether that man, Gödel, found the proof in that world. Suppose that Gödel exists in both world *A* and world *B* (perhaps in *A* he's a mathematician who is a rival of Schmidt's, and in *B* he's a market-gardener). It's obvious that (6) is false in both world *A* and world *B*, but true in the actual world. Since (6) is true in the actual world and false in some other possible worlds (worlds *A* and *B*), (6) is contingent.

Now turn to (8). To find out whether (8) is true in each world, you first find Gödel, and then ask whether that man, Gödel, is Gödel in that world. Obviously, (8) is true in every possible world in which Gödel exists.

Here's the difference, then, on Kripke's view. To find out whether a sentence involving a *description* is true in a given possible world, you first consider whoever satisfies the description *in that world*, and then ask whether the rest of the sentence applies. But to find out whether a sentence involving a *proper name* is true in a given world, you first consider the person who is *ordinarily* referred to by that name, and then ask whether the rest of the sentence applies to that person. That is to say, a description picks out in each possible world whichever object satisfies the description *in that world*, and in most cases this will vary from world to world. But a name picks out the *same* object – the object *ordinarily* referred to by the name – in every possible world.

That's the fundamental difference between proper names and definite descriptions, on Kripke's view. A proper name is what Kripke calls a *rigid* designator: it picks out the *same* object in every possible world (at least those in which that object exists).[7] Most definite descriptions, on the other hand – according to Kripke – are *non-rigid* designators: they pick out different objects in different possible worlds. This fundamental difference means that proper names cannot be equivalent in meaning to definite descriptions.[8]

There's one striking consequence of Kripke's view that ordinary proper names are rigid designators. Consider this sentence:

(9) If Vincent Furnier exists, Vincent Furnier is Alice Cooper.

This is true. It seems clear that it can only be known *a posteriori*: I need to know a little about rock music to know it. But on Kripke's account it is *necessary*. 'Vincent Furnier' refers in all possible worlds to the same person, the person ordinarily referred to by that name in the actual world. 'Alice

---

[7] What about worlds in which the object does *not* exist? What does the name do there? There is a nice argument for the claim that the name refers to the same object even in worlds in which that object doesn't exist. Don't we want to say that Gödel might not have existed? In that case, it seems, 'Gödel does not exist' *might* have been true. That is to say, there is some possible world in which 'Gödel does not exist' *is* true. But, of course, for it to be true in that world, 'Gödel' must refer (to Gödel, of course), even though Gödel does not exist in that world. For this point, see, e.g., A. D. Smith, 'Rigidity and Scope', *Mind*, 93 (1984), p. 180. Smith himself attributes it to Kaplan; for relevant considerations, see D. Kaplan, 'Afterthoughts', in J. Almog, J. Perry, and H. Wettstein, eds., *Themes from Kaplan* (Oxford: Oxford University Press, 1989), pp. 569–71, and 'Bob and Carol and Ted and Alice', in J. Hintikka, J. Moravcsik, and P. Suppes, eds., *Approaches to Natural Language* (Dordrecht: Reidel, 1973), appendix x.

[8] Sometimes people have attempted to characterize the difference between rigid and non-rigid designators in terms of scope. The idea is that proper names are always understood as having *wider* scope than contexts of necessity and possibility: we always understand a name as if it occurred before the phrase 'it is necessary that …' or 'it is possible that …' Definite descriptions, on the other hand, are not understood like this: at least sometimes we understand them as occurring *within* contexts of necessity and possibility – *after* the phrases 'it is necessary that …' or 'it is possible that …' Kripke himself objects to this characterization of the distinction between rigid and non-rigid designators, on the ground that names are rigid designators even when no issue of scope arises (as in (6), for example). For an account of rigidity in terms of scope, see M. Dummett, *Frege: Philosophy of Language*, 2nd edn (London: Duckworth, 1981), pp. 112–16; see also G. McCulloch, *The Game of the Name* (Oxford: Oxford University Press, 1989), pp. 101–11. For Kripke's response, see *Naming and Necessity*, pp. 10–15. For an independent argument in support of Kripke's central point here, see Smith, 'Rigidity and Scope'. And for more on this issue, see S. Soames, *Beyond Rigidity* (Oxford: Oxford University Press, 2002), pp. 25–39.

Cooper' refers in all possible worlds to the same person, the person ordinarily referred to by that name in the actual world. As it happens, both names refer to the same person in the actual world. So they must refer to the same person in all possible worlds. So (9), which says precisely that if Vincent Furnier exists at all, Vincent Furnier is the same person as Alice Cooper, must be true in all possible worlds. So (9) is necessarily true.

Some might conclude from Kripke's arguments that the Millian theory was right after all: there's no more to the meaning of a proper name, in a given use, than the fact that it refers to the object which it does refer to; proper names have reference but no Sense. Kripke himself seems to have been tempted to draw this conclusion. Certainly, the Millian theory would provide an explanation of the fact (assuming it is a fact) that proper names are rigid designators. If a proper name merely refers to an object, and doesn't say anything about it, it's hard to see that it could do anything but pick out that object – the same object – in all possible worlds.

Kripke complements his arguments against the description theory with an alternative account – he calls it a 'picture' – of how proper names work. The description theory is at root *individualist*: it imagines each individual being capable of picking out the object referred to by means of what she herself knows about that object. The meaning of a name in a community is nothing but the overlap between such individual conceptions. His own 'picture' runs the other way. According to Kripke, an object receives a name in some initial baptism, and that is then a device for referring to the object later on. Later uses of the name are intended just to refer to whatever was referred to by the earlier uses of the name. Individual speakers need know nothing significant about the object referred to: all they need to do is to tap into a historical tradition of use of the name. The name itself, as it were, carries the reference to the object: it doesn't simply ride on the back of an independent capacity to identify the object.

4.5 Defences of the description theory

Should we adopt a Millian theory of names? Recall the problem for a Millian theory which arose over pairs of sentences like these two:

(1) Art thinks that Alice Cooper is a rock musician.
(2) Art thinks that Vincent Furnier is a rock musician.

In the circumstances imagined, we naturally think that (1) is true but (2) is false. But a Millian theory will count both as true. This is an aspect of what I've called the Basic Worry for the view that the meaning of words concerns things in the world, rather than things in the mind. One of the principal reasons for offering a description theory of names was that it allows us to hold onto the natural view about pairs of sentences like (1) and (2). Is there any way of letting a description theory do that job, while preserving it from Kripke's arguments? There is at least something to be said.

Kripke's whole presentation of the description theory assumes that the basic point of the description theory is to provide an account of how it is that names manage refer to the objects they do refer to. If this is the point of the description theory, the descriptions associated with names will have to provide us with some way of identifying those objects independently of the names themselves. And this leads Kripke to focus on a particular range of descriptions associated with particular names: descriptions such as 'the Roman orator', 'the famous physicist', and so on. These descriptions are very evidently vulnerable to Kripke's arguments against (DN2), (DN3), (DN4), and (DN5). No one expects us to have identifying descriptions for every name we understand which will pick out a single object uniquely, and which can be known without experience to be true of that object.

But it's not obvious that everyone who offers a form of description theory of names needs to be committed to this descriptive account of how names manage to refer to objects. We may offer a descriptive account of names simply in order to provide an account of how (1) may be true and (2) false. In that case, all we will want will be some description which will plausibly be equivalent in meaning to each name – provided that a different description is associated with each different name. If this is the limit of our ambitions, and we're making no attempt to explain how names manage to refer, then there's a devastatingly simple proposal which needs to be considered. Why not take the name 'Alice Cooper' to be equivalent to the description 'the person called "Alice Cooper"', and the name 'Vincent Furnier' to be equivalent to the description 'the person called "Vincent Furnier"'? Let's call this a simple *nominal description theory*.[9]

---

[9] See, e.g., K. Bach, *Thought and Reference* (Oxford: Oxford University Press, 1987), chs. 7 and 8, and more recently his 'Giorgione was So-Called because of his Name', *Philosophical Perspectives*, 16 (2002), pp. 73–103. The version of the nominal description theory I develop here is different from Bach's in some respects. Two are worth singling

Of course, there are (no doubt) lots of people called 'Alice Cooper' and lots of people called 'Vincent Furnier', but this need not embarrass a nominal description theorist. We've already seen that definite descriptions need to be understood as being used in particular contexts of utterance, so that it's natural to expect the context to supply whatever is needed to fix uniqueness.[10] A nominal description can be expected to be equivalent to something like 'the person who ... and is called "Vincent Furnier"' - with context supplying some filling of the blank - or else to something like 'the person who is called "Vincent Furnier" on this use of the name'.

If the things which are believed to be true of the referent of a name in (DN1)–(DN6) amount to no more than *being the thing called by that name*, there is no obvious problem with any of (DN1)–(DN5). The nominal description theorist's versions of the first four commitments are relatively unproblematic. There doesn't seem much difficulty even with (DN5). Consider this sentence:

(10) If Vincent Furnier exists, Vincent Furnier is the person who is called 'Vincent Furnier'.

It's not obvious that there's any difficulty in saying that that can be known *a priori*.

(DN6) is trickier, however. The problem is that even if (10) can be known *a priori*, it's not obvious that it's *necessarily* true. Surely Vincent Furnier might have been called by another name? This was Kripke's central point. But a nominal description theorist has some reply even to this. There seems to be another way of hearing (10) – helped, perhaps, by a suitable surrounding context – according to which it *is* necessary. Suppose that the phrase 'the person who is called "Vincent Furnier"' has already been introduced, before we use (10), and we're picking up on that earlier introduction of the phrase when we use (10). In that case, (10) will mean something like this:

(10*) As for the person who is called 'Vincent Furnier': if Vincent Furnier exists, Vincent Furnier *is* that person.

out. First, as will become clear in a moment, I allow that the descriptions may be rigid (because they implicitly include reference to the actual world); and secondly, I do not assume that Russell is right about definite descriptions.

[10] This point arose in connection with Russell's theory of descriptions in ch. 3, § 3.7.

And (10*) is naturally understood as being necessarily true.

We might formalize this by saying that there is a reading of descriptions as meaning the person who *actually* satisfies the description – the person who satisfies the description in the *actual* world. 'Actualized' definite descriptions of this sort seem to be rigid designators. They refer in all possible worlds to the person who satisfies the description in the *actual* world.

This suggests a minor revision to our initial simple nominal description theory: we take a name to be equivalent to an *actualized* description, picking out the person who is *actually* called by that name. That means that in order to test the theory, we need to consider the following sentence, instead of (10):

(10a) If Vincent Furnier exists, Vincent Furnier is the person who is *actually* called 'Vincent Furnier'.

And this does indeed seem to be necessarily true, as (DN6) requires. The uses of the name 'Vincent Furnier' outside quotation marks in (10) are, of course, uses of the name here, in the actual world. It seems inevitable that these uses of the rigidly designating name will pick out the very same person in all possible worlds as is picked out by the description 'the person who is *actually* called "Vincent Furnier"'. This is because this description will pick out the same person in all possible worlds – it will pick out in every world the person who is called 'Vincent Furnier' in the *actual* world.[11]

Of course, this nominal description theory falls foul of the Kripkean non-circularity condition (NC), but it will protest that that condition is unfair. The reason is that the condition is meant to block circular attempts to explain how names manage to refer to their objects, and the nominal description theory under consideration here is not trying to do that at all. It is simply trying to explain the difficulty of swapping co-referential names within psychological contexts.

Is the nominal description theory acceptable, then? I suspect not. As we've seen, the nominal description theory insists on separating these two tasks:

---

[11] The nominal description theory may still be vulnerable to a development of Kripke's modal argument: for a complex modal objection, see S. Soames, *Beyond Rigidity*, pp. 48–9.

(i) Providing an account of how proper names succeed in referring to objects;

(ii) Providing an account of the contribution of proper names to the meaning of sentences.

It aims to fulfil the second task while ignoring the first. Unfortunately, it's not clear that it can do this. It's not obvious that the nominal description theory is compatible with every theory offered in fulfilment of the first task. It's not even clear that it's compatible with the most plausible account.

Here's a suggestion about how proper names work. After a name's first introduction, later uses are linked to the first use *anaphorically*. An anaphoric link is one of the kind which makes sense of the use of 'she' in the second sentence of this pair:

(11) A woman came into the room. She was the person everyone was looking for.

We might suppose that the name 'Carol' works in a rather similar way in the second sentence of the following pair:

(12) Carol came into the room. Carol was the person everyone was looking for.

The suggestion that names work anaphorically is quite plausible. It would explain the naturalness of Kripke's suggestion that the reference of a name is determined by a history of links back to an initial baptism. The difficulty is that it's hard to understand how this suggestion could be compatible with the nominal description theory. It may be that in context a description might exploit anaphoric connections. For example, in a given context, someone might use the description 'the object named by the name "Vincent Furnier"' and defer to some recent previous use to draw attention to just one of the several things called by that name. But this isn't enough to make the name 'Vincent Furnier' function anaphorically. What we want is the idea that the *name itself* carries the link – as the pronoun 'she' does in (11) and the name 'Carol' seems to in (12). And it's hard to see how something which is equivalent to a definite description could do that. This suggests that Kripke may have been right after all to take description theories of names to be committed to a particular kind of conception of how names manage to refer to objects, and therefore to insist that they meet the non-circularity condition (NC).

4.6 Sense and direct reference

If we reject every form of description theory of names, it seems that we have to think of names as *directly referential*, in the terms of the following definition of direct reference:[12]

> (DR) An expression is *directly referential* if and only if
>   (i) It refers to a particular object; and
>   (ii) It does not refer to that particular object, on every occasion of its use, in virtue of that object's satisfying some description.

In fact, it seems that the really crucial thing about proper names is that they are directly referential. This seems more fundamental than their being rigid designators. For one thing, some descriptions (for example, those involving 'actually') are rigid designators. For another, it seems plausible to say that it is *because* they are directly referential that proper names are rigid designators. A name is unstructured; it refers directly. That is why there's no room for it to be anything other than a rigid designator. But if proper names are directly referential, does this mean we have to adopt a Millian view of names?

It's standardly assumed that it does, but in fact the issue is not so clear. There is a way of offering a Fregean – or perhaps *neo*-Fregean – theory which allows proper names to be directly referential and still have Sense.[13] It's natural to read more than this into the notion of Sense in retrospect, but when it was introduced the notion was effectively defined as whatever it is about two expressions which allows them to differ in informativeness even when they have the same reference. Consider the following two sentences:

---

[12] The term 'direct reference' seems to have been introduced by David Kaplan. The definition of direct reference in the text is meant to be a non-metaphorical elucidation of the conception presented by David Kaplan in his 'Afterthoughts', pp. 568–9. It also accords with the conception of 'pure referentiality' introduced by Smith in 'Rigidity and Scope', p. 190. Kaplan himself talks of reference which is 'unmediated by any propositional component', but the notion of 'mediation' is quite obscure, and that of a 'propositional component' introduces a number of technical issues. The cautious phrase 'on every occasion of its use' is inserted into the definition here in order to allow that a name may be *introduced* in the first instance by means of a description without being equivalent in meaning to that description.

[13] This picks up the alternative conception of Sense, in which Sense depends on reference, which was considered in ch. 2, § 2.7, above.

(13) Alice Cooper is a rock musician;

(14) Vincent Furnier is a rock musician.

It seems obvious that it's possible to understand both sentences, and yet think that one is true and the other false. That on its own is enough to guarantee that there's a difference of Sense between them. And if there's a difference in Sense between (13) and (14), that can be used to give a semantic explanation of how (1) can be true and (2) false.

Frege himself was inclined to *explain* the Sense of proper names in terms of definite descriptions, and the descriptions he chose were the kind which would appeal to a description theory of reference. In part this was due to one interpretation of the notion of a *mode of presentation*. Frege seems mostly to have regarded a mode of presentation of an object – a way of giving an object – as a condition which something has to meet in order to count as being the object in question. This leads to one interpretation of the slogan 'Sense determines reference', and allows terms to have Sense without reference. But if we start just from the idea that Sense is simply what marks difference of informativeness despite sameness of reference, it's possible to give a different interpretation of the notions of Sense and mode of presentation.

If we are acquainted with an object, we are bound to be acquainted with it in some way: it may be by reading about it, but it may also be by direct perception. We can understand a mode of presentation as a way of being acquainted with an object. That there is some way in which we're acquainted with an object obviously doesn't mean that our acquaintance is *indirect* in any sense. It doesn't mean, for example, that we identify the object as the thing which satisfies a certain description. In the same way, the fact that we're acquainted with an object *under a certain mode of presentation*, on the present understanding of that phrase, doesn't mean that we're only indirectly related to it.

If this is accepted, it's clear enough that if an object is a real object – something in the real, objective world – it must be possible to be acquainted with it in more than one way: we can look at someone from one angle, for example, or from another. The moment this is possible, it must be possible not to realize that the object we're acquainted with in one way is the same as the object we're acquainted with in another way. And this is the basis of an alternative account of difference of Sense. We imagine two different names being associated with different ways of being acquainted with an object. A child in Detroit is introduced to a companion in the early 1950s: 'This is Vincent Furnier'. A rock musician appears on stage in the 1980s: 'That's Alice Cooper'. Once these two names have been associated with these two ways of being acquainted with what is in fact the same person, it's obviously possible for someone to think that (13) is true and (14) is false. And that means, on a Fregean theory, that we have two names with the same reference, but different Senses.[14]

But none of this requires that the names be equivalent, in anyone's mind, to definite descriptions. Nor does it require that a name refer to its referent indirectly, in virtue of the referent satisfying some description. So it seems that proper names can be directly referential and still have Sense. And that means that Kripke's attack on the description theory of names is not yet a decisive argument for a Millian theory of names.

4.7 Conclusion

Kripke's work on names created a revolution in philosophy whose effect is hard to recall now. One of its effects was to restore respectability to the Millian theory of names, in the face of the prevailing consensus that some form of description theory, often combined with an acceptance of Fregean Sense, was needed to cope with what I've called the Basic Worry about the view that the meaning of words concerns things in the world, not things in the mind. But Kripke's work also had a more general effect on our conception of language. The description theory of reference imagines each individual being able to single out anything she refers to by means of information she herself possesses. Kripke's theory makes our ability to refer depend on traditions of use within communities. This has some significance for natural-kind terms, as we'll see in the next chapter.

Of no less significance is the influence of Kripke's work on wider philosophical issues. Pride of place here goes to his separation of *epistemic*

---

[14] This kind of understanding of Frege's notion of Sense is prevalent among philosophers we might call *Oxford neo-Fregeans*: G. Evans, *The Varieties of Reference* (Oxford: Oxford University Press, 1984), is an extended treatment of singular reference within a neo-Fregean picture; J. McDowell, 'De Re Senses', *Philosophical Quarterly*, 34 (1984), pp. 283–94, provides a briefer presentation of the view. It has been attacked by David Bell, 'How "Russellian" was Frege?', *Mind*, 99 (1990), pp. 267–77.

and *metaphysical* or *ontological* considerations. *Epistemic* considerations concern how we *know* about things; *metaphysical* or *ontological* considerations are to do with how things are. Kripke's firm distinction between the two kinds of consideration is an expression of a kind of realism. *Realism* – as opposed, for example, to *idealism* – is the view that the nature of the world (how things are) is entirely independent of anything to do with how we think about it or know about it. Kripke's robust separation of the epistemic and the metaphysical overturned the approach of generations of philosophers, whose view of how things are had been shaped by their conception of how things are known.

Further reading

The classic presentation of a sophisticated description theory of names is John R. Searle, 'Proper Names', *Mind*, 67 (1958), pp. 166–73. A form of nominal description theory is propounded by Kent Bach, *Thought and Reference* (Oxford: Oxford University Press, 1987), chs. 7 and 8. G. Evans, 'The Causal Theory of Names', *Aristotelian Society Supplementary Volume*, 47 (1973), pp. 187–208, presents a development of Kripke's picture, with criticism of some aspects of it. G. McCulloch, *The Game of the Name* (Oxford: Oxford University Press, 1989) – especially chs. 4 and 8 – is a good advanced introduction to many of the issues of this chapter. S. Soames, *Beyond Rigidity: The Unfinished Semantic Agenda of* Naming and Necessity (Oxford: Oxford University Press, 2002), chs. 2 and 3, contains a sophisticated discussion of Kripke's views.

5   Natural-kind terms

Key texts

Saul Kripke, *Naming and Necessity*, 2nd edn (Oxford: Blackwell, 1980), lecture III; and H. Putnam, 'Meaning and Reference', *Journal of Philosophy*, 70 (1973), pp. 699–711.

5.1   Introduction

Saul Kripke's arguments against description theories of names inaugurated a revolution in the philosophy of language. One of the first acts of that revolution was an application of similar arguments against a similarly descriptive theory of another sort of expression – so-called *natural-kind* terms. Kripke himself claimed that natural-kind terms are rigid designators. In this he was supported by the semi-independent work of Hilary Putnam. Kripke and Putnam together are acknowledged as the creators of a new theory of such terms. This chapter focuses on the work by these two philosophers in which they first proposed that new theory.

But what *are* natural-kind terms? They differ from proper names in this: whereas proper names pick out individuals, natural-kind terms pick out *kinds*. Favourite examples are 'tiger' and 'water'. But natural-kind terms form a grammatically variegated class. Although they're all terms for kinds in some sense, they may be terms for kinds of *object* (like 'tiger', 'mammal', 'fish', 'whale') or for kinds of *stuff* (like 'water', 'gold', 'aluminium'). It's generally assumed that this difference is not important for the issues which Kripke is concerned with. What does matter is that the kinds in question are *natural* kinds. So what makes a kind *natural*? There are two broad conceptions of nature which seem to be at play in the focus on natural-kind terms. The first is what we may call the *science-relative* conception; we can explain it as follows:

(SRN) A natural kind is a kind about which some natural science is authoritative.

What is a natural science? This is unlikely to be precisely defined. We will have a list – physics, chemistry, biology – and we will have in mind certain contrasts – with art and with the human sciences (psychology, anthropology, sociology) – and we will probably expect this to be enough to explain the notion for the time being.

The other conception of nature is perhaps more fundamental: it certainly seems to have a more direct philosophical significance. We might call it the *real-kinds* conception; and we might tentatively offer the following as a formulation of it:

(RKN) A natural kind is a kind whose identity as a kind is fixed by reality, and not by human interests or concerns.

This conception is rarely explicit in the literature on natural-kind terms, but something like it seems to be implicit in much of it. (RKN) turns on a contrast between the respective contributions of reality and human interests to the fixing of concepts. We might doubt whether this contrast can really be made out: it might be claimed, for example, that it's impossible for us to grasp reality as it is entirely independent of human interests and concerns. I will not pursue that issue here. It is worth noting, however, that if anything like (RKN) is accepted, consideration of natural-kind terms takes on a special philosophical importance. If we accept (RKN), natural-kind terms are our handle on reality as it is in itself: it is through them that we get a grip on the fundamental nature of the world.

Someone may, of course, link the two conceptions. Indeed, it might be held that the distinctive point and value of the natural sciences is that they (and perhaps they alone) tell us how reality is in itself. This kind of view is often known as *naturalism*, and sometimes as *scientific realism*. Whether (RKN) is true, and whether (RKN) and (SRN) in effect define the same kinds, are large-scale metaphysical issues: that is to say, they are concerned with very general questions about the fundamental nature of things. One way the issue of natural-kind terms is important is that it connects philosophy of language with metaphysics.

5.2　A Lockean view of natural-kind terms: the individualist version

According to John Locke's general view of language (discussed in chapter 1), words are meaningful in virtue of signifying Ideas (something like mental images) in the minds of speakers. This general theory is applied to what we call natural-kind terms by means of this remark:

> [T]he *nominal Essence of Gold*, is that complex *Idea* the word *Gold* stands for, let it be, for instance, a Body yellow, of a certain weight, malleable, fusible, and fixed.[1]

This remark, and others in the surrounding text, have suggested that Locke himself held a counterpart – for the case of natural-kind terms – of the description theory of names which Kripke is concerned to undermine in the earlier parts of *Naming and Necessity*. In fact, there are complexities in Locke's own view which make it difficult to set him up precisely as the target of Kripke's and Putnam's criticism, but we can reasonably describe the view they attack as broadly *Lockean*.[2]

We can state the core of a Lockean theory of natural-kind terms with a studied lack of specificity, as follows:

(LK)　The meaning of a natural-kind term is determined by what is *believed* to be definitive of the kind in question.

(The reason for the lack of specificity will emerge shortly.) And we can lay out the commitments of such a theory, in a way which parallels the commitments of a description theory of names, as follows:

(LK1)　If '*K*' is a natural-kind term, there is a family of things associated with '*K*', an appropriate part of which is believed to be true of members of *K* and only members of *K*;

(LK2)　If '*K*' is a natural-kind term, then if an appropriate part of what is believed to be true of members of *K* is in fact true of something, then

---

[1] J. Locke, *Essay Concerning Human Understanding*, ed. P. Nidditch (Oxford: Oxford University Press, 1975), iii, vi, 2.

[2] The complications surround the fact that Locke accepts that there is such a thing as 'real' as well as 'nominal' essence, and that the terms 'essence' and 'property' have different meanings for him from what they have for us. Kripke's and Putnam's conception of a Lockean theory also includes features of W. V. Quine's views on necessity and possibility – for which see ch. 6 below.

that thing is indeed a member of K;

(LK3) If 'K' is a natural-kind term, then it is *a priori* that an appropriate part of what is believed to be true of members of K is in fact true of members of K;

(LK4) If 'K' is a meaningful natural-kind term, then it is necessarily true that an appropriate part of what is believed to be true of members of K is indeed true of members of K.

(LK1) is the counterpart to (DN1) and (DN2) of my presentation of the commitments of the description theory of names in chapter 4. (LK2) is the counterpart to (DN3), (LK3) to (DN5), and (LK4) to (DN6).[3] The phrase 'an appropriate part' is a gesture at the idea that not everything believed to be true of members of a kind is believed to be definitive of the kind: we would expect some features to be more central than others. This is parallel to the idea that the description theory of names holds that the most important of the things believed to be true of the referent of a name are thought to define the meaning of the name. I leave it open here whether an 'appropriate part' is a matter of simple majority, or an appropriate majority – or whether it depends on some other features.

The lack of specificity in all these formulations lies in the phrase 'is believed': believed by whom? Locke himself seems generally to endorse an individualist conception of language: each person is the authority over the use of her own terms; a word in one person's mouth can signify only that person's conception of things. In this respect, Locke's own view of natural-kind terms was close to the description theory of reference we considered in the last chapter. It is this individualist theory which is the target of the most direct of Kripke's and Putnam's criticisms, which are closely parallel to Kripke's objections to the description theory of names.

Take (LK1) first. Putnam says that he cannot tell the difference between elms and beeches, and indeed claims that there is no difference between his concept of an elm and his concept of a beech.[4] So (LK1), despite its modesty, looks false. This is parallel to the fact noted by Kripke, that most

---

[3] Note that I have included here no counterpart to (DN4), which gives the condition under which a name fails to refer. The issue of 'empty natural-kind terms' is not a live one, and there is some uncertainty about what it would involve: if nothing met the conditions associated with the term 'K', would this mean that there was no such kind, or merely that it had no actual members?

[4] Putnam,'Meaning and Reference', p. 704.

of us know very little (almost nothing, in fact) about many of the historical figures whose names we know.[5]

(LK2) is similarly doubtful. Suppose that what I think is definitive of tigers is just that they are large carnivorous quadripeds of cat-like appearance, tawny yellow in colour with blackish transverse stripes and white belly.[6] Kripke claims, plausibly, that there could be something of just this appearance which was of a different species, and so did not really count as a tiger.[7]

The crucial thing here is that the conception of members of a natural kind which ordinary speakers possess seems to relate principally to relatively superficial appearances. What Kripke's point suggests is that, intuitively, we do not regard such superficial appearances as really determining what counts as a genuine member of a natural kind. Instead the job is done by something which we might hope that a biologist would know, but most of us are ignorant of.

This is one of the points of Putnam's 'Twin-Earth' example.[8] Putnam imagines that there is another planet somewhere else in the universe, which he calls Twin Earth. Twin Earth is qualitatively indistinguishable from Earth, at least in relatively superficial appearance: that is to say, if you were instantaneously transported there, you wouldn't notice the difference. (Of course, this means that there is someone exactly like you on Twin Earth, and the same goes for everyone else.)

Despite all this superficial similarity, there is a fundamental difference between Earth and Twin Earth: whereas the chemical composition of the stuff in Earth rain, Earth rivers, and Earth lakes, which we call 'water', is H_2O, the chemical composition of the similar stuff on Twin Earth, which the Twin-Earthians call by a similar-sounding name, is something quite different – XYZ, let's say. Putnam claims (and it really is no more than a claim, though it is supposed to be intuitively compelling) that the stuff on Twin Earth, despite being superficially indistinguishable from water – it looks the same, tastes the same, wakes you up in the night by dripping the

---

[5] This point was considered in ch. 4, section 4.3, above.

[6] This is the definition Kripke offers, derived from the Shorter Oxford English Dictionary, but adapted as he suggests to avoid committing us to the thought that tigers are essentially feline: *Naming and Necessity*, pp. 119–20.

[7] *Naming and Necessity*, pp. 120–1.

[8] 'Meaning and Reference', pp. 700–2.

same – is not really water. What Putnam is claiming here, and trying to make vivid by means of his example, is that what counts as water is not determined by what ordinary speakers know. It is the knowledge of the scientist which is decisive, not the concepts which ordinary speakers have.

Given this, it should come as no surprise that the Kripke–Putnam view finds an intuitive difficulty over the next claim of the Lockean view, (LK3). Kripke shows how we can raise doubts about this by considering two kinds of possibility: the possibility that we might have been subject to some kind of illusion when we encountered those members of the kind on which our conception of the kind is based; and the possibility that the members of the kind we have encountered were in fact abnormal.

Suppose (for the first kind of case) that we have only come across gold in certain limited circumstances (in caves, perhaps, or burial chambers), and that our conception of the kind is based on this range of encounters. This being so, we could imagine that our conception of gold as being yellow in colour might have been due to an illusion.[9] (Perhaps we've only seen gold in the yellowish light of artificial lamps.) Now we have an ordinary conception of gold as being yellow, but it is clear that we don't know *a priori* that gold is yellow. This is because in order to find out that gold is *really* yellow, we need to do an experiment which will show that our original impression of colour was not just due to an illusion. (Perhaps we bring the stuff out into natural light.)

For the other kind of case, consider for the moment what would have happened if the only tigers we had come across had had three legs – whether through a series of coincidental accidents, or some unnatural deformity.[10] We might then have supposed that tigers were tripeds, not quadrupeds. But, as things are, we would have been wrong, because in fact tigers naturally have four legs. If this is a possibility, as it surely is, then it is surely also imaginable that the *four-legged* tigers we have actually come

---

[9] The example is Kripke's (*Naming and Necessity*, p. 118); but I am using it slightly differently in turning it to the issue of the truth of (LK3). The idea of turning this example to this issue is suggested by Kripke's observation that cats are in fact animals can be seen as a 'surprising discovery': *Naming and Necessity*, p. 125.

[10] Again, the example is in Kripke (*Naming and Necessity*, pp. 119–20), but its application to (LK3) is made more explicit here. That application is, however, suggested by Kripke's claim that 'The phrase "a three-legged tiger" is not a *contradiction in adjecto*' (*Naming and Necessity*, p. 119).

across might be unnatural specimens. And that seems to mean that we cannot know *a priori* that tigers are quadrupeds: we need to do some empirical work to discover that tigers are naturally four-legged.

We can construct a similar kind of case to this last one with gold too. When we talk about stuff kinds, we often seem to be concerned with the stuff in a pure state. It might be that the yellow colour of the gold we have come across was due to impurities in the gold. If that had been true, then gold would not really have been yellow. But that means that we cannot know *a priori* that gold is yellow: we need to know that the colour is not due to impurities, and to know that we need to do some experiments.

Can Kripke and Putnam give us reason to question (LK4), the Lockean claim that an appropriate part of what is believed to be true of a kind is *necessarily* true of the kind? Kripke himself imagines a case involving a term which is at least *like* a natural-kind term, 'heat'. He supposes that we have fixed the referent of this term by a contingent property of it, namely 'the property that it's able to produce such and such sensations in us'.[11] Surely it is not *necessary* that heat is able to produce those distinctive sensations in us: after all, we might not have existed, or might have been insensitive to heat. Similarly, we might identify water as the liquid which falls in rain, which flows in rivers, and which fills lakes and seas. This might be how we fix the reference of the term 'water', but it is surely not *necessary* that water does this: could there not have been water (on another planet, say), even if Earth had not existed, so that there were not *these* rivers, lakes and seas?

(LK4) looks implausible, then. Kripke and Putnam themselves seem to be more interested in a Lockean claim which looks almost the converse of (LK4). We might formulate it like this:

(LK5) If '*K*' is a natural-kind term, then nothing is necessarily true of members of *K* as members of *K* other than an appropriate part of what is believed to be true of members of *K*, or what follows logically from that.

This claim derives from a general trend in empiricism, rather than from Locke himself. Empiricism (to put it a little crudely) is the view that all knowledge derives from experience. Experience here includes perception by means of the five senses (and 'reflection' as well, in Locke's case), and

---

[11] *Naming and Necessity*, p. 132.

any kind of test which involves such perception. A crucial commitment of empiricism is the view that we cannot have any real knowledge of the world beyond what we can gain from experience. Within this basic philosophical approach, Hume made the following (plausible) claim: we cannot literally *perceive* (see, hear, smell, etc.) that something is necessary. If we accept that, it seems that an empiricist is bound to think that when we say that something is necessary (for example, that I am human as long as I exist), we are not talking about what can be got from the world itself. Instead, we must be talking about something which derives from our way of thinking of the world. This is precisely the view which underlies (LK5). If necessity derives from our way of thinking about things, rather than from the things themselves, it seems that what is necessarily true of a natural kind can only derive from the way we think of the kind.

Kripke and Putnam are concerned to deny (LK5) and the associated conception of necessity as being derived from our ways of thinking of things. Consider the following pair of sentences, for example:

(1) Gold is the element with atomic number 79;
(2) Water is H_2O.

Kripke and Putnam claim that statements like these are *necessary* – at least if they are true at all. If (1) is true at all, it is an essential property of gold that it has atomic number 79. If (2) is true at all, it is an essential property of water that it is H_2O. Although they are necessary (according to Kripke and Putnam), (1) and (2) are *a posteriori*: they can only be known through extensive experience and experiment. The possibility of a necessary *a posteriori* truth is made room for by a point we considered in chapter 4. Kripke is concerned to separate the *epistemic* issue of whether a truth is *a priori* or *a posteriori* (whether it can be *known* independently of experience) from the *metaphysical* or *ontological* issue of whether it *could* (objectively) have been false. But in insisting that (1) and (2) are necessary, Kripke and Putnam are attacking the empiricist conception of necessity which led people to conflate the epistemic and the metaphysical in the first place. The necessity of (1) and (2) seems to reside in the way the world is, rather than in anything to do with our ways of thinking of the world.

If (1) and (2) are necessary, that has consequences for our understanding of the terms involved. Recall Kripke's explanation of possibility and necessity in terms of possible worlds (ways things might have been). What is possible is true in at least one possible world; what is necessary is true in all possible worlds. Bearing this in mind, let's concentrate on (1), and think about the stuff we're describing as gold. It seems that (1) can only be necessary if both of the following are true:

(1a) The predicate 'x is the element with atomic number 79' applies to *that stuff* in all possible worlds;
(1b) The term 'gold' picks out *that stuff* in all possible worlds.

If (1) is true, then it seems that (1a) must be true. It looks as if giving the chemical constitution of some stuff must tell us something which is essential to the stuff. But (1b) is the interesting claim now. (1b) is just the claim that 'gold' is a *rigid designator* (a designator which designates the same thing in all possible worlds).

What this shows is that the claim that (1) and (2) are necessarily true (and with it the undermining of the traditional empiricist view of necessity) depends on the claim that ordinary natural-kind terms are rigid designators. In this respect, the Kripke–Putnam view of natural-kind terms makes them very like proper names, as Kripke's theory thinks of proper names.

5.3   A Lockean view without individualism

The simplest of Kripke's and Putnam's objections relate to an individualist version of a Lockean view of natural-kind terms, and these emphasize the similarities between natural-kind terms and proper names. But if we concentrate on the individualist version of the view, we're likely to miss what's really distinctive of Kripke's and Putnam's own approach to natural-kind terms.

In his opposition to the Lockean view, Putnam is keen to emphasize what he calls the *division of linguistic labour*. In a community, he suggests, there is a division between experts and lay people in the use of natural-kind terms. The experts are people who have the sort of knowledge which is relevant to the kind in question, and the rest of the community defer to them in their use of the terms. That is to say, the lay people use natural-kind terms to mean, in effect, whatever the experts mean by them. Putnam takes his own use of the terms 'elm' and 'beech' (which refer to kinds he knows almost nothing about) to be parasitic on the use of these terms by people who really know what is essential to being an elm or a beech.

But a Lockean view can be revised quite easily to accommodate this 'division of linguistic labour'.[12] Indeed, we can make it more complex: we can distinguish various layers of users within a community. In particular, we might want to distinguish ordinary competent users from both the experts and linguistic parasites. Ordinary competent users might be people, for example, who are quite good at telling elms from beeches when they're faced with standard examples of both species (and so know more than Putnam), but who would expect to defer to the knowledge of an expert when faced with an unusual instance of either kind. Any such complexity of division of linguistic labour is easily accommodated within a broadly Lockean view by means of a different way of making more specific the unspecific phrase 'is believed': what we need is simply for the kinds to be defined by the beliefs of experts.

This non-individualist form of the Lockean view is still opposed by the Kripke–Putnam approach. A fundamental difference emerges in the fact that the revised Lockean view insists that the experts to whom a community defers must already exist. So, according to the revised Lockean view, I cannot leave the true nature of a natural-kind to be determined by future scientists, or by reality.

Some such Lockean view may seem to fit well with some of our intuitions. Recall Putnam's Twin Earth. On Twin Earth everything is superficially exactly as things are on Earth; it's just that the liquid which fills the lakes and rivers, which people and animals drink, and which helps plants to grow, has the chemical composition XYZ rather than H_2O. Now think back to some time in the seventeenth century, before the chemical composition of water was discovered, but while the word 'water' was in use. It's plausible that 'water' was a natural-kind term then as much as now. Let's imagine ourselves using the word 'water' in its seventeenth-century use, and ask: is the stuff on Twin Earth *water*, in this sense, or not? According to Putnam, it's not: the word 'water', as a natural-kind term, always referred to the liquid with the composition H_2O; since the liquid on Twin Earth doesn't have that composition, it's not water – even in the

---

[12] David Smith pointed this out to me: see his 'Natural Kind Terms: A Neo-Lockean Theory', *European Journal of Philosophy*, 13 (2005), pp. 70–88.

seventeenth-century sense of the word. Many people, however – perhaps a majority of those who are untainted by philosophical theory – disagree. They think that the stuff on Twin Earth is water all right: just water with a different chemical structure. They might support their view by comparing the word 'water' with the word 'jade'. As Putnam himself notes, jade (the gemstone which is used in oriental jewellery) has two chemically distinguishable forms: jadeite and nephrite. Why shouldn't we think of water in the same way?

There are complications here: we'll come back to some of them in the next section. For the moment, we can note that a lot depends on the choice of example. Opinions may differ about water, but they seem to side more easily with Kripke and Putnam in the case of gold.

Suppose that contemporary chemists are right, and that it is essential to gold (as we use the term) that it is the (unique) element with atomic number 79. It is very intuitive to think that the kind *gold* is the same kind as that referred to by the Greek word used by Archimides in the third century BC. Take Archimedes to be the best expert of his time on the nature of gold, and take it that he took it to be essential to and distinctive of gold that it has the same density as a certain sample gold bar, *b*. (LK1) comes out true in this situation, on the appropriate understanding of 'is believed', but it looks as if we have enough here, with a few further reasonable assumptions, to allow the Kripke–Putnam view to deny all of (LK2)–(LK5) for the case of the term 'gold', even if it's only the beliefs of experts which count.

It seems to be essential to gold, the very kind about which Archimedes was the best third-century-BC expert, that it has atomic number 79. But that gold has atomic number 79 is clearly not something believed to be true of gold by Archimedes, so it's natural to follow the Kripke–Putnam view in denying (LK5).

(LK4) seems not to be true either in this case. Archimedes' test of gold depends on having a sample, *b*, which is presumed to be pure. But what if *b* was not in fact pure gold? In that case, what Archimedes believed to be essential to and distinctive of gold might not even be *true* of gold. That means that (LK2) will be false in this case too: for if *b* is not a pure sample of gold, having the same density as *b* will be distinctive of something which is *not* pure gold.

(LK3) seems doubtful too. It is presumably an empirical question whether *b* is in fact a good sample of pure gold: *b* will have been tested by whatever means were available to Archimedes. This suggests that Archimedes must have had some other criteria for being pure gold, with reference to which he tested the purity of *b*. Surely he will have done; but there is no reason for us or him to think that these criteria are finally decisive. They will simply reflect the tests available at the time; there is no reason for us or him to think that these tests could never be improved upon.

If we concentrate on the case of gold, it seems natural to think that the Kripke–Putnam view is vindicated, and that even the revised form of the Lockean view gets things wrong. And the problem with this one case is enough to cause trouble for the Lockean view as a general view about natural-kind terms. Whatever we say about water (or jade), it looks as if it is possible for there to be some natural-kind terms which fit the Kripke–Putnam model. That is something which the Lockean view finds unintelligible in principle.

5.4   How can there be Kripke–Putnam natural-kind terms?

How can our present use be deferential to the views of experts who don't even exist yet? I think there is a serious difficulty here, but I'll suggest the outline of an account which might deal with it. Interestingly, this account seems to give Kripke and Putnam what they want, while remaining within something like the spirit – if not the letter – of the Lockean view. This account makes important use of the notion of the *point* of using a term, and of the idea of what matters to us about the kind in question.

Let's begin by turning again to the controversial case of 'water', and trying to re-imagine the seventeenth-century use of the word. We can ask: what is the point of singling out a particular liquid as *water* in the way we did (in the seventeenth century)? Why does it matter to us (as we imagine ourselves in the seventeenth century) that something is water? If we ask this question, it's natural to think that what is important about water is that it quenches thirst in humans and animals, and helps plants to grow. What matters about it is that it's that liquid which produces these particular beneficial effects. These effects are defined biologically, in a very broad sense: they are effects of a certain kind within certain specific biological species (which we could point to). We might then count water, in this seventeenth-century sense, as a *biological* kind term.

Bearing this in mind, we can turn again to Putnam's Twin Earth. If we want to know whether the liquid in the lakes and rivers there is water, the natural question to ask now is this: what happens if (Earthian) human beings and Earthian animals drink it, or we try irrigating Earthian plants with it? If it has the same effects on Earthian animals and plants as the water on Earth does, it's quite natural to count it as water. But could this chemically alien liquid, XYZ, produce those effects? That seems to me an empirical question. It is possible that it is only a liquid with the core chemical composition H_2O which could produce water-like effects on Earthian animals and plants, the laws of nature being as they are. In that case, it seems to me, the Twin-Earth liquid will not be water. (Would you count it water if you travelled to Twin Earth and the liquid poisoned you when you drank it?) If it turned out to be true that only something with the chemical composition H_2O could possibly produce the relevant effects on the appropriate biological species, it would be clear enough that water is H_2O. If this were all true, then it would turn out that the essence of the kind referred to by the term 'water', as that term was used in the seventeenth century, was given by something which was unknown in the seventeenth century. This is possible because the seventeenth-century use of the word made room specifically for the intervention of later science: water was, in effect, defined as that liquid which produces such and such effects; and the production of effects is precisely something for science to investigate.

What does it mean to say that water was 'in effect' defined as that liquid which produces such and such effects? It may be that nobody in the seventeenth century had anything like this description explicitly in mind. It can nevertheless be true that the description is a fair rationalization of the point of using the word in the way it was used in the seventeenth century. The competent user uses words competently and knowledgeably, but – it may be – unreflectively. Someone might then reflect on the use of the competent user and rationalize it, in the way I've tried to rationalize the use of the word 'water' in the seventeenth century. That rationalization might then license a link with an investigative science, which would mean that even the competent and reflective user could find out something about the essence of a kind she is used to talking about.

What if it turned out that liquids with a wide variety of chemical compositions – including XYZ, perhaps – could quench the thirst of Earthian animals, and nourish Earthian plants? Could it still be true that 'water', in its seventeenth-century sense, referred to H_2O? If we continue to try to explain natural-kind terms by appeal to the point or rationale for their use, this will depend on the precise details of the proper rationalization of seventeenth-century use. Do we think that 'water' referred to the liquid which *in fact* quenches Earthian thirst and nourishes Earthian plants? Or do we think it is just any liquid which is *capable* of doing that? If we think the first thing, we'll continue to say that water is H_2O. If we think the second thing, we won't: instead, we'll say that there are several different kinds of water – H_2O, XYZ, and perhaps some others. This would make the case of water very like that of jade.

Would this mean that 'water' was not a natural-kind term? This isn't obvious. We might regard water as a *biological* kind (since it produces a uniform biological effect), but not a *chemical* kind (since the chemical composition of the various kinds of water are different, on this hypothesis). And we can say the same about jade. We might regard jade as a *jewellery* kind – unified enough for the science of the jeweller – but not a chemical kind, since the chemical composition of jadeite and nephrite is different. If we adopt this line, we are accepting a certain view about the relation between the different sciences. We are accepting, in effect, that sciences at different levels have a certain autonomy: biology might provide explanations by grouping together things which are dissimilar chemically, and chemistry might provide explanations by grouping together things which are dissimilar physically.

What we have here is an almost Lockean explanation of how there can be Kripke–Putnam natural-kind terms. The account is rooted in the commitments, if not the explicit beliefs, of competent users of the terms. On this picture, natural-kind terms turn out to be those terms the rationale for whose use provides a place for investigation by a natural science. Of course, this view has to operate at the outset with what I earlier called the *science-relative* conception of natural kinds, which defines natural kinds as those about which natural sciences are authoritative. But that doesn't rule out its adoption of the *real-kinds* conception, which defines natural kinds as those whose identity is fixed independently of human interests. It could be argued, for example, that natural sciences discover just those kinds whose identity is independent of human interests. It might be suggested that the particular success of natural sciences in explaining and predicting events in the natural environment is evidence that they deal with uniformities which are independent of human interests.

5.5   How can natural-kind terms be rigid designators?

According to the Kripke–Putnam view, natural-kind terms like 'gold', 'water', and 'tiger' are rigid designators: they designate the same kinds in all possible worlds. How can this be?

Kripke and Putnam treat natural-kind terms as very like proper names, and they seem to offer an account of their rigidity which is parallel to Kripke's picture of how proper names work. According to Kripke's picture, proper names are introduced by an initial baptism, or by means of a reference-fixing description, and later uses refer to whatever the name was originally introduced to refer to, in virtue of the historical links between the later uses and the original introduction. This allows us to see that proper names themselves are directly referential: their reference to objects does not depend on the objects' satisfying some description. And this directness of reference looks as if it explains how proper names come to be rigid designators.

Kripke and Putnam give accounts of how natural-kind terms come to be rigid designators which are strikingly (indeed, surely consciously) similar to this account of proper names. In the case of gold, Kripke imagines a 'hypothetical', though 'admittedly somewhat artificial' baptism, carried out by means of some such declaration as this: 'Gold is the substance instantiated by the items over there, or at any rate, by almost all of them'.[13] Putnam imagines that I give what amounts to an 'ostensive definition' (one which involves pointing to a sample), by saying '*This* liquid is water.'[14] Alternatively, he suggests, I may give an 'operational definition' (roughly, one which involves reference to relatively superficial properties) of water as something like 'the liquid which has such and such superficial properties *in the actual world*'. Kripke's 'baptism' and Putnam's

---

[13] *Naming and Necessity*, p. 135.   [14] 'Meaning and Reference', p. 707.

'definitions' look just like the different ways in which Kripke imagined the reference of a proper name might be fixed.

This might then be thought to suggest that later uses of natural-kind terms designate the relevant kinds in virtue of being historically connected to the first, introductory uses.[15] That might suggest that natural-kind terms, like proper names, are directly referential. And it might then seem that this non-descriptive directness is what explains the rigidity of natural-kind terms, just as it seems to in the case of proper names.

There are two reasons for thinking that this cannot be right. The first is that the supposed 'baptisms' and 'definitions' are clearly entirely artificial (as Kripke, of course, acknowledges). In fact, it's hard to see how all natural-kind terms *could* be introduced in this way. Such baptisms and definitions depend on taking for granted the identity of the kind being defined – or if not that kind, then some more general kind. Thus Kripke takes for granted the notion of a *substance*, and Putnam takes for granted the notion of a *liquid*. If 'gold' and 'water' are introduced by explicit baptism or definition, what about 'substance' and 'liquid'? At some point this regress needs to be stopped, and we have to reach terms which are not introduced by explicit baptism or definition, but by some kind of practice and training.

There's a crucial difference between proper names and natural-kind terms in this respect. When proper names are introduced, it is indeed against the background of certain other concepts – of a *person*, a *city*, or a *country*, for example – and these are taken for granted in the introduction of names. But for this reason, questions about identity also concern those background concepts. So we can ask what it is for someone identified on one occasion to be the same person as someone identified on another occasion, and this debate turns on the question of what it is to be a *person*. There is no such debate about what it is for someone to be J. Edgar Hoover, for example. On the other hand, there does seem room for genuine debate about what it is for something to be *gold*, or *water*, and this is not just a matter of what it is for something to be a substance, or a liquid. Indeed,

---

[15] It's worth noting here that Putnam's definitions, unlike Kripke's baptism, are probably not meant to provide an account of how a natural-kind term might be introduced in the first place; so it is hard to cite Putnam himself as a supporter of this historical-link direct-reference account of natural-kind terms.

there being issues of this kind here is presumed by the Kripke–Putnam account: after all, these are the issues which are settled by the scientific discovery that gold is the element with atomic number 79, and that water is H_2O. This is why a baptism, or explicit ostensive definition of the kind imagined by Putnam, is not really credible as an account of how most natural-kind terms get their meaning. Baptisms and ostensive definitions introduce terms which aren't themselves subject to identity disputes, on the basis of background concepts where such disputes are fought out. In the case of most natural-kind terms, identity disputes concern the natural-kind terms themselves, rather than any presupposed background concepts.

If Kripke's and Putnam's 'hypothetical' baptisms and definitions cannot be taken seriously as genuine baptisms and definitions, what are they? They are surely preliminary attempts to characterize the rationale of kind terms. And this leads to the second reason for thinking that natural-kind terms don't behave like proper names. In the last section I offered an explanation of how there could be Kripke–Putnam natural-kind terms – terms about whose application some *future* scientist might be authoritative. This explanation turned on the possibility of characterizing the *point* of the use of the terms in question. That characterization, in effect, produces a description of the natural kind, something which will prevent the relevant natural-kind term being directly referential. It was suggested, for example, that water is *the stuff which quenches our thirst and nourishes our plants*.

Suppose that description really does capture the point of the word 'water', as it is commonly used (and was used in the seventeenth century too). Then it looks as if there's some sense in which that description gives the meaning of the word 'water'. I'll come back to what that might amount to in a moment. If it's granted that the description 'the stuff which quenches our thirst and nourishes our plants' gives the meaning of 'water' (in some sense), that description ought to explain the rigidity of the term, if 'water' really is a rigid designator. How might it do this?

It's natural to think that the description should be read as some kind of actualized description – of the kind which seemed in chapter 4 to escape Kripke's modal argument against the description theory of names.[16] This

---

[16] See § 4.5 above.

might be spelled out in different ways, in line with different ways of making precise the rationale of the use of 'water'. In the last section I imagined two different conceptions of water, one which allowed that XYZ (the liquid on Twin Earth) is a kind of water, and one which did not. For the first view (supposing that XYZ is capable of quenching our thirst and nourishing our plants), the description is equivalent to something like this: any stuff which is *capable* of quenching our thirst and nourishing our plants, with the laws of nature, and the constitution of ourselves and our plants, as they *actually* are. For the second view, the description is equivalent to something like this: the stuff which is *actually responsible* for quenching our thirst and nourishing our plants. The reference to the actual world in these descriptions will ensure that they are rigid designators: they will pick out the same stuff in every possible world – though what counts as the same stuff will be different on the two different conceptions.

But in what sense could it be said that the description 'the stuff which quenches our thirst and nourishes our plants' gives the *meaning* of the word 'water'? Clearly no user of the word need have had it in mind. (And we should remember that there are some users of some natural-kind terms who know almost nothing about the kinds in question – like Putnam with 'elm' and 'beech'.) What we want is something like this: a competent user (unlike Putnam with 'elm' and 'beech') could recognize, by reflection alone, that the description does indeed capture the point of the word.

Do we end up with a form of description theory of natural-kind terms? Perhaps we do, but it's quite different from the sort of description theory of names which Kripke was concerned to undermine. For one thing, it is not an individualist theory. For another, the description is not supposed to be something which is in any sense in the mind of speakers. And, finally, the description is implicitly an *actualized* description, so that it allows natural-kind terms to be rigid designators.

Further reading

In addition to 'Meaning and Reference', it is also worth reading the longer (and arguably more famous) version of Putnam's paper: 'The Meaning of "Meaning" ', in K. Gunderson, ed., *Language, Mind and Knowledge*, Minnesota Studies in the Philosophy of Science VII (Minneapolis: Univerity of

Minnesota Press, 1975); reprinted in Putnam's own collection, *Mind, Language and Reality: Philosophical Papers Volume 2* (Cambridge: Cambridge University Press, 1975), pp. 215–71. Doubts about the Kripke–Putnam view are expressed by D. H. Mellor, 'Natural Kinds', *British Journal for the Philosophy of Science*, 28 (1977), pp. 299–312 and E. Zemach, 'Putnam's Theory on the Reference of Substance Terms', *Journal of Philosophy*, 73 (1976), pp. 116–27. An account of the introduction of natural-kind terms, broadly in sympathy with the Kripke–Putnam view, is to be found in J. Brown, 'Natural Kind Terms and Recognitional Capacities', *Mind*, 107 (1998), pp. 275–304. A. D. Smith, 'Natural Kind Terms: A Neo-Lockean Theory', *European Journal of Philosophy*, 13 (2005), pp. 70–88, gives a defence of a broadly Lockean theory for some natural-kind terms. A more technical account of natural-kind terms, relating especially to the issue of rigid designation, is to be found in S. Soames, *Beyond Rigidity: The Unfinished Semantic Agenda of* Naming and Necessity (Oxford: Oxford University Press, 2002).

6   Quine on *de re* and *de dicto* modality

Key text

W. V. O. Quine, 'Three Grades of Modal Involvement', reprinted in Quine's *The Ways of Paradox and Other Essays*, 2nd edn (Cambridge, MA: Harvard University Press, 1976).

6.1   Introduction

In the last two chapters we've looked at the works at the centre of a revolution in our thinking about reference and necessity. So far I've represented the revolution as being against views to be found in Frege, Russell, and Locke. But there was a more recent target than any of these: the great American philosopher and logician, Willard Van Orman Quine. Quine dominated the English-speaking philosophical world in the middle years of the twentieth century, with an enormous influence on both doctrine and style, in the United States in particular.

Quine followed Russell in his treatment of definite descriptions and proper names. Indeed, he went even further, proposing that *all* singular terms be replaced by, or reconstrued as, definite descriptions. He was also an ardent advocate of what he and his followers called *extensionalism*. Recall the core of Frege's conception of meaning, the part to which the notion of Sense is added. According to this, what matters about the meaning of various types of expression can be summarized as follows:

For sentences – whether they are true or false;

For singular terms – which objects they refer to;

For predicates – what difference they make to the truth and falsity of sentences, given any particular choice of names in place of the variables.

We can characterize Quine's extensionalism as insisting, as far as possible, on sticking to the conception of meaning characterized by these three clauses. Any kind of construction which didn't seem to fit this conception of meaning – and we'll see two in this chapter and the next – was either to be translated into one which did, or else avoided. In this Quine saw himself (very much as Russell did) as constructing a language suitable for science, everything about which would be clearly and precisely definable.[1]

Quine combined this austere approach to language with a similarly austere conception of the nature of the world. As an empiricist, he held that the nature of the world could only be discovered through experience, and most particularly in science. And as a Humean, he held that necessity could not strictly be experienced. As a result, he held that there is no necessity in the world: necessity is always a feature of what we bring to the world, rather than of the world itself.

By the time that Kripke gave his lectures on *Naming and Necessity*, Quine had succeeded in making these views something like orthodoxy among those at the forefront of philosophy in the English-speaking world – though, of course, he was working within a culture which was congenial to them, and on the back of the already respected work of others. Natural science was regarded as being of central and fundamental importance. The Humean view of necessity was generally accepted. Something like Russell's conception of reference was widely endorsed. And non-extensional constructions were regarded as being proper objects of suspicion.

In this chapter, we'll be focusing on Quine's views on one kind of construction which seems to be non-extensional: modal constructions (to do with possibility and necessity). 'Three Grades of Modal Involvement' represents the kind of view of necessity which Kripke was attacking.

6.2 Quine's three grades of modal involvement

Given his general philosophical views, Quine thinks that getting involved with modality (necessity and possibility) is something to be approached

---

[1] This can be seen as a bold response to what I've called the Basic Worry for the view that the meaning of words concerns things in the world, rather than things in the mind: see ch. 2, § 2.8, above.

with caution. He notes three stages of involvement: the first step is safe; the second can be made safe; but the third, he thinks, can and should be avoided.

Consider the following elementary arithmetical claim:

9 is greater than 5.

Quine's three grades of modal involvement can be represented by three different claims involving this bit of arithmetic. The first Quine writes like this:

(1) Nec '9 > 5'.

Here's how we might put it in English:

(1e) The sentence '9 is greater than 5' expresses a necessary truth.

Note the use of quotation marks here: we're talking about a linguistic expression, a sentence.

The second grade of involvement with necessity Quine writes like this:

(2) nec (9 > 5).

That is, in English:

(2e) It is necessarily true that 9 is greater than 5.

Note that no quotation marks are used here: we're not talking about linguistic expressions.

The third grade of modal involvement Quine writes like this:

(3) $(\exists x)$ nec $(x > 5)$.

That is:

(3e) Something is necessarily greater than 5.

Note again that no quotation marks are used in (3) or (3e).

What is the difference between these three grades? To understand this, we need to understand the difference between two kinds of expression: *predicates* and what Quine calls *statement operators*.

Formally speaking, a predicate is what you get when you start with a sentence containing one or more singular terms, and you knock out one or more singular terms and mark where they were with variables. So 'x is red' is a predicate (with one gap for a singular term), as is 'x is thinner than y' (though this has two gaps for singular terms). A predicate is an expression which needs one or more singular terms added to it to form a grammatical sentence. Since singular terms refer to objects, we can say that predicates are used to say something about objects: 'x is red' is used to say that an object is red; 'x is thinner than y' is used to say that one object is thinner than another.

What Quine calls *statement operators* are quite different. Statement operators – I'll call them just *operators*, for short[2] – are things you add to *whole sentences* to form other sentences. So 'It is not the case that … ' is an operator. If you put a whole sentence in the gap (say, 'Napoleon lost the battle of Waterloo') you get another whole sentence ('It is not the case that Napoleon lost the battle of Waterloo', which happens to be false). And ' … because – –' is an operator, this time with two gaps for whole sentences. So if you put the sentence 'Napoleon lost the battle of Waterloo' in the first gap, and the sentence 'the Prussians arrived' in the second gap, you get a new sentence: 'Napoleon lost the battle of Waterloo because the Prussians arrived' (which is probably true). Whereas a predicate needs one or more *singular terms* added to it to form a grammatical sentence, an operator needs one or more *whole sentences*. Operators are not used to say something about objects: they simply adapt or join sentences.

The crucial difference between Quine's three grades is created by the fact that Quine's 'Nec (…)', like the English phrase ' … expresses a necessary truth', is a *predicate* – it says something about an object – whereas his 'nec (…)', like the English phrase 'It is necessarily true that … ', is an *operator* – it adapts a sentence. To see this, consider what you have to add to the two different expressions to make whole sentences. To get a whole sentence out of ' … expresses a necessary truth', you need to put a *name* of something, or some other singular term, in the gap. What you put in the gap is not a sentence, but an expression which *refers* to a sentence. A common way of making an expression which refers to a sentence is to put quotation marks around that sentence, which is why there are quotation marks in (1) and (1e). But if we'd decided to use the

---

[2] The notion of an operator is in fact much more general than this. What Quine calls *statement* operators are generally known as *sentential* operators, since they take sentences as input to produce sentences as output. But there can be other kinds of operator, which take different kinds of input to produce different kinds of output.

word 'Archibald' as a name for the sentence '9 is greater than 5', then we could have written the following instead of (1e) to state the same fact:

(1e*) Archibald expresses a necessary truth.

But to get a whole sentence out of 'It is necessarily true that … ' you need to fill the gap, not with a name (whether of a sentence or anything else) but a *sentence*. That's why the sentence '9 is greater than 5' goes into it *unquoted* in (2e) – because quotation marks produce a kind of name of what's written between them. To see what would be wrong with that, consider again that use of the word 'Archibald' as a name of the sentence '9 is greater than 5'. If you insert that name into the gap in 'It is necessarily true that … ', you get this:

(2!) It is necessarily true that Archibald.

And that's just ungrammatical.

Clearly 'Nec' in (1) and 'expresses a necessary truth' in (1e) are *predicates*, whereas 'nec' in (2) and 'It is necessarily true that' in (2e) are *operators*. What, then, is the difference between (2) and (3), since both involve the *operator* 'nec'?

Consider another sentence which includes a statement operator:

(4) It is not the case that Catherine the Great loved Peter III.

This is formed by putting the sentence 'Catherine the Great loved Peter III' (which is false, as it happens) into the gap in the operator 'It is not the case that … ', to produce a whole sentence, (4) (which is true).

If you knock one of the names out of (4), you get a predicate:

(4a) It is not the case that *x* loved Peter III.

Frege's logic expresses generality (claims about *some* or *all* things of a given kind) by attaching *quantifiers* ('There is an *x* such that', 'Every *x* is such that', etc.) to the front of predicates. Do that to (4a) and you get, for example, this:

(4b) There is an *x* such that it is not the case that *x* loved Peter III.

Or, more colloquially:

(4be) Somebody didn't love Peter III.

In (4a) we see the operator 'It is not the case that ... ' forming part of a
predicate, rather than a whole sentence. And that remains its role in (4b),
because the whole sentence (4b) is formed by adding a quantifier to the
front of the predicate to *bind* (as it's called) the variable. When an operator
occurs in a sentence as part of a *predicate*, rather than just being attached to
a whole sentence, Quine describes it (rather confusingly) as functioning as
a *sentence operator*. The crucial difference between the second and third of
Quine's grades of modal involvement is this, then: at the third grade, but
not the second, 'nec (...)' appears as an operator in a sentence formed by
attaching a quantifier to a *predicate which contains that operator*.

This looks like a merely technical distinction: but the whole of Quine's
philosophy of necessity, one of the fundamental targets of Kripke's work,
hangs on it.

6.3   Referential opacity and Leibniz's law

There are nine planets. We can express that fact as follows:

(5) The number of planets = 9.

It is a basic law of identity that if *a* is the same thing as *b*, whatever is true
of *a* is true of *b*. That means that if we begin with a truth about an object,
in which the object is referred to by one name, we should still have a truth
if we refer to the same object by a different name. This is an informal
statement of what is known as *Leibniz's Law*.

Now we've already noted this interesting fact:

(6) 9 is greater than 5.

From this, the identity statement (5), and that basic law of identity
(Leibniz's Law), it seems that we can derive the following:

(7) The number of planets is greater than 5.

This is true, so everything seems fine and unproblematic. But now
consider what happens when we begin, not with (6), but with (2e):

(2e) It is necessarily true that 9 is greater than 5.

Recall (5) and apply Leibniz's Law to (2e), and we get this:

(8) It is necessarily true that the number of planets is greater than 5.

There is at least one reading – perhaps the most natural one – on which (8) is false. If the phrase 'the number of planets' is really being understood as occurring in the context of the operator 'It is necessarily true that … ', then (8) means something like this:

(8*) It is necessarily true that there are more than 5 planets.

And (8*) is surely false: surely there could have been only 5 planets, or fewer, if the history of the solar system had been slightly different.

Quine is unwilling to abandon Leibniz's Law, so he concludes that in (2e) the symbol '9' is not really referring (sometimes it seems: not simply referring) to the number, and (2e) is not really a truth *about* the number. This peculiarity in the use of the symbol '9' in (2e) is obviously due to the operator 'It is necessarily true that … '. On Quine's view, if a name occurs as part of a sentence which fills the gap in that operator, it's not functioning purely referentially; the operator doesn't, as it were, let us use the name to see straight through to the object referred to. The sentential context introduced by the operator is therefore, according to Quine, *referentially opaque*. Whatever names might be doing in referentially opaque contexts, they aren't simply – perhaps aren't really – referring to their normal referents.

This means that, according to Quine, constructions introduced by 'It is necessarily true that … ' involve uses of words which seem, on the face of it, to flout the rule of extensionality in at least this respect: we cannot say that all that matters here about the use of a singular term is which object it refers to.

In fact, it's obvious enough that constructions involving necessity and possibility flout the rule of extensionality in other respects too. Where extensionality reigns, we can say that all that matters about the meaning of a whole sentence is whether it is true or false. So where extensionality reigns, we can appeal to a rule which is rather like a sentential version of Leibniz's Law: if you begin with one sentence, whether it's true or false, it does no harm to substitute for it another sentence which has the same truth-value. Now it's certainly true that 9 is greater than 5. It's also true that I got up at six o'clock this morning. So the two sentences '9 is greater than 5' and 'I got up at six o'clock this morning' (as used by me now) have the same truth-value. But if I try substituting the latter for the former within (2e), I get this:

(9) It is necessarily true that I got up at six o'clock this morning.

And that's false: I could quite easily have got up later (I was rather tempted to, in fact).

What this shows is that there seem to be quite general problems with the rule of extensionality in constructions involving 'It is necessary that ... ' For this reason, contexts introduced by that phrase are counted *non-extensional*, or *intensional* (note the 's': intensional).

I've just introduced two technical notions, referential opacity and intensionality, in an informal way. Both are in quite widespread use, and are often treated as more or less interchangeable. But if we treat them as interchangeable, we miss some of the point of Quine's choice of words in coining the phrase 'referentially opaque', and we fail to note a crucial feature of his philosophy of modality.

What is clear, and agreed by everyone, is that a context counts as intensional if the rule of extensionality does not hold for it. That is, if something more matters about the meaning of a singular term than which object it refers to, if something more matters about the meaning of a predicate than which objects it's true of, or if something more matters about the meaning of a sentence than whether it's true or false.

What is not so clear is what 'referentially opaque' means. Quine introduces it in contrast with uses which are 'purely referential' ('referentially transparent'); this suggests that in referentially opaque contexts singular terms continue to refer all right – they just don't *simply* refer. But note (to dwell on Quine's metaphor for a moment) that there are two ways of not being transparent: being opaque – or being *translucent*. In the terms of the image, we would expect a context in which a singular term refers, but doesn't *simply* refer, to be referentially *translucent*. When Quine uses the phrase 'referentially opaque' we should, then, expect him to be talking about contexts in which singular terms don't really refer at all. It would follow from this that when we say something we're using a singular term inside a referentially opaque context, we're not really talking *about* the object normally referred to by the term at all.

In fact, I think this is precisely Quine's view.[3] Referentially opaque contexts, as he understands them, are those in which singular terms don't refer to their usual referents at all. Referentially transparent contexts are those in which singular terms refer to their usual referents, and do so 'purely' – that is, they have no other function. Quine doesn't seem to acknowledge the possibility of referential *translucent* contexts – those in which singular terms refer to their usual referents, but not 'purely' (that is: they have some other function there as well).[4]

6.4   Referential opacity and the three grades

Quine's view is that the use of the concept of necessity in (1) (and (1e)) is entirely innocent; that the use in (2) (and (2e)) can be rendered harmless enough; but that the use in (3) (and (3e)) is logically dubious and metaphysically repugnant. How is this?

The case of (1) and (1e) is obvious enough. Consider a very obviously bad argument. We recall that identity:

(5) The number of planets = 9.

---

[3] Thus, for example, he says: 'If "nec (… > 5)" can turn out to be true or false "of" the number 9 depending merely on how that number is referred to (as the falsity of [(8), below] suggests), then evidently "nec (x > 5)" expresses no genuine condition on objects of any kind' ('Three Grades', pp. 172–3: this sentence is quoted and discussed in § 6.5 of the main text). We find the same simple contrast between the 'purely referential' and the 'non-referential' in Quine's *Word and Object* (Cambridge, MA: MIT Press, 1960), pp. 142–3.

[4] This can be seen as a way of facing down one aspect of what I've called the Basic Worry about the view that the meaning of words concerns things in the world, rather than things in the mind. The worry is that this view seems to require two words which are associated with the same thing in the world to have the same meaning, although this is often counter-intuitive. Quine's policy is, in effect, to try to solve the problem by associating the words with the right things in the world in the relevant contexts. In a referentially transparent context, the words are associated with their normal referents, and nothing else matters about their meaning there. In referentially opaque contexts, on the other hand, the words are associated with something else entirely (on the view which Quine favours, they're associated just with *themselves*, rather than anything else in the world). What he can't allow is the possibility of referential *translucent* contexts, since these would be contexts in which words are still associated with the usual things in the world, but there is more to their meaning here than which things in the world they're associated with.

We also know:

(1e) The sentence '9 is greater than 5' expresses a necessary truth.

We try applying Leibniz's Law to (1e) on the basis of (5), to get this:

(10) The sentence 'The number of planets is greater than 5' expresses a necessary truth.

But (10) is false for the same reason as (8) – on its most natural reading – was: if the history of the universe had been different, there would have been fewer planets.

What's gone wrong here? The answer is simple: we cannot legitimately apply Leibniz's Law to (1e) on the basis of (5). This is because (1e) says something about the *sentence* '9 is greater than 5', and not about the arithmetical fact that nine is greater than five. Moreover, the symbol '9' occurs within the quoted sentence '9 is greater than 5', not as a name for the number nine, but as itself, the mere symbol. Since (10) involves an expression which refers to a different sentence – the sentence 'The number of planets is greater than 5' – there is no reason at all to expect what was true of the first sentence to be true of the second.

There's no violation of the policy of extensionality here, because when they appear within quotation marks, the crucial expressions don't function in their ordinary roles. The sentence '9 is greater than 5' doesn't really occur *as a sentence* when it is quoted: instead it appears as part of a *name* of a sentence (itself). The same goes for the symbols '9' and '5', and the predicate '*x* is greater than *y*' when they appear in quotation. Indeed, as Quine points out, it's a quite arbitrary fact (he calls it 'an orthographic accident'),[5] due just to the convenience of the notational system of quotation, that we happen to form names of symbols by using complex expressions which incorporate those symbols themselves. We could quite easily have used other names, whether for the individual symbols or for whole sentences (as I used 'Archibald' as a name for the sentence '9 is greater than 5').

The sentence (1e) in fact has just two components, according to the familiar grammar of Frege's logic. It has something which looks like a singular term, and it has a predicate. The singular term is the whole

---

[5] 'Three Grades', p. 161.

expression consisting of the sentence '9 is greater than 5' *together with* the quotation marks which surround it in (1e). This singular term refers to the sentence within the quotation marks, and all that matters about it, as far as Quine is concerned, is that it refers to that sentence. This is why (1e*) – 'Archibald expresses a necessary truth' – can be said to state the same fact as (1e). And all that matters about the predicate '*x* expresses a necessary truth' is, according to Quine, what the policy of extensionality says matters.

So much, then, for (1e). How can Quine deal with the problems which arise over (2) and (2e)? Here's (2e) again:

(2e) It is necessarily true that 9 is greater than 5.

Quine suggests that, strictly speaking, (2e) exploits a *predicate* use of necessity, rather than an *operator* use. That is, (2e) really means no more than this:

(2e*) *That-9-is-greater-than-5* is necessarily true.

Here the italicized and hyphenated phrase '*That-9-is-greater-than-5*' is a complex name or referring expression, which refers to something which is capable of being true. We don't need to speculate here on the kinds of thing which can be true or false, if they're not sentences: whatever they are, that's the kind of thing referred to by that phrase. And here, of course, the phrase as a whole acts as a name or singular term, and it's a matter of mere notational convenience that it is formed by means of a sentence which can express the truth in question. The treatment of (2e) is therefore very similar to the treatment of (1e).

In fact, Quine hopes to make it even more similar than it appears. He has no fondness for such abstract objects as *that-9-is-greater-than-5*. As a result, he hopes to be able to deal with all of the necessary truths he's prepared to acknowledge by means of a predicate which applies to *sentences* – like his original 'Nec ... ', or the English ' ... expresses a necessary truth'. And in traditional empiricist fashion, he seems to countenance only a very limited range of necessary truths. In fact, he has worries even about things which more traditional empiricists would have accepted: in 'Three Grades of Modal Involvement' he is prepared to count as necessary only those truths which might figure in mathematics or in that part of logic where the rule of extensionality holds. He claims that the necessity of all of these truths can be represented by the use merely of a semantical *predicate*. This is what section II of 'Three Grades of Modal Involvement' aims to show.

What, then, of the final grade of modal involvement, that manifested in these formulations? –

(3) $(\exists x)$ nec $(x > 5)$;
(3e) Something is necessarily greater than 5.

It is obvious, to begin with, that what is said here cannot be represented in terms of a predicate which applies to sentences. Consider, for example, an attempt to give a semi-colloquial version of (3) using the predicate ' … expresses a necessary truth':

(3!) There is an x such that '$x > 5$' expresses a necessary truth.

The trouble is that, as Quine wants to understand quotation – as simply forming a name of what lies between the quotation marks – the 'x' which appears in '$x > 5$' when that phrase appears within quotation is not being used with its ordinary (or indeed, any) meaning: it simply appears as itself, the 24th letter of the alphabet. That means that it can't be connected with the use of 'x' *outside* quotation marks in (3!). But if it's not connected with the use of 'x' outside quotation marks, then the whole expression '$x > 5$' has to be assessed on its own. Well, then: does '$x > 5$', taken all on its own, express a necessary truth? Of course not: if there is nothing to link the 'x' to, it doesn't say anything, true or false. It's simply a predicate. It is as if I'd asked whether ' … is greater than 5' expresses a necessary truth.

So with the third grade of modal involvement we reach a kind of modality which can't be represented by means of a semantical predicate which says something about sentences. But this is really a symptom of what Quine takes to be a malaise, rather than the illness itself.

The problem arises from the natural understanding of the quantifiers – phrases such as 'There is an x such that … ' or 'Every x is such that … '. These expressions are naturally understood as introducing claims about the kinds of *object* that we might have in mind when we make general claims. It's natural to take (3), for example, to be making the following claim:

(3*) There is an *object* of which it is necessarily true that *it* (the object) is greater than 5.

The point is even clearer in the colloquial form (3e), which surely just means that some *object* is necessarily greater than 5.[6] What this means is that (3) and (3e) require us to accept that necessity and possibility may attach to objects themselves, rather than simply to ways of describing them.[7] It forces us to accept necessity and possibility which *concerns the object*: the Latin phrase '*de re*' means precisely *concerning the object*, so (3) and (3e) require us to accept necessities and possibilities which are *de re*. The earlier grades, however, had required no more than necessity and possibility which depended on *ways of describing* things: that kind of modality *concerns a kind of description*. The Latin phrase '*de dicto*' means *concerning the saying* or *concerning the way it is expressed*; (3) and (3e) require us to accept necessities and possibilities which are not merely *de dicto*.

What Quine objects to is a view he describes as 'Aristotelian essentialism'. Essentialism is the view that objects, as the *objects* they are, and not simply in virtue of some way of describing them, have some qualities essentially: that is to say, those objects couldn't exist without them. In general (though not inevitably), these *essential* qualities will be contrasted with *inessential* or *accidental* or *contingent* qualities, which those objects need not have in order to exist. We might think, for example, that it was essential to a particular person, in order to be the particular person she is, that she is the offspring of just *those* parents: no one born of different parents could have been *this* person. On the other hand, we might

---

[6] There is a contrast to be drawn here between two ways of understanding the quantifiers of Fregean logic. On the standard ('objectual') interpretation, we begin with a (perhaps implicitly defined) pool, or *domain*, of objects. These objects may then be taken as the *values* of quantificational variables (roughly, what the variables may be temporarily taken to refer to). 'There is an *x* such that *x* is a cat' is then taken to be true if there is at least one object in our domain which the predicate '*x* is a cat' is true of, if that object is taken as the value of the variable '*x*'. The contrast is with a non-standard, 'substitutional' reading of the quantifiers. According to this, 'There is an *x* such that *x* is a cat' is true if and only if there is a singular term *t* which, when put in place of the variable '*x*' in the predicate '*x* is a cat' yields a truth. In the terms of the distinction shortly to be explained in the text, sticking to a substitutional interpretation of such sentences as (3) could ensure that all necessity was, etymologically at least, *de dicto*: necessity might only appear as a predicate of sentences. It's a more complicated question whether this would stop some claims of necessity being *de re*.

[7] This might be expressed in terms of objects having modal *properties* – being necessarily greater than 5, for example, or being possibly older than Nixon at the time of his resignation, or being only contingently long-haired.

think that it was inessential or accidental to a particular person that she is wearing a particular jacket on a particular day: her whole identity does not seem to depend on her wearing precisely that outfit.

Quine objects to the very idea of a contrast between essential and inessential qualities of an object, just as the object it is. And it seems that we must make the idea of such a contrast at least *intelligible* (even if it is never actually realized) if we accept *de re* necessity. To say that some things are necessarily true of an object, just in virtue of its being the object it is, requires us to make intelligible the idea of things which are true, but not necessarily true of that object, just in virtue of the object it is. So when Quine says that there is 'no semblance of sense' in the contrast between essential and accidental attributes or qualities, he is saying, in effect, that there is 'no semblance of sense' in *de re* modality.

Why does he think this? I think there are two kinds of reason. One kind is due ultimately to Quine's empiricism: that is, to his belief that substantial knowledge is all derived from experience. I'll examine this kind of reason in the section 6.6. The other kind of reason is that there is (according to Quine) something close to logical incoherence in the very idea of *de re* modality. I turn to this reason next.

6.5   Quine's logical problem with *de re* modality

Quine thinks that it's impossible to make sense of *de re* necessity while doing justice to the fact that contexts of necessity are intensional – that is, that they do not permit of the routine intersubstitution of sentences which have the same truth-value, predicates which are true of the same things, and singular terms which refer to the same objects.

The basic argument, I think, is very simple. Here is Quine's statement of it:

> If 'nec (... > 5)' can turn out to be true or false "of" the number 9 depending merely on how that number is referred to (as the falsity of [(8)] suggests), then evidently 'nec $(x > 5)$' expresses no genuine condition on objects of any kind.[8]

---

[8] 'Three Grades', pp. 172–3.

The argument here needs a little unpacking. Here's a more careful formulation of it:

(Q1) If something is necessary *de re*, it is necessarily true of an object just in virtue of its being the object it is;

(Q2) If something is necessarily true of an object just in virtue of its being the object it is, it makes no difference to its being necessarily true of that object whether we refer to the object in one way rather than another;

(Q3) If it makes no difference to something's being necessarily true of an object whether we refer to the object in one way rather than another, then it is always possible to intersubstitute two different expressions which refer to the same object within contexts of necessity, without affecting the truth of the whole;

(Q4) It is not always possible to swap two different expressions which refer to the same object within contexts of necessity without affecting the truth of the whole; *so*

(Q5) Nothing is necessary *de re*.

This looks like a compelling sequence of thought. (Q1)–(Q3) seem simply to spell out what's involved in the idea of *de re* necessity, and (Q4) seems undeniable, if we accept that

(2e) It is necessarily true that 9 is greater than 5,

is true, while

(8) It is necessarily true that the number of planets is greater than 5,

is false, on its most natural interpretation, in which the phrase 'the number of planets' occurs strictly within the context of necessity.

This argument for (Q4) depends on treating the phrase 'the number of planets' as a complex singular term. If we follow Russell, and analyse all definite descriptions as quantifier expressions (for which, see chapter 2), this argument will fail. So we could block Quine's formal argument against essentialism by adopting Russell's theory of descriptions.[9] (It's ironic that Quine himself officially endorsed Russell's theory.)

---

[9] Quine produces a brief technical argument in further support of (Q4), on pp. 163–4 of 'Three Grades'. This is a variant of an argument which can be traced back to Frege, and is now known as 'the Slingshot'. The argument is now generally recognized not to be decisive, though it's not quite clear how it should be challenged. Like the simple

There is, though, another way of resisting Quine's argument, which emerges from our earlier consideration of the meaning of the notion of referential opacity. We could deny (Q3). The idea of (Q3) is that if the necessity really concerns the object, what matters is that we refer to the right object; and as long as we refer to the right object, other features of our expressions are simply irrelevant. This seems very reasonable, but in fact it involves a crucial assumption which isn't made explicit.

The implicit assumption here is that expressions which refer to the object in question are *doing nothing else* apart from refer to the object. But if, in addition to referring to an object, an expression is doing something else – *saying something*, for example, either about that object or about something else – then we can't say that it doesn't matter which expression we use. (Q3) is only reasonable if it's assumed that the expressions in question refer to the object in question, and do nothing else.

If we look at the expressions which are involved in the difficulties with intersubstitution within contexts of necessity, we'll find that they don't seem to meet this condition. Take the phrase 'the number of planets', for example. If we accept that this is a singular term (which Russellians, of course, deny), we're likely to insist that it doesn't *just* refer to an object: it also, at least, *describes that object as the number of planets*.

On the other hand, if we look at expressions which might plausibly be supposed to refer to objects, and do nothing else, we'll find that there are no obvious problems with intersubstitution within contexts of necessity. It's not implausible to suppose that *proper names* are just that kind of expression. Suppose, then, that we treat the Arabic symbol '9' and the English word 'nine' as two different proper names of the same thing, the number nine. That is to say:

(11) 9 = nine.

Now, if we begin from

---

argument in the text, it relies on treating definite descriptions as singular terms, so can be resisted by adopting Russell's theory of descriptions. Interestingly, it can also be resisted by distinguishing between rigid and non-rigid designators. Either way, it is closely linked with themes which have already been explored. For more on the Slingshot, see D. Føllesdal, 'Quine on Modality', in R. Gibson, ed., *The Cambridge Companion to Quine* (Cambridge: Cambridge University Press, 2004), and S. Neale, *Facing Facts* (Oxford: Oxford University Press, 2001).

(2e) It is necessarily true that 9 is greater than 5,

and swap 'nine' for '9' on the basis of (11), we reach this:

(12) It is necessarily true that nine is greater than 5.

And (12), even if a little odd stylistically, is surely true.

The general point here affects Leibniz's Law, which lies behind the reasoning in the (Q1)–(Q5) argument. In section 6.3, I offered the following informal account of Leibniz's Law and its motivation:

> If *a* is the same thing as *b*, whatever is true of *a* is true of *b*. That means that if we begin with a truth about an object, in which the object is referred to by one name, we should still have a truth if we refer to the same object by a different name.

We now see that it's not unimportant that the principle is formulated here in terms of *names*; and it requires the implicit assumption that names are expressions which refer to objects and do nothing else.

This implicit assumption governs Quine's conception of singular terms, and indeed can now be seen to underlie his contrast between referential transparency and referential opacity. I noted earlier that, in the terms of the metaphor in play here, one option is not considered: referential translucency. We would have referential translucency if we found that an expression genuinely referred to an object, but did more than just refer to it. There's no place for such a thing as referential translucency in Quine's conception of the function of words. On reflection, that is hardly surprising, since Quine adheres strictly to his 'policy of extensionality', and according to this policy, nothing can matter about the meaning of a singular term, when it really is occurring as a singular term, other than which object it refers to. In the light of this, it's hardly surprising that Quine should find an assumption like (Q3) compelling.

Quine, in fact, acknowledges that a logical system could be devised which did not follow his own preferred policy of extensionality, though he clearly finds it unattractive.[10] If we accept the possibility of what I've called referential *translucency*, it's clear that Quine has no decisive argument against the logical coherence of *de re* modality. As far as the logic is concerned, his view seems to depend upon a certain austerity of

---

[10] See, e.g., 'Three Grades', p. 175.

taste, which favours extensionality, together with whatever pragmatic reasons may be offered in support of the theoretical simplicity of extensional systems.

6.6   Quine's metaphysical worries about *de re* modality

Quine's deepest concerns about *de re* necessity seem to depend on his metaphysical outlook – his view of the fundamental nature of the world. According to his Humean conception of necessity, necessity is not found in the world itself, but is rather introduced by the *conceptions* which we bring to the world. This is the basis of the thought that all necessity must really be *de dicto*, concerning a way of *describing* the world, rather than the way the world is in itself.

Since Kripke and Putnam, we are happier with the idea of *de re* necessity than people were before they wrote. And we are less impressed with empiricist arguments which insist that we cannot experience necessity: after all, haven't Kripke and Putnam shown that there can be necessary *a posteriori* truths (necessary truths which can only be known by experience)? But Quine's general Humean view of necessity has not been destroyed by Kripke's and Putnam's work. It's not clear, for example, that we simply observe that it's *necessary* that gold has atomic number 79. According to a natural elaboration of the Kripke–Putnam story, gold is defined (implicitly, perhaps, within a certain practice) as the stuff which a certain sort of natural science will count as authoritative about; and then the appropriate science delivers its results. It is the first stage which establishes what counts as necessary to gold, and this is not something observed by science, but something which is central to the point of the practice of using the word 'gold'. This practice leaves room for the findings of experience to contribute what they may; and that allows the final result to be *a posteriori*. But we needn't accept that it's simply observed that it's necessary that gold has atomic number 79. So much for the precise point about the necessary *a posteriori*. At a more general level, the idea that the world itself simply happens to be a certain way, but *need not* have been, remains compelling.

The issues here are vast, and this is not the place to examine them thoroughly. Instead, I'll simply lay out some options. Quine's view seems to depend on the following claim:

(A) It is not essential to an object's being the object it is that it is described
     or conceived of in a certain way.

Quine seems to need something like this claim to maintain the contrast
between *de re* and *de dicto* necessity: it is only because something like (A) is
true that what follows necessarily from *describing* an object in a certain way
is not a necessary truth about the object itself.

There are two things to note about (A). The first is that it's an extremely
natural claim: it seems absurd to suppose that the nature of things as they
are in themselves depends on *our* ways of thinking of them or describing
them. The whole thing about the real world is that it is real, independent
of us, lying there to be discovered, not a figment of our imagination. But
the second thing to note is that to give this natural thought its due force
requires us to read (A) itself as involving *de re* necessity. The explanation
which I've just appealed to of the independence of the world as it is in
itself from any way of thinking of it depends on reading (A) as the denial of
a particular claim of *de re* necessity: the particular claim being denied is
that it is essential to objects being the objects they are that they are
described or conceived of in certain ways. Our denial of this particular
claim depends on a conception of what is *really* essential to things as they
are in themselves. It doesn't rest on a blanket rejection of all *de re*
necessity.

So we seem to be in a curious position. We seem driven to accept (A);
acceptance of (A) seems (if Quine is right) to undermine the very idea of
de re necessity; but (A) itself implicitly depends on accepting *de re* necessity.

How might we deny (A)? It can seem natural to accept this pair of
thoughts:

(B) It is essential to an object's being the object it is that it is an object of the
     particular *kind* it is;
(C) An object's being of the particular kind it is depends upon its being
     described or conceived of in a certain way.

Take a simple example in support of (B): I couldn't be *me*, the very
individual I am, without being a *person*. I couldn't have existed without
being a person; and when I cease to be a person, I cease to exist. (B), then,
seems very natural.

But now consider (C). The concept of a person seems a very particular concept, dependent on the particular interests of people in general, and also, plausibly enough, on a particular kind of culture. It seems implausible to suppose that this particular way of categorizing objects is simply a reflection of the way the world is in itself. Now, of course, my being a person (to continue with the example) doesn't depend on anyone actually thinking of me, and describing me as a person; but it does seem to depend upon the *possibility* of so describing me, and that possibility seems only to have been made available as a result of certain features of human interests.

Accepting both (B) and (C) might, then, seem a natural way of denying (A). But there is also a third option. We can have both (A) and *de re* necessity if we accept (B) (as well as (A)) but deny (C). That is, we can suppose that our classification of objects, at some fundamental level, reflects the way the world is in itself. We might say that for something to be of the kind it is depends ultimately just on the world, and not on our schemes of classification.

We seem, then, to have three intelligible positions, but each of them seems to face large difficulties. First, there is the *Quinean* position. This accepts (A), because of its commitment to the independent reality of the world. In order to maintain its commitment to the Humean conception of necessity – necessity depends on our conceptions of things, rather than the things themselves – this position will then deny (B) while accepting (C). The difficulty with this position is that it leads to a denial of *de re* necessity, while apparently depending on *de re* necessity in its conception of the independent reality of the world.

Secondly, we have a position which we may call *conceptualist*.[11] This accepts both *de re* necessity and the empiricist conception of necessity, by endorsing both (B) and (C); it therefore has to deny (A). But in that denial of (A) it seems to be rejecting the independent reality of the world as it is in itself, and that seems almost impossible to do.

And, thirdly, we have a position which we may call *non-empiricist realist*. This accepts both the independent reality of the world, by endorsing (A), and *de re* necessity, in endorsing (B), but it denies the empiricist conception

---

[11] This term is used by David Wiggins to describe his own (similar, I think) position, in his *Sameness and Substance Renewed* (Cambridge: Cambridge University Press, 2001), ch. 5.

of necessity by denying (C). And the difficulty with this for many people is just that the Humean conception of necessity can seem so compelling.

Although I won't attempt to pursue these issues further here, this little taste should be enough to show something of the attraction of Quine's way of doing philosophy, even to those who disagree with him. What he does is to express, in the adoption of formal positions on technical issues, a very large conception of the nature of reality. The most technical philosophy of language becomes the most fundamental metaphysics.

Further reading

An earlier version of Quine's views on these issues is to be found in 'Reference and Modality' in his *From a Logical Point of View*, 2nd edn (New York: Harper and Row, 1961). A later version appears in his *Word and Object* (Cambridge, MA: MIT Press, 1960), pp. 195–200. A useful introductory book on Quine is A. Orenstein, *W. V. Quine* (Chesham: Acumen, 2002); ch. 7 considers the issues of this chapter. A more advanced introduction to Quine's work is C. Hookway, *Quine* (Cambridge: Polity Press, 1988); ch. 7 considers the issues of this chapter. A useful discussion of Quine's views on modality is to be found in A. Plantinga, *The Nature of Necessity* (Oxford: Oxford University Press, 1978), ch. 2 and the Appendix.

7 Reference and propositional attitudes

Key text

W. V. O. Quine, 'Quantifiers and Propositional Attitudes', *Journal of Philosophy*, 53 (1956), pp. 177–87.

7.1 Introduction

Linguistic constructions count as *intensional* if they raise problems for the rule of extensionality. Where extensionality reigns we can swap singular terms which refer to the same object, predicates which are true of the same things, and sentences which have the same truth-value (either both true or both false), without affecting the truth-value of the whole sentence in which such expressions occur. In chapter 6 we looked at problems which arise in connection with one kind of intensional construction – modal constructions (to do with possibility and necessity). In this chapter we'll look at some related problems with another kind of intensional construction – propositional-attitude constructions. Intensional constructions in general are of central interest in the analytic tradition, because they are a principal focus of what I've called the Basic Worry about the view, which has been adopted enthusiastically in the analytic tradition, that the meaning of words is concerned with things in the world, rather than things in the mind. The relevant aspect of Basic Worry is that this world-directed view seems to require two words which are associated with the same thing in the world to have the same meaning, but that seems counter-intuitive in some contexts. Intensional constructions are the most obvious contexts in which it seems counter-intuitive.

A *propositional attitude* is a state of mind whose nature can be characterized using a whole sentence embedded within a 'that'-clause.

So we might say Joan of Arc *believed that she was called by God to save France*; or we might say the English *hoped that a religious trial would stop them being blamed for her death*, or we might say the Church authorities *desired that the threat she presented to male authority should be removed*. (This last we might express more colloquially by saying that they wanted to remove the threat she presented to male authority.) In such constructions, the 'that'-clause tells us *what* is believed, hoped, desired (etc.); it gives us what's sometimes called the *content* of the propositional attitude. The thing believed, hoped, desired (etc.) is also sometimes called the *object* of the propositional attitude. In one sense of the word 'proposition', it is the *proposition* to which the *attitude* (hope, belief, desire, etc.) is taken.[1]

This chapter focuses on a famous paper which is concerned with problems which arise when someone has a propositional attitude which is directed to, or concerned with a particular individual object: it might be a belief about a particular thing, or a hope or desire which is directed to some particular thing. Willard Van Orman Quine's 'Quantifiers and Propositional Attitudes' deals with a problem very like the problem of *de re* modality which we considered in the last chapter. And Quine adopts what is, in essence, a very similar approach. In particular, he uses the dichotomy between referential *opacity* and referential *transparency*. According to this approach, if a singular term genuinely refers to an object, then it can be replaced by other, co-referring singular terms; so if there is a problem with such intersubstitution, that means that the singular term in question is not really referring to an object at all as it occurs in such constructions. This article galvanized interest in propositional-attitude constructions for decades, and has shaped the use of much of the technical terminology which is applied in the field.

7.2   Quine's problem

Consider the following sentence:

(1) Ralph believes that someone is a spy.

This is ambiguous, even if one of the readings takes some seeing. The two construals can be rendered in English as follows:

---

[1] In this sense, 'proposition' means *what is meant by a declarative sentence*.

(1a) There is someone whom Ralph believes to be a spy;

(1b) Ralph believes that there are spies.

(1a) represents what Quine calls a *relational* sense of (1): it takes (1) to be concerned to describe a relation between Ralph and a particular person. This reading of (1) takes it to be describing what we may call a *de re* belief: it is a belief which is specifically concerned with a particular object.

(1b), on the other hand, represents what Quine calls a *notional* sense of (1); on this reading no relation between Ralph and any particular person is described. In the area of modality, as we saw in chapter 6, the *de re* is contrasted with the *de dicto*: it is a contrast between necessity which *concerns an object* (*de re*) and necessity which *concerns a way of describing objects* (*de dicto*). The familiarity of that contrast in the area of modality has led the sense of (1) which is represented in (1b) to be described as a *de dicto* construal, even though there is no obvious sense in which (1b) represents Ralph's belief as being concerned with a *saying* or a *way of describing*.

Quine's problem in 'Quantifiers and Propositional Attitudes' is how to understand the difference between (1a) and (1b). The problem is made sharp for him by the attempt to render (1a) and (1b) into quantifier-variable notation. (1a) seems naturally represented like this:

(1a*) $(\exists x)$(Ralph believes that x is a spy)

('There is an x such that Ralph believes that x is a spy'); and (1b) seems naturally represented like this:

(1b*) Ralph believes that $(\exists x)$(x is a spy)

('Ralph believes that there is an x such that x is a spy.')

Quine finds (1a*) problematic for the same reason as the reason he objected to *de re* modality. If (1a*) represents a genuinely *de re* belief, Quine thinks, it ought to be possible to swap co-referring singular terms in the position of the 'x' within the 'that'-clause in (1a*). But this seems not to be possible, because belief constructions are *intensional*. Quine illustrates the point by imagining that (1a) is true, and telling the following story:

> There is a certain man in a brown hat whom Ralph has glimpsed several times under questionable circumstances on which we need not enter here; suffice it to say that Ralph suspects his is a spy. Also there is a gray-haired man, vaguely known to Ralph as rather a pillar of the community, whom

Ralph is not aware of having seen except once at the beach. Now Ralph does not know it, but the men are one and the same. Can we say of this *man* (Bernard J. Ortcutt, to give him a name) that Ralph believes him to be a spy?[2]

Now it seems clear from the story that this is true:

(2) Ralph believes that the man in the brown hat is a spy.

And the following is also true:

(3) The man in the brown hat = the man seen at the beach.

In the last chapter, we came across the familiar logical principle known as *Leibniz's Law*, which we can state informally like this: if we begin with a truth about an object, in which the object is referred to by one name, we should still have a truth if we refer to the same object by a different name. If we accept Leibniz's Law, it may seem that from (2) and (3) we should be able to derive this:

(4) Ralph believes that the man seen at the beach is a spy.

But (4) is naturally taken to be false. According to Quine, if we hold that (2) and (3) are true and (4) is false, 'then we cease to affirm any relationship between Ralph and any man at all'.[3]

This is Quine's doctrine of the dichotomy between referential transparency and referential opacity, which we saw at work in his distrust of *de re* modality. Here we see Quine claiming that if there is a difficulty with the intersubstitution of co-referring singular terms in a certain construction – that is, if the construction is not referentially *transparent* – then those singular terms are not really referring there at all[4] – that is, the construction is referentially *opaque*.

But Quine now faces a problem which is sharper for him than that which arose in the case of modality. He had difficulty making sense of the logic of *de re* necessity, but then he was quite happy to dispense with it altogether: after all, *de re* necessity involves a non-Humean conception of

---

[2] 'Quantifiers and Propositional Attitudes', p. 179.

[3] Ibid. Note, however, that there is only even the appearance of a problem here if we take definite descriptions to be singular terms, which Quine, officially at least, does not, since he follows Russell's approach to descriptions.

[4] At least, not to their usual referents: Quine allows that they may be regarded as referring to themselves.

modality which he was anyway committed to denying. Things are different with propositional attitudes, however: the contrast between (1a) and (1b) seems undeniable. There seems an obvious difference between having a particular person in mind and merely holding general beliefs. And the problem does not just concern belief: as Quine points out, the same difficulties precisely affect striving, wishing, and wanting.

7.3   Quine's proposed solution

Quine's problem is raised by the ambiguity of construal which we found in (1). His proposed solution is to explain this in terms of an ambiguity of *construction*. In its simplest version, this amounts to saying that the ordinary propositional-attitude verbs ('believes', 'hopes', 'desires', etc.) are themselves systematically ambiguous.

Quine begins the presentation of his solution by appeal to what he calls *intensions*. Intensions correspond either to whole sentences or to predicates. An intension, for Quine, is, roughly, what is *said* by a sentence or a predicate. An intension of degree 1 is what is said by a *one*-place predicate: that is, a predicate with *one* variable to mark a place where a singular term may go. Thus *ugliness* is an intension of degree 1: it is said truly of Socrates (for example) by saying that he is ugly – that is, by using the predicate 'x is ugly' to describe him. Quine would represent the intension corresponding to the predicate 'x is ugly', as follows: x (x is ugly). I shall use the slightly more natural locution: x's being ugly. An intension of degree 2 is what is said (of two objects, taken in order) by a *two*-place predicate; and an intension of degree 3 is what is said (of three objects, taken in order) by a *three*-place predicate, and so on. An intension of degree 0 corresponds to a whole sentence: Quine calls an intension of degree 0 a *proposition*, following one traditional use of that term. A proposition, in this use, is what is said by a whole sentence. We naturally refer to propositions (in this sense) by means of 'that'-clauses: we might talk of the proposition *that there are spies*.

In the first instance, then, Quine explains his solution to the problem of *de re* propositional attitudes in terms of these intensions. Recall the *notional* (not *de re*) reading of (1):

(1b) Ralph believes that there are spies.

According to Quine, a proper representation of this sentence sees it as being formed from a *two*-place predicate, 'x believes$_1$ y'. (I use the subscript '$_1$' to mark off this two-place belief predicate from others which we'll encounter soon.) To reach (1b) you put a name of a person ('Ralph') in place of the first variable, and a name of a proposition ('that there are spies') in place of the second variable. The notional reading of (1) is captured by means of a two-place predicate which expresses a two-place ('dyadic') relation (*believing*) between a person and a proposition. On this under-standing, (1b) falls within the rule of extensionality, because the whole expression 'that there are spies' is taken to be (in effect) a singular term which refers to a proposition; it can be replaced by any other expression (in a different language, for instance) which refers to the same proposition.

What, then, of the other reading of (1),

(1a) There is someone whom Ralph believes to be a spy?

Quine thinks that this is formed from a *three*-place predicate, expressing a *triadic* relation, which we might write like this:

x believes$_2$ y of z.

(I use the subscript '$_2$' to distinguish 'believes$_2$' from 'believes$_2$', and from any other belief predicates that may be needed.) To get a whole sentence, we can put the name of a believer (in our case, Ralph) in place of 'x', the name of an intension of degree 1 (in our case, *being a spy*, or *y's being a spy*) in place of 'y', and the name of the object the belief is about (in our case, Bernard J. Ortcutt) in place of 'z'. So there is a *de re* belief which can be truly reported like this, in Quine's story:

(5) *Ralph* believes$_2$ *y's being a spy of Ortcutt.*

Now (1a), of course, merely says that there is *someone* whom Ralph believes to be a spy: it doesn't name that person. So to get a proper representation of (1a) we need to replace the name 'Ortcutt' in (5) by a variable, and attach a quantifier to the resulting predicate. That will give us this:

(1a**) There is an x such that Ralph believes$_2$ *y's being a spy of x.*

We can do the same thing with *de re* beliefs involving more than one person. Quine's example is this:

(6) Tom believes that Cicero denounced Catiline.

If we take this to express a *de re* belief which Tom has about both Cicero and Catiline, we would, according to Quine, express (6) as follows:

(6a) Tom believes$_3$ x's denouncing y of Cicero and Catiline (in that order).

(Note that we've now introduced a *third* belief predicate, 'w believes$_3$ x of y and z'.)

In all of these constructions the singular terms occur in referentially transparent positions. In (5) we can replace the name 'Ortcutt' with any other expression which refers to the same man (including both 'the man in the brown hat' and 'the man seen at the beach'); and we can replace 'y's being a spy' with any other expression which refers to the same intension of degree 1. In (6a) we can replace 'Cicero' and 'Catiline' with any other expressions which refer to the same people (for example, 'Tully' and 'the principal conspirator', respectively); and we can replace 'x's denouncing y' with any other expression (in French, for example) which refers to the same intension.

What about these two sentences:

(2) Ralph believes that the man in the brown hat is a spy;
(4) Ralph believes that the man seen at the beach is a spy?

We understood these earlier in such a way that (2) was true (given Quine's story) and (4) was false. Quine will now understand them as ambiguous. He will suppose that they both have a *notional* reading (which some may call '*de dicto*'), which we can represent using the two-place predicate 'x believes$_1$ y', as follows:

(2n) Ralph believes$_1$ *that the man in the brown hat is a spy*;
(4n) Ralph believes$_1$ *that the man seen at the beach is a spy*.

(2n) is true, on the story, and (4n) is false. But there is no temptation to swap 'the man seen at the beach' for 'the man in the brown hat' here. This is because, on Quine's view, these two expressions are not functioning here as singular terms for a particular man (Ortcutt) at all, and so we should not expect them to be intersubstitutable. They function merely as parts of what are in effect singular terms for *propositions*. The only singular terms in (2n), on this view, are 'Ralph' and the whole clause 'that the man in the brown hat is a spy'. The only singular terms in (4n) are 'Ralph' and the whole clause 'that the man seen at the beach is a spy'. In both sentences the 'that'-clauses as wholes are, in effect, singular terms which refer to propositions. Since they are different propositions, there's no licence to swap one clause for the other, so there is no inconsistency in maintaining that (2n) is true and (4n) false.

But Quine's view allows that there is an alternative, *relational (de re)* reading of (2) and (4), which he would represent as follows:

(2r) Ralph believes$_2$ *x's being a spy* of the man in the brown hat;

(4r) Ralph believes$_2$ *x's being a spy* of the man seen at the beach.

(2r) contains three singular terms on Quine's analysis: 'Ralph', which refers to Ralph, of course; '*x*'s being a spy', which refers to an intension of degree 1; and 'the man in the brown hat', which refers to Ortcutt. Now since these all occur in referentially transparent positions, it's possible to put co-referring singular terms in their place. In particular, it is possible to put 'the man seen at the beach' in place of 'the man in the brown hat'. That means that we can legitimately derive (4r) from (2r) (given (3)). And since (2r) is true, (4r) must be true too. But this is not a problem, because (4r) *doesn't* imply (4n): that is to say, it doesn't imply that Ralph believes that the man seen at the beach is a spy, as we would ordinarily understand that (the reading on which it is false). So the move from (2r) to (4r) is harmless.

As a result of these manoeuvres, propositional-attitude constructions are brought within the rule of extensionality. Every singular term or referring expression, if it is taken really to be acting as a singular term or referring expression, can be replaced with any other singular term or referring expression which refers to the same object. So Quine seems to have found a way of making sense of the difference between notional and relational readings of the same sentence, without flouting the rule of extensionality.

He is not himself content with this analysis, however, because it depends on referring to intensions, which he thinks are 'creatures of darkness'.[5] This is ultimately because, on his account, they can only be defined in terms of sameness of meaning, which is a notion he is sceptical about.[6] He therefore offers for consideration a proposal which is exactly analogous to the attempt to reformulate all claims about necessity as

---

[5] Ibid., p. 180.

[6] See his 'Two Dogmas of Empiricism', in his *From a Logical Point of View*, 2nd edn (New York: Harper and Row, 1961), pp. 20–46.

involving a semantical predicate, which we saw him undertake in the last chapter. He considers treating propositional attitudes as involving, not relations to intensions, but relations to *sentences* and *predicates*. Quine suggests that for this purpose, we will have to replace 'believes' with 'believes-true', but otherwise it seems easy enough to see how the reformulations will go. For example, the 'notional' reading of (2) will be rendered as follows:

(2n*) Ralph believes-true$_1$ 'The man in the brown hat is a spy'.

And the relational reading of (2) will be rendered like this:

(2r*) Ralph believes-true$_2$ 'x is a spy' of the man in the brown hat.

Quine is not entirely happy about this proposal, however. There are two reasons for this. One is that (2n*) cannot be strictly be regarded as equivalent to (2), even on a notional reading. This emerges in translation. A French translation of (2) would be this:

(2nf) Ralph croit que l'homme au chapeau brun est un épion.

But a French translation of (2n*) would look like this:

(2n*f) Ralph croit-vrai$_1$ «The man in the brown hat is a spy».

Clearly a French person who knew no English could understand what Ralph believes from (2nf), but not from (2n*f).[7]

But Quine is actually more worried about the second reason for discontent with the analysis in terms of quoted sentences and predicates. He treats words and sentences as things whose nature is entirely defined by their shape (when they're written) and their sound (when they're spoken).[8] Clearly, then, it is possible for the same word to have different meanings; it could even belong to different languages. So what is said by (2n*), for example, is not even fixed until we have specified the language or scheme of interpretation by whose lights we are to understand the quoted sentence. We need to expand (2n*) to make that explicit, in some such way as this:

---

[7] This point is made by A. Church, 'On Carnap's Analysis of Statements of Assertion and Belief', *Analysis*, 10 (1950), pp. 97–9.

[8] This is a version of the Lockean assumption (L8), which we encountered in ch. 1.

(2n*) Ralph believes-true 'The man in the brown hat is a spy' *as that is understood in English.*

And the problem is that the notion of an English understanding or interpretation of a sentence looks likely to be as difficult to explain as the notion of meaning was.

So it seems that Quine has found no way of dealing with propositional attitudes without referring to something at least as difficult to understand as the notion of meaning. But he does seem to have a solution to his technical problem: he has found a way of coping with the difference between 'notional' and 'relational' construals of such sentences as (1), without violating his policy of extensionality.

The core of his solution depends upon assimilating a distinction between types of *state of mind* to a distinction between types of *linguistic construction*. The reason why the distinction between the 'relational' and the 'notional' construals of (1) cannot be abandoned is that there is a genuine difference in state of mind between a belief which is *about a particular object* – genuinely *de re* – and one which is not. Quine's extensionalism requires that if a belief is genuinely about an object, then the expression which refers to that object must be open to replacement by any other expression which refers to the same object. So genuinely *de re* beliefs must be represented by some construction (such as that in (2r) and (2r*)) in which those referring expressions occur *outside* the 'that'-clauses which impose restrictions on substitution. It follows that if any referring expression occurs *within* the 'that'-clause of some proposi-tional-attitude construction – if, that is, it cannot be automatically replaced by any other expression which refers to the same object – then the propositional-attitude being described cannot really be *about a particular object*: it cannot be genuinely *de re*.

This assimilation of the distinction of states of mind to a distinction between types of construction has been preserved in much discussion of propositional attitudes, although Quine's reasons for making it have largely been forgotten. This has had two quite striking effects. The first concerns the use of the terms '*de re*' and '*de dicto*' in connection with propositional attitudes. We have seen that the term '*de re*' has ready application both to modality (necessity and possibility) and to proposi-tional attitudes: there is an issue about propositional attitudes concerning an object, just as there is an issue about necessity which is due to the nature of an object itself. But the term '*de dicto*' is very oddly applied to propositional attitudes: here it can only mean *not de re*.

As we have seen, whether or not a belief is *de re* seems fundamentally to concern the belief, the state of mind, itself: it is an issue of whether the believer has a particular object in mind. Consequently, a *de dicto* belief – being just a non-*de-re* belief – ought just to be a belief which does not concern a particular object: it ought to be a belief which someone could have without having a particular object in mind. But if we assimilate this distinction between types of state of mind to a distinction between types of construction, it will now seem legitimate to talk of *de re* and *de dicto linguistic constructions*. We will call a construction *de re* if it has a singular term position for the thing the belief is about *outside* the 'that'-clause; and we will call a construction *de dicto* if it has *no* singular term position outside the 'that'-clause for the thing the belief is about.[9] This assimilation of the distinction between types of state of mind to a distinction between types of construction – and hence, the appearance of the idea of *de re* and *de dicto* constructions – will shortly be put in question. For the time being, it's important to note that the terms '*de re*' and '*de dicto*' are often used to characterize both distinctions.

The other effect of the assimilation of these two kinds of distinction has been to raise questions about the relation between the so-called *de re* and *de dicto* constructions. Consider this Quinean construction:

(1a**) There is an x such that Ralph believes$_2$ y's being a spy of x.

This is a relational construction, reporting a *de re belief*. Suppose that this was all we knew of Ralph. Would we already know that something reportable using a 'notional' construction must have been true? Would we know, that is, that something of the following form must have been true:

(1c) Ralph believes$_1$ *that [α] is a spy* –

where '*α*' expresses some way in which Ralph thinks of the man in question? Does the truth of a 'relational' (so-called *de re*) construction claim

---

[9] Sometimes, of course, the singular term position will be occupied by a variable bound by a quantifier, as in (1a*).

depend on there being some true 'notional' (so-called *de dicto*) construction claim?

And then there is a question looking the other way. Suppose we have some 'notional' construction claim, such as this:

(2n) Ralph believes₁ *that the man in the brown hat is a spy.*

We might wonder: what *else* has to be true for us to be able to derive from (2n) a 'relational' construction claim?

This issue is then given a particular twist, if we forget the distinction between types of state of mind and types of construction. For it might then seem that what we need to know is what needs to be added to a *de dicto* (that is, *non-de-re*) *belief* for us to have a genuinely *de re* belief. Remember that a *de dicto belief* (as opposed to a 'notional' *construction*) is one which does not concern any particular object. Consider the following claim:

(7) Ralph believes that the shortest spy is a spy.

This is ambiguous between two construals, which Quine might render as follows:

(7a) Ralph believes₁ *that the shortest spy (whoever that is) is a spy;*
(7b) Ralph believes₂ *x's being a spy* of the shortest spy.

Now (7a) reports a *de dicto* belief: Ralph could have this belief without knowing any spies at all, just in virtue of thinking that there are spies and (because it's likely enough) that one is shorter than all the others. If we confuse types of state of mind with types of construction, we may be tempted then to ask what needs to be added to the *de dicto* belief reported in (7a) to enable us to conclude that Ralph has a *de re* belief, such as that reported in (7b). If we don't make this confusion, it's unclear that this question need ever arise.

7.4 Perry and the essential indexical

A serious threat to Quine's solution is posed by indexical expressions (words whose reference depends on the circumstances of their use). The problem was raised most explicitly by John Perry, in his paper 'The Problem of the Essential Indexical'.[10] Perry makes his point by means of

---

[10] J. Perry, 'The Problem of the Essential Indexical', *Noûs*, 13 (1979), pp. 3–21.

several examples (concerning indexicals referring to people, times, and places), but we can concentrate just on the first. Perry says:

> I once followed a trail of sugar on a supermarket floor, pushing my cart down the aisle on one side of a tall counter and back the aisle on the other, seeking the shopper with the torn sack to tell him he was making a mess. With each trip around the counter, the trail became thicker. But I seemed unable to catch up. Finally it dawned on me. I was the shopper I was trying to catch.[11]

What comes to be true when the truth dawns on him would have been expressed at the time by Perry himself as follows:

(8p) I realize that I am making a mess.

We might now express it like this:

(8w) John Perry realized that he was making a mess.

(8p) and (8w) capture a fact which is of considerable explanatory significance: it explains why Perry at that point stopped circling the aisles and attended to his sugar-bag. We don't get the same explanatory power if we replace the indexical 'I' within the 'that'-clause in (8p) (or 'he' in (8w)) with any non-indexical expression. Suppose, for example, that we replace 'I' in (8p), and 'he' in (8w), with the name 'John Perry' (with a suitable adjustment to the verb in the case of (8p)). We get these formulations:

(8pa) I realize that John Perry is making a mess;
(8wa) John Perry realized that John Perry was making a mess.

These don't explain why Perry changed his behaviour, unless we also assume what Perry at the time might have expressed like this:

(9p) I believe that I am John Perry;

or, as we would now put it:

(9w) John Perry believed that he was John Perry.

This suggests quite a different explanation (as if Perry had first heard a voice over the sound system saying something like 'Would John Perry please attend to his sack of sugar', and then took a while to realize that the

---

[11] 'The Problem of the Esssential Indexical', p. 3.

voice was referring to him). And, in any case, the crucial indexical returns in (9p) and (9w).

Similar problems infect any other attempt to find a non-indexical substitution for the indexical in (8p). There are two basic difficulties. First, it's not clear that Perry (or anyone else) need have a non-indexical way of describing or thinking of himself. And even if someone does have such a non-indexical description of herself, it seems inevitable that putting that description in place of the indexical in a sentence like (8p) will give us a different kind of explanation. Nor is the problem confined to beliefs which concern oneself: the same difficulty will arise with any belief naturally described using indexicals (for example, the belief that it is *now* time to go to the meeting, or the belief that *that* is the path home). The indexical, it seems, is essential.

7.5   The problems for Quine's solution

The problem of the essential indexical seems devastating for Quine's attempt to accommodate *de re* belief while adhering to his policy of extensionality. Intuitively, 'I' in (8p) and 'he' in (8w) are expressions which refer to John Perry. But they cannot be replaced by just any other expressions which refer to John Perry, as the problems with (8pa) and (8wa) show: at the very least, if John Perry happens to have forgotten his name, (8p) and (8w) will be true while (8pa) and (8wa) are false.

This means that the indexical terms 'I' and 'he' have to be regarded as occurring genuinely *within* the 'that'-clauses of (8p) and (8w), respectively. That means that they must be given 'notional' formulations, according to Quine. And because of Quine's rigid dichotomy between referential transparency (pure referentiality) and referential opacity (non-referentiality), that means that in (8p) and (8w), on Quine's view, 'we cease to affirm any relationship' between Perry and anyone at all. That is to say, the belief reported in (8p) and (8w) cannot be *de re*.

But that is surely absurd: Perry's belief is surely *about himself*, and therefore about some particular object. And this is confirmed by the fact that there *are* alternative formulations of the belief: (8w) describes the belief just as well as (8p) does. What links (8w) to (8p), of course, is that it uses an indexical which is appropriate from our perspective ('he') to refer to the same thing as is referred to by the indexical which is appropriate from Perry's perspective ('I'). That is to say, it is clear that the *reference*, as well as the indexicality, of the 'I' in (8p) is crucial to its use there. So (8p) and (8w) must describe a *de re* belief.

The obvious solution is to find a middle way between referential transparency (the purely referential) and referential opacity (the non-referential). It is natural to suggest, as I suggested in the last chapter, that we need the notion of referential *translucency*: we need the idea of terms appearing in contexts where they really do refer, but they don't *just* refer. So 'I' in (8p) and 'he' in (8w) really do refer to John Perry; but they don't just refer to him – their indexicality is crucial too.

What this amounts to, of course, is nothing less than the abandonment of the policy of extensionality. It is a cornerstone of that policy that nothing more matters about the meaning of a singular term, when it is really functioning as a singular term, than which object it refers to. It seems hard not to conclude that this policy is unsustainable in the light of the problem of the essential indexical.

But we also need to abandon the neat assimilation of types of propositional attitude to types of construction. (8p) and (8w) seem clearly to describe a *de re* belief, but, because of the difficulties of swapping co-referring terms for the indexicals, they use what is known as a *de dicto* construction. In fact, the idea of a *de dicto* construction now seems to collapse: for we might have expected, at the very least, that *de dicto* constructions would describe *de dicto* propositional attitudes.

Furthermore, we should look again at the questions about the relationship between the *de re* and the *de dicto* which seemed to arise in connection with propositional attitudes. Consider the 'relational' reading of (1):

(1a) There is someone whom Ralph believes to be a spy.

Does the truth of (1a) depend on something of the following form being true:

(1c*) Ralph believes that [α] is a spy?

It is not absurd to think it does. But then there seems no special difficulty about finding an appropriate replacement for 'α' here, given enough knowledge of Ralph's state of mind: after all, all we need is some expression which both refers to the person whom Ralph is thinking of, and shows how Ralph is thinking of that person – and we can use indexicals to form such expressions ('that person', perhaps). We do not need to find some non-referential descriptive phrase to put in place of 'α'. It seems that there is a question to be asked here, but it looks as if it has an easy answer.

Something similar holds for the question which runs the other way. Under what conditions can we derive something like (1a) from something of the form of (1c*)? There is a natural and simple answer: when, and only when, 'α' is an expression which genuinely refers to some object. This means that from,

(8w) John Perry realized that he was making a mess,

we are immediately entitled to infer,

(8wr) There is someone whom John Perry realized was making a mess.

On the other hand, we should be suspicious of any attempt to add something to

(7a*) Ralph believes that the shortest spy (whoever that is) is a spy,

in order to be able to conclude that (1a) is true. To suppose that the truth of (1a) depends upon something like (7a*) with something added is to commit oneself to a contentious conception of the relation between thought and reality. The idea would be that thought as it is in itself is purely general: we simply think that there are things which meet certain conditions (being a spy shorter than any other spy, being a unique King of France, and so on).[12] And then, it would be supposed, these purely general thoughts are hooked up to the world by certain causal relations. The connections with real objects would always be external to thought itself. But once we see that there need be no link between a propositional-attitude construction being wholly intensional – with no space where co-referring terms may be freely swapped – and its describing a belief which is non-*de-re*, at least one reason for being tempted by this picture is removed.[13]

---

[12] There are clear connections here with the descriptive theory of reference, expressed in commitments (DN3) and (DN4) of the description theory of names which is Kripke's target in *Naming and Necessity*. See ch. 4, § 4.2 above.

[13] Perry himself offers a different diagnosis of the problem, which traces it to what he calls 'the doctrine of propositions'. In my view, although the doctrine of propositions

7.6 Consequences

Quine's 'Quantifiers and Propositional Attitudes' attempts to deal with a direct threat to his policy of extensionality. I think his solution fails, and Perry's problem of the essential indexical shows why. The failure of Quine's solution is important for two reasons. First, it shows that there is serious doubt whether the policy of extensionalism can really be sustained in the analysis of language. We have only seen one attempt to preserve the policy fail in this chapter, of course: extensionalism is not yet dead, but it does face serious questions.

Secondly, the issues raised by the failure of Quine's solution raise serious questions about what it is for thought to be related to the world. Since Quine's solution fails, it seems that we don't need to think that thought itself is merely general, and is related to the world by some hook – a causal connection of some kind, no doubt – which attaches general thoughts to reality. That is, if we reject Quine's treatment of *de re* thoughts, we can allow that the connection with reality is built into the nature of thoughts themselves. Such a view is known as *externalism* in the philosophy of mind (roughly because the external world is involved in the nature of thoughts themselves).

We can see an illustration of externalism in a variant of the kind of Twin-Earth case we considered in connection with natural-kind terms. Suppose I pick up a piece of chalk and think that it is dusty. On Twin-Earth (a place indistinguishable from Earth in superficial respects) an exact Twin of me will be picking up a piece of chalk at the same time and thinking that *it* is dusty. If externalism is right, we will be thinking different thoughts: mine will be about my piece of chalk, and this will enter into its content; my Twin's will be about *his* piece of chalk, and that will affect its content. Externalism of this kind has been the focus of much recent debate in the philosophy of mind. Quine's attempt to preserve extensionalism is a crucial part of the background to that debate.

Further reading

It is worth reading John Perry's famous paper in full (even though I think he offers a misdiagnosis of the problem he's addressing): J. Perry, 'The

---

may have had some influence among philosophers, it is not the obvious thing to find fault with in Quine's picture.

Problem of the Essential Indexical', *Noûs*, 13 (1979), pp. 3–21. The literature on *de re* belief and externalism in the philosophy of mind is extremely rich. One particularly productive seam concerns the connection between *de re* belief and Fregean views of thought. Within this field it is worth considering: another paper by John Perry, 'Frege on Demonstratives', *Philosophical Review*, 86 (1977), pp. 474–97; two papers by Tyler Burge, 'Belief *De Re*', *Journal of Philosophy*, 74 (1977), pp. 338–62 and 'Sinning Against Frege', *The Philosophical Review*, 88 (1979), pp. 398–432; two papers by John McDowell, '*De Re* Senses', and 'Singular Thought and the Extent of Inner Space', both in his *Meaning, Knowledge, and Reality* (Cambridge, MA: Harvard University Press, 1998); and two works by Gareth Evans, 'Understanding Demonstratives', in his *Collected Papers* (Oxford: Oxford University Press, 1985), and *The Varieties of Reference* (Oxford: Oxford University Press, 1982), which is a sustained attempt to make sense of *de re* Senses.

8 The semantics of propositional attitudes

Key texts

Saul Kripke, 'A Puzzle about Belief', in A. Margalit, ed., *Meaning and Use* (Dordrecht: Reidel, 1979), pp. 239–83; Donald Davidson, 'On Saying That', in his *Inquiries into Truth and Interpretation* (Oxford: Oxford University Press, 1984), pp. 93–108.

8.1 Introduction

Semantics is the attempt to give a systematic explanation of how the meaning of sentences depends upon the meaning of their parts. Modern semantics began with Frege, whose logical system depends on the semantics of the sentences which can be constructed using its grammar. Frege's semantics was extensional: in general, whole sentences may be swapped when they have the same truth-value, singular terms may be swapped when they refer to the same object, and predicates may be swapped when they're true of the same things.

Propositional-attitude constructions – constructions involving a psychological verb ('believes', 'hopes', 'wishes', 'fears', etc.) and a 'that'-clause – have presented a challenge to extensionalism from the beginning. It's clear that more matters about sentences which occur in such 'that'-clauses than their truth-value, and it seems that more matters about singular terms which occur here than which object they refer to, and about predicates than which things they're true of. How, then, are we to explain what the words are doing in these 'that'-clauses? How can we provide a semantics for propositional-attitude constructions?

This chapter focuses on two articles which address the problems in surprising ways. Saul Kripke's paper 'A Puzzle about Belief' raises serious questions about the reasoning which seems to lie behind the idea that propositional-attitude constructions are not extensional; but if we abandon the idea that these constructions are not extensional, we seem to abandon the idea of propositional attitudes altogether. And this is Kripke's main point: there is a serious *puzzle* about propositional attitudes. Donald Davidson's paper 'On Saying That' takes a quite different approach: it seems to suggest that propositional-attitude constructions pose no problem for semantics at all. These are both ways of addressing one aspect of what I've described as the Basic Worry for the view that the meaning of words concerns things in the world, rather than things in our minds. As we've seen several times already, this aspect of the worry is that the world-directed conception of meaning seems to require two words which refer to the same thing to have the same meaning, while this is counter-intuitive, particularly in propositional-attitude constructions. Kripke can be understood as, in effect, facing down the worry by suggesting that the constructions which seem to cause the problem are not themselves in good shape. Davidson can be understood as saying that propositional-attitude constructions can be dealt with, while leaving the Basic Worry on one side.

8.2   Kripke, names, necessity, and propositional attitudes

One of the fundamental points of Kripke's *Naming and Necessity* is that *modal* and *epistemic* distinctions need to be kept separate. The difference between what is *necessary* and what is *contingent* is a modal distinction, and it concerns the nature of things themselves: it's a *metaphysical* or *ontological* distinction. The difference between what is *a priori* and what is *a posteriori* (between what can and what cannot be known independently of experience) is an *epistemic* distinction. Since these distinctions are made on quite different bases, we shouldn't expect them to coincide.

Now consider this sentence:

(1) If there is any such person as Vincent Furnier, Vincent Furnier is Vincent Furnier.

That seems both necessary and *a priori*. That is to say, the following two claims are both true:

(1a) It is necessarily true that if there is any such person as Vincent Furnier, Vincent Furnier is Vincent Furnier;

(1b) It can be known independently of experience that if there is any such person as Vincent Furnier, Vincent Furnier is Vincent Furnier.

(1a) and (1b) both seem to involve intensional (non-extensional) contexts: (1a) involves a *modal* intensionality, whereas (1b) uses a slightly complex propositional-attitude context.

We also know that *this* is true:

Vincent Furnier is the same person as Alice Cooper.

Kripke has argued that proper names are *rigid* designators: that is, a name refers to the same object in all possible worlds. More importantly, perhaps, it seems that proper names are *directly referential*: that is to say, they refer to objects, and not in virtue of those objects satisfying any descriptive condition. Their function, one might say, is *just* to refer. Now in the case of *modal* constructions, like (1a), it seems that proper names do nothing but refer to their objects. Since 'Vincent Furnier' and 'Alice Cooper' are two proper names which refer to the same person, it seems that it shouldn't matter which of them we use in modal constructions. So, if (1a) is true, this ought to be true too:

(2a) It is necessarily true that, if there is any such person as Vincent Furnier, Vincent Furnier is Alice Cooper.

And Kripke does indeed argue that such claims are true. But what if we had swapped the name 'Alice Cooper' for the name 'Vincent Furnier' within (1b)? We would have ended up with this:

(2b) It can be known independently of experience that, if there is any such person as Vincent Furnier, Vincent Furnier is Alice Cooper.

But this strikes us as false: don't we need to know a little musical history – something we can't get without experience – to know that Vincent Furnier is Alice Cooper?

It seems central to Kripke's whole point about the difference between modal and epistemic distinctions that co-referring names *can* be swapped within modal contexts (such as (1a)), but *can't* be swapped within propositional-attitude contexts, such as (1b). And this itself suggests something which might seem to run against the spirit of what Kripke was doing in *Naming and Necessity*. Kripke seems at least to be tempted to the view of proper names advocated by J. S. Mill: that they refer, but 'have, strictly speaking, no signification'.[1] This might seem to be saying, in Fregean terms, that names have reference but not Sense. But in 'Über Sinn und Bedeutung', Frege seems to take it to be one of the defining features of the notion of Sense that Sense is that aspect of words, whatever it is, which is distinct from reference and which matters for their use in propositional-attitude contexts. It seems from the falsity (as it strikes us) of (2b) that *something* other than the reference of names matters for their use in propositional-attitude contexts. So it seems that names must have Sense as well as reference.

Kripke's 'puzzle' about belief is designed to show that the reasoning which leads us to believe that (2b) is false is faulty, and therefore that this anti-Millian conclusion is not so easily drawn.

8.3 Kripke's Pierre

Why should we think that it cannot be known independently of experience that, if there is any such person, Vincent Furnier is Alice Cooper? Here is a natural thought: this cannot be known just in virtue of understanding the words involved. Reflection on this suggests that our use of propositional-attitude constructions depends upon links between propositional attitudes and people's understanding of sentences. These links can be formulated in terms of principles which it's natural to accept about propositional attitudes and sentences. Kripke formulates two such principles in his paper. I shall offer instead a pair of principles which do the work which Kripke wants his principles to do, but which are simpler than Kripke's, and also more plausible. I will call them *sentence-belief* principles. Here they are:

(SB1) If someone understands a sentence and thinks it is true, then she believes what the sentence says;

(SB2) If someone understands a sentence and does *not* think it is true, then, provided she is rational, she does *not* believe what the sentence says.

---

[1] J. S. Mill, *A System of Logic* (London: Longmans, Green, Reader, and Dyer, 1875), I, ii, 5, 5.

It's natural to think that these principles underlie some of our feelings about propositional-attitude constructions, and in particular our feeling that they are non-extensional. The natural view that (2b) is false, for example, looks as if it is a result of applying (SB2) to the understanding of the following sentence:

> (2) If there is any such person as Vincent Furnier, Vincent Furnier is Alice Cooper.

It seems that someone could understand (2) without thinking it's true. According to (SB2) she would not believe what the sentence says. So she wouldn't *know* what it says (since knowledge requires belief).

To get the first version of Kripke's puzzle, we need to add to (SB1) and (SB2) the following *translation principle*:

> (TP) A good translation of a sentence can be used to say what the original sentence says.

The English sentence 'Snow is white' is, we may suppose, a good translation of the French sentence 'La neige est blanche.' According to (TP) we can use this English sentence to show what the French sentence says. That is to say, we can say that the French sentence says that *snow is white*. And that seems quite plausible.

Enter now Kripke's Pierre. Pierre is brought up in France, and is taught about the world in French. He comes to accept the following sentence as true:

> (3) Londres est jolie.

Later on he moves to England, learns English by the direct method, and settles in a very ugly part of London. One of his neighbours says, ironically:

> (4) London is pretty.

Pierre understands the sentence, as well as the irony, and agrees with his neighbour that the sentence is false.

But here's the catch: Pierre never realizes that the city he heard referred to as *Londres* in his youth is the same as the city in which he now lives, which he knows as *London*. So he is still prepared to accept (3), even though he thinks (4) is false: he just thinks that the childhood information concerned a different city.

Now if we apply (SB1) to Pierre's acceptance of (3), we can say:

(5) Pierre believes what (3) says.

And since 'London is pretty' is a good translation (we may suppose) of (3), we can say what Pierre believes as follows:

(6) Pierre believes that London is pretty.

Now, since Pierre doesn't realize that *Londres* is the same city as London, he is ill-informed but not irrational. That means that we can apply (SB2) to his non-acceptance of (4) to get this:

(7) Pierre does not believe what (4) says.

But, of course, (4) says that London is pretty. So we get this:

(8) Pierre does not believe that London is pretty.

And now we seem to have a contradiction between (6) and (8). It seems that the very principles which lead us to reject extensionality in the case of propositional-attitude constructions commit us to a contradiction. But not rejecting extensionality in the case of propositional-attitude constructions would amount to giving up propositional attitudes altogether: what could be left of belief, if we allowed that anyone who believed one truth believed all truths, or that anyone who believed one falsehood believed all falsehoods?

And the puzzle is more general than the case of Kripke's Pierre suggests – in two respects. First, as Kripke himself points out, although the case in which two languages are involved provides a vivid example, no principles of translation are in fact necessary. Paderewski was a famous romantic pianist who became prime minister of Poland in later life. Pierre's English-speaking cousin Peter comes across his name in two different contexts: in a record catalogue, and in a list of those involved in the Treaty of Versailles. When he comes across the name in connection with the Treaty of Versailles, Peter is happy to accept this:

(9) Paderewski is a politician.

But when the conversation turns to recordings of Chopin, and Peter is asked whether the pianist in the catalogue was also a politician, he assumes that the questioner has muddled his Paderewskis: in this context, where 'Paderewski' refers to the pianist, Peter thinks (9) is false.

Peter seems clearly to understand (9), on both of these occasions. So in virtue of the occasion when he is reading about the Treaty of Versailles, (SB1) entitles us to conclude:

(10) Peter believes that Paderewski is a politician.

And in virtue of the occasion when he is looking at the record catalogue, (SB2) entitles us to conclude:

(11) Peter does not believe that Paderewski is a politician.

This time we seem to have a contradiction without any use of the translation principle (TP).

The second respect in which Kripke's puzzle can be generalized is that it doesn't seem to be restricted to belief constructions involving just *proper names*. Kripke himself considers extending the puzzle to natural-kind terms, and wonders whether it might spread even further.[2] Surely it does have wider application. The Paderewski case shows that all we need to create a puzzle case is for someone to think wrongly, but rationally, that a particular word is ambiguous, while still counting as understanding the word enough for (SB1) and (SB2) to apply. This looks as if it is a possibility for almost *any* kind of word, although I will not pursue that here.

8.4   Referential solutions to the puzzle

The first thing to note about Kripke's puzzle is that it strikes right to the heart of Frege's theory. Frege introduced the notion of Sense initially in a way which defined it in terms of informativeness: two expressions which differ in informativeness count as differing in Sense. What is it for expressions to differ in informativeness? Two sentences differ in informativeness if it is possible for someone who understands both rationally to think that one is true and not think the other is true.[3] Frege then applied the notion of Sense which was introduced in that way to deal with the intensionality of propositional-attitude contexts. That seems to commit him immediately to (SB1) and (SB2).

---

[2] See S. Kripke, 'A Puzzle about Belief', n. 36.

[3] This is, in effect, Evans's 'intuitive criterion of difference': G. Evans, *The Varieties of Reference* (Oxford: Oxford University Press, 1982), p. 19.

Nor can anyone easily deny that they can actually be applied in the puzzle cases, if they are true at all. It is hard to believe that Pierre doesn't really understand one or other of 'Londres' and 'London', or that Peter doesn't really understand 'Paderewski'. The difficulty here is that it looks as if in all of these cases the various subjects have as good an understanding of the words as we normally think of ourselves as having. If they don't really understand their words, it seems hard for us to claim that we understand ours.

Could we deny either (SB1) or (SB2), as part of a generally *non*-Fregean view? Someone who holds a Millian conception of names will naturally deny (SB2). On such an account, there is nothing a proper name *can* do but refer to its object. Now consider this sentence:

(12) Vincent Furnier is a man.

Many people think this is true. My friend Frankie is one. Given that and (SB1), we can say:

(13) Frankie believes that Vincent Furnier is a man.

But on a Millian view of names, the name 'Vincent Furnier' can do nothing but refer to its object in (13). 'Alice Cooper' is another proper name of the same person, so there can be no harm in putting it in place of 'Vincent Furnier' in (13). So there's a sense in which the following is true:

(14) Frankie believes that Alice Cooper is a man.

But Frankie knows nothing about rock music, and doesn't think *this* sentence is true:

(15) Alice Cooper is a man.

If we applied (SB2) on the basis of that fact, we'd get the following claim:

(16) Frankie does not believe that Alice Cooper is a man.

(16) contradicts (14), on a Millian view. And since (16) could only be true while (14) was true if the name 'Alice Cooper' was doing something more than just refer to its object – which is what the Millian denies that names can do – it follows that the Millian has to reject (16), and hence the principle (SB2) on which it is based.

The Millian view is the simplest form of what we may call a *world-directed* or *referential* theory of both meaning and propositional attitudes. Referential theories in general take their lead from the opposition to the notion of Sense which is found in Russell's writings on the philosophy of language. According to Russell, 'the essential business of language is to describe facts'.[4] On a theory of his kind, we take singular terms to refer to objects, predicates to refer to qualities and relations, and sentences to correspond to states of affairs. Communication is not a matter of passing something internal from one mind to another, but of one person informing another of how things are in the objective world.

This referential view of language in general can also be applied to propositional attitudes. In saying what someone thinks, on this view, we are saying how things have to be in the world for her to be right; in saying what someone wants, we are saying how things have to be in the world for her to be satisfied. The business of the words in the 'that'-clauses of propositional-attitude constructions is not to characterize some internal state of the person, but to describe a possible state of the objective world.[5]

There are ways of adapting the simple Millian view in order to try to make its initial counter-intuitiveness less disturbing. One is suggested by Nathan Salmon; his version offers a different way of dealing with Kripke's puzzle.[6] Here is a simplified presentation of his proposal. At its core is a world-oriented conception of language. We say that the business of

---

[4] B. Russell, Introduction to L. Wittgenstein, *Tractatus Logico-Philosophicus* (London: Routledge and Kegan Paul, 1922), p. x.

[5] For such a view see, e.g., J. Barwise and J. Perry, *Situations and Attitudes* (Cambridge, MA: MIT Press, 1983), ch. 1.

[6] N. Salmon, *Frege's Puzzle* (Cambridge, MA: MIT Press, 1986). A different adaptation of the Millian view is provided by S. Soames, *Beyond Rigidity: The Unfinished Semantic Agenda of Naming and Necessity* (Oxford: Oxford University Press, 2002), especially ch. 8. Simplifying considerably, Soames's view is that the meaning of propositional-attitude constructions is what the Millian says it is (so that (13) and (14) in the text, for example, mean the same), but in particular contexts sentences may be used to express other things which are naturally formulated descriptively, even though those other things are not strictly meant by the sentences. My feeling is that this is only likely to be convincing if we're already convinced that every other way of coping with propositional attitudes while insisting that language is fundamentally world-directed is hopeless (Soames hopes to have done enough for that, in chs. 2–7 of *Beyond Rigidity*). I choose to present Salmon's proposal in the text, just because it shows how tempting something like the Fregean view is.

a sentence is to *encode information* about the world. The notion of 'information' used here is a technical one, so I'll capitalize the word. The crucial thing about it for the present issue is this:

> Two singular terms which refer to the same object encode the same Information.

It's clear from this that if propositional attitudes were regarded just as attitudes to Information, Salmon's theory would be no different from the simple Millian theory we've already considered. But Salmon introduces a complication. Just as it's possible not to recognize a person you know if she appears in a disguise, so it's possible not to recognize *Information* you know, if it's dressed up in unfamiliar words, in a different sentence. According to Salmon, Information never comes to us naked, but always in some 'guise'.

This means we shouldn't simply talk of believing *some Information*: we should always bear in mind the guise in which we receive or grasp it. We can use this to analyse Kripke's puzzle cases. In the Paderewski case, we seemed entitled to say both of the following:

> (10) Peter believes that Paderewski is a politician;
> (11) Peter does not believe that Paderewski is a politician.

Salmon can now analyse (10) in something like the following way:

> (10a) There is some guise such that Peter believes the Information that Paderewski is a politician *under that guise*.

And we can analyse (13) somewhat as follows:

> (11a) There is some guise such that Peter does *not* believe the Information that Paderewski is a politician *under that guise*.

But (10a) and (11a) – unlike the original (10) and (11) – do not contradict each other. This is because there are two *different* guises of the same Information expressed by the same sentence, 'Paderewski is a politician'. (10a) is true in virtue of one of them (the Treaty of Versailles guise), while (11a) is true in virtue of the other (the record catalogue guise). So Salmon's view allows us to resolve Kripke's puzzle by claiming that, despite initial appearances, the puzzle sentences do not actually contradict each other.

Unlike the simple Millian view we considered earlier, Salmon's view enables us to accept a modified form of both (sb1) and (sb2). The modifications are as follows:

(SB1a) If someone understands a sentence and thinks it is true, then there is a guise under which she believes what the sentence says;

(SB2a) If someone understands a sentence and does *not* think it is true, then, provided she is rational, there is a guise under which she does *not* believe what the sentence says.

This is because it is has a way of disarming the objection to the simple Millian theory which leads it to deny (SB2). Salmon, like the simple Millian, thinks that if this is true,

(13) Frankie believes that Vincent Furnier is a man,

then the following is true too:

(14) Frankie believes that Alice Cooper is a man.

But Salmon has some defence against our intuitive rejection of (14). That intuitive reaction depends on applying (SB2) to Frankie's rejection of (15) to derive the following:

(16) Frankie does not believe that Alice Cooper is a man.

But accepting (16) gives us no reason for rejecting (14), on Salmon's view. This is because (14) and (16) are more precisely formulated as follows, according to Salmon:

(14a) There is some guise such that Frankie believes the information that Alice Cooper is a man *under that guise*;

(16a) There is some guise such that Frankie *does not* believe the information that Alice Cooper is a man *under that guise*.

As with (10a) and (11a), there is no contradiction between (14a) and (16a), because there are two different guises involved. So (14) and (16) can be accepted as being strictly true. Salmon can, however, accept that (14) is, though true, *misleadingly put*. This is because we *expect*, for various conversational reasons, that the sentence which is used to *encode* the information believed will also *express the guise* under which the person believes it. That is, we expect the words in the 'that'-clause to *express the guise* as well as merely encoding the information.

8.5   A Fregean response

My suspicion is that most of us think that (14) is worse than misleading: we think it's just false. In that case, if we're tempted by the world-orientation of Salmon's theory, we may be inclined to accept a modification of it. The modification is obvious: what Salmon says is merely *expected*, we take to be part of the *meaning* of propositional-attitude constructions. We take the words in the 'that'-clauses of propositional-attitude constructions to *express the guise* under which the person believes the information as well as merely encoding encoding the information. That is to say, we take (14) to be properly analysed as follows:

(14a*) There is some guise expressed by the sentence 'Alice Cooper is a man' such that Frankie believes the information that Alice Cooper is a man *under that guise*.

We take (14a*) – and therefore (14) – to be false. But surely if (14) is false, it must be denied by (16): how can we make sense of that? We can say that there are two readings of (16), depending on whether we understand the negation in it as having *wide* or *narrow* scope. The narrow scope reading is just a modification of Salmon's (16a):

(16a*) There is some guise expressed by the sentence 'Alice Cooper is a man' such that Frankie *does not* believe the information that Alice Cooper is a man *under that guise*.

But there is a wide scope reading:

(16b) *It is not the case that* there is some guise expressed by the sentence 'Alice Cooper is a man' such that Frankie believes the information that Alice Cooper is a man under that guise.

We naturally take (16) on the wide scope reading (it might be suggested): that is, as analysed by (16b). And this really does deny (14) (as analysed by (14a*)).

If we modify Salmon's theory in this way, what we end up with looks very like a Fregean theory. There are two reasons for this. We preserve some form of (SB1) and (SB2), which are fundamentally Fregean. And Salmon's notion of the *guise* in which Information may be presented seems very similar to one natural understanding of Frege's notion of a *mode of presentation* of an object; and Frege uses that notion to explain the notion of

Sense. It's hard not to think that in his notion of 'guises' Salmon has brought in Sense by another name.

Can we, then, simply resurrect a Fregean theory, and solve Kripke's puzzle like that? Let's return to the case of Pierre. We found ourselves led by Fregean assumptions to accept both of the following:

(6) Pierre believes that London is pretty;
(8) Pierre does not believe that London is pretty.

Now there seems nothing deeply puzzling *psychologically* about Pierre. We can explain his state of mind by saying these two things, instead of (6) and (8):

(6a) Pierre believes that the city he heard of in his youth is pretty;
(8a) Pierre does not believe that the city in which he now lives is pretty.

There seems no contradiction here. Can this fact be used to claim that (6) and (8) don't really contradict each other either?

Kripke rejects this way out. First of all, he insists that the fact that there is no problem with such formulations as (6a) and (8a) is no argument on its own for saying that there is no problem with such formulations as (6) and (8), since (6) and (8) were derived quite properly, in their own right, by principles we find it hard to reject. This is surely right: it is no argument – *on its own*. But we might think that there was a way of linking (6) to (6a) and (8) to (8a) which would allow there to be such an argument. After all, we had no difficulty in thinking of the descriptions involved in (6a) and (8a), and we can see their relevance to (6) and (8).

The fact that (6a) and (8a) don't contradict each other can only be used to argue that (6) and (8) don't contradict each other if we can claim that, as it is used in (6), the name 'London' somehow *means* the city Pierre heard of in his youth, and that, as it's used in (8), it somehow *means* the city in which Pierre now lives. And this, of course, is a traditional Fregean way of understanding the Sense of proper names. Kripke argues against this suggestion in ways which will be familiar from the discussion in *Naming and Necessity*. He offers two arguments against the suggestion here. First, he claims that many of us will not associate a uniquely identifying description with any particular name on any particular use: so someone might know no more about Feynman than that he was a famous physicist. And secondly, even if someone did associate a uniquely identifying description with a particular name, it might be the *same* description in both of the uses which create a puzzle case. Perhaps this is not very plausible for the cases we've considered, but it seems hard to rule out.

These objections of Kripke's are not very compelling, however. When we suggest (6a) and (8a) as ways of explaining what is going on in (6) and (8), we are not considering what descriptions Pierre himself might associate with any name. We are simply explaining the two different ways in which Pierre is related to the city: as the city he heard of in his youth, and as the city in which he now lives. Pierre himself need have no such descriptions in his mind at all. This means that the Fregean claim that the names, as they are used in (6) and (8), somehow *mean* what is expressed in the descriptions in (6a) and (8a) has to be understood with care; but the claim is not altogether ruled out.

The claim still faces two significant difficulties, however. The first is that it needs to be explained in what sense, precisely, the name can be said to *mean* what is expressed by these two descriptions; and as part of that explanation, we need to understand how the same name could come to mean those different things. This is not a small task. But the second difficulty is perhaps more substantial, and it goes right back to the problems we found with Frege's original introduction of the notion of Sense.

The problem is that the notion of Sense is supposed to be a property of linguistic expressions *as such*. We're supposed to be able to talk about *the* Sense of a linguistic expression, and not merely its Sense for this or that particular speaker. This is crucial to Frege's rejection of psychologism. It's also crucial to Frege's attempt to provide an account of the semantics of propositional-attitude constructions. Such an account is supposed to show how the meaning of a whole propositional-attitude sentence depends upon the meaning of its parts – including the parts within the 'that-clause. But surely the word 'London' hasn't changed its *meaning* between (6) and (8): Pierre might have thought he was dealing with two different proper names – or with a name which has two different meanings – but he was wrong. So whatever it is which explains how (6) and (8) don't contradict each other, it seems that it can't be what we can properly call *the* meaning of the name 'London'. It looks as if the Fregean solution to Kripke's puzzle – which involves denying that (6) and (8) really contradict each other – is bought at the cost of giving up all hope of explaining the semantics of propositional-attitude constructions.

8.6 Davidson's proposal

It is on just this point that the central proposal of Davidson's famous paper, 'On Saying That', seems to have something to contribute. Davidson follows Quine, and the mainstream of the tradition reaching back to Frege, in having a preference for extensional constructions. He also prefers, as far as possible, to make do with the resources provided by the grammar of Frege's logic. This leads him, like the bulk of the tradition, to treat propositional-attitude constructions as involving – in the basic case, at least[7] – two-place predicates. On this approach, 'Galileo said that the Earth moves' uses the two-place predicate 'x said y', and 'Frankie believes that Vincent Furnier is a man' involves the two-place predicate 'x believes y'.

Most of the tradition has treated the whole 'that'-clause in this kind of construction as a complex singular term. According to Frege, we can understand a sentence like (6) as saying something like this:

(6f) Pierre believes *that-London-is-pretty*.

Here the whole italicized phrase refers to the Sense of the sentence 'London is pretty', which Frege calls the Thought that London is pretty. Quine preferred to reform ordinary English, and replace the 'that'-clause by a singular term which referred to an appropriate entity. Quine's rendition of (6) might be formulated like this:

(6q) Pierre believes-true 'London is pretty'.

One strange result of both of these theories is that they cannot let the words in the 'that'-clauses of propositional-attitude constructions do what they do elsewhere. On Frege's proposal, they cease to refer to their normal referents, and instead refer to their normal Senses. If we took Quine's proposal to be an analysis of ordinary English – instead of a suggestion for linguistic reform – the words in the 'that'-clauses would suddenly refer to

---

[7] Quine, of course, treats 'relational' constructions as involving predicates with more than two places, as we saw in ch. 7.

themselves instead of their normal referents. To this Davidson makes the following compelling objection:

> If we could recover our pre-Fregean semantic innocence, I think it would seem to us plainly incredible that the words 'The earth moves', uttered after the words 'Galileo said that', mean anything different, or refer to anything else, than is their wont when they come in other environments.[8]

Davidson's principal focus is on constructions of indirect speech. Consider this sentence:

(17) Galileo said that the earth moves.

Davidson's proposal is that this is not really one sentence, but two. We might write them as follows:

(17a) The earth moves. Galileo said that.

Or else, simply like this:

(17b) Galileo said that. The earth moves.

The idea here is that one sentence here consists of a two-place predicate, 'x said y'. As Davidson understands it, the 'y' position is filled with a *demonstrative*, 'that'. This word is used to point to, or demonstrate, something else. What it points to here, according to Davidson, is the utterance of the sentence which is written alongside it ('The earth moves'). This idea of a sentence being written *alongside* another, without being part of it, gives Davidson's analysis its technical name: it is known as a *paratactic* analysis (one which represents the sentence in the 'that'-clause as *drawn up alongside* the main sentence, rather than contained within it).

In order to make sense of this, we need to understand the meaning of the word 'said' in a particular way: we must understand it as describing something which can be explained by our uttering a sentence. We might, then, paraphrase the whole of (17), as Davidson understands it, as follows:

(17c) *Galileo* spoke to an effect which we can capture with *this utterance*. The earth moves.

Here the italicized words, 'Galileo' and 'this utterance', are singular terms which fill the gaps in the predicate 'x spoke to an effect which we can

---

[8] D. Davidson, 'On Saying That', p. 108.

capture with *y*'. And that rather complicated predicate is meant just to give the meaning of the more humdrum '*x* said *y*'.[9]

Davidson himself has no proposal for propositional attitudes, but we could give a Davidsonian analysis of (10), perhaps as follows:

(10c) *Peter* is in the kind of state of mind which would lead him, if he were in my present position, to produce *this utterance*. Paderewski is a politician.

Here the italicized words 'Peter' and 'this utterance' are singular terms which fill the gaps in the predicate '*x* is in the kind of state of mind which would lead him, if he were in my present position, to produce *y*'. And that complicated predicate is meant just to give the meaning of the more mundane '*x* believes *y*' (though this version should be regarded as no more than a first attempt).

In dealing with propositional-attitude constructions, we face two issues. First, there is the problem of understanding the semantics of the whole sentence – explaining how the meaning of the whole depends on the meaning of the parts. And secondly, there is the problem of understanding the meaning of the propositional-attitude verbs which are at their core ('believes', 'hopes', 'wishes', 'fears', etc.). Davidson's proposal does two things. First, it keeps the two issues quite separate from each other. And, secondly, it simply dissolves the semantic problem. The difficulty was understanding how the meaning of the whole sentences in propositional-attitude constructions could depend on what we can ordinarily recognize as the meaning of the words which occur in the 'that'-clauses in these constructions. Davidson's paratactic analysis simply denies that the words which occur in the 'that'-clauses are really part of the main sentence. The principal sentence simply finishes after 'that' in (17); so it is just not the business of *semantics* to explain how the choice of words after the word 'that' here affects the truth of what leads up to it.

What are the words in the 'that'-clause doing, then? We might compare their use to the use of a drawing to illustrate a point. We might say:

(18) Jack and Jill were sitting like *this* –

---

[9] Davidson himself understands '*x* said *y*' in terms of the notion of 'samesaying' (roughly: Galileo says the same as we say when we utter the following words). In fact, he ought to be happier with something like the formulation I have offered, for reasons which will emerge in ch. 9.

and then explain how they were sitting by drawing a picture. Now clearly the picture is not part of (18), and we don't need to explain how it contributes to the meaning of (18) as part of a general semantic project: it's simply something pointed to by a word in the sentence. But this doesn't mean that any old picture will do. Of course not: the picture I use must show how Jack and Jill were really sitting. In the same way, on a Davidsonian view, the sentence 'Paderewski is a politician' is used to illustrate Peter's state of mind in (10), but without it being part of the sentence which says that he believes that. It matters which sentence I use to illustrate Peter's state of mind, of course, in just the same way as it matters what I draw to illustrate how Jack and Jill were sitting.

8.7   Can Davidson's proposal solve Kripke's puzzle?

What Kripke's puzzle seems to threaten is the idea of providing an account of the semantics of propositional-attitude constructions: at the very least, what matters for the use of words inside the 'that'-clauses of these constructions seems to depend on things which are too specific to the particular person and the particular time to count as part of the meaning of the words. It might seem that Davidson's proposal – which makes the words in the 'that'-clauses of such constructions irrelevant to the semantics of such constructions – is well suited to dealing with this difficulty. But we are not out of the woods yet.

In the first place, we need to find an appropriate way of interpreting the word 'believes'. I suggested that the principles which are used to create Kripke's puzzle – principally (SB1) and (SB2) – are plausible. If that is right, it seems that we can only solve the puzzle if we can find a way of understanding the following two sentences which does not take them to contradict each other:

(6) Pierre believes that London is pretty;
(8) Pierre does not believe that London is pretty.

If we adopt my provisional explanation of 'x believes y' (see (10c) above), then we can give the following Davidsonian paraphrases of these two sentences:

(6b) Pierre is in the kind of state of mind which would lead him, if he were in my present position, to produce *this utterance*. London is pretty.

(8b) Pierre is not in the kind of state of mind which would lead him, if he were in my present position, to produce *this utterance*. London is pretty.

These paraphrases seem only to allow (6b) not to contradict (8b) if the position referred to as 'my present position' in (6b) is different from that referred to as 'my present position' in (8b). We have to suppose that (6b) and (8b) – and therefore (6) and (8) – are uttered from different perspectives. This may seem reasonable; or there may be a better analysis of '*x* believes *y*' which would remove the appearance of contradiction more plausibly. This is an issue which would need to be pursued further.

Suppose that these difficulties could be solved: would that show that Davidson's proposal was right? It's not quite clear. One issue is whether the 'that' which introduces the 'that'-clauses in propositional-attitude constructions is really a demonstrative, and if it is, what it refers to. In ordinary speech it doesn't *seem* like a demonstrative, and there are languages with similar constructions which don't appear to involve anything which could be construed as a demonstrative. Further, even if it is a demonstrative, it's far from clear that Davidson is right to think it refers to the *utterance* of the sentence which follows (rather than, for example, the sentence itself, or the meaning of the sentence)?[10]

We can stand aside from many of the technical issues involved in these questions if we ask this simple question: can we get the advantages of the Davidsonian approach without thinking that a demonstrative is involved?

---

[10] Ian Rumfitt, for example, suggests that in cases where it is appropriate to treat 'that' as a demonstrative – and this is not all cases – the demonstrative refers to the proposition (effectively the Fregean Thought) expressed by the utterance which follows: see his 'Content and Context: The Paratactic Theory Revisited and Revised', *Mind*, 102 (1993), pp. 429–54. Many of the the objections to Davidson's proposal are really concerned with the choice of object referred to. Davidson's suggestion that 'that' refers to an *utterance* is implausible: for example, if I simply *repeat* (17), then, according to Davidson's construal, I report Galileo as having said *two* things – one for each utterance by me of the sentence 'the earth moves'; and that's absurd. This point was made by Ian McFetridge in 'Propositions and Davidson's Account of Indirect Discourse', *Proceedings of the Aristotelian Society*, 76 (1975), pp. 131–45. A series of objections to Davidson's theory, which depend on Davidson's view that 'that' is a demonstrative referring to utterances, can be found in S. Schiffer, *Remnants of Meaning* (Cambridge, MA: MIT Press, 1987), pp. 126–37. Other objections which seem to have the same specific target are to be found in T. Burge, 'On Davidson's "Saying That"', in E. Lepore, ed., *Truth and Interpretation: Perspectives on the Philosophy of Donald Davidson* (Oxford: Blackwell, 1986), pp. 190–208.

We can certainly get some benefits, but we can't get everything which Davidson himself seemed to be after.

We should remember that Davidson was aiming to deal with propositional-attitude constructions within the framework of a policy of extensionalism; he also seemed to be trying to follow, as far as possible, the grammar of Frege's logic. This led him to regard propositional-attitude constructions as involving two-place predicates. If these expressions are construed as predicates, we should expect them to be followed (or completed) by a singular term (in the '*y*' position). And if we are looking for a singular term, what we need (given the rest of Davidson's proposal) seems to be a demonstrative. But if we don't feel bound by the grammar of Frege's logic, we can imagine various alternative construals which seem to be within the spirit of Davidson's proposal – for example, something like this in place of (17c):

(17d) Galileo spoke to an effect which we can capture as follows: the earth moves.

Here there is no singular term which points to the sentence following the colon: we simply have a construction which leaves space for that sentence to be written. There is, as it were, a demonstrative effect, without any evident demonstrative singular term.

This preserves one crucial feature of Davidson's proposal: keeping what is being done with the words in the 'that'-clause of the original separate from the semantics of the main sentence. But we might feel that there is a risk that we have lost some of our earlier clarity about the task of semantics. If we help ourselves to construals like (17d), there seems no reason why we should not adopt paratactic analyses of any statement operator – such as 'It is necessary that . . .', and '– because . . . ' – which our basic semantics finds it hard to cope with.[11] Consider the bearing of this on the policy of extensionalism. We have seen Quine labouring to preserve extensionalism despite severely counter-intuitive consequences. But if we allow ourselves construals like (17d), which enable us to use paratactic analyses without any simple restriction of our grammatical resources,

---

[11] There is a hint that Davidson himself might have been tempted to move this way: see, e.g., his proposal to treat constructions involving 'mood-setters' paratactically in 'Moods and Performances', in his *Inquiries into Truth and Interpretation*, pp. 109–21.

then there is a risk that it will be too easy to preserve extensionalism: whenever there is any difficulty, we simply bring in a paratactic analysis, and exclude the drawn-up-alongside sentence from the field of semantics. And then the project of providing a semantic theory seems in danger of losing much of its point.

Further reading

The literature on this topic is vast, but mostly quite technical. Nathan Salmon's *Frege's Puzzle* is a readable advanced text in the field: it presents in detail the view which is described in a simplified form in section 8.5. A large number of papers, some of them quite technical, can be found in Nathan Salmon and Scott Soames, eds., *Propositions and Attitudes* (Oxford: Oxford University Press, 1988): this collection is oriented towards the kind of view I described as 'referential' in section 8.5. Soames himself presents a refined form of referential view in *Beyond Rigidity: The Unfinished Semantic Agenda of* Naming and Necessity (Oxford: Oxford University Press, 2002). Ian Rumfitt, 'Content and Context: The Paratactic Theory Revisited and Revised', *Mind*, 102 (1993), pp. 429–54, presents a sophisticated version of Davidson's theory.

9 Davidson on truth and meaning

Key text

Donald Davidson, 'Truth and Meaning', in his *Inquiries into Truth and Interpretation* (Oxford: Oxford University Press, 1984), pp. 17–36.

9.1 Introduction

The meaning of sentences depends upon the meaning of their parts. This basic truth about language must be at the heart of any philosophy of language. In the analytic tradition, it guides the project of semantics, which attempts to provide a systematic theoretical explanation of precisely how the meaning of sentences depends on the meaning of their parts. We've seen this issue shaping all of our discussions so far. What does a definite description contribute to sentences of which it can form part? Is it an object referred to, together with the way in which it is given (as Frege thought), or does it, in context, assert the unique existence of something which satisfies some condition (as Russell proposed)? A parallel question arises for proper names: do they work in sentences in the way that definite descriptions do (whatever that is), or do they do something quite different? Again, should we give a descriptive account of what natural-kind terms contribute to the meaning of sentences involving them, or should they be regarded as directly referential? And the whole discussion of propositional-attitude constructions, from Frege himself onwards, is shaped by the difficulty of explaining what the words in the 'that'-clauses of such constructions are contributing to the sentences which report propositional attitudes, given that they seem to be subject to peculiarly strict restrictions on substitution.

There is a sense, however, in which these discussions fail to confront the most basic question: what is it to explain the way in which the meaning of a sentence depends upon the meaning of its parts? We've looked at cases in which more or less seems to matter for the meaning of sentences than some people have supposed. But we haven't considered what is involved, in general, in explaining the way in which the meaning of a sentence depends on the meaning of its parts – even when there's no dispute about whether we're packing too much or too little into our conception of the meaning of the parts. What kind of explanation should we be providing? What kind of explanation can we provide?

These are the issues on which Donald Davidson's seminal paper 'Truth and Meaning' made a decisive contribution – one which has shaped all work in the philosophy of language since its publication. In fact, its impact has been so profound that it's hard for philosophers of language now to realize that its central idea was once new.

In this paper, and a series of others on related topics, Davidson proposed that work in semantics should take a particular form. He suggested that we should be aiming to provide what he called *theories of meaning* for particular languages (such as English, perhaps). A theory of meaning for a particular language is not a general account of what meaning is. It is, instead, an attempt to show, in a particular theoretical way, how the meaning of sentences of that language depends on the meaning of their parts.

The crucial feature of this theoretical approach to semantics is that it demands that we be completely explicit about the meaning of sentences and their parts. A theory of meaning for a particular language must include an explicit statement of the meaning of every basic expression in the language. And from these explicit statements of the meaning of the basic expressions, it attempts to *derive* an explicit statement of the meaning any sentence in the language. This is how a theory of meaning for a language shows how the meaning of a sentence depends on the meaning of its parts: it shows an explicit statement of the meaning of the sentence to be *derivable* from explicit statements of the meaning of the parts.

Davidson himself doesn't always give as much prominence as this to the project of explaining how the meaning of sentences depends upon the meaning of their parts. Often he presents himself as concerned to show

how it's possible for someone with finite capacities to be in a position to understand any one of the potential infinity of sentences which can be constructed in ordinary natural languages. But I think the project of explaining how the meaning of sentences depends on the meaning of their parts is the more basic one. For if we can explain how the meaning of sentences depends on the meaning of their parts, we will be able to explain how someone could be in a position to understand any one of a potential infinity of sentences on the basis of a finite capacity. And the meaning of sentences can still depend on the meaning of their parts, even in a language in which only a finite number of sentences can be constructed. Suppose, for example, that we had a language whose basic vocabulary consisted just of ten proper names and ten predicates. It would seem that there cannot be more than one hundred sentences which could be constructed in this language, but the meaning of each of these sentences must surely depend upon the meaning of the ten names and ten predicates, if we're right to think that the language has these names and predicates at all.

9.2 Meanings as entities

How might we set about showing how an explicit statement of the meaning of sentences can be derived from explicit statements of the meanings of their parts? What might such explicit statements look like? We might be tempted to think that such statements must all have this form:

(M!) E means M,

where 'E' is a name of a linguistic expression, and 'M' is a name of what it means. This seems to treat meanings as entities which are correlated with expressions to make them meaningful. Davidson rejects such approaches, on the grounds that it's hard to see how a theory of the appropriate form could be generated by using them. The central difficulty arises from attempting to answer this question: how can we see the entity meant by a sentence as a function of the entities meant by its parts? We can approach the problem by looking, to begin with, at different theories of *reference*.

Frege and Russell offered different theories of the reference of sentences and their parts. Frege's theory of reference, in outline, is this:

Sentences refer to truth-values (either the True or the False);
Singular terms refer to objects;
Predicates refer to Concepts (functions from objects to truth-values). [1]

Now consider a particular sentence:

(A) Bucephalus is a horse.

This is true (Bucephalus – 'Ox-head' – was the horse of Alexander the Great). It now seems that we can state the semantic facts about this sentence, according to Frege's theory, as follows:

(1f) The sentence 'Bucephalus is a horse' refers to the True;
(2f) The singular term 'Bucephalus' refers to Bucephalus (Alexander's horse);
(3f) The predicate 'x is a horse' refers to the Concept horse.

Because of the way Frege thinks of Concepts (as functions from objects to truth-values), Frege can clearly explain how the reference of sentences is a function of the reference of their parts. But it is obviously absurd to take Frege's conception of the reference of sentences as giving their *meaning*:[2] that would take all true sentences to have the same meaning, and the same would go for all false sentences. And Frege does nothing to explain how the *meaning* of sentences, in any ordinary sense of the term, can be understood as a function of the meaning of their parts.

Russell's theory differs from Frege's in offering a richer conception of the reference of predicates and sentences.[3] This makes it more plausible to suppose that in giving the reference of sentences we're giving their

---

[1] Recall that Frege uses the notion of a 'Concept' eccentrically. He doesn't use it to refer to part of the content of thought, as we would: that would put his 'Concepts' in the realm of Sense. Instead, he uses it to refer to something in the sphere of reference. A Concept, in Frege's senses, is just a special kind of function: it is one which yields a truth-value for any choice of object. I use a capital letter to indicate that this is, in effect, a technical use.

[2] In 'Truth and Meaning', Davidson sometimes uses 'meaning' as a word for Fregean Sense.

[3] What is described here is, strictly, just one of Russell's theories, held for a period from around the time of 'On Denoting', *Mind*, 14 (1905), pp. 479–93.

meaning, on an ordinary understanding of that term. If we use the word 'proposition' (as Russell sometimes did[4]) to mean a kind of objective correlate of a sentence, we can state a Russellian theory in outline like this:

Sentences refer to propositions;
Singular terms refer to objects;
Predicates refer to properties and relations.

And in the particular case of sentence (A), the result is as follows:

(1r) The sentence 'Bucephalus is a horse' refers to the proposition that Bucephalus is a horse;
(2r) The singular term 'Bucephalus' refers to Bucephalus (Alexander's horse);
(3r) The predicate 'x is a horse' refers to the property of being a horse.

Davidson thinks views like this Russellian one are just untenable: he thinks that if we take sentences to refer to anything, we have to suppose (like Frege) that all true sentences refer to the same thing, as do all false sentences. He offers a brief technical argument for this view in 'Truth and Meaning'.[5] That argument is a development of an argument which Frege first used in 'Über Sinn und Bedeutung',[6] but it is hotly disputed. It's not easy to find a version of it which avoids begging the question against Russellian views, so I shall not consider it here.[7]

But even if this argument is not convincing, Russellian theories face a different problem, which is an aspect of the problem of the unity of the sentence which was mentioned in ch. 1 (§ 1.5).

If we suppose that we can refer to the referents of predicates, as well as the referents of singular terms, by means of expressions which themselves look like singular terms, we seem to have difficulty explaining the difference between a sentence and a list. We began with this sentence:

---

[4] See, e.g., Russell, *Principles of Mathematics*, 2nd edn (London: George Allen and Unwin, 1937), § 51, p. 47.

[5] 'Truth and Meaning', p. 19.

[6] Frege, 'Über Sinn und Bedeutung', *Zeitung für Philosophie und philosophische Kritik*, 100 (1892), p. 35.

[7] The argument which Davidson offers is a variant on an argument known as the Slingshot. For an extensive discussion of the Slingshot, see S. Neale, *Facing Facts* (Oxford: Oxford University Press, 2001).

(A) Bucephalus is a horse.

A Russellian theory states that this sentence consists of two expressions, each of which refers to something. So it looks as if (A) ought to be equivalent, on a Russellian account, to the following list:

(A*) Bucephalus, the property of being a horse.

But (A*) isn't a sentence. It doesn't form a complete unity: we can add other words to it at will without offending any constraints of grammar.

We might try to deal with this by insisting that (A*) misses something crucial about (A). We might suppose that the meaning of (A) is captured by *this*, rather than (A*):

(A**) Bucephalus *instantiates* the property of being a horse.

But now we need to understand the semantics of (A**). A Russellian theory of reference presumably has something to say about the word 'instantiates' – something like this:

(4r) The predicate '*x* instantiates *y*' *refers* to the relation of instantiation.

And if we adopt that view, we need to explain how (A**) is different from *this* list:

(A***) Bucephalus, the relation of instantiation, the property of being a horse.

And now we are evidently launched on a regress.[8]

We might, perhaps, claim that the regress here is not a vicious one. But I suspect that that won't be the end of the matter. The real problem is just to explain why (A*) wasn't a satisfactory representation of the meaning of (A) in the first place. After all, (A*) seems to do everything which the Russellian theory says is done by (A): it consists just of expressions which refer to two different items. What exactly is the difficulty? A proposition (in the sense relevant to (1r)) is, intuitively, something which itself has a certain unity and completeness: it is not merely an aggregate of objects and qualities. The proposition that Bucephalus is a horse (or, if you

---

[8] This regress is known as *Bradley's Regress* after a similar regress which F. H. Bradley claimed undermined the notion of relations; see, e.g., F. H. Bradley *Appearance and Reality* (Oxford: Oxford University Press), p. 18.

prefer: *Bucephalus' being a horse*) is not, intuitively, just an aggregate of Bucephalus and horsiness. Unfortunately, the account of the reference of singular terms and predicates leaves it unclear how anything referred to by a sentence could have the appropriate unity and completeness.

This problem may not be insoluble, but it does at least help us to see the attraction of following Davidson in turning away from theories which treat meanings as entities. If we adopt a Fregean theory, we have a neat explanation of how the *reference* of a sentence can be understood as a function of the reference of its parts. But since, on Frege's theory, the referents of sentences are just the truth-values, this doesn't help us to see how the *meaning* of sentences can be understood as a function of the *meaning* of their parts. And no comparably neat account is to be found in Frege's theory of Sense. On the other hand, if we adopt a Russellian theory, it may be more plausible to suppose that the entities which are assigned to sentences as their referents are indeed the *meanings* of those sentences; but it is hard to see how they can be regarded as functions of the referents of their parts.

If we are not going to appeal to meanings as entities to explain how statements of the meaning of sentences are derivable from statements of the meaning of their parts, where can we turn? According to Davidson, to the work of Alfred Tarski.

9.3   Tarski's 'definition' of truth

Tarski was concerned with the semantics of formal systems like that of Frege's logic. Since the notion of truth is central to logic, he was especially concerned to explain how sentences within such formal systems could be true or false. But here he seemed to face a problem. In ordinary languages, like English, it appears to be possible to construct sentences like this one:

(B) Sentence (B) is false.

But it seems obvious that if (B) is true, then it's false, and if it's false, it's true. Either way it seems to contradict itself. This is a form of the Liar Paradox.

Tarski, naturally enough, didn't want the crucial semantic notion of truth to lead him into contradiction in specifying the semantics of formal systems. So what he wanted to do was to show how we could provide rules for applying the concept of truth to sentences in formal systems without risk of contradiction. What is known as his 'definition' of truth is precisely such a set of rules. In a sense it is unlike an ordinary definition: it doesn't explicitly say what truth is – though Tarski also has something to say on that – but it does fix how the concept is to be used.

We don't need to go into the details of Tarski's solution to the Liar paradox here. There are just two things that matter about Tarski's 'definition' of truth for our purposes. First, he showed how to provide a rule for the application of a certain predicate, 'x is T', to formulae which can be constructed in a symbol system. And secondly, he provided an argument for the claim that this mystery notion 'T' is tantamount to *truth*.

Let's begin with that second point. Tarski's approach to truth is inspired by the fact that when you say that a sentence is true, you are, in a way, endorsing what the sentence says. So (to use Tarski's example), when you say that the sentence 'Snow is white' is true, you are, in a way, saying that snow is white. We can express this fact as follows:

(E) The sentence 'Snow is white' is true if and only if snow is (in fact) white.

This says that something you can say *about* a sentence – namely that it's true – is somehow equivalent to just using the sentence to say something for yourself. Tarski himself understood the 'if and only if' here as expressing what's known as *material* equivalence: it requires the sentences on each side either both to be true or both to be false, but they don't need to be connected in any other way.

Now consider a schematic formula:

(T) The sentence s is T if and only if p.

The letter 's' here is supposed to be capable of being replaced by some expression which refers to a sentence: the most obvious thing is a sentence written within quotation marks. So, for example, I can refer to sentence (A) above like this: 'Bucephalus is a horse.' The letter 'p' here is supposed to be capable of being replaced by a sentence – not a sentence in quotation marks, just a sentence.

We can write out explicitly an instance of (T) which concerns the sentence (A), like this:

(Ta) The sentence 'Bucephalus is a horse' is T if and only if Bucephalus is a
horse.

Notice that we *refer* to the sentence 'Bucephalus is a horse' on the left of
the 'if and only if' by quoting it: the clause 'The sentence "Bucephalus is a
horse" is T' says something *about* that sentence. But we don't refer to that
sentence on the right of 'if and only if': we simply *use* the sentence here.
On the right-hand side of (Ta) we're no longer talking about the sentence:
we're talking about Bucephalus. (Ta), again, will be understood by Tarski as
a material bi-conditional: (Ta) is true provided that the sentences on each
side of the phrase 'if and only if' are either both true or both false, but they
don't need to be connected in any other way.

The schematic formula (T) contains an undefined predicate 'x is T'. What
Tarski wants to show is that if its application is fixed in a certain way, this
undefined concept 'T' will be tantamount to truth. In order to show that,
he needs a test which will determine when some concept is tantamount
to truth. The test he comes up with is what's known in English as
Convention T. We'll just be concerned with a crucial part of it, which I'll call
Tarski's Test.

Tarski's Test is concerned with the schematic formula (T). Here's an
informal expression of it:

(TT) If you always get a truth from the schematic formula (T) when you
replace the letter 's' with the name of a sentence, and the letter 'p' with
a sentence which gives the meaning of that sentence, then 'T', in
effect, means *true*.

This test is a way of expressing that basic fact about truth which inspired
it. It's distinctive of truth that if you say that a sentence is true you are, in a
way, saying what the sentence says. But what is meant by the vague clause
'"T", in effect, means *true*' here? Just this: if the condition is met, the
predicate 'x is T' applies to all the true sentences, and only the true
sentences, of the symbol system.[9]

How, then, can we fix the application of the predicate 'x is T' in a way
which passes Tarski's Test? For our purposes, we don't need to go into the

---

[9] Note that there may be predicates which don't strictly mean *true*, but which apply to all
and only the true sentences of a system. For example, if there is an omniscient God, the
predicate 'x is thought by God to be true' will apply to all and only the true sentences.

details of Tarski's original proposal (although these details involve his most significant formal achievements). Instead, we can use a toy version of Tarski's system. We can imagine that we have a symbol system which includes just a few proper names and a few simple predicates. We want a way of specifying the meaning of the proper names and predicates which we can use to define our semantic predicate 'x is T', which applies to whole sentences.

We can give the meaning of the proper names with a clause like this:

(sb) The thing referred to by the name 'Bucephalus' = Bucephalus.

And we can introduce a special notion – call it *satisfaction* – to explain the meaning of predicates. An example of the specification of the meaning of a predicate using this notion might be this:

(sh) Something satisfies the predicate 'x is a horse' if and only if it is a horse.

Finally, we introduce a rule for the use of the special predicate 'x is T' in the case of very simple sentences:

(st) A sentence consisting of a name and a one-place predicate is T if and only if the thing referred to by the name satisfies the predicate.

Now we're in a position to apply the predicate 'x is T' to our original sentence (A) ('Bucephalus is a horse'). We can assume that this is true:

(A1) The sentence 'Bucephalus is a horse' consists of a name ('Bucephalus') and a one-place predicate ('x is a horse').

Given (st) we can say this:

(A2) The sentence 'Bucephalus is a horse' is T if and only if the thing referred to by the name 'Bucephalus' satisfies the predicate 'x is a horse'.

Since, according to (sb), the thing referred to by the name 'Bucephalus' is just Bucephalus, we can replace the phrase 'the thing referred to by the name "Bucephalus"' with the name 'Bucephalus'. That will give us this:

(A3) The sentence 'Bucephalus is a horse' is T if and only if Bucephalus satisfies the predicate 'x is a horse'.

And since, according to (sh), to satisfy the predicate '*x* is a horse' just is to be a horse, we can replace the phrase 'satisfies the predicate "*x* is a horse"' with the simpler phrase 'is a horse'. And that will give us this:

(A4) The sentence 'Bucephalus is a horse' is *T* if and only if Bucephalus is a horse.

Now surely if any sentence can be used to give the meaning of any sentence, we can use the sentence 'Bucephalus is a horse' to give its own meaning. (It doesn't matter that it won't be very interesting if you already understand the sentence: the more trivial such a statement of meaning seems, the more likely it is to be correct.) So it looks as if the sentence used on the right of 'if and only if' gives the meaning of the sentence quoted on the left. And if this applies to all applications of the predicate '*x* is *T*', then '*T*' in effect means *true*. And that will mean that we are entitled to say this:

(A5) The sentence 'Bucephalus is a horse' is *true* if and only if Bucephalus is a horse.

We've therefore provided a way of specifying the conditions under which that sentence is true.

This is only a very simple model of what Tarski did, but it is easy enough to see how to produce specifications of the meaning of other names and predicates. Sentential connectives like 'and', 'or', and 'if' are quite simple too. Suppose our simple symbol system includes these. Here's a rule for the sentential connective 'and':

(sa) A sentence consisting of the sentence *s* followed by 'and' followed by the sentence *t* is *T* if and only if the sentence *s* is *T* and the sentence *t* is *T*.

Rules can be given which provide the semantics of sentences involving quantifiers ('all', 'some', etc.), but these involve the full technicalities of Tarski's definition, which I've left out here.

9.4 Davidson's use of Tarski

Recall Davidson's problem, as we left it at the end of section 9.2. He was looking for a way of explicitly stating the meaning of parts of sentences which would enable us to derive explicit statements of the meaning of whole sentences. Referential theories seemed not to help, so he was looking for a new approach. This is just what Tarski's work seems to provide.

Davidson himself doesn't have precisely Tarski's worries about the Liar Paradox, and for this reason he doesn't need to construct a rule for applying a concept which he can then show to be tantamount to truth. He can begin with the notion of truth from the outset. And that means that he doesn't need to get at the truth of sentences by means of the notion of *satisfaction* of predicates, although he in fact does use that notion. In fact, it's hard to see how the notion of satisfaction can be understood entirely independently of the notion of truth, in any case. It seems that something's *satisfying* a predicate is just the same thing as the predicate's *being true of* it. And in many ways it avoids confusion if we just state the meaning of predicates in these terms.

If we do that, we should replace (Sh) and (St) with these two modifications of them:

(sh*) The predicate 'x is a horse' is *true of* something if and only if that thing is a horse;

(st*) A sentence consisting of a name and a one-place predicate is *true* if and only if the predicate is *true of* the thing referred to by the name.

These modified claims are enough to show the decisive change in the approach to semantics which Tarski's work made room for. The crucial thing is that there's no use of the notion of reference in connection with predicates or whole sentences. Instead, we fix a semantic property of a predicate – *truth-of* – by using a predicate on the right-hand side of the connective 'if and only if'. And we fix a semantic property of a sentence – *truth* – by using a sentence on the right of 'if and only if'. We never need to find an *entity* to be the reference of the predicate or of the sentence.

The result is that it's easy to see how the semantic property of a sentence – *truth* – can be derived from semantic properties of its parts – reference and truth-of. We can use a variant of the derivation of truth from satisfaction and reference which was given in the last section. So Tarski's work shows how we can derive a certain semantic property of *sentences* from certain semantic properties of parts of sentences.

But does it show us how to derive the *meaning* of sentences from the *meaning* of their parts? This is where Davidson makes his boldest move.

Let's ask what an explicit statement of the meaning of a sentence would look like. It's natural to suggest that it might have this form:

(M) The sentence *s* means that *p*.

Here, as in the schematic formula (T), the letter '*s*' is supposed to be capable of being replaced by the name of a sentence (such as a sentence within quotation marks), and the letter '*p*' is supposed to be capable of being replaced by a sentence (not quoted) which says what it means. (Again, it looks as if a safe – though trivial – way of saying what a sentence referred to by '*s*' means is by using that very sentence in place of '*p*' in something like (M).)

It's not obvious how to construct explicit statements of the meaning of parts of sentences from which we could derive statements which have the form of (M). This is at least in part due to the fact that 'means that' – like 'believes that' and 'says that', which we considered in chapter 8 – introduces an intensional context which imposes significant restrictions on substitution. If you look again at the way in which (A4) was derived from (A), you'll see that it depended upon substitutions at crucial points. We got to (A3) from (A2), by replacing one singular term with another which referred to the same object. And we got to (A4) from (A3) by replacing one predicate with another which was true of just the same things. These substitutions would not obviously be legitimate within the 'that'-clause in something of the form of (M), so it's not immediately clear how we could derive (M)-like statements of meaning sentences from statements of the meaning of their parts.

What Davidson, in effect, proposes is devastatingly simple: that we *count* statements of the reference of names, and of the conditions under which predicates are true of things, *as* statements of the meaning of names and predicates; and that we *count* the derivation of explicit statements of the truth-conditions of sentences, from such statements about names and predicates, *as* the derivation of statements of the meaning of sentences from statements of the meaning of their parts. That is, we count a Tarskian way of specifying the application of the predicate '*x* is true' to sentences in a language *as* a theory of meaning for that language, in the sense of a theory which explains how statements of the meaning of sentences are derived from statements of the meaning of their parts.

Davidson himself doesn't present it quite as baldly as this, but I think he might as well have done. What he does is offer an argument which attempts to mimic Tarski's procedure. That is, he supposes that we're considering something like the Tarskian schematic formula (T). And he imagines that we're attempting to put enough constraints on the use of the predicate 'x is T' to ensure that we always get a truth from (T) if we replace 's' with a name of a sentence, and 'p' with a sentence which gives the meaning of that sentence.

Davidson then notes that if we have met this condition, we have passed Tarski's Test, the so-called Convention T. He concludes:

> [I]t is clear that the sentences to which the predicate 'is T' applies will be just the true sentences of [the language].[10]

It follows from this that if the sentence which replaces 'p' gives the meaning of the sentence named by 's', then the letter 'T' here means, in effect, *true*. What does not follow is what Davidson needs in order to have a good argument here: that if 'T' means *true*, then the sentence which replaces 'p' gives the meaning of the sentence named by 's'. That means that Davidson is not strictly entitled to what he says on the following page:

> There is no need to suppress, of course, the obvious connection between a definition of truth of the kind Tarski has shown how to construct, and the concept of meaning. It is this: the definition works by giving necessary and sufficient conditions for the truth of every sentence, and to give truth conditions is a way of giving the meaning of a sentence.

This last claim is what Davidson is not entitled to. What he is entitled to is, rather, the converse claim: that giving the meaning of a sentence is a way of giving its truth conditions.

I think we should not cavil at the weakness of the argument here: instead we should examine the bold proposal. We know how to derive a statement of the truth-conditions of a sentence from statements of the reference and truth-of conditions of its parts. We might call a theory which was capable of doing this for every sentence in a language a *theory of truth for that language*. Let's propose, then, that a theory of meaning for a language must take the form of a theory of truth for a language. This, I

---

[10] *Inquiries into Truth and Interpretation*, p. 23.

think, is Davidson's suggestion. It's not quite clear yet what it means: this will emerge as we consider objections to it.

9.5   The obvious objections to Davidson's proposal

The obvious objections to Davidson's proposal derive from the very thing which led Davidson to make it. It seems that, strictly speaking, what we're after is a way of deriving explicit statements of the meaning of sentences which have this form:

(M) The sentence *s* means that *p*.

Because it's hard to see how to derive anything of that form, Davidson suggests that instead we aim to derive what we take to be statements of the meaning of sentences which have *this* form:

(T) The sentence *s* is true if and only if *p*.

The crucial difference between (M) and (T) – the difference which led Davidson to prefer (T) in the first place – is that in (M) '*p*' occurs in an *intensional* context, whereas in (T) it occurs in an *extensional* context. You can only swap sentences after 'means that' if they *mean* the same, whereas after 'if and only if' (as Davidson understands it) you can swap them if they just have the same truth-value.

Now suppose that you've used your theory of truth for English to derive the following:

(Ts) The sentence 'Snow is white' is true if and only if snow is white.

Since the sentence 'Grass is green' has the same truth-value as the sentence 'Snow is white' – they're both true – you can swap one for the other in (Ts) to reach this:

(Ts*) The sentence 'Snow is white' is true if and only if grass is green.

But while (Ts) might be regarded as a statement of the meaning of 'Snow is white', (Ts*) surely cannot be. What's happened here is that we have encountered, yet again, a version of the Basic Worry which faces the view that the meaning of words concerns things in the world, rather than things in the mind.[11] The form of the worry which has dogged us most is

---

[11] See ch. 2, § 2.8, above.

that if two words are linked to the same thing in the world, they seem bound to have the same meaning, but this seems unacceptable. In Davidson's theory the worry takes on an abstract form: according to his theory the meaning of a sentence is given by a statement of material truth-conditions, so two sentences with the same truth-value should have the same meaning; but this seems absurd.

Davidson has two responses to this. One is that sentences such as (Ts) are supposed to be the product of empirical theories which describe the speakers of a language, and so should have the status of empirical laws. So we should ask ourselves: was (Ts*) bound, as a matter of empirical law, to be true while the words continued to have the same meaning in that community? The answer is clearly 'No': all that would be needed would be for grass to be a different colour, while snow was the same colour. There is no law-like connection between the meaning of the sentence 'Snow is white' and the colour of grass, so (Ts*), unlike (Ts) couldn't have the status of an empirical law.

The second response is this: (Ts) is supposed to be derived directly from explicit statements of the reference and truth-of conditions of the terms and predicates it involves. In order to derive (Ts*) directly from such explicit statements, the statement of the truth-of condition of the predicate 'x is white' would have had to be something like this:

(Sw*) The predicate 'x is white' is true of something if and only if that thing is green.

But it's just not plausible that this could be a true and lawlike statement of the truth-of condition of that predicate in English.

Neither of these responses is adequate. Imagine that from (Ts) we had derived the following, instead of (Ts*):

(Ts**) The sentence 'Snow is white' is true if and only if snow is white and the area of a circle is πr^2.

(Ts**) is just as lawlike as (Ts): it couldn't fail to be true while the words continued to have the same meaning. But surely (Ts**) is absurd as a statement of the meaning of 'Snow is white': 'Snow is white' is about the colour of snow, and has nothing to do with the area of circles.

That sidesteps the first response to the problems raised by (Ts). And we can sidestep the second equally easily. For (Ts**) could perfectly well have been derived directly from statements of reference and truth-of conditions which are themselves true and lawlike. All we need is to imagine this eccentric statement of the truth-of condition of the predicate '*x* is white':

>   (Sw**) The predicate '*x* is white' is true of something if and only if that thing is white *and* the area of a circle is πr^2.

This is surely both true and lawlike, it would enable us to derive (Ts**) directly (given a suitable statement of the reference of 'snow'), but it surely does not give the meaning of the predicate '*x* is white': '*x* is white' is about colour, not the area of circles.

What these points show is that there is only one way of understanding Davidson's proposal which leaves it with any plausibility. That is, that the way to show how the meaning of sentences depends on the meaning of their parts is indeed to provide a theory of truth for the language in question: that is, we show how the truth-conditions of sentences are derived from the reference and the truth-of conditions of sub-sentential parts (together with appropriate statements for connectives and quantifiers). But not all theories of truth count as theories of meaning. They don't all show how the *meaning* of sentences depends on the *meaning* of their parts. To get a theory of truth which *does* count as a theory of meaning, we need to see it as meeting some extra conditions. Davidson himself supposes that these extra conditions are supplied by what we have to do to understand the language as it is used by native speakers. His view of what that involves is the topic of chapter 10.

9.6   Truth and the possibility of general semantics

Davidson's concern is to provide a framework in which it will be possible to explain how the meaning of every sentence in any language depends upon the meaning of its parts. His suggestion is that this be done by the peculiarly explicit means of providing what he calls a theory of meaning for each language. And his bold proposal is that we can use a theory of truth as such a theory of meaning.

But remember the goal: to be able to explain how the meaning of *every* sentence in a language depends on the meaning of its parts. There's an obvious problem: not every sentence is capable of being true or false.

There are two ways in which this problem might seem to manifest itself. First, there are clearly sentences whose grammatical form makes them incapable of being true or false. Questions and commands, for example, cannot be true or false. Secondly, we might suppose that there is not really a question of truth or falsehood in certain subject-areas. We might think that there cannot really be such a thing as truth or falsehood about moral issues, for example, or about questions of taste, or about what is funny.

The first problem is a technical one, and needs a technical solution. Those sentences whose grammatical form makes them capable, other things being equal, of being true or false are known as *declarative* sentences. Davidson's response is to treat all *non-declarative* sentences (imperatives and interrogatives, for example) as consisting, in essence, of two parts: a declarative core, and something else (Davidson calls it a 'mood-setter') which determines how the declarative core is to be *taken* (imperatively or interrogatively, for example). The words in the declarative core will have their function explained in the regular way, by means of a truth theory for the language. And then there will be a special part of the theory specifying truth-conditions for the mood-setters. In this way, everything about the meaning of even non-declarative sentences will be capable of being explained by a truth-theory.

This is not the place to assess whether this kind of response will really work.[12] Instead, I'll look briefly at the second problem which faces the idea of using a truth-theory to explain the meaning of every kind of sentence. This is the issue of those subject-areas in which we might think that there is no question of truth and falsehood. There is no simple grammatical reason why the sentences involved here should not be true or false: 'Deliberate killing is sometimes legitimate', '*The Rite of Spring* is a great work', and '*Monty Python* is very funny' are all declarative sentences. If we think that there's no possibility of truth and falsehood here, it's because we think both that what's true and false concerns what can genuinely be thought to be facts about the world itself, and that there are no real facts about morality, artistic value, or humour.

---

[12] Davidson makes a beginning on the task in 'Moods and Performances', in his *Inquiries into Truth and Interpretation*, pp. 109–21.

The proper Davidsonian response to this objection is clear. It is to deny the conception of truth which the objection presupposes. The Davidsonian will insist that there is very little more to the notion of truth than is captured by Tarski's Test.[13] Provided we're dealing with meaningful declarative sentences, the notion of truth applies, because there's no more to there being a *truth-condition* for such a sentence than there being a way of saying what it says.[14] Davidson assumes that we can use a declarative sentence to say what it itself says – as in (E) and (Ta). In that case, all that's needed for such a sentence to have a truth-condition is that it should say *something* – that is, that it be meaningful. The objection, on the other hand, presupposes the existence of some further and independent criterion for what is genuinely a fact about the world: it assumes that there is not a genuine fact for every meaningful declarative sentence. The Davidsonian will then challenge the objector to find some way of motivating any such independent criterion.

This Davidsonian response to the second aspect of the problem looks surprisingly robust. It turns out to be extremely difficult to find a serious motivation for any independent criterion for what is to count as a genuine fact about the world – beyond being the counterpart of some meaningful declarative sentence. Moreover, many of the reasons for thinking that there cannot be genuine truths about particular subject areas turn out to be quite superficial. The issues here are not closed, of course. The Davidsonian programme in semantics leads directly into some central questions in metaphysics.

9.7   One final worry

There is another worry which might be raised about Davidson's proposal, even though it's seldom voiced. The clarity of focus which Davidson's approach gives to the task of semantics depends on the explicitness which it demands. The aim is to show how the meaning of sentences depends on

---

[13] This is the basis of a tradition of Davidsonian defences of the view that there can be genuine moral and aesthetic truths; see, e.g., M. Platts, *Ways of Meaning* (London: Routledge and Kegan Paul, 1979), ch. x.

[14] There may be sentences which don't say anything, because they're not really meaningful. For example, a sentence like 'Colourless green ideas sleep furiously' might be thought not to say anything, in which case it has no genuine truth-condition.

the meaning of their parts by showing how *explicit statements* of the meaning of sentences can be derived from *explicit statements* of the meaning of their parts. When this is made clear, it also becomes clear that the clarity of focus is bought at the cost of a bold assumption. The assumption is that linguistic meaning is something which can be captured in an explicit statement.

This assumption is not just obviously true. To see this, consider another use of the notion of meaning. We think of works of art (pieces of music, works of literature, paintings, and so on) as meaningful: they have some significance, and there is something to be understood about them. Moreover, it seems clear that the significance of a whole work of art depends on the significance of its parts (although it is also true, as with the case of sentences, that the significance of the parts is a matter of their contribution to the significance of the whole). But we do not in general think that the significance of a work of art can be captured in an explicit statement. In fact, what seems to draw us back to works of art and to keep us looking at or listening to the same works again and again, is the fact that no explicit statement can ever really completely capture what they mean.[15]

The Davidsonian approach to meaning assumes that things are different with ordinary linguistic meaning. No argument is provided for that assumption, and in general it's not questioned within the analytic tradition. But it should at least be noted that something non-trivial is being taken for granted.

Further reading

Davidson's approach to theories of meaning for ordinary languages is sketched out in a number of papers which appear in his *Inquiries into Truth and Interpretation* (Oxford: Oxford University Press, 1984), particularly the five papers in the first section ('*Truth and Meaning*'). His response to the problem about non-declarative sentences appears in 'Moods and Performances', in the same volume. Alfred Tarski's original work on the definition of truth is 'The Concept of Truth in Formalized Languages', in his *Logic, Semantics, Metamathematics* (Oxford: Oxford University Press, 1956).

---

[15] I owe this thought about works of art to Paul Davies.

A simplified explanation and defence of his approach is to be found in his 'The Semantic Conception of Truth and the Foundations of Semantics', *Philosophy and Phenomenological Research*, 4 (1944), pp. 341–75. This latter paper is also an object-lesson in simplicity and precision in laying out technical issues. A very helpful introduction to Davidson's work on semantics is to be found in the Introduction to G. Evans and J. McDowell, eds., *Truth and Meaning* (Oxford: Oxford University Press, 1976). A more general (and more introductory) introduction to Davidson's work is B. Ramberg, *Donald Davidson's Philosophy of Language: An Introduction* (Oxford: Blackwell, 1989).

10   Quine and Davidson on translation and interpretation

Key texts

W. V. O. Quine, *Word and Object* (Cambridge, MA: MIT Press, 1960), ch. 2; Donald Davidson, 'Radical Interpretation', in his *Inquiries into Truth and Interpretation* (Oxford: Oxford University Press, 1984), pp. 125–40.

10.1   Introduction

So far we've been concerned with the kind of meaning different kinds of linguistic expression have, and with the way in which the meaning of sentences depends on the meaning of their parts. But there might seem to be more basic issues in the philosophy of language. Don't we need to understand the role of language in people's lives?

This issue will occupy us, in various forms, over the next few chapters. In this chapter we'll be examining the conception of language and meaning proposed by Willard Van Orman Quine and developed by Donald Davidson. They're concerned to show what kind of phenomena languages are, and what it is to make sense of them. Since the meaning of words is what there is to make sense of in them, an account of making sense of language is bound to be illuminating about meaning. Indeed, Davidson uses it to try to supply what we found to be missing from his semantic proposal, considered on its own.

The general picture of language developed by Quine and Davidson has been hugely influential. There are some differences between them on questions of detail, as will be clear shortly; and people have differed from both of them on other points. But the general conception of what language is, and of what it is to understand it, has been shared by the large majority of philosophers working on language within the English-speaking tradition.

10.2 Quine and radical translation

When we think about language, most of the time we think of words we understand in a language we understand. Quine's fundamental thought is that the familiarity of languages we understand makes it hard for us to see the nature of languages themselves, and of the assumptions which we have to make if we're to make sense of understanding languages at all. So if we're to see languages as they really are, and the understanding of language as it really is, we need to think instead of a quite different kind of situation.

What we need to concentrate on, according to Quine, is the situation of someone he calls a 'field linguist' engaged in what he calls 'radical translation'. The field linguist finds herself in a place where people speak a language which she knows nothing about. She's entitled to assume nothing about this language, beyond what has to be assumed for it to count as a human language at all. The language, we might say, is *radically* foreign to her. Superficial similarities of construction or word-form, of writing or vocalization, between this foreign language and her own cannot be taken to indicate any real similarity of grammar or meaning. The foreign language presents itself to her as an object of scientific study. Within such a context, it's known as the *object language*.

The linguist's task, therefore, is to approach this object language as a scientist, and to try to work out, on the basis of the evidence which is objectively before her, what the sentences in it mean. Quine takes this to be the task of getting into a position to provide a translation in her language of any given sentence of the foreign language. Since it may be possible to construct an infinite number of sentences in the foreign language, she needs some way of going about it systematically. What she needs to do is to construct a *translational manual*, which will provide a recipe for producing a translation for any given sentence of the foreign language – the object language – into her own language – which we may call the *home language* or *subject language*. Since she's engaged in translating sentences in a radically foreign language, we may describe her as engaged in *radical translation*.

Quine's thought is that the situation of the radical translator shows us clearly both what languages are and what it is to understand them. According to Quine, a language really is just what might present itself to a radical translator: everything else we might think belongs to language is just a projection of habits created by dealing with familiar languages. And, in some sense, on Quine's view, nothing can really be involved in understanding a language other than what is involved in producing a translation manual within the situation of radical translation. As Quine himself memorably puts it: 'radical translation begins at home'.[1] The idea is that even when we're dealing with the speech of our friends and family, and others whom we take to be speaking our language, the status of our understanding of that speech is not essentially different from that of the radical translator's understanding of the radically foreign language which is the object of her study.

It's natural to understand this as a thorough development of the common idea (which we found in Locke, for example) that words are arbitrary signs which are not intrinsically meaningful: on this view, if we take words as they really are in themselves, they give no indication of what they mean. The situation of radical translation is just a situation in which this is made extremely obvious. But whereas Locke thought that words get their meaning through association with invisible things (Ideas) in a speaker's mind, Quine is concerned to explain the meaning of people's words in terms of what is objectively available to an observer.

As far as language is concerned, Quine thinks that the basic facts which are objectively available are facts about speakers' dispositions to assent to and dissent from sentences. Even these aren't always obvious, though: a sign of assent in one culture may look very like a sign of dissent in another. So the field linguist has some work to do before she can be confident even of these basic facts.

Of course, different sentences provoke different kinds of disposition to assent and dissent. We know, for example, that we're inclined to assent to 'That's a dog' when a dog is pointed out, and not when what is pointed to is a fish, or when nothing at all is pointed out. Some obvious sentences like these sometimes provoke assent, and sometimes dissent, but we would expect all similarly placed English speakers to react in the same way. So in these cases assent and dissent vary with circumstances, but not from speaker to speaker. Other sentences have a different profile. Consider

---

[1] W. V. Quine, 'Ontological Relativity', in his *Ontological Relativity and Other Essays* (New York: Columbia University Press, 1969), p. 46.

the sentence 'God exists'. Show a speaker a dog or a fish or nothing at all, and it will make little difference to whether she assents to or dissents from this sentence. But different speakers have markedly different attitudes to it: some consistently assent to it, while others consistently dissent from it. Here assent and dissent vary between speakers, but not with circumstances. Other sentences again provoke consistent responses from all speakers in all circumstances. Speakers of English unhesitatingly accept '$2 + 2 = 4$', and unhesitatingly reject '5 is greater than 9'.

This knowledge we have of our own language can be used by the field linguist as a way of dealing with the radically foreign language of the people she's studying. What she can do is observe the assent and dissent profiles of individual sentences, and pair them with sentences in her own language which have similar assent and dissent profiles. She observes that the speakers of the object language assent to one sentence when there's a dog present, and not otherwise, so she tentatively pairs it with her sentence 'That's a dog.' Another sentence provokes consistent assent among speakers when a fish is spotted in the water, so she tentatively pairs it with her sentence 'That's a fish.' Something which seems to contain both of these two object-language sentences provokes assent on one occasion when a dog comes out of a river with a fish in its mouth: she tentatively pairs it with the conjunction 'That's a dog and that's a fish', and makes a record of the object-language sentence-part that looks as if it might be paired with the word 'and' in her language.

This is a cartoon version of the kind of procedure which Quine imagines the field linguist adopting. Her basic evidence concerns dispositions to respond to whole sentences, but some of these sentences will seem to contain parts which recur in other sentences. If we pair groups of object-language sentences which seem to have common parts with groups of subject-language (home-language) sentences which have common parts, we can begin to predict the ways in which different combinations of the same parts will be reacted to. We can then test our predictions by presenting the native speakers of the object language with sentences of their language which we have constructed ourselves, which we have not heard on their lips, and see whether they provoke assent or dissent. If the native speakers react as we expect, then our hypothesis is confirmed; if not, then we need to revise something about our pairing of object-language sentences with subject-language sentences.

Proceeding by trial and error in this way, Quine's field linguist will hope to build up a complete translation manual. This will involve pairing parts of sentences of the object language with parts of sentences of the subject language, in order to provide a recipe for producing a pair in the subject language for any sentence which can be constructed in the object language. The fundamental requirement is that the subject-language counterpart to each object-language sentence should have the same assent and dissent profile as the original. If assent to and dissent from the object-language sentence is constant across speakers, but varies with the circumstances of utterance, then the same should go for the subject-language counterpart; moreover, it should provoke assent and dissent in just the same circumstances. If assent and dissent varies between speakers, but not between circumstances, in the case of the object-language sentence, the same should apply to the subject-language counterpart. If assent or dissent is invariant between speakers and circumstances, this also should be matched in the subject-language. We can imagine other matches too: for example, it may be that whole groups of sentences provoke assent in one group of natives and dissent in another group; we should then find counterparts in the subject language which show similar tendencies to provoke common group responses.

The important thing to remember here is that the situation of the field linguist is not supposed to be an exotic or unusual one. Although it will not generally seem like that, our own situation in understanding the language of those around us is not fundamentally different from that of the field linguist, on Quine's view. So this account of what the field linguist has to do, and what she has to go on, is supposed to tell us what the real facts about language and meaning are – even for us, working in our own languages. What this means is that the basic facts about meaning are just the facts about assent and dissent profiles. And there is no more to the meaning of the words in a language than could be represented in a pairing with words of another language which generated a best possible match of assent and dissent profiles between the two languages.

10.3   Davidson and radical interpretation

Quine's view is extremely – and characteristically – austere. Much of this austerity is due to two features of his approach: his insistence that the basic evidence available to the linguist is just of dispositions to assent and dissent; and his view that what the field linguist has to do is produce what Quine calls *translations*. Davidson's approach follows Quine's in its concentration on the situation of the field linguist, but it differs from Quine's precisely in those features which make Quine's view so very austere.

Davidson thinks that the task of the field linguist is not radical translation, but radical *interpretation*. This is because of his conception of the task of semantics, and of the link between semantics and the project of the field linguist. As we saw in the last chapter, Davidson sees the task of semantics as being to show in an explicit way how the meaning of sentences depends on the meaning of their parts. He takes it to be a requirement of a semantic theory for a language – what he calls a *theory of meaning* for a language – that it should enable one to *derive* an *explicit statement* of the meaning of any sentence from an *explicit statement* of the meaning of its parts. Crucially, then, semantic theories need to issue in explicit statements of the meaning of sentences. He then makes the natural suggestion that it is the business of the field linguist to produce a semantic theory – a theory of meaning, in his sense – for the language which is the object of her study.

This marks a significant contrast with Quine. Quine's field linguist is looking for a recipe (a translation manual) which will enable her to pair sentences in the object language with sentences in the subject language which have very similar assent and dissent profiles. But, as Davidson points out:

> [W]e can know which sentences of the subject language translate which sentences of the object language without knowing what any of the sentences in either language mean.[2]

This is clearly right, if we have Quine's notion of 'translation' in mind: we could, in principle, observe two *different* alien tribes, and discover matches of assent and dissent profiles in the sentences of their two languages, without knowing the meaning of any sentence of either language. But we couldn't provide a *theory of meaning* for an alien language, in Davidson's sense of that term, without knowing what any of the sentences of that language mean.

---

[2] 'Radical Interpretation', p. 129.

This is because a theory of meaning for a language issues in explicit statements of the meaning of the sentences of the language. If we understand what the theory says, and know that it's true, we must know the meaning of the sentences whose meaning is explicitly stated in the theory.

Moreover, Davidson's version is clearly superior to Quine's if we're to take the situation of the field linguist dealing with a radically foreign tongue as a model for all our understanding of language. And Davidson is no less firm than Quine in this: he says, 'All understanding of the speech of another involves radical interpretation.'[3] We cannot possibly accept that our understanding of the speech of the people we interact with every day is no better than an ability to match assent and dissent profiles – which, as we've just seen, can be possessed by someone who understands nothing.

The other respect in which Davidson's version differs from Quine's is in the evidence which Davidson takes to be available to the field linguist working in a radically foreign land. Davidson is happy to accept that the basic evidence for the field linguist is not the natives' dispositions to assent to or dissent from sentences, but beliefs and desires about sentences. In the original and simplest version of his view, Davidson holds that the basic evidence available to the field linguist is which sentences the natives think are true and which they think are false. He supposes that the field linguist can tell which sentences the natives think are true, without yet knowing what the sentences mean or what other beliefs the natives have. The idea is that we use this basic evidence to work out simultaneously what the sentences of the native language mean, and what else the natives believe.[4]

What Davidson needs for this purpose are principles like two which we've come across already, in considering Kripke's puzzle about belief:

(SB1) If someone understands a sentence and thinks it is true, then she believes what the sentence says;

(SB2) If someone understands a sentence and does *not* think it is true, then, provided she is rational, she does *not* believe what the sentence says.

The field linguist assumes that the natives understand their own sentences; she can tell which ones they think are true and which they

---

[3] Ibid., p. 125.

[4] We will also, of course, have to fit what we think the natives *believe* into a more general conception of their mindset, including their desires and values.

don't think are true; so she knows a little about what the natives believe. She knows that they believe what is said by the sentences they think are true, and don't (insofar as they're rational) believe what is said by the sentences they do not think are true.

But what *is* said by these sentences? At this point, Davidson's procedure depends on some version of what's known as the *Principle of Charity*. Davidson himself offers different formulations of the principle in different papers, and others following him have offered others again. The detail is not important just at the moment (though we'll return to it in the next section). The crucial thought is just this: in interpreting someone, we're aiming to make *sense* of her; but we don't count as making sense of someone if we represent her as being inexplicably foolish. What this means is that in interpreting someone, we should take her to believe what is sensible for someone in her situation to believe, unless we can explain how she might have ended up with beliefs which are not sensible.

This means that, on the whole, we should presume that what someone believes is true, and reasonable for the circumstances. And this tells us something about what her sentences mean. If someone understands a sentence and thinks it's true, then we should take the sentence to mean something which it's reasonable for her to believe in the circumstances in which she finds herself. Here we can use the same kinds of evidence which are available to Quine about assent and dissent profiles. If someone thinks a sentence is true in some circumstances but not in others, then we should suppose that it means something which it's reasonable to believe in some circumstances and not others (and in the right circumstances, of course). If someone thinks a sentence is true, no matter what the circumstances, then we should think that it means something which it's reasonable to believe, no matter what the circumstances. And so on.[5]

As in Quine's picture, we begin with provisional statements of the meaning of sentences. The meaning of sentences must depend on the meaning of their parts, so we need to suggest provisional statements

---

[5] Although I haven't mentioned it in the main text, it's clear that what we take someone to *believe* is interconnected with what we take her to *want*. Someone who holds her hand in a flame might still believe that the flame will burn her – provided she wants to be burned, or, at least, doesn't mind about being burned. Again, in making sense of someone's wants, we have to avoid representing her as inexplicably foolish, just as we do in the case of beliefs.

of the meaning of the parts from which we can derive those provisional statements of the meaning of whole sentences. Once we've done that, we can use the provisional statements of the meaning of the parts of sentences to construct new whole sentences to which we can also assign a provisional meaning. We can then test these new sentences on our native speakers. If they think those sentences are true which mean things – according to our provisional assignment of meaning – which we think are true, then our provisional theory is confirmed. If they think that those sentences are true which mean things – according to our provisional assignment of meaning – which we think are false, then our provisional theory needs to be revised, unless we can find some explanation of the supposed difference of view. Proceeding in this way, by trial and error, the Davidsonian field linguist will build up a large repertoire of statements of the meaning of parts of sentences, together with rules for deriving from them statements of the meaning of whole sentences. Bit by bit, she'll build up a theory of meaning for the language she's interpreting.

Davidson's approach to semantics is located in the context of a total conception of language. A theory of meaning for a language is essentially something which is arrived at as the result of a process of interpretation. And the interpretation we use in our everyday dealings with people who speak the same language as us is not fundamentally different in status from the radical intepretation pursued by a field linguist studying a language about which she can make no special presumptions, beyond those which are involved in the idea of interpretation itself.

Two questions naturally arise at this point. First, how precisely does the context of interpretation affect what can be regarded as an acceptable statement of the meaning of a sentence? And, secondly, how does a theory of meaning which is reached through the process of interpretation relate to what speakers themselves know about their own language? We'll look at these two questions in the next two sections.

10.4   Statements of meaning and propositional attitudes

In the last chapter (in section 9.5), we considered some obvious objections to Davidson's principal semantic claim, that a theory of meaning for a language could be given by providing a theory of truth for that language. The basic worry was that statements of the truth-conditions of sentences seem to permit more substitutions than statements of the meaning of sentences do. As a result, something could count as an acceptable statement of the truth-condition of a sentence, even if it could not plausibly be regarded as an acceptable statement of its meaning. One example was this:

> (Ts**) The sentence 'Snow is white' is true if and only if snow is white and the area of a circle is πr^2.

(Ts**) is true (given a suitable understanding of 'if and only if' – the one which Davidson intends). But the following seems obviously unacceptable as a statement of the *meaning* of the crucial sentence:

> (Ms**) The sentence 'Snow is white' means that snow is white and the area of a circle is πr^2.

We saw in the last chapter that (Ts**) is not ruled out as a proper statement of the meaning of 'Snow is white' by either of the two moves Davidson is initially inclined to make. Now that we have seen how radical interpretation works, can we find any further constraints which we can use to rule that (Ts**) cannot count as a way of stating the *meaning* of the sentence 'Snow is white'?

It might seem that we can. Recall that on Davidson's view we find out what the natives believe and what their sentences mean *at the same time*. In particular (though Davidson himself is never quite explicit about this), we need to make use of principles like this one:

> (SB1) If someone understands a sentence and thinks it is true, then she believes what the sentence says.

The idea was to use this kind of principle in conjunction with the Principle of Charity to ensure that we only take sentences which natives hold true to mean things which they might reasonably believe. What this seems to do is to use the contexts of propositional attitude (in particular, belief)[6] to block substitutions which would be legitimate in mere statements of truth-conditions.

Consider how this might work in connection with (Ts**). Almost all native English speakers, irrespective of their knowledge of geometry,

---

[6] Though Davidson insists, reasonably enough, that we can only understand what someone believes in the context of also understanding her desires and values.

think that the sentence 'Snow is white' is true. Since they understand the sentence, it follows from (SB1) that they believe what it says. So the sentence has to say something which almost all English speakers believe, irrespective of their knowledge of geometry. Now suppose that we took (Ts**) to give the meaning of that sentence. It would follow that almost all English speakers, irrespective of their knowledge of geometry, believe that snow is white and the area of a circle is πr^2. But English speakers would surely be inexplicably foolish (not to say otherwise incomprehensible) if they believed that complex proposition *irrespective of their knowledge of geometry*. That seems to be ruled out by the Principle of Charity. So (Ts**) assigns to the sentence 'Snow is white' a truth-condition which cannot reasonably be regarded as giving its meaning.

What this shows is that principles like (SB1) and (SB2), combined with a judicious and apparently reasonable use of the Principle of Charity, can prevent certain obviously bizarre statements of truth-conditions from counting as statements of meaning. Is this what Davidson is proposing? Unfortunately, this isn't quite clear, because of the variations in his formulations of the Principle of Charity.

Sometimes Davidson seems to endorse what we might think of as an *extensional* version of the Principle of Charity.[7] According to this, what we need to do is simply to *maximize* agreement between the native speakers and ourselves, as radical interpreters. Our task is to make the natives right about as much as possible, by our lights. This puts very little constraint on the kinds of thing we might suppose the natives to be thinking. Certainly, there would be nothing here to stop us supposing that almost all English speakers, irrespective of their knowledge of geometry, believe that snow is white and the area of a circle is πr^2. After all, it as true that snow is white and the area of a circle is πr^2 as it is that snow is white.

---

[7] This seems to be his view at 'Truth and Meaning', *Inquiries into Truth and Interpretation*, p. 27; something similar is said in 'On Saying That', *Inquiries into Truth and Interpretation*, p. 101 (though we are also apparently supposed to take account of whether the attributed beliefs are 'weird'). In 'Radical Interpretation' (p. 136), Davidson uses the notion of maximization, but says that it cannot be taken literally; on p. 137 he uses the idea of *optimizing* agreement. In 'Belief and the Basis of Meaning', *Inquiries into Truth and Interpretation*, p. 153, he says we must avoid 'too much unreason': 'too much' suggests some quantitative measure, 'unreason' suggests a different kind of consideration.

Sometimes, again, Davidson seems to endorse what we might describe as a *weighted extensional* version of the Principle of Charity. According to this, what we need to do is to *optimize* agreement between native speaker and radical interpreter.[8] That is to say, we have a conception of which are the things it is important for people to get right, and we set it down as a requirement on acceptable interpretations that they show the natives to be right as often as possible when the issue concerns one of the things which it is important for people to get right. Again, however, this won't stop (Ms**) counting as an acceptable statement of the meaning of 'Snow is white.'

But sometimes Davidson seems to appeal to the intuitive idea I've already exploited – that we should not attribute to natives *inexplicable* error or foolishness.[9] And at this point it seems that quite independent considerations about what kinds of error are reasonable or explicable can be brought in. In effect, it looks as if we can bring in here something which gets close to a general theory of concept-possession, which might yield such truisms as that it's unreasonable to attribute knowledge that the area of a circle is πr^2 to someone who has not thought about geometry at all.[10]

10.5   Theories of meaning and speakers' knowledge

A theory of meaning for a language offers a theoretical characterization of the way in which the meaning of sentences in the language depends upon the meaning of their parts. According to Davidson, authoritative

---

[8] The term 'optimize' is used in 'Radical Interpretation', p. 137 (as just noted), and also in 'Thought and Talk', p. 169: it is natural to understand this (especially in the latter case) as I have in the main text, but even here Davidson may be moving towards the richer conception of charity which I consider next.

[9] Appeal to what is explicable is explicit in 'On the Very Idea of a Conceptual Scheme', *Inquiries into Truth and Interpretation*, p. 197. But we may also find the same richer conception of charity implicit in the worry about 'weird' beliefs in 'On Saying That', p. 101, and the appeal to rationality in 'Thought and Talk', p. 159.

[10] A further complication is that Davidson sometimes insists that we cannot get at what someone believes independently of deciding what her sentences mean (see, e.g., 'Belief and the Basis of Meaning', p. 144). If we really stuck to that, it's hard to see how we could use judgements about what it's reasonable to believe – which the intuitive version of the Principle of Charity depends on – to constrain statements of what sentences mean.

knowledge of such a theory is to be discovered through the process of radical interpretation. A theory of meaning is therefore an empirical theory, offered as a hypothesis in order to explain certain evidence – ultimately the behaviour of speakers.

But what precisely does such a theory show about the speakers of a language? Here's a natural suggestion:

(spk) A theory of meaning for a language is a statement of what competent speakers of that language know.

Call this the *speakers' knowledge* conception of theories of meaning. According to (spk), a theory of meaning for a language should tell us something about the actual state of the minds of people who can speak the language.[11]

Davidson himself does not regard theories of meaning as forays into the psychology of speakers, even if some psychological work needs to be done to reach a correct theory of meaning through radical interpretation.[12] Instead, he accepts what I'll call the *sufficient knowledge* conception:

(suk) A theory of meaning for a language is something knowledge of which *would suffice* to enable someone to understand that language.

There's no suggestion here that those who currently speak the language actually know any such theory; the idea is, rather, that knowing a theory would get one into a position as good as that of the native speakers of the language, even if by a different route.

What difference might this make? One natural thought is that it will make a difference to the way we represent the structure of sentences within a language. On Davidson's conception, the fundamental business of a theory of meaning for a language is to be able to yield a correct statement of the meaning of every *sentence* in the language. As long as a theory does that, it's fine. But it looks as if two theories of meaning for the same

---

[11] This interpretation is found, e.g., in M. Dummett, 'What is a Theory of Meaning? (i)' and 'What is a Theory of Meaning? (ii)', both in his *The Seas of Language* (Oxford: Clarendon Press, 1993), in B. Loar, 'Two Theories of Meaning', in G. Evans and J. McDowell, eds., *Truth and Meaning* (Oxford: Clarendon Press, 1976), pp. 138–61.

[12] This is clear from the opening paragraph of 'Radical Interpretation', on p. 125, and 'Reply to Foster', *Inquiries into Truth and Interpretation*, p. 171. There are hints that he at one time toyed with the view I contrast with it, in 'Theories of Meaning and Learnable Languages', *Inquiries into Truth and Interpretation*, pp. 3–16.

language could do equally well at the level of sentences, while differing quite widely in what they take to be the meaning of *parts* of sentences, and in the way in which they take the meaning of sentences to be derived from the meaning of the parts. As far as Davidson is concerned, such differences have no importance. Provided that the two theories yield equally good results at the level of sentences, they do all that such theories could hope to do. They both provide us with enough to enable us to understand all the sentences which can be constructed in the language; so they both enable us to understand the language.

Someone who accepts the speakers' knowledge conception won't be content with this, however. She'll want to know how speakers actually reach conclusions about the meaning of whole sentences. If their derivation follows one route rather than another, that should be reflected in a theory of meaning. All kinds of evidence might be brought to bear to help us decide this. We might notice that speakers tend to acquire (and lose) the ability to speak sentences in clusters; in that case, according to the speakers' knowledge conception, we might expect a theory of meaning to show links between the sentences in any cluster. Or we might find that some sentences take speakers longer to understand than others, despite containing a similar number of words. In that case, the speakers' knowledge conception would naturally suggest that the derivations of their meaning must have a different complexity.

The hope of the speakers' knowledge conception is that we will be able to produce theories of meaning for particular languages whose grammar is *psychologically real*. That is to say, our representation of the structure of the sentences in the language, and of the way in which conclusions about their meaning is derived, matches the processes which speakers actually go through when they read and hear sentences, and come to understand what they mean. It is in this sense that a theory of meaning is supposed to say what speakers know.[13]

This suggestion needs to be handled with some care, of course. In particular, it's often remarked that the theoretical concepts which need to be deployed in a theory of meaning go far beyond the knowledge of ordinary speakers of a language. It's accepted that very few of us actually

---

[13] Reasoning like that of this paragraph and the previous two is to be found, e.g., in R. Larson and G. Segal, *Knowledge of Meaning* (Cambridge, MA: MIT Press, 1995), pp. 56–62.

have an explicit understanding of the theoretical concepts of different parts of speech, or of the semantic concepts appropriate for the explicit statement of their meaning. But according to the speakers' knowledge conception of theories of meaning, there's still a sense in which such a theory can properly be said to state what competent speakers know. Those who hold this view will say that the knowledge in question is *tacit* knowledge, rather than explicit knowledge.[14] That is to say, it's knowledge of a kind which can be possessed without a full comprehension of the concepts which are needed to state it explicitly.

Those who accept the speakers' knowledge conception tend to portray Davidson, and others who hold the *sufficient* knowledge conception, as failing to acknowledge that there are real facts about the state of speakers' minds. Those who hold the sufficient knowledge conception tend to be portrayed as holding something quite close to a behaviourist view in the philosophy of mind. As long as we get the right results at the level of *input* – the circumstances in which speakers find themselves, and the sentences they hear – and *output* – the sentences speakers utter in particular circumstances – nothing else matters, according to this portrayal of those who hold the sufficient knowledge conception. It is as if there aren't really any relevant facts beyond that. And those who hold the *speaker*'s knowledge conception then seem quite reasonable in their rejection of such a picture.

But there's another way of understanding the dispute. Why should we think that an account of what a *language* means must tell us anything about the *minds* of speakers? There's one conception of language which makes this natural: it holds that there's no more to a language than what its speakers know.[15] This is what lies behind the speakers' knowledge

---

[14] This use of the notion of tacit knowledge seems to derive from Noam Chomsky: see his *Aspects of the Theory of Syntax* (Cambridge, MA: MIT Press, 1965). For an introduction to the issues (from Chomsky's side) see Larson and Segal, *Knowledge of Meaning*, pp. 542–53.

[15] This seems integral to much of Chomsky's work; see, e.g., his 'Language and Problems of Knowledge', in A. P. Martinich, ed., *Philosophy of Language*, 4th edn (Oxford: Oxford University Press, 2001), pp. 581–99. What I call the *subjective* view Alexander George calls the 'no-error' view of language: see A. George, 'Whose Language is it anyway? Some Notes on Idiolects', *Philosophical Quarterly*, 40 (1990), pp. 275–98. He contrasts it with both a 'communitarian' view (roughly, my 'objective' view), and his own view which seems effectively to define the language which a person speaks in terms of what that person *would*, on reflection, count as correct and incorrect.

conception of theories of meaning. The idea is that in talking of languages we are precisely talking about structures in people's minds. We might call this the *subjective* view of language. On this view, each individual person has her own language: it's a matter of the way she uses her words and what she means by them. An individual cannot be deeply wrong about her own language, on this conception.[16] If the subjective view of language is right, then an account of what a language means might indeed be thought to be a matter of psychology.

If we hold the *sufficient* knowledge conception, by contrast, we may hold that languages are more objective than this. On what I shall call an *objective* view, a language is something which exists independently of any particular speaker. Its words mean what they do independently of what any speaker takes them to mean. They can be used correctly or incorrectly; they can be understood and misunderstood. In learning a language, what we do is attempt to master something whose true nature is independent of us.[17] On this objective view, what words mean is not a matter of what anyone means by them; it seems to follow that psychology has nothing to say about what a language means.

The difference between these views comes out clearly in their attitude to familiar languages like English, German, and Japanese. On the subjective view, the fundamental facts about language are facts about the psychology of individuals. Of course, individuals will differ, so we will expect there to be differences between the theories of meaning attributed to different people. In fact, it's not immediately obvious that there will be any theoretical reason for talking about familiar common languages like English, German, or Japanese, at all. We'll only have reason for talking about languages like these, in addition to the particular individual

---

[16] A deep error is one that cannot be explained as a matter of failing to work out or execute something one really knows or knows how to do.

[17] Something like the objective view is to be found in D. Wiggins, 'Languages as Social Objects', *Philosophy*, 72 (1997), pp. 499–524. George, in his 'Whose Language is it Anyway?', calls this the 'communitarian' view. George himself, as just noted, supposes that there is a kind of middle position, which allows that someone can be wrong about her own language without there being such a thing as a language whose meaning is determinate independently of what anyone *would* say, after reflection. I doubt myself whether this gives proper sense to the idea that we can be wrong about the words of the language we speak.

languages – called *idiolects* – spoken by individual speakers, if we find that there's some explanatory advantage to be had from considering what's common to individual speakers of what we pre-theoretically think of as the same language.

According to the objective view, by contrast, it's likely to be precisely languages like English, German, or Japanese which should be the centre of our attention. There's no harm in studying the psychology of individual speakers. We may well be able to make sense of the tacit knowledge which they have of the language they speak. And there may or may not be interesting generalizations to be made about the psychology of speakers of the same language. But worthwhile though such studies may be in their own right, according to the objective view of language they're not relevant to understanding what *languages*, properly conceived, mean. On this objective view, the business of a theory of meaning is to do nothing other than describe the objective facts about a language, as such.

If we think of the debate in these terms, the difference between the speakers' knowledge and the sufficient knowledge conception of theories of meaning doesn't seem to depend on a difference of view about whether there are real facts about psychological mechanisms. Instead, it reflects a fundamental difference between two very general conceptions of language.

Davidson's own position in this debate is not altogether clear. He clearly favours the sufficient knowledge conception of theories of meaning. On the other hand, his view of the status of such common languages as English, German, and Japanese, is very like that of the subjective view.[18] In fact, one might think that his insistence on setting theories of meaning within the context of radical interpretation suggested a bias towards the subjective view. It's tempting to see the basic goal of radical interpretation as being to make sense of *people*. Understanding a person's language seems then to be interesting, ultimately, only because it is an integral part of understanding the person herself.

10.6   How fundamental is radical interpretation?

Quine and Davidson agree in giving a fundamental importance to the situation of the field linguist engaged in radical translation or

---

[18] See, e.g., 'A Nice Derangement of Epitaphs', in E. Lepore, ed., *Truth and Interpretation: Perspectives on the Philosophy of Donald Davidson* (Oxford: Blackwell, 1986), pp. 433–46.

interpretation. It might seem a strange and exotic experiment, rather like deciphering Linear B, to see if one could make sense of a language in this way; but according to Quine and Davidson, this situation in fact reveals our true relation to language – even to our own mother tongue.

We can express the commitment their view depends on as follows:

(RT) Every fact about the meaning of any words in any language, which can be known at all, is available in principle to someone to whom those words are initially radically alien, who proceeds by means of the methods of radical interpretation.

The fundamental idea here is that we could only need two things to get at the meaning of the words in any language: first, evidence which is in principle available to anyone; and, secondly, rationality, in working from that evidence in the construction of a theory. Seen in this light, (RT) looks as if it is a special case of a general principle – we might call it the *perspective-neutrality* principle:

(PN) Every fact of any kind, which can be known at all, can be known on the basis of evidence which is available in principle to everyone, together with the application of reason.

(PN) is an expression of a commitment to the power of a certain kind of science. The idea is that sciences of this kind do not depend on any particular perspective: their evidence can be gathered and tested from different points of view. And they proceed from that evidence just by being rational.

Is (PN) plausible in general? It seems very demanding. To see this, consider the case of so-called secondary qualities, such as colours. Secondary qualities are typically thought to be available primarily, or authoritatively, only through a particular sense. We might think that *redness*, for example, was primarily or authoritatively available to us only through *sight*. If we thought that, it seems likely that we would think that people who could not see, or whose sight was somehow defective (being colour-blind, for example), would not always be able to tell whether or not something was red. It is natural, therefore, to think that redness is a quality which is not available to just everyone. If we accept (PN), we have to reject this apparently natural view of redness. We have to think that if redness is real, it is definable in terms of some science (physics, perhaps) which appeals only to evidence which really is available to everyone. But can we define redness in such scientific terms – in terms of physics, for example? That seems open to doubt.

It might seem that (RT) is more plausible than the utterly general claim of (PN). After all, facts about meaning don't seem to be linked with any particular sense. There doesn't seem to be the same kind of perspective-dependence of meaning as it seems plausible to suppose is present in the case of colours. But there's still room for doubt even about (RT). We might think, for example, that learning a language involves acquiring very general habits and a distinctive cast of mind. Such habits and casts of mind might be thought to depend on some kind of non-rational training. It might be like transforming one's character, rather than getting to understand a theory. If learning a language does depend on some kind of non-rational training, it seems that it won't be able to be acquired simply on the basis of the exercise of reason in the face of evidence which is available to everyone.

But perhaps (RT) itself requires something even more modest. Someone might acknowledge that to speak a language at all – to speak *any* language – we have to acquire certain very general habits and a distinctive cast of mind. And she might acknowledge that such habits and casts of mind are acquired through a form of non-rational training. Nevertheless, she might say, once you've got in the way of *one* language, you're in a position to interpret any language at all. This may seem a tempting picture, and it's probably coherent. The difficulty is finding a motivation for it. Once we've acknowledged that learning language at all requires acquiring, by some non-rational means, certain habits and casts of mind, it's hard to insist that it's impossible that different languages might require different habits and casts of mind, and therefore different non-rational training. It's difficult to find a reason for accepting (RT) which does not depend upon a more general insistence on perspective-neutrality.[19]

---

[19] Davidson himself gives what amounts to a defence of (RT) in his famous paper, 'On the Very Idea of a Conceptual Scheme', *Inquiries into Truth and Interpretation*, pp. 183–98. But his defence amounts to a range of *ad hominem* arguments against certain formulations of conceptual relativism: it's not clear that there is no better formulation of a denial of (RT).

Further reading

Introductory chapters on radical interpretation and related issues can be found in B. Ramberg, *Davidson's Philosophy of Language* (Oxford: Blackwell, 1989), chs. 6–10, and in S. Evnine, *Donald Davidson* (Cambridge: Polity Press, 1991), chs. 6–8. A number of significant articles on these topics appear in E. Lepore, ed., *Truth and Interpretation: Perspectives on the Philosophy of Donald Davidson* (Oxford: Blackwell, 1986), parts IV and V. An advanced piece on radical interpretation, developing in detail the principles an interpreter needs to appeal to, is D. Lewis, 'Radical Interpretation', *Synthèse*, 23 (1974), pp. 331–44. The kind of perspective-relativism which is rejected by the importance given to radical interpretation is sometimes associated with the later work of Wittgenstein: see, e.g., L. Wittgenstein, *On Certainty* (Oxford: Blackwell, 1977). A work in that Wittgensteinian tradition is P. Winch, 'Understanding a Primitive Society', *American Philosophical Quarterly*, I (1964), pp. 307–24.

11   Quine on the indeterminacy of translation

Key texts

W. V. O. Quine, *Word and Object* (Boston, MA: MIT Press, 1960), ch. II; 'On the Reasons for Indeterminacy of Translation', *Journal of Philosophy*, 67 (1970), pp. 178–83.

11.1   Introduction

We've seen that Quine's and Davidson's insistence on the centrality of radical translation or interpretation to our understanding of language is an expression of a fundamentally scientific attitude to language. In Quine's case, this formed part of a concerted and longstanding attack on traditional conceptions of meaning. At each end of the central decade of his philosophical career, he produced dramatic claims about meaning which have continued to seem profoundly sceptical – though Quine himself didn't see them in quite that way. In 'Two Dogmas of Empiricism'[1] (first published in 1951), Quine attacked the use, within empiricism, of the traditional notion of analyticity, which is bound up with the idea of sameness of meaning. In *Word and Object* (first published in 1960), he advocated what he called the *indeterminacy* of translation, which again calls into question the extent to which it makes sense to speak of sameness of meaning.

These two challenges to traditional conceptions of meaning have had rather different histories. The first (the attack on analyticity in 'Two

---

[1] W. V. Quine, 'Two Dogmas of Empiricism', in his *From a Logical Point of View*, 2nd edn (New York: Harper and Row, 1961), pp. 20–46 (an earlier version of the paper appears in *The Philosophical Review*, 60 (1951), pp. 20–43).

Dogmas') remains quite widely accepted, particularly in the United States. It has shaped, and continues to shape, the whole conception of their subject held by many philosophers in the English-speaking world. The second (the thesis of the indeterminacy of translation) has remained a topic of continual puzzlement: it has seemed unclear exactly what the arguments for Quine's claim are, and whether the thesis is really significant. Quine himself has not helped: he has returned to the issue on several occasions, though he has emphasized different things each time. The interpretation offered here is derived from the most famous of Quine's returns to the thesis, his article 'On the Reasons for Indeterminacy of Translation'.

My principal concern in this chapter is with the thesis of the indeterminacy of translation. I'll offer a brief sketch of 'Two Dogmas' just as background.

11.2 'Two dogmas of empiricism'

In his famous paper, 'Two Dogmas of Empiricism', Quine attacked the prevailing orthodoxy among philosophers of his time, and sketched an alternative picture of the relation between philosophy and science. The 'empiricism' of his title was what Quine calls *logical empiricism*, and others have called *logical positivism*.[2] The logical empiricists were *logical*, in that they used the logical techniques of Russell and the early Wittgenstein, and *empiricist*, in that their general world-view was that of quite traditional empiricism – Hume's, in particular.

---

[2] Logical empiricism, or logical positivism, began with a group of people known as the Vienna Circle, who were heavily influenced by Ludwig Wittgenstein's *Tractatus Logico-Philosophicus* (London: Routledge, 1922). Wittgenstein's views were presented, in a way which emphasized the continuities with Humean empiricism, by Bertrand Russell, in 'The Philosophy of Logical Atomism', reprinted in B. Russell, ed. R. Marsh, *Logic and Knowledge* (London: Allen and Unwin, 1956), pp. 177–281. The most influential member of the group was Rudolf Carnap, who moved to America in the 1930s, and was Quine's philosophical mentor. The classic statement of logical empiricism is Carnap's *Der Logische Aufbau der Welt* (Berlin: Weltkreis-Verlag, 1928), translated as *The Logical Structure of the World and Pseudoproblems in Philosophy*, trans. R. George (Berkeley: University of California Press, 1967). In Britain, logical empiricism was promulgated most notably by A. J. Ayer, particularly in his *Language, Truth and Logic* (London: Gollancz, 1936).

The core of the logical empiricists' view is encapsulated in their verificationist conception of meaning which we can express as follows:

(VM) Every meaningful statement is *either*

(a) True or false in virtue of meaning alone; *or*

(b) Verifiable or falsifiable by immediate experience.[3]

The 'two dogmas' of Quine's title are connected with the two clauses of (VM). Statements which are true in virtue of meaning alone are known as *analytic* truths: the first 'dogma' is that there is a genuine distinction between analytic and non-analytic (*synthetic*) truths. Quine argues that there is no such genuine distinction, on the grounds (to cut a long story short) that the notion of analyticity cannot be satisfactorily defined.

As for (b), the logical empiricists seem to have held that individual statements are verifiable or falsifiable by immediate experience.[4] This requires each individual statement to have specifiable consequences for experience, of something like this form: if this statement is true, then such and such experiences can be expected. This specification of the experiential consequences of an individual statement was held by the logical empiricists to give the statement's meaning. Quine's objection to this is that statements always come as part of whole theories, and whole theories face what he calls 'the tribunal of sense experience', not individually, but only as a 'corporate body'.[5] If experience does not live up to our expectations, there's no particular individual statement to which the blame is automatically attached. *Something* in the theory may have to be changed, but the choice of what to change is not made for us. We have to decide what to revise, and in doing so, our choice can only be made for pragmatic reasons – reasons of convenience or simplicity, for example.

---

[3] This is, in effect, a restatement of what is known as 'Hume's Fork': Hume's claim that all truths are either mere 'relations of ideas' or 'matters of fact' (D. Hume, *Enquiry concerning Human Understanding*, IV, 1). Hume's view is restated with some force by Rudolf Carnap, in 'The Elimination of Metaphysics Through Logical Analysis of Language', in A. J. Ayer, ed., *Logical Positivism* (Glencoe, IL: The Free Press), pp. 60–81.

[4] A distinction is often made between *strong* and *weak* verification or falsification. A claim or theory is *strongly* verified or falsified if it is *conclusively* verified or falsified. It is *weakly* verified or falsified if it is *confirmed* or *disconfirmed* (made more or less reasonable to accept). My formulations below are intended to be compatible with the *weak* understanding of verification and falsification, though I think no very important issues depend on the point.

[5] 'Two Dogmas', p. 41.

Quine takes the whole body of our beliefs to comprise a kind of scientific theory, and he likens this theory to a field of force whose boundary conditions are experience. Within this field, different beliefs are nearer to or further from the boundaries – the periphery. Those near to the periphery are those which we ordinarily think of as simple judgements of experience; those further away, nearer the core of the theory, are those we think of as theoretical commitments. But all are linked together. If I make what seems a straightforward report of experience – such as 'The cup on my desk is white' – this depends on a conception of what cups and desks are, and of what it is for something to be white. Suppose I think that the cup on my desk is white, and then look to see if I am right. I look at what I take to be my desk, single out what I take to be my cup on top of it, and find that it seems *not* to be what I take to be white. It seems that I am wrong here, but this does not mean that I should withdraw my judgement that the cup on my desk is white. It may be that instead I should revise my conception of what it is for something to be a cup (so that I don't think what I'm looking at is really a *cup*), or of what it is for something to be a desk (so that it's not a cup on a *desk* that I'm looking at), or of what it is for something to be white (so that the cup on my desk might count as white after all).

These different kinds of revision require different kinds of upheaval in my beliefs. On the face of it, revising my judgement that the cup is white, while keeping constant my conceptions of cups, desks, and whiteness, might seem the simplest option: revising my conceptions of cups, desks, and whiteness will have ramifications across a large range of my beliefs. But if I keep finding myself surprised in judgements of the kind which I take to be ordinary judgements of experience, it may in fact be simpler to make a revision of something more fundamental, and thereby adjust a whole range of expectations. On Quine's view, the decision is always just a pragmatic one: it's a question of weighing up the gains and losses of the different possible revisions. A given revision may be more convenient in one respect, but less convenient in another. These factors need to be considered in coming to our decision, but there is nothing beyond such pragmatic considerations to settle the issue.

Quine takes this to be nothing more than the thorough working out of the abandonment of the first 'dogma' of empiricism – the view that there is a fundamental distinction between analytic and synthetic truths.

According to Quine, to hold that there is such a fundamental distinction is to hold that the choice of what to revise in the face of the failure of our experiential predictions is not merely a pragmatic matter: it is to hold that some choices are fixed in advance of all possible experience. In effect, he claims, the two 'dogmas' are at root the same.

As one might expect, Quine's suggestion has consequences for the whole of philosophy. In particular, it undermines the idea of philosophy as being independent of science. In Quine's view, philosophy can be no more than highly theoretical science: it deals with beliefs a long way from the periphery, in his field-of-force image. Philosophical views – even views about what to count as elementary logical truths – are in principal open to revision in the light of experience, just as all views are. On the whole, it will seem simpler to make revisions in what we ordinarily count as empirical judgements than to change these very basic beliefs; but in some circumstances – when considering quantum mechanics, for example – it may be that the simplest way out of an experimental difficulty is to deny a principle of logic. Philosophy can no longer be regarded as separate from, and prior to, science.

This is not the place to engage in a serious consideration of the 'Two Dogmas' position. It is enough here to note two things which might make one hesitate to adopt it. First, it's not clear that Quine is right to think that the two 'dogmas' are inextricable. It looks perfectly possible to hold on to the analytic-synthetic distinction and also accept some of what Quine says about statements facing the 'tribunal of experience' as a 'corporate body', rather than individually. This latter view is a relatively uncontroversial thesis about confirmation in science, traditionally associated with Pierre Duhem.[6] And secondly, it's not clear that it's as easy to do without the idea of analytic truths as Quine suggests. In fact, there are two features of his own view which seem to depend on something very like analyticity.

First, in what sense do our beliefs form a *body*, which has to confront the 'tribunal of sense experience' as a whole? The natural suggestion is this: our beliefs form a body in that there are rational interconnections between them. What this means is that it's at least *difficult* rationally to give up one belief without also revising certain others, or that it's *difficult*

---

[6] P. Duhem, *The Aim and Structure of Physical Theory*, trans. by P. Wiener (Princeton: Princeton University Press, 1954).

rationally to preserve one belief without abandoning certain others.[7] If this is right, it seems that to believe in the idea of my judgements forming a body is to believe that there are some true claims of the form 'X cannot easily be rationally abandoned without revising Y', or 'X cannot easily be rationally preserved without revising Y'. These claims themselves look like claims which depend on the meaning of the relevant Xs and Ys, and so seem to be analytic.

Secondly, consider the idea that experience may be, as Quine puts it, 'recalcitrant':[8] sometimes experience goes against our theory. But what is it for experience to go against the theory? We imagine that what is involved is for experience to show that something in the theory would be better revised. That is to say, it's at least not *easy* rationally to leave the theory unrevised in the face of experience. This looks as if it requires there to be a rational connection between the theory as a whole and experience. And this again seems to depend upon the meaning of the theory. So it seems that to believe in the very idea of experience going against a theory we have to suppose that the very meaning of the theory requires *something* to count as undermining it. And this looks as if it requires there to be analytic truths of the same general type as the ones which Quine rejects – connecting our statements with conditions of verification – with the simple difference that all of our statements are interconnected.

11.3   Indeterminacy and inscrutability

Quine's dramatically pragmatic conception of theory-choice forms the background to his views on radical translation. Recall the assumption which gives radical translation or interpretation its importance:

(RT) Every fact about the meaning of any words in any language, which can be known at all, is available in principle to someone to whom those words are initially radically alien, who proceeds by means of the methods of radical interpretation.

---

[7] The reference to *difficulty*, rather than *impossibility*, here is meant to take account of the fact that a logical empiricist may accept that verification and falsification can be less than conclusive.

[8] 'Two Dogmas', p. 43.

What Quine claims is that what is available in principle to someone in the position of a radical interpreter is not enough to decide between what seem, on traditional conceptions of meaning, to be different interpretations of the meaning of words.

Quine makes this claim at two levels: the level of whole sentences, and the level of subsentential expressions. At the level of subsentential expressions the claim is known as the thesis of the *inscrutability of reference*. We might formulate it like this:

> (IR) Even if we accept that the truth-values of all the whole sentences of a language are fixed, there is nothing available, even in principle, to the radical interpreter which determines the reference of subsentential expressions.

Note that, although its name might suggest that it was really concerned with a difficulty of *knowing* the reference of subsentential expressions, the thesis of the inscrutability of reference is actually a thesis about what facts there are, rather than about what can be known. Quine's crucial claim is not the *epistemological* claim that we cannot *know* what subsentential expressions refer to; it is rather the different claim – which we might call *metaphysical* or *ontological* – that there is no *fact* of the matter about what they refer to. It follows from (RT) that if nothing available to the radical interpreter fixes the reference of subsentential expressions, then there is no fact of the matter about their reference.

Quine's claim at the level of whole sentences is known as the thesis of the *indeterminacy of translation*. We might formulate it like this:

> (IT) There is nothing available, even in principle, to the radical interpreter, which determines the truth-value of all the individual sentences of a language.

Again, it's important to be clear about what this thesis means. Given (RT), (IT) is a thesis about what *facts* there are: the claim is that there is no fact of the matter about the truth-value of all the sentences of a language.

It's easy to be misled by the name of the thesis of the indeterminacy of translation, and take it to be an expression of what we think of as a familiar fact about different languages. It is often thought, for example, that there's no such thing as a *correct* translation of a French or Greek text into English: after all – we often suppose – there are no precise English *equivalents* to French and Greek words. We begin by observing that the nuances of words cannot be captured in foreign languages, and then we notice (as we suppose) that the difficulties of translation are deeper than that: it seems to turn out that what in one language is presented as a single concept, has to be translated into another language by a variety of terms between which no obvious link can be found, from the perspective of that second language. An example familiar to philosophers is the Greek word *logos*, which is variously translatable, in different contexts, as *speech*, *word*, *reason*, *reckoning*, or *account* (and the list could be continued).

But this is not at all the kind of thing which is involved in Quine's thesis of the indeterminacy of translation. The reason is that the familiar thinking which supposes that texts have no absolutely correct translations in other languages depends on denying (RT). We think that we cannot precisely capture the meaning of *logos* in English, because there is something about the meaning of that word which is only available to someone who understands Greek – from the inside, as it were. We think that there are facts about the meaning of Greek words which cannot be captured in other languages. But this is just what (RT) denies.

Why, then, does Quine believe the theses of the inscrutability of reference and the indeterminacy of translation? The thesis of the inscrutability of reference is supported initially by the famous 'Gavagai' example in *Word and Object*.[9] A native cries out 'Gavagai' when a rabbit scurries past. We think he means something like 'Lo, a rabbit!' But might he not equally mean 'Lo, an undetached rabbit-part!' or 'Lo, a temporal stage of a rabbit!'? The sentence itself doesn't decide the matter. It seems that the term 'gavagai' might refer to rabbits, or to undetached rabbit-parts, or to temporal stages of rabbits: wherever we get one, we seem bound to get the others.

This example on its own is unlikely to be convincing: we expect there to be more tests which will rule out some of the alternatives. We'll find that 'gavagai' makes sense in verbal combinations in which several of the alternatives would not make sense. But the point is really quite an abstract one, and doesn't depend on the effectiveness of this example. The point really depends, at root, on the thought that the radical interpreter's evidence always comes, in the first instance, at the level of whole

---

[9] See *Word and Object*, pp. 51–2.

sentences. From the perspective of radical interpretation, the reference of subsentential expressions, including individual words, is nothing more than a theoretical construction designed to yield appropriate interpretations for whole sentences.

Recall Davidson's view, that what the radical interpreter is trying to do is provide what he calls a 'theory of meaning' for the foreign language she's interpreting. For Davidson this means that she needs to able to state the truth-conditions of each of the potential infinity of sentences in the language. She discerns structure in sentences, and assigns reference to the parts thus identified, just in order to be able to do that. The assignment of reference to parts of sentences has no higher status than this, on Davidson's theory: it's done simply in order to generate acceptable statements of the truth-conditions for whole sentences. It follows that any assignment of reference to subsentential parts which delivers acceptable results for whole sentences will do. If two different assignments do equally well at the level of whole sentences, there's no fact of the matter about which is right. And the simple thought which leads to the thesis of the inscrutability of reference is then just this: isn't it *obvious* that different assignments of reference to subsentential parts might do equally well at the level of whole sentences?

Davidson himself makes this vivid by means of a simple example.[10] Suppose that we begin with an assignment of reference which works for all the sentences we have encountered. Our theory of meaning for the foreign language which we are interpreting contains, let us suppose, the following two clauses:

(Refa) The thing referred to by 'a' = Jane;
(TF) The predicate 'x is F' is true of something if and only if that thing is witty.

These two clauses enable us to give the following statement of the truth-condition of the sentence 'a is F':

(T1) 'a is F' is true if and only if Jane is witty.

---
[10] D. Davidson, 'The Inscrutability of Reference', in his *Inquiries into Truth and Interpretation* (Oxford: Oxford University Press, 1984), pp. 227–41.

But now suppose that everything in the universe has a shadow. If that's true, then we can reinterpret all the singular terms in the language as referring, not to the original things, but to their shadows, and all the predicates as being true, not of the original things, but of their shadows. In particular, we will offer the following two alternative clauses in our alternative theory of meaning for the language:

(Refas) The thing referred to by '*a*' = Jane's shadow;

(Tfs) The predicate '*x* is *F*' is true of something if and only if that thing is the shadow of a witty thing.

These alternative clauses will enable us to give the following alternative statement of the truth-condition of the sentence '*a* is *F*':

(T1s) '*a* is *F*' is true if and only if Jane's shadow is the shadow of a witty thing.

And this statement of truth-conditions has at least the following virtue: it will show the sentence '*a* is *F*' to be true in just the same circumstances as the original (T1) shows it to be true.

If we take this to show that there is nothing to choose between these two statements of truth-conditions, from the perspective of the radical interpreter,[11] then we have here an argument for the inscrutability of reference. But this kind of consideration doesn't lead directly to the thesis of the indeterminacy of translation, which relates to whole sentences, since our alternative interpretation was designed precisely to ensure that no difference was made to the truth-values assigned to whole sentences. Quine nevertheless imagines that there might be some way of moving from the inscrutability of reference to the indeterminacy of translation. An argument of that form is what Quine, in his paper 'On the Reasons for Indeterminacy of Translation', would call *pressing* the doctrine of indeterminacy *from below*.[12]

---

[11] Of course, this itself is quite doubtful, since the different statements of truth-conditions will require us to attribute to the natives different kinds of belief and desire. They'll only be equivalent if we adopt a rather weak understanding of the Principle of Charity: see ch. 10, § 10.4. This issue is dealt with in the next section.

[12] 'On the Reasons for Indeterminacy of Translation', *Journal of Philosophy*, 67 (1970), p. 183.

It's not immediately clear how we could have a convincing form of such *pressing from below*. It seems that it would have to work something like this. We would attempt to show that two alternative assignments of reference to subsentential expressions made no difference to the truth-value of a *certain range* of sentences, and we would then try to claim on this basis that there was no real fact about which of the two assignments was correct: each, we would claim, did its job of generating acceptable truth-conditions of whole sentences within the range equally well. And then we would find some further sentences, *outside* the original range, which came out true on one assignment of reference to subsentential parts, and false on the other. The problem with such an argument is obvious: what could have given us the right to exclude these problematic sentences from the original range of sentences for which we were trying to generate correct truth-conditions?

In fact, in his presentation of the situation of the radical translator, Quine does give us a reason to distinguish between different ranges of sentences. Some sentences are assented to by all speakers in certain circumstances, and dissented from by all speakers in other circumstances, and the assent and dissent of speakers is not significantly affected by any supplementary information we might provide. These sentences are naturally regarded as reports or descriptions of what is available to experience on particular occasions. Quine calls them *observation sentences*. These have a special status: their translation is particularly secure, since they are naturally translated by a sentence in the translator's own language which reports or describes the relevant state of affairs. The translation of other sentences is less simple, according to Quine: speakers may not always agree, and supplementary information may make a difference to their tendency to assent or dissent; nor do the observable circumstances at the time of utterance seem to be so crucial.

Given this distinction – vague and gradual as it may be – between observation sentences and others, we might be able to use it to provide a version of the 'pressing from below' argument for indeterminacy of translation. Let's suppose that the translations 'rabbit' 'undetached rabbit-part', and 'temporal stage of a rabbit' work equally well for all occurrences of the word 'gavagai' in *observation* sentences. That is to say, it makes no difference to the truth-value of observation sentences which translation we choose. Nevertheless, we might suppose, a choice could make a difference to some sentences further away from observation sentences: to what we might think of as *philosophical* sentences, for example.

Does this give us a reason to conclude that there is no fact of the matter about the truth-value of these highly theoretical sentences? Why shouldn't we just say that the difference of truth-value among the highly theoretical sentences simply shows that the different translations of 'gavagai' were not, after all, equally good?

I think there's only one response which can be made to this, and that takes us on to the other argument for indeterminacy which Quine mentions – the style of argument he calls *pressing* the doctrine of indeterminacy *from above*.[13] It also takes us back to some of the central claims of 'Two Dogmas of Empiricism'. The response involves these two assumptions:

(ITa) There is no more to the truth or falsity of non- observational sentences than their tendency to be confirmed or falsified by the truth or falsity of observation sentences;

(ITb) Non-observational sentences are only confirmed or falsified by observation in *groups* (theories).

(ITa) and (ITb) evidently represent some of the central features of Quine's 'empiricism without the dogmas', set in the context of radical translation. (ITa) is a form of verificationism about meaning, not far from one aspect of (VM). And (ITb) is a statement of Duhemian holism of confirmation.

Given (ITb), it seems clear that there will be different ways of accommodating the falsification of a group of non-observational sentences by the tribunal of experience. A theory can be regarded as a long conjunction of sentences (it will have the form 'p and q and r and ... '). If the theory is falsified, that just means that *at least one* of its component sentences is false. Unless we have some other indication that one particular sentence must be to blame, there's nothing to stop us revising the theory in several different ways: counting one component sentence false on one revision, and another on another revision. And (ITa) tells us, in effect, that there can be no other indication that one particular sentence must be to blame. So there's nothing to rule one revision right and another wrong – unless we take into account merely pragmatic considerations

---

[13] 'On the Reasons for Indeterminacy of Translation', p. 183.

(of convenience and simplicity, for example). Moreover, even pragmatic considerations may not always urge us in the same direction: one revision may produce something more convenient for one purpose, another for another.

If we hold (ITa) and (ITb), it seems that we can begin to sketch out a reason for thinking that two translation manuals which assign different truth-values to theoretical sentences in an alien tongue might be equally – and, indeed, perfectly – good. Suppose that there are (at least) two theoretical sentences of the alien tongue which use the word 'gavagai': call them $S1$ and $S2$. Suppose that if we translate 'gavagai' as 'rabbit', we have to take $S1$ to be true and $S2$ false, whereas if we translate 'gavagai' as 'undetached rabbit-part', we have to take $S1$ to be false and $S2$ true. Suppose (absurdly, but the absurdity is irrelevant to this issue) that these are the only possible translations of 'gavagai' into English. And finally suppose that if we try to see which of $S1$ and $S2$ the speakers of the language assent to, there is nothing to choose between the two sentences: either the speakers all assent to both, or they all dissent from both, or as many assent to each as assent to the other.

All this looks quite possible. But in these circumstances (the argument goes) there is no reason to favour one translation over the other. It is either quite arbitrary, or at best a matter of our own convenience as translators, which we choose. Given (ITa) and (ITb), it seems that there is no absolute fact about the truth-value of $S1$ and $S2$. $S1$ is counted true by the 'gavagai'-means-*rabbit* manual, and $S2$ is counted true by the 'gavagai'-means-*undetached-rabbit-part* manual, but neither can be regarded as being true or false independently of all translation manuals. In effect, a translation manual is taken to be equivalent to a particular choice of revision of

theory: since, according to the view of 'Two Dogmas of Empiricism', choices of revision of theory are ultimately arbitrary, the choice of translation manuals is arbitrary too.

Even here, however, the argument is not quite straightforward. We should pause for a moment to note an assumption which is needed if we are to get to the full indeterminacy thesis. We might formulate it like this:

(ITc) If there is no fact of the matter about which of two theoretical
        sentences, $S1$ and $S2$, is true, then there will be no fact of the matter

which of two interpretations of speakers of the language of *S1* and *S2* –
one mapping *S1* onto a true sentence and *S2* onto a false one, and the
other *vice versa* – is correct.

The crucial thought here is that if nothing fixes which of the individual
theoretical sentences is *true*, there will be nothing *else* which decides which
of the possible rival interpretations is correct. The choice between such
interpretations can only be pragmatic.

What we have here remains, strictly speaking, a form of *pressing* the
doctrine of indeterminacy *from below*. That is, it begins from inscrutability
of reference at the level of observation sentences, and leads to the full-
fledged thesis of the indeterminacy of translation. But, if I am right, it only
gets there with the addition of two central assumptions of the general
conception of empirical theories to be found in 'Two Dogmas of
Empiricism'. And once they are added, we are in a position to press the
doctrine of indeterminacy *from above* – directly, without first introducing
the inscrutability of reference.

Pressing for indeterminacy *from above*, in Quine's terms, is arguing for
indeterminacy on the basis of the assumption that scientific theories are
under-determined by all possible evidence. It's important to be clear about
this assumption. It's not merely the assumption that scientific theories are
posited before all the evidence is in; nor is it the assumption that we will
only ever have a finite amount of evidence, or that the evidence is only
evidence about what has actually happened, which will be compatible
with many different theories about what *would* have happened if things
had been otherwise in any of an indefinite number of respects. It is rather
the assumption that even if we had had all *possible* evidence – if we had
known what would have happened in every possible experiment – we
would might still end up with a number of alternative theories, between
which there was no reason to choose – apart from reasons of convenience.
This seems quite a strong assumption, but it looks as if it follows
immediately from the holistic claim (ITb). If theories are verified or
falsified as wholes, rather than sentence by sentence, it seems obvious that
a falsified theory might be revised in different ways. Each such revision
might be compatible with all possible evidence, although the alternative
revisions will be incompatible with each other. So all the possible evidence
fails to determine one theory as uniquely correct.

How does this lead to the thesis of indeterminacy of translation? It seems that we need to make the same claims as we needed to complete the process of 'pressing from below'. We need to assume (ITa), or else the fact that all possible evidence fails to determine one theory as uniquely correct will not show that one theory is not, in fact, uniquely correct – although unverifiably so. And we need to claim that when we have one interpretation which understands the theoretical sentences of a language in line with one possible satisfactory theory, and another which understands them in line with another, there's nothing else which might make one interpretation better than the other. That is to say, we need to assume (ITc).

This seems to obliterate any substantial difference between the two routes to the indeterminacy thesis: pressing from below (via the inscrutability of reference) and pressing from above (using just the abstract considerations about the way in which theoretical sentences are verified or falsified). What we need to add to the thesis of the inscrutability of reference to get the thesis of the indeterminacy of translation are just the assumptions which are enough to get indeterminacy on their own. Pressing for indeterminacy from below seems little more than pressing for indeterminacy with an illustration: we identify the alternative theories as theories which assign different referents to subsentential expressions (for example, as theories which give different interpretations to the word 'gavagai').

11.4   Resisting Quine on indeterminacy: some simple ways

Quine seems to have regarded the thesis of the inscrutability of reference and the thesis of the indeterminacy of translation as just obvious. We can understand this, because the two theses turn out to depend on assumptions which we can understand Quine thinking are obvious, even if we might want to question them ourselves.

One of these assumptions is (RT) itself, of course – the assumption which makes the situation of the radical interpreter so central to Quine's philosophy. I noted briefly, in chapter 10, that this is not completely compulsory.

We've seen that the indeterminacy thesis depends on a form of verificationism about meaning in (ITa). Again, we might doubt that. Is it obvious that the truth of non-observational sentences turns on nothing more than how they might be verified or falsified in observation? It seems, for example, that something might be posited as the *cause* of something observable, without itself being observable. We can imagine two different theories, which posited different kinds of cause of something observable. We might suppose that the two theories were equally good at explaining all the observable facts, and hence that no observation could confirm one at the expense of the other. Would it follow that there was really no fact of the matter as to which, if either, was right? Surely, we might think, the cause of something observable might be a certain way, even if we could never show that it was.

But we might think that there was a simpler way of resisting both the inscrutability of reference and the indeterminacy of translation – even while accepting both (RT) and (ITa). Mightn't we suppose that an appeal to a form of the Principle of Charity, which we considered in the last chapter, would rule out some of these alternative interpretations. Consider the case of the inscrutability of reference. Doesn't it make a considerable difference to how we think of the speakers of a language if we suppose that they're thinking primarily of *shadows*, rather than familiar objects, or that they're thinking of *undetached rabbit-parts*, or *temporal stages of rabbits*, rather than rabbits? Won't these alternative attributions require us at some point to ascribe very peculiar concerns to these people, and to interpret their actions in quite bizarre ways? It might seem unclear that we can really be making sense of them at all.

A similar point arises in connection with the indeterminacy thesis. This time it's focused on assumption (ITc). Why should we think that an interpretation of speakers which maps *S1* onto a true sentence and *S2* onto a false one must make as much sense of speakers as one which makes the opposite mapping – provided only that there's no fact of the matter which of the two sentences is actually true? Mightn't it always be clear that one interpretation made more sense of speakers than the other?

Quine's treatment of the Principle of Charity isn't always clear, but it seems that he regards it as a *pragmatic* principle, rather than one which determines what counts as *correctness* of interpretation. It's more convenient for us to take alien speakers as believing the kinds of thing which we believe, and saying the kinds of thing which we say; but doing this doesn't take us any closer to the *truth* about them. It's not clear that this view is ultimately defensible. It seems to depend on taking for granted that we do ourselves really believe and say certain determinate things. But that itself looks as if it ought to be undermined by the indeterminacy thesis. The theses of the inscrutability of reference and the indeterminacy of translation seem to depend on claiming that there are genuinely distinct interpretations between which no choice can be made, except on pragmatic grounds, however much evidence is available to us. But the genuine distinctness of the supposed interpretations seems to be threatened by these indeterminacy theses themselves.

Even if we don't think it's incoherent to regard the Principle of Charity as a merely pragmatic principle, it's clear that someone could deny that it had that status. In the end, Quine offers no clear argument for his view.

Further reading

There are several introductions to Quine's work, most of them quite sympathetic to Quine. One is C. Hookway, *Quine* (Cambridge: Polity Press, 1988): ch. 2 discusses 'Two Dogmas of Empiricism', and relates it helpfully to the work of Rudolf Carnap; chs. 8–10 discuss indeterminacy. Another is A. Orenstein, *W. V. Quine* (Chesham: Acumen, 2002): ch. 4 discusses 'Two Dogmas', and ch. 6 indeterminacy. A famous early objection to Quine's 'Two Dogmas' is H. P. Grice and P. F. Strawson, 'In Defense of a Dogma', *Philosophical Review*, 65 (1956), pp. 141–58. A robust rejection of Quine's indeterminacy thesis is R. Kirk, *Translation Determined* (Oxford: Oxford University Press, 1986).

12 Austin on speech acts

Key text

J. L. Austin, *How to do Things with Words*, 2nd edn, J. O. Urmson and M. Sbisà, eds. (Oxford: Oxford University Press, 1975), especially lectures I, V, VI, VIII, and XI.

12.1 Introduction

Truth has some claim to be the central topic of philosophy. It is therefore not entirely surprising to find *philosophers* of language (as opposed to students of linguistics and grammarians, for example) concentrating particularly on truth in their treatment of language. Analytic philosophy of language may be said to begin with Frege's determination that the fundamental thing about the meaning of a sentence is its truth-value. And we've seen Davidson's related claim, that the meaning of a sentence may be given by giving its truth-conditions, forming the core of his philosophy of language.

This focus on truth has led to a corresponding focus on the kind of sentence which can be used to say something true: the *declarative* sentence – the kind of sentence which it makes grammatical sense to insert in the gap in the phrase 'Simon says that ... ' It has therefore come to seem natural to regard sentences of this grammatical type as the *basic* kind of sentence, and to regard their meaningfulness as being closely connected with what is involved in their being true or false.

In a series of lectures, worked on over several years in the 1950s and eventually published as *How to Do Things with Words*, the British philosopher J. L. Austin set out to challenge this apparently natural view. He began in what may seem a peculiar way: not by focusing on sentences which are not of the grammatical type known as declarative, but by considering sentences which seem to belong grammatically to that type, but which look odd in a more unsettling way. These sentences, which Austin called *performatives*, seem not to describe anything in the world at all, and so seem not to be true or false. Instead, they seem to *get something done*. Austin himself appeared to argue that these performative sentences cannot finally be set apart as a wholly peculiar class; but he thought that they could only be understood if we altered quite radically our conception of the nature of language.

If we focus on sentences which are capable of being true or false, we can think of sentences as things which we might hold up against the world, like pictures. This takes sentences out of the context of our everyday lives. Austin's focus on performatives – sentences which we can *do* things with – leads to a general concern with the *acts* we may perform when we use sentences, and to a whole dimension of evaluation of such acts which is distinct from the simple evaluation of statements in terms of truth and falsity. If we follow Austin, our interest in language is shifted from the concentration on truth which characterizes the bulk of work in the analytic tradition, to a general concern with the various ritual and conventional procedures involving language with which we carry on our everyday lives.

12.2   Performative utterances

Consider these sentences:

(1) I promise that I'll be there;
(2) I name this ship the Enterprise;
(3) I give notice that the next meeting will be held on 1 August;
(4) I sentence the prisoner to 14 years' hard labour;
(5) I declare the festival open.

You will naturally expect these sentences to be spoken in particular contexts: (1) by someone giving a promise to somebody else; (2) by someone naming a ship in a public ceremony; (3) by the chairman or secretary of a society in publishing the date of a meeting; (4) by a judge as she passes sentence; and (5) by some dignitary opening a festival. These are, we might think, the *natural* uses of these sentences.

All of these sentences are of the grammatical form known as declarative. But in these natural uses they don't seem to be used to *describe* the world: instead, they seem to be used to *do* something, to *perform* some action. In a natural use of (1), I don't (it seems) report the fact that I am promising: I actually promise. In a natural use of (2), I don't tell you what I call the ship: I give it a name. In a natural use of (3), I don't describe my giving notice: I actually give notice. And so on. It seems, intuitively, as if nothing true is said in these natural uses of such sentences. Instead, these uses are *performative*: they are *performances* of acts of certain kinds. Austin accepted the intuitive view that performative uses of sentences are not uses in which anything true or false is said, and so contrasted these *performative* uses with those he called *constative*. Constative uses, in Austin's sense, are precisely uses in which something true or false *is* said.

It's a striking fact that sentences (1)-(5) include verbs which may be used to describe acts we can perform by speaking or writing; and these verbs appear here in the first person of the present tense. But the presence of such verbs in the first person of the present tense is neither necessary nor sufficient for uses of sentences to be performative. The acts which are performed by natural uses of sentences (1)–(5) could equally well be performed by using the following sentences instead, provided that they're uttered with appropriate intentions and in the right contexts:

(1a) I will be there;
(2a) This ship is the Enterprise;
(3a) The next meeting will be held on 1 August;
(4a) The prisoner will serve 14 years hard labour;
(5a) The festival is now open.

On the other hand, there are uses of (1)–(5) in which they can be taken to be reports of fact. Imagine an entry in the diary of a busy judge and local celebrity:

10 am: call from festival organizer worried about the afternoon ceremony; I promise that I'll be there. 10.30: rush to shipyard, where I am hustled onto a platform beside a huge ship; as rather boringly instructed, I name this ship the Enterprise. 12 noon: brief preliminary meeting of GP executive committee; I give notice that the next meeting will be held on 1 August. 2 pm: in court for sentencing in Abercrombie case; I sentence the prisoner to 14 years hard labour. 4.35: after a quick change, I arrive at the festival site, to be greeted by the organizer (extremely worried, because I'm 5 minutes late); I declare the festival open. 7 pm: back home with a splitting headache; and so to bed.

These rather simple-seeming points raise a number of quite large issues about language. The first and most straightforward one is the nature of the distinction between performative and constative uses of sentences. There seems a very clear difference here: the use of sentences (1)–(5) in the imagined diary entry seems clearly different from their natural, performative, uses; and sentences (1a)–(5a) all have quite simply descriptive uses, which seem clearly distinct from the performative uses in which they seem almost equivalent to sentences (1)–(5). But how precisely is that distinction to be characterized? And here's a related question: is Austin right to think that performative uses do not say anything true or false? If I say, 'I promise', do I merely promise, or do I also say truly *that* I promise?

There are larger questions about meaning involved here too. Crucially, consideration of performatives shows that there is a difference between the meaning of words and sentences, on the one hand, and the meaning or significance of *uses* of words and sentences, on the other. It seems that there's no ambiguity of meaning in the word 'promise' between the performative and the diary-entry uses of (1), or between its use in (1) and its use in either of these two sentences:

(1b) I promised that I would be there;
(1c) She promises that she'll be there.

And yet there seems a clear difference in what's being done between the performative and diary-entry *uses* of (1), or between the performative and the obviously descriptive *uses* of (1a)–(5a). What, then, is the relation between the significance of a *use* and the meaning of a word or sentence? Does the use presuppose the meaning of the words, or is the meaning of words to be explained in terms of the significance of uses of them?

12.3   Towards a general theory of speech acts

Austin began with the idea that there was an important contrast between *performative* utterances – in which something is *done* in the uttering of words – and *constative* utterances – which can be true or false. Clearly this distinction is a conflation of two different distinctions, which might, in principle, diverge. On the one hand, there's the supposed distinction between utterances in which something is done and those in which nothing is done (or nothing like that). And, on the other hand, there's the supposed distinction between utterances of declarative sentences which are true or false and utterances of declarative sentences which are not true or false. In this section, we'll look further at the performative/non-performative distinction. In the next, we'll consider the claim that performative utterances cannot be true or false.

Despite beginning with the idea of a contrast between performative and constative utterances, Austin ended up concluding that there was no way to characterize performative utterances which did not count constative utterances as performative.[1] What does a performative utterance have to be like? We might think that it needs a special performative *verb* – a verb which describes a kind of act which might be performed by speaking, such as 'promise', 'order', 'baptise', and so forth. And we would then expect that verb to be in the first person of the present tense. But we've already seen that this condition is neither necessary nor sufficient for an utterance's being performative. Not necessary, because an utterance can be performative without containing such a verb in the first person of the present tense: (1a)–(5a) can be used in performative utterances, for example (and there are also performatives which use the second or third person – 'You are hereby warned', for instance – as Austin points out).[2] And not sufficient, because utterances of sentences which meet these grammatical criteria need not be performative, as the example of the judge's diary shows.

Austin's eventual criterion was something like the following. Utterances of sentences which contain no performative verb – sentences like (1a)–(5a) – are performative if they are 'equivalent', in some sense, to utterances of sentences which do contain a performative verb – sentences like (1)–(5). Take the first in each list of examples, in particular, beginning with the sentence without a performative verb:

(1a) I will be there.

---

[1] F. Recanati thinks that Austin's change of mind depends, in effect, on a change in the meaning of 'performative'; see his *Meaning and Force: The Pragmatics of Performative Utterances* (Cambridge: Cambridge University Press, 1981), pp. 70–2.

[2] *How to Do Things with Words*, p. 57.

This sentence might be used to make a prediction ('I will be there, I expect – I usually go'). But if it's used performatively, that use will be equivalent, in some sense, to a use of the following sentence:

(1) I promise that I'll be there.

Again, (1) could be used non-performatively (as in our judge's diary entry), but not in a use which is equivalent to a use of (1a). And we can make (1) unambiguously performative by means of some self-referential device, as in the following sentence:

(1*) I *hereby* promise that I'll be there,

even if this might seem rather formal for everyday use.

Austin's idea is that a sentence like (1a) can be used in what he calls a *primary* performative (the kind of performative utterance which could be made before there were words to describe types of linguistic act). The performative is then made *explicit* in the reformulation involving a performative verb (like (1)). The thought is that in an explicit performative someone performs the same act – promising to be there, for example – as is performed in the corresponding primary performative: it is just that the words make it explicit what act is being performed.

If this is the test of performativity, then it seems that Austin's original 'constative' (statement-making or descriptive) utterances will count as performative too. Consider the following sentence:

(6a) The cat is dead.

A statement-making utterance of (6a) is a constative utterance, if anything is. But If 'promise' is a performative verb, because it describes an act which can be performed in speaking, then surely 'state' is also a performative verb. And in that case, it seems that I can make explicit what I'm doing in uttering (6a) by uttering the following sentence instead:

(6) I state that the cat is dead.

Austin would regard the use of (6) as 'equivalent' to the use of (6a) in just the same sense as the use of (1) is 'equivalent' to the use of (1a) to make a promise. So it seems that constatives are performatives too.

Austin's reaction to this is to move from the rather specific contrast he began with, between performative and constative utterances of declarative sentences, to the outline of a general theory of speech acts. In any ordinary use of language, he suggests, a speaker will be performing acts of at least two, and possibly three, importantly different kinds.

In the first place, she will be performing what Austin calls a *locutionary* act. This is more than merely uttering sounds: it's speaking the words with the meaning they have (or have here). It's what we might call *saying something*. Secondly, as Austin puts it, she will be doing something *in* saying that. In using those words, she might be asking a question, giving an order, making a promise, stating a fact, and so on. These are all what Austin calls *illocutionary* acts. And finally, she might achieve something *by means of* saying what she says: she might draw someone's attention to something, convince her of something, get her to do something, and so on. Austin calls these acts of achieving something by means of saying something *perlocutionary* acts.

When someone speaks she may be performing acts of all of these kinds. Suppose someone utters the sentence 'Shut the door!' If she uses this sentence with the meaning it standardly has, she has, as we might say, *said something*: she's performed a *locutionary* act, rather than merely made some noises. In all probability, she's also given an order: this is an *illocutionary* act. And it may be that the order is obeyed, and her audience shuts the door. In that case, she's performed the *perlocutionary* act of getting someone to shut the door. There's a sense in which these are all different acts, in that they're all different things which she can be said to have done. But she doesn't need to do them all separately: she does all these things just by uttering the sentence 'Shut the door!'

Austin's focus on the acts which people perform when they speak can seem like a breath of fresh air in the intense atmosphere of analytic philosophy of language. We seem to have moved away from the logic-oriented, theoretical approach to language which has dominated the analytic tradition; instead language seems to be placed in the middle of real lives. This reaction is understandable, but it needs to be treated with some caution. Austin was, in fact, concerned to distance himself from *two* different approaches to language, not one. One part of the analytic tradition has concentrated simply on the meanings of words and sentences: this is the line which descends from Frege, whose concern is with semantics. But another part, reaching back to Locke at least, has always been concerned with the role of language in people's lives. Language has standardly been thought to have a function: immediately one of communication, but ultimately one of making people's lives safer and better. Too strong an emphasis on this idea of the *ultimate* point of language is itself one of the things which Austin opposes.

Austin's particular concern is with the class of *illocutionary* acts – the questionings, orderings, promisings, and statings which may be performed in uttering sentences. He thinks there's a tendency to try to assimilate illocutionary acts to acts of one of the other two kinds – either to mere sayings, or to the things we achieve by means of saying things. The tendency to assimilate illocutionary acts to locutionary acts – mere sayings – may be associated with the theoretical, semantically-oriented line of the analytic tradition. Austin himself is not at all sceptical about this tradition. Indeed, he seems to adopt without question the idea that words have both Sense and reference, and is in that respect an orthodox Fregean. His point is rather that concentration on the meaning of words misses something central about language.

Nor is that central thing to be understood by thinking of language as a tool by means of which certain desirable results can be achieved. To rush too quickly from concentration on locutionary acts – mere sayings – to focus on what can be achieved by means of language is to ignore the importance of illocutionary acts from the other side, on Austin's view. This is manifested in the tendency to assimilate illocutionary acts to *perlocutionary* acts. Austin's concern is to make us focus on *illocutionary* acts, which are, in a sense, intermediate between the locutionary and the perlocutionary.

But why should the illocutionary act be particularly important? Consider the two obvious uses of a sentence like (1a):

(1a) I will be there.

We expect this to be uttered in the making of a promise, but it could (given a suitable context) be used to make a prediction. On Austin's view, if an utterance of (1a) is the making of a prediction, then we will have something which is true or false (according to whether or not the utterer is, in fact, in the place in question at the relevant time); but if it is the making of a promise, there will be nothing for which the question of truth and falsity even arises. Whether or not we have a bit of language (to put it deliberately loosely) which is capable of truth or falsehood seems to depend on which illocutionary act is being performed. If this is right, it has both a specific significance in the history of the philosophy of language, and a general significance for understanding what matters about language.

The specific significance is that if Austin is right, it will at least be more complicated to take a Fregean or Davidsonian approach to semantics, and explain the meaning of words in terms of the truth of sentences. For declarative sentences, on their own, will not be true or false: we will only have something capable of truth or falsity once an appropriate illocutionary act has been performed.

The general point about language follows on from that. If Austin is right, many of the most important features of the language we encounter will depend on the illocutionary act being performed, rather than on the meaning of words and sentences. When we're faced with someone saying something, it's evidently of fundamental importance whether we're being faced with a question or a statement or a command. The issue will not be determined just by grammar – though we might expect grammar often to provide a clue – but will depend on what illocutionary act is being performed.

12.4 Truth and performatives

On Austin's view, both of the following sentences may be used to make the same promise:

(1) I promise that I'll be there;
(1a) I will be there.

And both of the following sentences can be used to make the same statement:

(6) I state that the cat is dead;
(6a) The cat is dead.

According to Austin, nothing true is said by either (1) or (1a) (on this use) and just one thing is stated by both (6) and (6a) – that the cat is dead – and this can be true or false. The role of the phrases 'I promise that' and 'I state that' is, on his view, just to make explicit what illocutionary act is being performed in the utterance of the sentence which follows. If I utter (1) in the way which makes it roughly 'equivalent' to (1a), or (6) in the way which makes it roughly 'equivalent' to (6a), I do not state *that* I promise or *that* I state, nor do I describe myself as promising or stating.

The difficulty with this view is in finding an answer to Davidson's famous question (asked in another context): what are these familiar words doing here?[3] How can we explain what the word 'promise' is doing in (1) or what the word 'state' is doing in (2), while both respecting Austin's view and avoiding treating these words as being ambiguous? It's clear that these words do *something*: at the very least they introduce intensional contexts in (1) and (6) which are not present in (1a) and (6a). It's not obvious what should be said. In the light of this difficulty, some have supposed that utterances of (1) and (6) do, after all, make statements about the illocutionary acts being performed.

Kent Bach and Michael Harnish, for example, suggest that in uttering (1) I state that I promise that I will come.[4] This statement is true just in case I do, in fact, promise that I will come. Where and when do I actually make the promise? We may suppose that (1) is the only relevant sentence I utter. In that case, the promise must be contained in (1) itself. That is to say, in uttering (1) I make a statement (that I promise) which is made true by my uttering of that very sentence, (1), itself. We can now explain what the word 'promise' is doing in (1): it is doing exactly the same as the thing it does in the following two sentences:

(1b) I promised that I would be there;
(1c) She promises that she'll be there.

According to Bach and Harnish, in uttering (1) to make a promise, I'm really performing *two* illocutionary acts: I'm stating that I promise to be there, and – because that statement is true – I'm promising to be there. The same analysis is applied to utterances of such sentences as (6).

I think the principal reason why we might feel uncertain about this is probably what underlies Austin's insistence that if I utter (1) to make a promise, I don't state anything. (Austin himself offers no clear reasons.) Bach's and Harnish's view requires such an utterance of (1) to be *self-verifying*. There's a common intuition that what makes a statement true

---

[3] D. Davidson, 'On Saying That', *Inquiries into Truth and Interpretation* (Oxford: Oxford University Press, 1984), p. 94.

[4] K. Bach and R. M. Harnish, *Linguistic Communication and Speech Acts* (Cambridge, MA: MIT Press, 1979), pp. 203–9.

must be somehow independent of that statement itself. This is part of what lies behind the correspondence theory of truth, according to which a true statement is one which *corresponds* to a fact.[5] It seems part of the notion of correspondence that correspondence involves two independently existing entities, which happen to be correlated, but might not have been. Bach's and Harnish's suggestion seems to conflict with this correspondence intuition.

The intuition is not indubitable, though it's not indefensible either. The issues here are complex, and I can only hint at some of them here. We might note that if anyone manages to mean anything by uttering 'I exist', it seems bound to be true, and this might be thought to be a form of self-verification. But this doesn't seem to violate the original intuition, because the point remains that a person's existence is independent of her *saying* she exists. Again, it's natural to think that if someone says 'I am speaking', her utterance is self-verifying. But in most actual cases in which we might imagine this sentence being used (by an exasperated teacher addressing a class, for example), it's the utterance of the *surrounding* sentences, rather than that one, which is naturally understood to make the statement true. On the other side, we might think that there's a connection between this issue and the liar paradox. The liar paradox arises in the case of sentences like this:

(L) (L) is false.

It's not unnatural to think that the liar paradox is to be solved by insisting, in the manner of the correspondence theory, that what makes a statement true must be independent of that statement itself. But the proper treatment of the liar paradox is an enormous subject on its own; at the very least, it's far from obvious that there's no way of solving it while accepting Bach's and Harnish's account of performatives.[6]

Is there any alternative to Bach's and Harnish's account of what the word 'promise' is doing in (1) or the word 'state' in (6), which might allow us to follow Austin in denying that a promising use of (1) is true or false, or that an explicitly performative use of (6) states more than one thing? One suggestion that is worth pursuing is introducing the idea of special speech

---

[5] Austin himself seems to have accepted some form of correspondence theory of truth: see his 'Truth', *Aristotelian Society Supplementary Volume*, 24 (1950), pp. 111–29.

[6] For a brief introduction to the liar paradox, see R. M. Sainsbury, *Paradoxes*, 2nd edn (Cambridge: Cambridge University Press, 1995), ch 5.

acts of *referring*. We might suppose that whatever other speech acts we perform when we speak – acts of promising, stating, questioning, or whatever – we always also perform acts of referring by means of our words. We might here adopt a relatively orthodox world-directed view (in the anti-Fregean tradition started by Russell), and take uses of singular terms to involve acts of referring to objects, uses of predicates to involve acts of referring to qualities and relations, and uses of sentences to involve acts of referring to combinations of objects and qualities or relations, which we might call *states of affairs* or *situations*.[7]

This kind of theory faces two sorts of difficulty if it is to be offered as an alternative to the Bach–Harnish view. First, it needs to be explained how sentences can refer to states of affairs without being true or false. And secondly, it needs to deal with the various difficulties which have led Davidson and others to abandon referential accounts of meaning.[8] But if these problems can be dealt with, it may be that Austin's original intuition can be preserved.

12.5   Issues for a theory of speech acts

Austin's emphasis on the importance of illocutionary acts raises some questions for everyone concerned with the philosophy of language, and some questions specifically for those who aim to develop a theory of speech acts.

One central issue arises over the meaning of words. It seems undeniable that the meaning of words is, in some sense, prior to each individual illocutionary act. When I perform an illocutionary act, I exploit this prior meaning of the words I use. Austin himself seems to have a simple, conservative view of the meaning of words and sentences: they just have Sense and reference. He seems to suppose that this is something quite independent of speech-act theory. The difficulty is that it seems that truth and falsity only enter the picture once it has been determined that an illocutionary act of stating is being performed. This means that it's not

---

[7] A view of this general kind is offered by Stephen Barker, *Renewing Meaning: A Speech-Act Theoretic Approach* (Oxford: Oxford University Press, 2004).

[8] For Davidson's worries, see the opening pages of 'Truth and Meaning', in his *Inquiries into Truth and Interpretation* (Oxford: Oxford University Press, 1984), pp. 17–36. A related set of worries was considered in ch. 9, § 9.2.

clear how the meaning of words can be explained in terms of the truth of sentences. Indeed, it's hard to see how sentences can be true at all, on this view: they cannot even be true relative to an *occasion* of utterance, because it's the kind of illocutionary act being performed, rather than merely the reference given to each of the component words, which determines whether we have something capable of truth and falsity.

This raises a difficulty for everyone – including, most obviously, Frege and Davidson – who hopes to explain the meaning of words in terms of the truth of sentences. What else might we propose? There are two natural alternatives.

First, we might adopt some form of referential theory of meaning, as has just been suggested in offering an alternative to the Bach–Harnish view. We might suppose that singular terms refer to objects, predicates to properties and relations, and sentences to states of affairs or situations. Again, it will have to be claimed that we can make sense of sentences referring to states of affairs without being true or false; and we will have to deal with the traditional worries about referential theories.

Or, secondly, we might try building speech-act theory more thoroughly into our conception of semantics. We might attempt to explain the meaning of sentences in terms of the illocutionary acts that *could* be performed with them. Meaning will be explained in terms of illocutionary-act *potential.*[9] This suggestion itself is not without difficulty, however. After all, we've seen that the very same sentence can be used to perform quite different illocutionary acts – even when the words seem to have the same meaning. This was what we found with the groups of sentences (1)–(5) and (1a)–(5a).

Here's a natural way of dealing with that difficulty. Consider this sentence again:

(1a) I will be there.

If I use this to make a promise, the promise I make will be the promise *that I'll be there*; and if I use it to make a statement, the statement I make will be the statement *that I'll be there*. This idea can be generalized. If I use a sentence to ask a question, then *what* question I ask will be determined by

---

[9] This approach is championed by William Alston in his *Illocutionary Acts and Sentence Meaning* (Ithaca: Cornell University Press, 2000), although the details presented below are not his.

the meaning of the sentence. If I use a sentence to give an order, then *what* order I give will be determined by the meaning of the sentence.

We may then suggest that the meaning of a sentence is a matter of what *particular* illocutionary act would be performed by it, once it is determined what general *type* of illocutionary act it is. Can we perhaps formalize that suggestion, with a view to giving an explicit semantic theory for a language? Here's how we might begin, at the level of sentences at least.

(IAM) A sentence *s* means that *p* if and only if

For any illocutionary act type *A*, anyone who *As* in uttering *s* thereby *As* that *p*.

So it will follow that, if *s* means that *p*, if someone makes a *promise* in uttering *s*, she will be promising that *p*, and if someone makes a *prediction* in uttering *s*, she will be predicting that *p* – and so on. If we begin with something like (IAM) as the account of the meaning of sentences, some work will have to be done to explain what it is for words to have meaning, and how the meaning of sentences is dependent on the meaning of the word of which they are composed. But it may be that existing semantic theories can be adapted to the purpose.[10]

If this and some form of referential theory are the two natural options for a speech-act theorist who's concerned to explain word-meaning, it's arguable that speech-act theory introduces nothing very radically new to the study of semantics.[11] The general shape of the options seems not much different from what was available before we considered speech acts: on the one hand, a referential theory; on the other, a theory which aims to use sentences to state the meaning of sentences within statements of the familiar form '*s* means that *p*'.

In that case, the fundamental task for speech-act theories is to understand the character of the acts which are performed in the use of words and sentences. One central question is this: what determines what illocutionary act is performed when someone speaks? It's natural to think that the intention of the speaker has something to do with it. A further

---

[10] Note that an extensional theory, like a Tarskian truth-theory will face at least the usual problems, since '*x* As that … ', where '*A*' is schematic for some illocutionary verb, introduces an intensional context.

[11] Though presumably this claim would be challenged by Barker: see his *Renewing Meaning*.

question is whether an illocutionary act needs to conform to rules established by convention. Austin's view seems to have been that the various kinds of illocutionary act are established by convention, and someone counts as performing a particular kind of illocutionary act (promising, say, or asserting) in virtue of meeting the conventionally established conditions for performing acts of that kind. It is not entirely clear what kind of convention Austin had in mind, but we can develop something which seems in the spirit of his work by beginning with the case of promising, and generalizing some of its crucial features.

At the beginning of his book, much of Austin's focus is on certain kinds of illocutionary act which seem obviously institutional. The naming of a ship, the sentencing of a criminal, the official opening of a festival, giving notice of a meeting, are all acts which take place within institutions. Acts of these kinds are evidently bound by rules, which set boundaries for the acts' being properly performed: they need to be performed by the right people, in the right way, on the right occasions, and so on. The institutions and the rules which bind them are naturally thought to be conventional. These institutions are not natural objects – they don't simply grow like trees – so their constitutive rules are, in a sense, arbitrary: other institutions, with different constitutive rules, could have been established. Moreover, these institutions are established and kept in place by the agreement and connivance of their members and the people who interact with them.

Promises are not exactly like these obviously institutional acts, but they may seem to have some affinity with them. We may speak of an institution of promising – the fact that we give and accept promises, and act on the basis of them – but this isn't an institution like a club or society, nor is it one like a judicial system. Nevertheless, the practice of making promises need not have existed, and seems to depend for its continued existence on the attitudes and behaviour of the group of people who accept each other's promises. Within this 'institution' we can recognize certain kinds of rules for promises to be genuine promises: we can see that there are questions about who can legitimately promise what, and on whose behalf, for example.

It's not obvious that the same applies to the large majority of illocutionary acts, however. It's natural to think, for example, that the illocutionary acts of informing and of asking questions are essential to the nature of language itself. There may be some sense in which language as a whole is conventional, but that doesn't immediately make these particular types of illocutionary act conventional. Austin's view that all types of illocutionary act are conventional seems to require that there could be languages without acts of informing or questioning: these have to be thought of as particular routines which happen to have sprung up in particular languages and are sustained by the consent of their speakers – although they could, in principle, be abandoned.

Others oppose Austin's view. According to Bach and Harnish, for example, the fundamental types of illocutionary act are fixed by the states of mind which they express; and there need be nothing conventional about them. One fundamental type (Bach and Harnish call them *constative*, for obvious reasons) are expressions of *belief*: if I assert that the cat is dead, for example, I express the belief that the cat is dead. Bach and Harnish call another fundamental type *directives*, which they define as expressions of the speaker's attitude towards some prospective action by the hearer:[12] if I ask Winnie to shut the door, for example, I'm expressing my desire that she shut the door. On their view there are no specific procedures which have to be followed to perform an act of one of these types. There are no conventional rules which have to be followed in order to perform them.

So what is it to perform an illocutionary act, on such a view? It is, fundamentally, to intend to do something which is an expression of a particular attitude (belief, desire, or whatever). If we put this together with the preliminary account of sentence meaning proposed in (IAM), we have an account of meaning on something like the following lines. What a sentence means is a matter of what would be believed, desired (or whatever) by someone who really had the attitude she intended to express in uttering the sentence. This anticipates the account of meaning proposed by H. P. Grice, which is the subject of the next chapter.[13]

Further reading

The classic text in speech-act theory, after Austin's *How to Do Things with Words*, is John Searle's *Speech Acts* (Cambridge: Cambridge University Press,

---

[12] Their full taxonomy of types of illocutionary acts is to be found in *Linguistic Communication and Speech Acts*, ch. 3.

[13] This is hardly surprising, of course: Bach and Harnish make extensive use of work on the Gricean account of meaning.

1969). Searle follows Austin in thinking that speech acts presuppose institutions with rules for performing particular types of illocutionary act. This view is opposed by P.F. Strawson, 'Intention and Convention in Speech Acts', in his *Logico-Linguistic Papers* (London: Methuen, 1971), an article which is also significant in the development of Grice's account of meaning (the topic of chapter 13 below). Kent Bach and Michael Harnish develop a theory of speech acts which follows Strawson rather than Searle in this respect: K. Bach and R.M. Harnish, *Linguistic Communication and Speech Acts* (Cambridge, MA: MIT Press, 1979). A recent revival of the Austin-Searle tradition in this respect is W. Alston, *Illocutionary Acts and Sentence Meaning* (Ithaca: Cornell University Press, 2000): this work also develops an 'illocutionary act potential' theory of sentence meaning. A thoroughly worked (and therefore quite technical) attempt to do speech-act semantics, using the idea that sentences represent states of affairs, is S. Barker, *Renewing Meaning: A Speech-Act Theoretic Approach* (Oxford: Oxford University Press, 2004).

13   Grice on meaning

Key text

H. P. Grice, 'Meaning', *The Philosophical Review*, 66 (1957), pp. 377–88.

13.1   Introduction

In the last few chapters, we've been circling round what may seem to be the most basic question in the philosophy of language: what is it for linguistic expressions to have meaning at all? Quine's and Davidson's insistence on the central importance of radical interpretation does say something relevant to this question. They claim, in effect, that what is meant in one language is always open, in principle, to being captured in another language. And they make it central to meaning that it is something to be understood in the course of a general project of understanding people. Working from another angle, Austin's work places language among the actions that are performed in getting things done. But none of this seems to address the basic question directly.

And the basic question can seem very pressing – almost bewildering, in fact. For suppose we think, as it can seem very natural to think, that words are, at bottom, just types of mark or sound: things which have no meaning in themselves.[1] How *could* something like that have any meaning at all? This is the question which Paul Grice seems to be addressing in a series of papers, beginning with the ground-breaking 'Meaning', which is the focus of this chapter. The precise details of his answer have often been questioned, but many of the questioners (who include Grice himself) have been in broad sympathy with his approach. Grice's original paper

---

[1] This is the Lockean assumption which we identified as (L8) in ch. 1.

inaugurated a whole research programme within the philosophy of language, which has dominated one side of the analytic tradition. And the influence continues, even if it is not always acknowledged. Something like Grice's answer to the basic question can seem irresistible as long as we think that a language is a system of intrinsically meaningless things which (somehow) have meaning.

13.2 Grice's overall strategy

Insofar as he's concerned with language at all, Grice's ultimate aim is to explain the notion of meaning as it applies to linguistic expressions (such as sentences, words, or phrases). He wants to define this notion of linguistic meaning in terms which he takes to be more fundamental. The definition itself is quite complex, and has been subject to numerous objections and revisions, so that what might now be offered as a plausible Gricean definition is even more complicated than Grice's own version. Nevertheless, the basic idea is quite simple, and it may be tempting to think that some version of it must survive all of the objections which have been made to the various detailed proposals produced within the Gricean programme.

Grice takes himself to be trying to understand the everyday notion of meaning, which has much wider application than just to linguistic expressions. He begins by making a division within this general notion of meaning, between what he calls *natural* and what he calls *non-natural* meaning. As an example of *natural* meaning, we might suggest this:

(1) Those spots mean that she has measles.

And as an example of *non-natural* meaning, we might suggest this:

(2) Three rings on the bell mean that the bus is full.

Despite the similarity in form of these two statements of meaning, Grice thinks that there's something fundamentally different going on in them. I think Grice's own account of the difference slightly disguises the reasoning which underlies his whole approach to linguistic meaning. Here, slightly differently put, are the basic marks of difference Grice finds:

(i) In the case of *natural* meaning, 'X means that p' implies that it is true that p (in our case, (1) implies that she really does have measles); this does not hold for *non-natural* meaning (so, in the case of (2), the bell might have been rung three times by mistake);

(ii) In the case of *non-natural* meaning, what follows 'means that' could be put in quotation marks (the rings meant 'the bus is full'); this is not possible with natural meaning;

(iii) Natural meaning can be understood as the significance of certain *facts* (such as the fact that she has spots), whereas non-natural meaning is concerned with the significance of certain *objects* or *features of objects*.

These three marks of difference seem to go with another:

(iv) Statements of *non-natural* meaning of the form '*X* means that *p*' imply that *somebody* meant that *p* by *X* (in the case of (2), that *somebody* meant that the bus was full by three rings on the bell); but this is not the case with natural meaning.

If we see Grice's marks of difference in this way, we can see that his distinction between natural and non-natural meaning in fact provides the basis of an intuitive *argument* for his account of linguistic meaning. The argument will become easier to see when we realize that it's not really a distinction between what is and what is not *natural* which provides the basis of the differences which Grice finds between cases like (1), on the one hand, and (2), on the other. The real difference between (1) and (2) lies, I think, in the fact that (2) expresses a *teleological* conception of meaning, whereas (1) does not. Teleology, in general, is concerned with what has a goal, or purpose, or point. The kind of meaning involved in (2) is the meaning of something which is *supposed* to show something, in some sense: those three rings of the bell are there *in order* to show that the bus is full. This, I think, explains (i)–(iii) of the Gricean marks of difference. The fact that something is *supposed* to show that the bus is full allows that it can be faulty – in our example, that it can be produced even when the bus is not full. This same point explains why it is natural to express the meaning in quotation: the quotation isolates what seems to be shown from the actual facts. And it is objects, or features of objects, which have purposes – not facts.

This accounts for the Gricean marks (i)–(iii). Mark (iv) now appears in a slightly different light, and in fact to be overstated. It's not that statements of non-natural meaning *imply* that somebody meant something: it's rather that this is the best – perhaps the only conceivable – *explanation* of how they could be true. So there's no strict *implication* from (2) that some *person* meant that the bus was full; it's rather that we cannot understand how (2) could be true unless that was the case. If it's right that marks (i)–(iii) express the difference between a teleological and a non-teleological notion of meaning, then the Gricean mark (iv) is really an application to the notion of meaning of a general claim about teleology – we might call it the *Creation Condition*:

(CC) No mere object can really have a purpose unless somebody has made it have that purpose.

Once this assumption is exposed, we can think about questioning it: I'll return to it at the end.

As far as language goes, Grice's target is an account of the meaning of linguistic expressions. Consider the case of a simple declarative sentence (a sentence of a kind suitable for stating something). Suppose that E is such a sentence. Then the task is to explain what has to be true for something of the following form to be true:

(E) E means that p.

This is clearly a statement of 'non-natural' (that is to say, teleological) meaning. (To show this Grice carefully writes '$_{NN}$' after every use of 'means' when it's 'non-natural' meaning which is at issue. Since we'll *only* be concerned with 'non-natural' – that is, teleological – meaning from now on, this careful precaution is unnecessary.) In that case, given (CC), something like (E) can only be true in virtue of somebody having somehow made E have that meaning. That is to say, the truth of something like (E) depends, in the end, on facts about speakers. Suppose that S is a speaker; then the core facts on which statements like (E) depend are of this form:

(S) S means that p by E.

Grice, however, thinks that there's an important difference between statements of expression-meaning (like (E)) and statements of speaker-meaning (like (S)), which these formulations conceal. I cannot make an expression really mean something just by meaning something by it. The meaning of an expression is something stable, which resides in the expression itself, in some sense; whereas what I mean by an expression may depend just on the circumstances of a moment. Moreover, we may think that I can mean by an expression something other than what the expression itself means. (So we may think that someone may use the word 'refute' to mean *reject*, when that's not what the word means.) Grice expresses the distinction by saying that the meaning of an expression is *timeless*, whereas a speaker will only mean something by an expression on particular occasions. If we remember that we're dealing with teleology, we might compare this with the difference between a table-leg, the very point of whose existence is to hold up one corner of a table, and a pile of books, which I might use to prop up my table on a particular occasion.

In his original paper, 'Meaning', Grice offers a simple link between speaker-meaning (what is stated by sentences of the form of (S)) and expression-meaning (what is stated by sentences of the form of (E)). If we borrow something of the careful informality which is characteristic of Grice's own formulations, we can express the core of his original definition of expression-meaning in terms of speaker-meaning (for the case of simple declarative sentences), as follows:

(SE) *E* means that *p* if and only if 'people' (vague) mean that *p* by *E*.

Although Grice is not explicit about this, the suggestion here seems to be that for an expression to mean something (this is what Grice calls *timeless* meaning) is for people habitually or conventionally to mean something by it on particular occasions.

Grice is not content merely to explain expression-meaning in terms of speaker-meaning, however. He even offers an account of speaker-meaning. But even in the case of speaker-meaning, Grice seems – in the original paper, at least – still to be concerned with the meaning of an object or of a feature of an object. When we say something like (S), we're stating the speaker-meaning *of an expression*. That is to say, we're concerned with a meaning which an expression has, even if only temporarily and in the mouth of a particular person.

If this is right, what Grice is concerned with in speaker-meaning is something's playing temporarily, and for a particular person, the kind of role which a linguistic expression plays less fleetingly in a language. So when someone means something by an expression, that expression has, temporarily and for that person, the same kind of function as expressions in general have in languages. (This is comparable to the pile of books I use to prop up my table: that pile of books has, temporarily and for the circumstances, the same function as a table leg has in its very nature.)

What kind of function do expressions have in languages? Here Grice appeals to a very traditional conception of language – we found it in Locke – according to which it is the business of language to communicate. So when a speaker means something by an expression, what she does is somehow bestow on that expression a certain communicative function.

If we accept the creation condition (CC), we will think that the basis of something's having a function will be somebody's deliberate action. And at the basis of deliberate action is intention. So the core of Grice's account of speaker-meaning is the idea of someone using an expression with a certain communicative intention. Let us consider the case of an expression, E, which is a declarative sentence, used to describe something. Grice's 'first shot' at analysing this can be expressed as follows:

(S1) S means that p by E if and only if S produces E with the intention of getting an audience to believe that p.

But Grice finds this unsatisfactory: he thinks it fails to capture the difference between *telling* someone something (which is what he wants for genuine communication) and merely *letting her know*.

The crucial thing, according to Grice, is that for genuine communication to take place, the audience must recognize what the speaker is trying to do, and this must play a role in how the audience is affected. His revised account of speaker-meaning (for the case of declarative sentences) can be formulated like this:

(S2) S means that p by E if and only if S produces E with the intention of getting an audience A to believe that p by means of A's recognition of that very intention.

The basic idea here, I think, is that genuine communication between a speaker and her audience requires the audience to know what the speaker is up to when she produces some linguistic expression: in some sense, everything must be in the open between speaker and hearer.

13.3 Sympathetic objections to Grice's account of speaker-meaning

Grice's proposal has faced a very large number of objections. Many of these have been produced by people who are broadly sympathetic with Grice's view, and the objections have inspired them to produce modifications of their own within the larger Gricean programme. Other objections are more deeply hostile. In this section and the next, I'll deal with some objections of the first kind.

To begin with, though, it's worth noting a kind of objection which I won't pursue in any detail. The core of Grice's notion of speaker-meaning is the idea that what a speaker means by an expression is a matter of her *communicative* intentions. But perhaps not all uses of language are communicative: am I trying to communicate something if I write a shopping list, or if I write a poem? It's not obvious. The Gricean could say one of two things in response to this worry. First, she could claim that these uses are communicative after all. Or, secondly, she could claim that the meaning of expressions is really established by the communicative uses, and any non-communicative uses are simply parasitic on these. I won't consider here whether either of these responses is finally satisfactory.

Within the broadly sympathetic objections, we can distinguish between those which are objections to the account of speaker-meaning, and those which are objections to the account of expression-meaning in terms of speaker-meaning. A whole sequence of problems with the definition of speaker-meaning was inaugurated by P. F. Strawson.[2] First, Strawson offers a less informal specification of what he takes to be Grice's analysis of speaker meaning. Adapting it to the specific case of declarative sentences, we can write Strawson's version as follows:

(S3) S means that p by an utterance of E if and only if
   (i) S intends that the utterance of E should get an audience A to believe that p;
   (ii) S intends that A should recognize the intention (i); and
   (iii) S intends that A's recognition of the intention (i) should be part of A's reason for believing that p.

We'll see in section 13.6 that this formulation introduces a significant divergence from the letter – if not, perhaps, from the spirit – of Grice's original proposal.[3] But let's leave that on one side for the moment, and concentrate on Strawson's point.

---

[2] P. F. Strawson, 'Intention and Convention in Speech Acts', *Philosophical Review*, 73 (1964), pp. 439–60.

[3] Grice himself adopts something very like it in 'Utterer's Meaning and Intentions'.

Strawson presses further Grice's point about the difference between *telling* and *letting know*.[4] If genuine communication requires that the audience knows what the speaker is up to, and the speaker wants to be genuinely communicating, Strawson thinks clauses (ii) and (iii) of (S3) won't be enough. Doesn't genuine communication require the audience to recognize other intentions beyond the one described in line (i)? Strawson thinks we need to add at least one further clause:

(iv) *S* intends that *A* should recognize the intention (ii).

We might suspect that we're now embarked on an indefinite series of refinements: every extra intention we mention needs itself to be intended to be recognized, if the speaker really wants the hearer to know what she's up to. This is in effect what Stephen Schiffer has argued.[5] He claims that there's an infinite regress here: the Gricean analysis cannot be completed. And Grice himself came later to accept the point.[6]

But how should a Gricean react to this? The literature contains at least three broadly Gricean responses. First, there's Schiffer's own.[7] Schiffer elaborates and formalizes the idea that in genuine communication everything is open between speaker and hearer. He thinks that there's a familiar phenomenon, which he calls *mutual knowledge**. Here's a version of the example he introduces to explain the notion. Sally and Harry are enjoying a candlelit dinner. They're seated opposite each other, and on the table between them is a large and conspicuous candle; they sit watching the reflection of the candle (and themselves) in each other's eyes. Sally knows that there's a candle on the table; she also knows that Harry knows that too. Furthermore, she knows that Harry knows that she knows that he knows that. And she knows that Harry knows that she knows that he

---

[4] Strawson himself doesn't put the issue like this. His revision is supposed to be shown to be required by an intuitive consideration of a counter-example. I think the counter-example is less intuitive – and certainly less easy to understand – than the principle about communication which I think it's supposed to support.

[5] S. Schiffer, *Meaning* (Oxford: Oxford University Press, 1972), ch. 2. Again, Schiffer doesn't make his point by appeal to a simple principle about genuine communication, as I have here. Instead he uses a series of increasingly – indeed, bewilderingly – complex counter-examples. Once again, I think the principle is much more intuitive than any response to the counter-examples.

[6] H. P. Grice, 'Meaning Revisited', in his *Studies in the Ways of Words*, pp. 283–303.

[7] Schiffer, *Meaning*, pp. 30 ff.

knows that she knows that he knows that. And so on. It seems that there is an infinite number of things which Sally knows. And, of course, Harry on his side of the table knows just as much.

There's clearly some kind of regress here, but Schiffer claims that it's entirely harmless: it's a simple consequence of the common and innocent situation in which, as he puts it, all the relevant facts are 'out in the open'.[8] In general, two people S and A will have mutual knowledge* that p just in case:

  (i) S knows that p;
 (ii) A knows that p;
(iii) S knows that A knows that p;
 (iv) A knows that S knows that p;
  (v) S knows that A knows that S knows that p;
 (vi) A knows that S knows that A knows that p;
And so on.[9]

Schiffer uses the idea of mutual knowledge* to make a single once-and-for-all revision of the Gricean definition (S3). Here is a formulation which captures the heart of his proposal:

(S4) S means that p by an utterance of E if and only if S intended that the utterance of E should bring about a state of affairs M with the following feature:
  M is sufficient for S and an audience A to mutually know* –
  (i) that M obtains;
 (ii) that S intends that the utterance of E should get A to believe that p;
(iii) that S intends that A should recognize the intention (ii); and
 (iv) that S intends that A's recognition of the intention (ii) should be part of A's reason for believing that p.

Here we can see clauses (i)–(iii) of (S3) appearing embedded within clauses (ii)–(iv) as part of what the speaker means to be mutually known*.

---

[8] Ibid., p. 32.

[9] This idea is modified slightly by David Lewis, in his 'Languages and Language', in K. Gunderson, ed., *Language, Mind and Knowledge* (Minneapolis: University of Minnesota Press, 1975), pp. 3–35. Lewis imagines that it will be enough that the speaker and the audience would have each piece of knowledge if they bothered to think about it.

This proposal seems to close off the regress which was felt to threaten (S3), but it's still forbiddingly complex. Moreover, one might doubt that the infinite complexity of knowledge involved in Schiffer's technical notion of mutual knowledge is really as harmless as he claims: do we really have psychological states of that complexity?

Grice himself eventually reacted differently to the regress which seems to threaten (S3).[10] He returned directly to the spirit of the original proposal, and drew out something which he felt was implicit there, without being acknowledged. The original proposal made implicit appeal to something like *genuine* or *true* communication. In a later work, Grice suggested that there is something ineliminably *evaluative* about the conception involved here; and he proposed to bring that out explicitly. He therefore suggested the following very simple account of speaker-meaning, for the case of a declarative sentence:

(S5) S means that p by an utterance of E if and only if in uttering E S is in a state which is *optimal* for communicating that p.

And he suggested that this analysis can be correct even if it turns out that the conditions which are optimal for communicating that p cannot possibly be realized. Genuine communication is a kind of ideal, which we never quite reach. But in everyday life we can *say* that we're communicating, provided we're close enough to the ideal for the everyday purposes we have in mind. In just the same way, although we can never draw a perfect circle, it's quite all right for everyday purposes to say that someone has drawn a circle on a board.

The third response to the apparently infinite proliferation of complexity in Gricean analyses is disarmingly simple. In his original review of Schiffer's book, Gilbert Harman suggested that the difficulties only arise because Griceans (including Grice himself, after his original article) were concerned to avoid appealing to reflexive, or self-referential intentions.[11] Notice that my formulation of Grice's original proposal (which is entirely true to Grice's article in this respect) appeals to a self-referential intention:

---

[10] In 'Meaning Revisited'.

[11] G. Harman, *Review of* Meaning, *by Stephen Schiffer*, *Journal of Philosophy*, 71 (1974), pp. 224–9.

(S2) S means that p by E if and only if S produces E with the intention of getting an audience A to believe that p by means of A's recognition of *that very intention.*

But by the time we get to the Strawsonian reformulation (S3), that self-referential intention has been removed in favour of stratified intentions. Harman claims that (S2) is simply not vulnerable to the infinite series of counter-examples which face (S3) and its successors. Moreover, he says, we should acknowledge that all intentions are self-referential anyway: if I intend to do something, I always intend to do it in virtue of that very intention.

This solution won't please everyone, despite its attractive simplicity. There seems to be something worryingly unspecifiable about the content of a self-referential intention. Where (S2) mentions the phrase 'that very intention', it seems that we should be able to specify the intention in question. So we start trying to put in its place a specification of the intention: 'that A believe that p by means of A's recognition that … ' At this point we realize that we have to put the same words again in the gap marked by those dots; and so on indefinitely. Well, we might ask, can there really be an intention whose content cannot be specified?

13.4   Sympathetic objections to Grice's account of expression-meaning

The crucial feature of Grice's account of expression-meaning is that it explains expression-meaning in terms of speaker-meaning. I shall count any objection to Grice's account of expression-meaning a *sympathetic* objection, if it preserves this crucial feature, while disagreeing with the letter of Grice's original proposal.

Here was my formulation of Grice's original proposal, for the case of declarative sentences:

(SE) E means that p if and only if 'people' (vague) mean that p by E.

As I noted, this suggests that an expression's meaning something depends on there being a *custom* or *convention* to mean that by the expression. This suggestion has been explored and elaborated in great detail.[12] Sympathetic

---

[12] See D. Lewis, *Convention* (Cambridge, MA: Harvard University Press, 1969); S. Schiffer, *Meaning*, ch 5.

objections to Grice's proposal deny that any custom or convention is required, while accepting that expression-meaning is to be explained in terms of speaker-meaning.

A particularly dramatic objector is Davidson.[13] He draws our attention to the existence of *malapropisms*. A malapropism (named after Mrs Malaprop, a character in Sheridan's play, *The Rivals*) is a use of one word (or near-word) where another would have been, in some sense, more appropriate. A famous example of Mrs Malaprop's own is this:

She is as headstrong as an allegory on the banks of the Nile.[14]

Davidson's view of malapropisms seems to commit him to the following claims:

(i) Mrs Malaprop here means *alligator* by the word 'allegory';
(ii) Her audience (us, for example) understands her to mean *alligator* by the word 'allegory' here;
(iii) Given (i) and (ii), 'allegory' *does* mean *alligator* here.[15]

Davidson's view (expressed in (iii) here) seems to be that an expression means what someone can be understood to mean by it. And he takes the existence of malapropisms to show that no convention or custom of an expression's meaning that p is needed for someone to be capable of being understood to mean that p by it. Nor need there have been any convention in the past. In this situation, according to Davidson, we manage somehow to work out what Mrs Malaprop means, on the basis of our previous knowledge (what Davidson calls our *prior* theory). But this previous knowledge may itself be no more than what we have acquired in making sense of particular people in particular situations in the past – in just the same way as we are now making sense of Mrs Malaprop. If our making sense of Mrs Malaprop now depends on no convention, then our previous

---

[13] D. Davidson, 'A Nice Derangement of Epitaphs', in E. Lepore, ed., *Truth and Interpretation: Perspectives on the Philosophy of Donald Davidson* (Oxford: Blackwell, 1986), pp. 433–46.

[14] R. B. Sheridan, *The Rivals*, Act 3, Scene 3. Davidson in fact concentrates on another example from the same scene of the same play: 'If I reprehend anything in this world, it is the use of my oracular tongue, and a nice derangement of epitaphs.' But this example needs more explanation than the one I've chosen.

[15] In fact, of course, there are crocodiles, not alligators, on the banks of the Nile.

success in making sense of other people on particular occasions depends on no convention either.

What this means is that Davidson has no use for what Grice calls *timeless* meaning, and others have called the *standard* meaning of expressions. In fact, he has no use for languages, in the ordinary sense of that term: according to Davidson, there is never any theoretical point in appealing to such languages as English, French, German, or Japanese. He claims still to be able to distinguish between speaker-meaning and expression-meaning: he thinks that the distinction is needed to understand figurative uses of language, in which a speaker uses the meaning of the words in order to say something which would not normally or standardly (in some sense of those terms) be said by means of those words. But expression-meaning has become a transitory thing, fixed to particular circumstances of use.

Davidson's claims are not beyond question. To begin with, it's not clear that (i) is true. Mrs Malaprop surely intended to be using the word 'allegory' in its ordinary sense: she was just wrong (or careless) about its ordinary sense. We might then say that she meant *allegory* by 'allegory', but thought that allegories were predatory reptiles. And we needn't accept (iii) either: even if we can understand what someone meant to say when she used a word, there can still be such a thing as *the* meaning of the word, which she is simply wrong about. And we might still think that this notion of *the* meaning of a word is to be explained by convention.

The other sympathetic (or sympathetic-seeming) objection to Grice's original account of expression-meaning comes from Grice himself. He came to think that what an expression means may have some connection with what people mean by it on particular occasions, but there's no necessary connection with convention. For, he says:

> I can invent a language, call it Deutero-Esperanto, which nobody ever speaks. That makes me the authority, and I can lay down what is proper.[16]

He thinks this use of the evaluative concept of what is *proper* is not incidental here. It is, indeed, the crucial thing: convention may be one way of establishing what's proper, but it's not the only way. Grice therefore suggests an explicitly evaluative revision of his original proposal, which we might formulate like this:

---

[16] 'Meaning Revisited', p. 298–9.

(SE*) E means that p if and only if it is *proper* to mean that p by E.[17]

There is a risk that this will turn out to be a more significant revision to the original proposal than it seems. The original proposal seems to be trying to explain how what seem to be mere objects – certain marks and sounds – can have meaning. The difficulty was to see how the meaning could, as it were, attach to the objects themselves. Grice's original proposal seems to work like this. The core concept is that of a *person* meaning something. That seems relatively unmysterious. If we explain the meaning of an expression as conventional person-meaning, we seem to be able to preserve that unmysteriousness. In effect, we're never really talking about the expression, as such, meaning anything: we're simply using the notion of person-meaning, but because we have a convention in place, we no longer need to mention any particular people. Very roughly, expression-meaning is understood as person-meaning without reference to any particular person.

It's not clear that this is preserved in (SE*). For *whom* is it proper to mean that p by E? A natural answer is: for whoever is speaking the language to which E belongs. But here we're appealing to a conception of a language as something which has meaning. The difficulty is that we're now making implicit use of an unexplained notion of expression-meaning. We may be able to explain the circumstances in which a particular expression has a particular meaning, but we no longer seem to be addressing the question which made the Gricean programme so compelling in the first instance. We no longer seem to be explaining how it makes sense for such a thing as a mark or sound to have meaning at all. If this is right, this Gricean revision is not quite as sympathetic as it originally seemed to be.

13.5   An unsympathetic objection to Grice's account of expression-meaning

Recall again my formulation of Grice's account of expression-meaning, which uses Grice's own informal terms:

(SE) E means that p if and only if 'people' (vague) mean that p by E.

---

[17] Grice's own formulation uses the notion of what is *optimal*, but (SE*) is simpler.

Mark Platts has raised the following objection to this proposal.[18] It's possible to construct an infinite number of sentences in most languages. Even if the number of sentences which can be constructed in a language is just very large, we can be sure that a large number of them will never have been used. If they've never been used at all, then they will obviously never have been used with particular meanings, and there will be no habit or convention of 'people' (however vague) to mean anything by them. So at the very least, (SE) needs to be amended to something like this:

(SE**) E means that p if and only if, if 'people' (vague) *were* to use E, they *would* mean that p by E.

But what does (SE**) depend on? What makes it true that people *would* mean something by an as yet unused sentence? Surely, suggests Platts, the reason why people *would* mean that by the sentence is that that's what the sentence means. But if this is the answer we give, then it seems that the Gricean account fails to explain expression-meaning in terms of speaker-meaning, since its account of speaker-meaning depends on expression-meaning.

There is certainly something the Gricean can say to this, which may be enough to deal with the difficulty. There seems to be a way of accepting that what people *would* mean by an unused sentence is determined by what the sentence means, and still giving an account of that in terms of speaker-meaning. Here's one way of doing it. The meaning of a certain finite stock of sentences is explained in terms of speaker-meaning. The meaning of these sentences is determined by the fact that 'people' (vague) mean something by them. But these sentences have parts. Once the meaning of the sentences is fixed, the meaning of the parts is fixed too. And once the meaning of the parts is fixed, then the meaning of any sentence which can be constructed from those parts is also fixed – even it has never been used.

Some Griceans have put the matter in another way.[19] They take languages to be, not historical entities like English, German, or Japanese,

---

[18] M. Platts, *Ways of Meaning* (London: Routledge and Kegan Paul, 1979), pp. 229 ff.

[19] The suggestion derives from Lewis, 'Languages and Language'. It is followed in B. Loar, 'Two Theories of Meaning', in G. Evans and J. McDowell, eds., *Truth and Meaning: Essays in Semantics* (Oxford: Oxford University Press, 1976), pp. 138–61, and C. Peacocke, 'Truth Definitions and Actual Languages', in the same volume, pp. 162–88.

which have traditions of use in real populations, but abstract entities which consist essentially of pairings of symbols with interpretations of them. A language, in this abstract sense, is therefore an assignment of meanings to signs. There's a sense in which a language like this can exist even if no one ever uses it: as long as it's *possible* for these signs to have such an interpretation, the language may be said to exist. A language, in this sense, comes with its own theory of meaning. The language has a fixed grammar, which determines what the words are, and how they may be combined to form sentences. And a meaning is assigned to all of the words, in such a way as to allow us to derive the meaning of every sentence which can be constructed from them.

We may imagine, then, that there's an indefinite number of languages, in this abstract sense: that is, there's an indefinite number of possible assignments of meaning to all the possible signs. When we come to consider a particular population, the question we need to ask is: which of all these possible languages is the language which they actually speak? Which language is their *actual* language? And this question can be given a broadly Gricean answer. A language (in the sense of an assignment of meanings to signs) is the actual language of a given population if the communicative intentions of the population are made sense of by supposing that that's the language they are deploying. If we adopt a conventionalist version of a Gricean account, we'll say something like this: for a language *L* to be the actual language of a population is for there to be a convention in that population to use sentences with the meaning which *L* in fact assigns to them.

The Gricean may yet face a challenge: these two proposals make use of the notion of parts of sentences having meaning, but how is the meaning of parts of sentences to be characterized on either of them? It may seem that it will have to be in quite familiar terms (for example, in terms of reference for names, and truth-of for predicates).[20] And then it might seem as if the fundamental notion of expression-meaning – as it applies to *parts* of sentences – has not been explained in terms of speaker-meaning. I think this challenge can be met, however. The solution is for the Gricean to insist that the meaning of parts of sentences is nothing more than their

---

[20] These are, of course, the central notions in a Davidsonian truth-theoretical account of meaning.

contribution to the meaning of whole sentences of which they can be parts.[21] She should insist, further, that the notions which are brought in to characterize the meaning of parts of sentences (reference, truth-of, or whatever), have no more status than that of being whatever is needed to generate the meaning of whole sentences.[22] So it's not clear yet that the Gricean needs to appeal to any notion of expression-meaning which cannot be explained in terms of speaker-meaning.

13.6   An unsympathetic objection to Grice's account of speaker-meaning

Grice's account of *speaker*-meaning has also faced a number of hostile objections. The most famous is the one produced by John Searle,[23] although Searle himself understands this as providing what I've called a sympathetic objection – one which is to be incorporated in a revised version of Grice's proposal. Searle imagines an American soldier in Italy in the Second World War, during the period when the Italians and the Germans were allied against the Americans and the British. The American encounters some Italian soldiers. He speaks no Italian, but wants to suggest that he's on their side. He decides to try to pass himself off as a German. Unfortunately, he knows very little German. He does, however, remember a famous line of Goethe's: '*Kennst du das Land wo die Zitronen blühen?*' ('Do you know the land where the lemon-trees flower?'). So he utters this German sentence, meaning the Italians to take him to be telling them that he is a German soldier. All the relevant Gricean intentions seem to be in place. But, says Searle, he does not mean that he is a German soldier by that sentence. Searle thinks that when you use a sentence, you cannot mean what you like by it; you can only mean by it something which it already means.[24]

---

[21] This, of course, is Frege's Context Principle, which we first encountered in ch. 2, § 2.2.

[22] This is actually Davidson's view anyway: see, in particular, 'Reality without Reference', in his *Inquiries into Truth and Interpretation* (Oxford: Oxford University Press, 1984), pp. 215–25.

[23] J. Searle, *Speech Acts: An Essay in the Philosophy of Language* (Cambridge: Cambridge University Press, 1969), pp. 44–5. His objection is one in a line which originates with P. Ziff, 'On H. P. Grice's Account of Meaning', *Analysis*, 28 (1967), pp. 1–8.

[24] The point is derived from L. Wittgenstein, *Philosophical Investigations*, I. 510.

If we take this objection at face-value, and the point is sound, it completely undermines the attempt to explain expression-meaning in terms of speaker-meaning, because speaker-meaning itself turns out to depend on expression-meaning.

Searle's own treatment of the counter-example is slightly confusing. Although his main point seems to be that you can only mean by words something which the words themselves mean, he sometimes puts this point in a way which seems to undermine it. Thus he says, 'Meaning is more than a matter of intention, it is also at least sometimes a matter of convention.'[25] The difficulty is this: if you take the meaning of a common language to be held in place by convention, you seem to be assuming that the meaning of expressions in a language is dependent on what individual speakers mean by them. The idea seems to be that we could each mean what we like by our words, but that we adopt a convention to mean the same as each other, because that leads to smoother social interaction. If that's right, Searle cannot both object that expression-meaning is prior to speaker-meaning and take expression-meaning to be conventional.

Griceans tend not to be moved by Searle's objection. It's noticeable that they take great trouble to deal with the worries which were considered in section 13.3, but they tend to dismiss this one quite quickly. One Gricean response is, in effect, to accuse Searle of confusion here: he is bringing to the notion of speaker-meaning considerations which are only strictly relevant to expression-meaning.[26] This kind of Gricean is happy to find a place for convention, as Searle does: but that place is in the account of *expression*-meaning, not speaker-meaning.

Grice himself, and Schiffer following him, offer a different response, which is, I think, more deeply revealing. They think it's not obvious that Searle's case is a genuine counter-example.[27] That is, they think that on at least one understanding of the case, the American does indeed mean that

---

[25] *Speech Acts*, p. 45.

[26] See A. Avramides, *Meaning and Mind* (Cambridge, MA: MIT Press, 1989), p. 74.

[27] They think that whether the case provides a genuine counter-example depends on the reasoning the American wants the Italians to go through. The details don't matter here, but if the American intends them to reason in one way, they claim, we have no counter-example, whereas if he intends them to reason in another way, we just have a counter-example of a kind familiar to Griceans as developments of Strawson's theme. See Grice, 'Utterer's Meaning and Intentions', pp. 161 ff; and Schiffer, *Meaning*, pp. 28 ff.

he is a German soldier. I won't elaborate on the various possible understandings of the case which they suggest, but it's worth taking particular note of something significant about the analysis offered by Grice and Schiffer. Here's what Searle denies:

(c) The American means that he is a German soldier by the sentence 'Kennst du das Land wo die Zitronen blühen?'

But here is what Schiffer asserts (on one understanding of the case, at least):

(c*) The American means that he is a German soldier by *uttering* the sentence 'Kennst du das Land wo die Zitronen blühen?'

Searle claims that you can't mean by a *sentence* something which that sentence does not mean. Schiffer thinks that there is no such restriction on what you can mean by *uttering* a sentence. It seems that Searle and Schiffer are talking about different kinds of meaning. Searle is talking about the meaning of linguistic expressions – sentences and words. Schiffer is talking about the meaning of *actions* – the actions of uttering linguistic expressions.

There's an uncertainty here which reaches right back to the beginning of the Gricean programme. Although Grice seems to be offering an account of the meaning of expressions, we find him talking about utterances even in his original article. We certainly find Strawson considering what it is for a speaker to mean something by *uttering* an expression, and this is continued throughout the later tradition of the Gricean programme. (Look back at my version of Strawson's formulation of Grice's proposal, in section 13.3, and you'll see that the attention has switched to the meaning of *utterances*.) Grice's original account seems to be concerned wholly with the meaning of a certain kind of *object* (an expression, we assume): it aims to explain what it is for such an object to have meaning in a stable ('timeless') way in a common language; and it explains this kind of 'timeless' meaning in terms of the temporary and make-shift meaning which such an object can be given by a particular speaker. But Strawson, following hints in Grice himself, seems to imagine an account which deals wholly with the meaning of *actions*: in effect, the goal becomes that of explaining the meaning of a conventional or institutional action (whatever, exactly, that might be) on the basis of the meaning of particular actions performed on particular occasions.

Although Searle himself doesn't put the matter explicitly in these terms, he can be understood to be making two fundamental claims in presenting his famous counter-example:

(1) The meaning of an expression (on an occasion) is not the same thing as the meaning of an action of uttering that expression (on that occasion);

(2) It is impossible to mean anything by an expression which the expression does not (already) mean.

(2) is the claim which directly opposes the Gricean programme; but it depends for its plausibility on accepting (1). For if (1) were false, (2) would be saying something like this: someone can only intend by an action what that action is standardly taken to mean – and that is surely absurd. If the Gricean can reasonably deny (1), she can reasonably deny (2).

Denying (1) seems to depend on asserting that expressions are themselves types of action. And as it happens, it's common within the Gricean programme to find expressions identified with *types of utterance*.[28] But I think this kind of formulation fudges the issue we're concerned with. The word 'utterance' is ambiguous: it can refer *either* to an act of uttering *or* to the thing which is uttered in such an act; either to the process of producing something, or to the product of the process. It is only the meaning of the *act* or *process* which is plausibly explained in terms of intentions; but it is the product which is naturally identified with words or sentences, or with something composed of words and sentences.

And there are certainly reasons for denying that expressions are types of action, and that the meaning of expressions is the meaning of actions. Grice's own point about Deutero-Esperanto provides one: Grice doesn't just *use* Deutero-Esperanto however he likes – he first *establishes* the meaning of its words (by stipulation, apparently), and then uses those words in their then established meaning.[29] Grice himself seems to be giving the words a kind of meaning which precedes the meaning of any particular action of using the words. Moreover, the moment we think of words and sentences as a *resource* to be used in actions of uttering, rather than as mere features of such actions, the Searlean claim (2) becomes very

---

[28] See, e.g., Schiffer, *Meaning*, chs. 5 and 6.

[29] Grice, 'Meaning Revisited', p. 299.

plausible. If words and sentences are such a resource, they must bring their own properties with them. And that will mean that you cannot mean what you like by them. It will no longer be plausible to suggest that they mean, even on a particular occasion, what you intend them to mean on that occasion. For it will be clear that the whole point of your using the words is to use them to mean what they already mean.

This, I think, is the most significant challenge to the Gricean programme. If the meaning of expressions is not just the meaning of the acts of using them, what a speaker means by an expression will be dependent on what the expression itself means, so it will be impossible to explain expression-meaning in terms of speaker-meaning.

13.7   After Grice

If the Gricean programme has gone wrong, where has it gone wrong? It's natural to think that the trouble should be traced back to the place where speaker-meaning was introduced in the first place – the place where what I called the *Creation Condition* was introduced. Here is that condition again:

> (CC) No mere object can really have a purpose unless somebody has made it have that purpose.

(CC) combines with the idea that linguistic expressions are, in some sense, 'mere objects' to lead to the idea that the meaning of linguistic expressions must depend on speakers' intentions. If we want to reject the Gricean programme, it seems that we need *either* to deny that linguistic expressions are 'mere objects', *or* to find some other way for 'mere objects' to have purposes.

Let's begin with the second option: finding a way for 'mere objects' to have purposes. My calling the crucial assumption the *Creation Condition* was bound to suggest comparisons with evolutionary theory. Evolutionary theory might seem to offer a way of explaining how objects can have purposes without anybody ever having given them those purposes. A heart, for example, can be there *in order* to pump blood; and we might suppose that this fact has an evolutionary explanation. Perhaps the explanation is this: if our ancestors' hearts had not pumped blood, our hearts wouldn't have existed. Perhaps we can explain linguistic meaning in some similar way: if these (or similar) words hadn't been used in a particular way in the past, they would not now be used at all.[30]

I'm not myself convinced that such an appeal to evolution, or theories of the same kind, will really work. It's not obvious that evolution provides us with an account of purposes which avoids appeal to a creator. It seems just as natural to say that evolution provides us with an account of what *seems* to be purposive, without actually introducing any purposes.[31] If that's right, it seems we need to fall back on our other option: this would involve saying that words are not really 'mere objects' – not really just types of mark and sound. If we deny that words are just types of mark and sound, we can allow that they are intrinsically meaningful; and if they are intrinsically meaningful, then we don't need an account of how they come to have meaning.

Unfortunately, this is not easy either to accept or to make sense of. The view that words are just types of mark and sound is very deeply entrenched: so deeply, in fact, that it's hard to begin to make sense of an alternative.[32] This means that we're left in a difficult position, if we accept that Gricean theories are fundamentally misconceived. We need either to find some theory which offers a convincing alternative to (CC) as an account of the purposiveness of mere objects, or to find some way to make sense of the idea that words are intrinsically meaningful.

Further reading

There are three significant papers by Grice (in addition to the original 'Meaning') which pursue the Gricean Programme: 'Utterer's Meaning and Intentions', 'Utterer's Meaning, Sentence-Meaning, and Word-Meaning', and 'Meaning Revisited': these are all reprinted (along with the original 'Meaning') in Grice's *Studies in the Ways of Words* (Cambridge, MA: Harvard University Press, 1989). Stephen Schiffer's book, *Meaning* (Oxford: Oxford

---

[30] A full-blooded and thoroughly worked-out theory of the kind gestured at by this loose and provisional explanation is provided by Ruth Millikan, *Language, Thought, and Other Biological Categories* (Cambridge, MA: MIT Press, 1984).

[31] This is the view of Jerry Fodor, 'A Theory of Content I', in his *A Theory of Content* (Cambridge, MA: MIT Press, 1990), p. 79.

[32] What is here being questioned is the assumption which was identified as (L8) in Locke's conception of language in ch. 1.

University Press, 1972), is perhaps the classic statement of a developed Gricean view. P. F. Strawson suggests the possibility of a marriage between the Gricean and the Davidsonian programmes in 'Meaning and Truth', in his *Logico-Linguistic Papers* (London: Methuen, 1971), pp. 170–89. A helpful introduction to Gricean theories is Anita Avramides, 'Intention and Convention', in B. Hale and C. Wright, eds., *A Companion to the Philosophy of Language* (Oxford: Blackwell, 1997), pp. 60–86. Her *Meaning and Mind* (Cambridge, MA: MIT Press, 1989) is an extended, and ultimately critical, discussion of the programme.

14 Kripke on the rule-following paradox

Key text

Saul Kripke, *Wittgenstein on Rules and Private Language* (Oxford: Blackwell, 1982).

14.1 Introduction

We've seen the difficulty of explaining what it is for linguistic expressions to have meaning. But what if it could be shown that there's no fact of that matter at all about what our words mean? This dramatic sceptical claim was presented by Saul Kripke, in his *Wittgenstein on Rules and Private Language*. This work had an immediate effect, in two ways. First, it presented a striking challenge to everyone who believed that words really mean something, and provoked a minor industry of work designed to avoid the scepticism which it proposed. And, secondly, because Kripke claimed to derive his sceptical arguments from some sections of Wittgenstein's *Philosophical Investigations*, it led to a renewed interest in Wittgenstein's later philosophy.[1]

In fact, it's probably better not to stress the links with Wittgenstein too heavily. Kripke himself is quite modest about the status of his work as an interpretation of Wittgenstein: he claims to be doing no more than present 'that set of problems and arguments which I personally have gotten out of

---

[1] It is important to note that an interpretation of Wittgenstein which overlaps Kripke's in a number of ways was provided independently by Robert Fogelin: see R. Fogelin, *Wittgenstein*, 2nd edn (London: Routledge, 1987), chs. 11 and 12. There is no doubt, however, that it is Kripke's presentation which has had the dramatic influence. This is partly due to Kripke's personal reputation; but it is also due to the accessibility of Kripke's style.

reading Wittgenstein'.[2] And it's now quite widely agreed that, in certain crucial respects at least, Kripke misrepresents Wittgenstein.[3] Nor is the scepticism presented here one which Kripke himself endorses: what we have is, in Kripke's words, just 'Wittgenstein's argument as it struck Kripke, as it presented a problem for him'.[4] For this reason I will refer to the proponent of the argument of Kripke's book, not as Wittgenstein or Kripke, but as *KW* – a relatively anonymous hybrid of the two.

14.2   The sceptical challenge

The focus of the argument, to begin with, is a particular mathematical example. Consider addition, that simple arithmetical operation, which we refer to (as we suppose) by means of the word 'plus' and the symbol '+'. Addition is well defined for the full range of positive whole numbers (and many more). That is to say, if you take any two such numbers, however large, then the rule for addition fixes what the result is if you add them together. Since there are infinitely many positive whole numbers, the rule for addition fixes the result of infinitely many sums.

Now consider how I might stand in relation to this rule. I think I can add: I can certainly do elementary addition sums with relative ease. And I think I understand the words 'add' and 'plus', and the symbol '+': even if I occasionally make mistakes in adding, I can understand my error when it's pointed out to me. There seems no difficulty in saying that when I use the words 'add' and 'plus', and the symbol '+', I mean *addition*. But it's clear that although addition is well-defined for infinitely many cases, I myself can only have done a finite number of sums. Suppose that I've only done sums involving numbers less than 57. The particular limit doesn't matter: it's obvious enough that there will be a limit, and it's easier for exposition if we choose a relatively small number.

Now suppose that I try an addition sum I've never done before. What is 68 + 57? I answer, with relatively little hesitation: 125. Now why is that

---

[2] Kripke, *Wittgenstein on Rules and Private Language*, p. 5.

[3] Many have pointed to the fact that Kripke links his 'sceptical paradox' to the use of the word 'paradox' in the first paragraph of Wittgenstein, *Philosophical Investigations*, I. 201, without noticing that in the second paragraph of the same section Wittgenstein shows that to think there is a paradox here is to misunderstand things.

[4] Kripke, *Wittgenstein*, p. 5.

the right answer? According to KW, the reason is something like this. '125' is the right answer to the question 'What is 68 + 57?' because that's the answer which is determined by the rule for addition which I have learned. What is the rule for addition which I have learned? It's the rule which I intended to be following – the rule I meant – in the past. On KW's view, my present answer '125' is right because it keeps faith with what I meant by '+' in the past.

But what did I mean in the past? At this point KW considers the possibility of a peculiar sceptic. Might it not be, the sceptic asks, that when I used '+' in the past, I did not mean *addition*, but a different function, which delivers the same results for all the examples I had considered until then? Perhaps, for example, I used '+' to mean, not *plus*, but '*quus*', a bizarre function which can be symbolized (for convenience of exposition) by means of '⊕'. We can define '⊕' as follows:

$x \oplus y = x + y$, if x and y are both less than 57
          $= 5$ otherwise.

Let's say that applying the function '⊕' is *quadding*. Then the definition of '⊕' states that if you *quadd* together two numbers which are both less than 57, the result is the same as if you had *added* them; but if either number is 57 or larger, the result is 5.

Now suppose that (whatever I now think) I had actually meant *quus* by the symbol '+', as I used it in the past, and that I was in fact *quadding*, rather than adding. In that case, according to KW, the right answer for me to give to the question 'What is 68 + 57?' would be '5', not '125'. This is because, according to KW, what it's right for me to say now depends on what I mean now by '+', and what I mean now by '+' is determined by what I meant by it in the past. But it seems utterly incredible that the right answer to the question 'What is 68 + 57?' might be '5'. If we are confident of anything, we can surely be confident that *that*'s wrong!

And, of course, although the mathematical case is simple to set up, the same issue arises over any word which we think can be applied correctly or incorrectly. For any such word, correct application can be seen as a matter of following a rule. Following a rule is always, according to KW, keeping your present use in line with your past intentions. Your past intentions can only have been displayed in a finite series of cases. And every word is (we imagine) well defined for a potential infinity of cases.

What exactly is the sceptic challenging? So far I've represented the sceptic as asking us a question: 'What *did* I mean by "plus"?' But what exactly is the difficulty of answering this question meant to show? There are two kinds of scepticism which might be involved here. One is *epistemological*: it claims we cannot *know* what we mean. The other is not about knowledge, but about the facts: we might call it a *metaphysical* scepticism. If the scepticism is metaphysical it claims that there's no fact of the matter about what we mean. In the particular case of 'plus', the two basic sceptical claims are these:

(ES1) I cannot *know* what I meant by 'plus' in the past;
(MS1) There is no *fact* of the matter about what I meant by 'plus' in the past.

And since, according to KW, I mean now just to be keeping faith with my past use when I use 'plus', these two basic sceptical claims carry forward to the present:

(ES2) I cannot know what I mean by 'plus' now;
(MS2) There is no fact of the matter about what I mean by 'plus' now.

Which form of scepticism – epistemological or metaphysical – is KW presenting? The original setting up of the case might suggest that the problem is primarily epistemological. The addition example looks parallel to a familiar scepticism about induction, which derives from Hume.

The problem of induction, put briefly, is this. Learning from experience (which Hume thinks is the basis of all substantial knowledge) is a matter of applying the lessons of the past to our everyday lives. All of my daily activities involve this. To start my car in the morning, I turn the key in the ignition, rather than just sitting still and whistling; this seems to be because I've learned that the key has started the car in the past, and I expect that lesson to hold good for the future. The same point applies to even more basic cases. When I walk, I put my foot on the ground with confidence. This seems to be because I've learned that the ground has held my weight in the past, and I expect the same to be true now. In all this, I seem to be assuming a certain uniformity in nature: that in examples like these, the cases I have not yet encountered will follow the pattern of the cases I have. Hume's question is: what justifies that belief in nature's uniformity?

This is clearly an epistemological challenge: how do I *know* that nature is uniform in this kind of respect? – what *reason* have I for *thinking* that it is uniform? It raises no question about whether or not nature is in *fact* uniform. The initial setting up of the meaning-sceptic's position suggests that it too is a form of epistemological challenge. It looks just like the problem of induction: just because what I do has matched the requirements of addition in the past, how do I know that it will continue to do so in the future?

In fact, however, the challenge of KW's sceptic is meant to be primarily *metaphysical*. What he wants to show is that there is no fact of the matter about what I mean by my words, and therefore no fact of the matter about what is the right answer to any question. The scepticism he presents is fantastically dramatic: it seems that there is no such thing as meaning or truth at all. The way the sceptic works is by asking what the fact of my meaning *plus* rather than *quus* might be. What is it about me which determines that it is one thing rather than the other that I meant? I seem to need there to be some fact which ensures that I really do mean one rather than the other.

This seems a straightforwardly metaphysical challenge, but it does have an epistemological dimension. This is because KW imposes an epistemological restriction on what the fact which ensures that I mean one thing rather than another could be. Kripke writes:

> [T]here is a condition that any putative candidate for such a fact must satisfy. It must, in some sense, show how I am justified in giving the answer '125' to '68 + 57'.[5]

There may be some difficulty in my knowing all the relevant facts, but the idea is that if I knew all there was to know, and there really was a fact of the matter about what I meant by my words in the past, then I would know something which I could use to justify giving one answer rather than another now. We can formalize this point by suggesting this link between the metaphysical and the epistemological sceptical issues in the case of 'plus':

> (ME) If there is a fact of the matter about what I meant by 'plus' in the past, it can be used to justify my use of 'plus' now.

---

[5] Ibid., p. 11.

The sceptic's challenge, then, is to find some fact which meets this condition. What might it be? KW considers a range of possibilities. It cannot be that I had explicitly thought about this case, and decided that 68 + 57 was 125. The point of deviation between *plus* and *quus* was fixed comically low for dramatic effect, but it's clear that we can only have run through a finite number of examples, so there must be *some* possible deviations I have not thought about and explicitly ruled out. Nor can the crucial fact be that there is a special introspectible feeling which somehow fixes that I meant *plus* by '+'. In the first place, it seems quite possible to understand a word without having any such associated introspectible feeling. And even if I do have such a feeling, it's hard to see how anything about it could determine what I mean: after all, the feeling itself seems open to interpretation.

The suggestion which Kripke spends most time on is a *dispositional* conception of meaning. According to the simple version of such a view, what I mean is a matter of what I'm disposed or inclined to say. So I mean *plus* by the symbol '+' if I'm disposed to give answers to questions involving '+' which are the right answers to questions about *addition*, and I mean *quus* by the symbol '+' if I'm disposed to give answers which are the right answers to questions about *quaddition*. What would I say if I were asked what 68 + 57 is? '125', of course. According to the dispositional conception, that just shows that I can't mean *quus* by '+', since, if I had meant *quus*, I would have answered '5'.

Kripke has two objections to this suggestion. The first is that my dispositions are finite, just as the number of addition sums I have actually done is. It's true that I may be disposed to give answers to addition problems which I have not yet considered. There may be a large number of cases for which we can say that there is an answer which I would give if I were asked, even if I haven't been asked yet. But, Kripke claims, even this large number is finite: if the numbers I'm asked to add get too large, I'll just be at a loss – I won't even be able to comprehend them. This means that if our sceptic had decided to focus on a function which deviated from ordinary addition only when we got to these huge numbers (instead of the comical *quus*, which deviates at only 57), the dispositional conception would have had nothing at all to say in response.

Kripke's second objection to the dispositional view is the one which has had most influence. The objection is that the dispositionalist gives an account of meaning in *descriptive* terms, but meaning is a *normative* notion.[6] That is to say, the dispositionalist says simply what someone *will*, or *would*, do if asked, whereas meaning is concerned with what she *should* do. The question is not whether I *would* or *do* say '125' in response to the question 'What is 68 + 57?', but whether I *should* give that answer. According to Kripke, if I mean *plus* then I *should* answer '125', whereas if I mean *quus*, then I *should* answer '5' – whatever I am disposed to do. Indeed, I might be disposed to make mistakes: for example, there might be certain numbers which I habitually confuse. This surely makes sense, but it's incoherent on a dispositionalist view: since whether I am right is determined by what I mean, and what I mean is determined by what I am disposed to do, on a dispositionalist view, I cannot be disposed to make mistakes.

This ties up with the epistemological condition (ME). The problem with the dispositionalist account, it seems, is that it might enable us to *predict* how I will use the words, but it will not *justify* any particular way of using them. The notion of justification is essentially normative. Kripke concludes that the dispositionalist account cannot answer the sceptic's challenge, and since there seem to be no other candidates, the challenge goes unanswered.

14.3   The 'sceptical solution'

How should we respond to the sceptic? KW contrasts two kinds of 'solution' to a sceptical paradox. One is what he calls a 'straight' solution: this would involve showing that there is some fault in the argument to the sceptical conclusion. The other is what he calls a 'sceptical' solution: this would involve accepting all of the sceptic's claims, but insisting that the situation can nevertheless be lived with. KW proposes a 'sceptical solution' to the meaning scepticism he has presented.

The details of KW's sceptical solution are not entirely clear. Presenting it as neutrally as possible, we might say that KW accepts that there is no *fact* which justifies my using 'plus' in one way rather than another, but there is *something* which does (within limits, at least). This *something*, however, is not the kind of thing we were looking at before: it's not something about the individual (me, in the imagined case) considered in

---

[6] Ibid., p. 37.

isolation. It's something which appears only when we 'consider' the individual 'as interacting with a wider community'.[7] Let's look at this a little closer.

The idea seems to be that I can be counted as meaning *plus* rather than *quus* when I use the word 'plus' – insofar as there is a real distinction here at all – if there is some justification for my making the responses appropriate to *plus* rather than those appropriate to *quus*. How can my responses be justified? They will be justified if they match the responses which would be given by appropriate members of the community. But KW says that although this gives me the right to *assert* (for example) that 68 + 57 is 125, this does not make '68 + 57 = 125' *true*. That statement has, strictly speaking, no *truth* conditions: it only has *assertibility* conditions, which are determined by whether or not it agrees with what the appropriate members of the community would say.

This switch from *facts* and *truth conditions* to *assertibility conditions* is quite puzzling. Why can't we say that there is a fact which determines whether or not I should answer '125' to the question 'What is 68 + 57?' – only it's a fact about what appropriate members of my community would say, rather than a fact just about me? There are hints of two separate considerations in Kripke's text.

The first relates to Michael Dummett's worries about the notion of truth.[8] Dummett – influenced by Wittgenstein, in fact – was concerned to question the uncritical use of the notion of truth by Davidson, in the construction of theories of meaning for particular languages.[9] Dummett's basic claim (which I won't examine further here) is that there's nothing about what speakers of a language do which justifies the use of what he calls a *realist* notion of truth in characterizing the meaning of the sentences of that language. A *realist* notion of truth is one which allows that something can be true even if it's impossible to verify that it is true. Dummett thinks that all that can be got from an understanding of what speakers actually do are the conditions under which sentences in their language may *justifiably be asserted*. We have no right to describe their

---

[7] Ibid., p. 89.

[8] Kripke refers to Dummett on p. 73.

[9] For Dummett's discussion of Davidson's notion of a theory of meaning for a language, see his two papers, 'What is a Theory of Meaning? I' and 'What is a Theory of Meaning? II', both reprinted in his *The Seas of Language* (Oxford: Oxford University Press, 1993).

sentences by means of a notion of truth which outruns what can justifiably be asserted.

It seems to me that whatever the merits of Dummett's worries about the realist notion of truth, the conclusion that we should *replace* truth conditions with assertibility conditions is mistaken. What Dummett should strictly say instead is simply that the truth conditions of sentences can *be* no more than assertibility conditions. There are two reasons for this. First, if Dummett is right in his objection to realism, there can be no properly ordered notion of truth which outruns what can justifiably be asserted: so he cannot himself think that there are truth conditions which are distinct from assertibility conditions. And, secondly, we cannot just give up the notion of truth and make do with the notion of assertibility instead. This is because the notion of assertion itself presupposes the notion of truth: what is asserted is always asserted *as true*.

This means that Dummett's worries give us no reason to think that there is no *fact* of the matter about how I should use 'plus' if we adopt KW's 'sceptical solution'. There is indeed a fact of the matter: I am right, in *fact*, when I use 'plus' in agreement with the appropriate members of my community. It's simply that the fact is not, as we might put it, a *realist* fact. That is to say, there are only facts about what I should say to the extent that there are facts about what the appropriate members of my community would say; and since they won't say anything in cases where the answer can't be known, there won't be any unverifiable facts.

There is, however, another factor which occasionally seems to surface in Kripke's text, which might explain KW's claim that there are no facts about meaning, according to the 'sceptical solution'. There are times when KW seems to suggest that there's no fact of the matter about which community I belong to. I've already borrowed the cautious formulation KW uses, when he says that whether someone is justified in using a word in a particular way depends on whether we '*consider* him as interacting with a wider community'.[10] This formulation perhaps suggests that it's simply up to us whether we count someone as belonging to a particular community. The same suggestion emerges in KW's treatment of Robinson Crusoe. The original Robinson Crusoe was shipwrecked on an island: he already spoke English, and went on speaking English. For KW's point, we

---

[10] Kripke, *Wittgenstein*, p. 89 (the emphasis here is mine).

really need to consider a supposed *lifelong* Crusoe, who never learns any language from anyone, but invents a language for himself. The question is whether this lifelong Crusoe can be said to follow rules. What KW says is this:

> [I]f we think of Crusoe as following rules, we are taking him into our community and applying our criteria for rule following to him.[11]

KW seems to think that there is little problem with 'taking Crusoe into our community' in this way:

> Remember that Wittgenstein's theory is one of assertibility conditions. Our community can assert of any individual that he follows a rule if he passes the tests for rule following applied to any member of the community.[12]

KW here seems to be suggesting that the move to assertibility conditions instead of truth conditions is tied up with there being no real fact about whether an individual belongs in a community – other than whether that individual's practice happens to agree with the community's. And, of course, the agreement need be no more than rough: after all, an individual might often make mistakes, so a certain amount of deviation from the community's norm is tolerated.

If this is what KW is advocating, the 'solution' to the sceptical paradox can indeed be regarded as being a sceptical one. Suppose I'm a frequent user of the word 'plus', although I don't regard myself as terribly strong mathematically. Presumably I have a disposition to answer questions of the form 'What is $x + y$?' in a certain way; but I imagine that I quite often make mistakes, and I get bewildered by large numbers relatively easily. Suppose that as a matter of fact I'm disposed to offer a certain number z as the result of an application of '+' to two smaller numbers, m and n. Now suppose that there are in the world just two communities of people who use '+', A and B. The answers given to questions of the form 'What is $x + y$?' in these two communities differ quite strikingly (though not, perhaps, as comically as in the *quus* case). My 'plus' disposition doesn't precisely match what either community would say, but it diverges equally from both: each community would count me right just as often, and wrong just

---

[11] Ibid., p. 110.

[12] Ibid., p. 110. It should be said, however, that Kripke shows some uncertainty in the footnote to this passage about whether Wittgenstein really held this view.

as often, as the other – though, of course, they would count me right and wrong on different sums. It turns out that my answer 'z' to the question 'What is $m + n$?' matches what one community (community A) would say, but not what the other community (community B) would say.

Now am I right or wrong? It looks as if there's just no fact of the matter, on KW's picture. We have two options, it seems. *Either* my disposition diverges too much from what both communities would say for either community to count me as belonging to it; *or* my disposition is close enough to what both communities would say for each community to be able to count me as belonging to it. In the first case, I belong to no community – since, by hypothesis, there were only these two – and so have no standard to meet; that means, according to the 'sceptical solution', that there's no such thing as what I *should* do. In the second case, I'm right by A's lights and wrong by B's, but there's no sense beyond that in which I'm *really* either right or wrong.

This is a savage and bewildering form of scepticism, it seems to me. We might call it a *relativist* scepticism, since correctness is always relative to the apparently arbitrary choice of what community to count someone as belonging to. In fact, the problem gets quickly worse. If it's arbitrary what community to count an individual as belonging to, it seems bound to be arbitrary which individuals to count as forming a community in the first place. And in that case, it turns out to be quite arbitrary what we should count as a community. We can draw any number of community boundaries, including more people or fewer, according to how tightly we decide (again quite arbitrarily) to set the standards of uniformity of practice.

Is this relativist scepticism what KW is advocating as a 'sceptical solution'? That's not entirely clear, because it's not entirely clear why KW thinks that there's no fact of the matter about what I mean by my words; nor is it entirely clear what KW is building into the notion of a fact. It seems to me that Dummett's worries about a realist notion of truth don't provide KW with good reason to abandon altogether the idea that there is a fact of the matter about what I mean. This would more properly be described as an *anti-realist* solution, rather than a *sceptical* solution to the paradox.

But the situation is different if we take KW to be propounding the relativist scepticism I've just sketched out. Since, on this view, it's entirely arbitrary what community to count me as belonging to, there's a very serious sense in which there remains no fact of the matter about what I mean – even when considerations of community are brought into play. Moreover, it looks as if we do get a real distinction between assertibility and truth (even on a non-realist conception of truth). This is because, according to this relativist scepticism, warranted assertibility is not incompatible with warranted *deniability*. What makes my answer '125' to the question 'What is 68 + 57' assertible is just there being *some* community by whose standards that answer is right. But obviously, this doesn't rule out there being *another* community by whose standards that answer is wrong. Since it's hard to see how we can make sense of a genuine notion of truth which allows that what is true may also be false, assertibility seems to come apart from truth. Of course, it remains the case that whatever I assert I assert as *true*, but in the end this has to be understood as a kind of inevitable illusion. When I'm engaged in arithmetic (or any use of language) I seem bound to think of myself as making claims which are objectively true or false, and as stating what are genuine facts. But really (if this relativist scepticism is right), I am doing something which is just *counted* as true when taken one way – though it can equally be counted as false when taken in another way.

A solution like this would count as genuinely sceptical, and it would justify some of the melodrama of Kripke's exposition. For that reason, I will take this relativist scepticism as KW's final position. The issue won't matter all that much in the long run: I will consider a more modest community-based solution anyway.

Where do we stand? KW presents a scepticism which seems utterly disastrous: there is no fact of the matter about what we mean by our words. The relativist scepticism which I am taking to represent KW's 'sceptical solution' is hardly any better. We cannot really live with the idea that whether what we say is true or false depends simply on whether some arbitrarily defined group agrees with our general practice. We cannot really believe that our claims to truth are not really true or false at all. I think we have to find some 'straight solution' – some way of resisting the sceptic's arguments. I'll consider very briefly three such ways, which I think are representative of trends to be found in discussions of KW's rule-following paradox.

14.4   A community-based response

An appeal to the standards of a community can form the basis of a 'straight' solution to KW's sceptical paradox. Such a solution adopts a form of dispositionalism about what words mean within a community. What's meant by 'plus' within a community is a matter of what the community (or its acknowledged experts) *would* say. If the community would give the results of *addition* in answer to questions of the form 'What is $m + n$?', then the word 'plus' and the sign '+' mean *plus* in that community. On this view, there's no issue about what the community *should* do: there is simply what it does.

Where exactly does this community-based solution resist KW's sceptical argument? It claims that KW has not considered all the relevant facts about the individual. On this view, it's a fact about the individual – even if not, perhaps, a fact about the individual 'considered in isolation'[13] – that she belongs to a certain community. Given that she belongs to a community, she's right when she gives the answer the community would give, and wrong when she gives a different answer.

The basic problem with such a community-based view is that it's hard to see how dispositionalism at the level of the community is any better than dispositionalism at the level of the individual. It may be that KW's arguments against dispositionalism can be resisted, but it's unclear that they are more easily resisted at the level of the community. Let's ask to begin with: how is the relevant community to be defined? It had better not be defined just as the community which speaks a certain language (English, for example). For if that's the only way of defining the relevant kind of community, the basic facts about meaning will be of this form: this individual means *plus* by 'plus', because *plus* is what 'plus' means in English. And we then end up with a basic fact of meaning, that 'plus' means *plus* in English, which looks as if it will not provide the kind of justification for any particular use of the word which (KW) is after. (I'll be returning to this general issue in section 14.6.)

So it seems that the community must be defined by referring to a particular group of people, or as the people who stand in certain relations of interdependence with some particular group of people. Then the claim

---

[13] Kripke, *Wittgenstein*, p. 87.

has to be: whatever *these* people (whichever way we define the community) would say is right. It's true that there's room here for some kind of distinction between the tendencies of *individuals* and what's right for them, but there is no possibility of such a distinction between the tendencies of the *group* and what's right for it. And that seems to be wrong, if dispositionalism in general is wrong. If we define our community either by referring to a particular group of people, or as the people who stand in relations of interdependence with some particular group of people, it seems obviously to make sense to suppose that these people might go wrong. Indeed, it seems to make sense to suppose that they might have a *disposition* to go wrong: there are certain mistakes they *tend* to make, or *would* make in certain circumstances.

It looks, then, as if a community-based 'straight' solution will only work if some answer can be found to KW's arguments against dispositionalism. And then it looks as if the appeal to the community will be unnecessary.

14.5 Can dispositionalism be defended?

KW makes two objections to dispositionalism about meaning. Can they be rejected?

The first objection is that dispositions are finite, but addition (for example) is determinate for an infinite range of cases. The dispositions in question are specified in terms of subjunctive conditionals, which involve considering what I *would* do in certain circumstances. The dispositional view of meaning, in its simplest form, offers something like the following as its account of the fact which makes it the case that I mean *plus* by '+':

(MD) For any m and n, if I were asked 'What is $m + n$?', I would name in answer the number which is in fact the result of *adding* m and n.

The objection is that when m and n get large enough, there is simply nothing I would say: the numbers will just bewilder me.

It's not clear that this objection works. It's natural to think that there's some understanding of (MD) which abstracts from the actual finitude of my mind. This has something to do with subjunctive conditionals in general. Consider this pair of claims:

(1) If Berlioz had been the same nationality as Verdi, he would have been Italian;

(2) If Verdi had been the same nationality as Berlioz, he would have been French.

Each of these is naturally heard as being true, provided that they're not heard together. If they're heard together, they seem together to imply this:

(3) If Berlioz and Verdi had been the same nationality, Berlioz would have been Italian and Verdi would have been French.

And that's absurd. What this shows is that subjunctive conditionals are always understood in a certain way: we keep certain features of the actual facts constant when we work out what *would* be true in an imagined situation. In (1), we keep constant Verdi's actual nationality (Italian); in (2) we keep constant Berlioz's actual nationality (French). What we keep constant about the actual facts is often determined quite vaguely, by context (including, in this case, a natural understanding of the word-order of English sentences).

It's natural to think that in (MD) we're meant to keep constant my actual reasonable competence with addition – but *not* my tendency to get muddled in the face of very large numbers. On this natural understanding of (MD), my 'disposition' is as unlimited as the application of addition itself. If that's right, Kripke's first objection lapses.

Kripke's other objection to dispositionalism is more direct. It is that meaning is a *normative* notion, concerned with what I *should* say, while a dispositional account will be merely *descriptive*, saying just what I *would* say. What is the objection here?

The objection seems to be a very old one: that *normative* or *evaluative* notions cannot be defined in *non-normative* or *non-evaluative* (sometimes referred to as *natural*) terms.[14] This objection dates back at least to Plato, and can be found very clearly in Hume's famous 'is'-'ought' distinction.[15] We might call those who think that the normative *can* be defined in terms

---

[14] This is identified as the standard interpretation, and linked to Hume, as here, by J. Zalabardo, 'Kripke's Normativity Argument', *Canadian Journal of Philosophy*, 27 (1997), pp. 467–88. Zalabardo thinks this interpretation is wrong: he thinks that Kripke's normativity is concerned specifically with *justification*. I think his view depends on mislocating the significance of the epistemological constraint (ME) on proposed facts which might determine what I mean by 'plus'. I return to that issue in section 14.6, below.

[15] D. Hume, *A Treatise of Human Nature*, iii, i, 1, § 27.

of the non-normative *naturalists*, and those who think it *cannot non-naturalists*. Kripke's main objection to dispositionalism about meaning seems to be just a special case of the claim that naturalism about value is false.

What is the argument? We could put the point like this: we only have a genuine value if we can make sense of the possibility of going *wrong*. If we just define the right answer as the answer I *would* give, we seem to lose that possibility; and that means that we seem to have lost the essence of the notion of rightness too.

This point might be accepted by a more sophisticated form of dispositionalism than the one we've considered so far. A more sophisticated dispositionalism will acknowledge that we make errors, and that it's even possible for someone to be *disposed* to make mistakes. It will naturally define what I mean, not in terms of what I would do in ordinary circumstances, but in terms of what I would do in *ideal* circumstances. To return to the simple arithmetical case, the fundamental fact which makes it the case that I mean *plus* by '+' will not be (MD), according to this more sophisticated dispositionalism – but *this*:

> (MD*) For any m and n, if I were asked 'What is $m + n$?' *in ideal circumstances*, I would name in answer the number which is in fact the result of *adding* m and n.

But 'ideal', of course, is an evaluative term. This means that the challenge for the naturalist is transformed, but not removed: she needs to explain what count as *ideal* circumstances without re-importing some evaluative notion.

So far, however, it remains only a challenge. Opinions differ over whether some form of naturalism is defensible. The most popular modern version appeals to evolutionary theory, or to parallels with evolution. It's widely thought that evolution actually provides grounds for certain kinds of value and norm. A bodily organ, for example, is normally understood to have a function: it works *well* when it performs that function, and *badly* when it doesn't. And its having the function might be thought to be explained by evolution. The explanation will be of something like this form: if ancestors of this organ (in ancestors of this body) had not done this, this organ would not be there now. An organ performs its function if it does something the doing of which by its ancestors explains its being there now. This might not provide us with a defence of a simple dispositionalist account of meaning, but it would offer us a naturalist straight solution to the sceptical paradox, and so would do what the dispositionalist was hoping to do.

We've come across this kind of theory already, in connection with Gricean theories. And the same worry about it recurs here. It's not clear that evolution really does provide grounds for certain kinds of value or norm. We can understand evolution in a different way: it can be understood as showing that we can explain the *appearance* of value without really dealing with any kind of value at all.[16] The issue of the tenability of some form of naturalism about meaning remains undecided, as long as the general question of the acceptability of naturalism about value needs to be resolved.

14.6   Anti-reductionism and radical interpretation

If a community-based straight solution is unsatisfying, and the jury is still out on naturalism, is there anywhere else we can turn for a way of resisting the sceptic? Is there any other kind of fact we can appeal to in order to justify the natural thought that it's right to answer '125', rather than '5', when we are asked 'What is 68 + 57?'

Perhaps there is: something so obvious that it never occurred to us. Might the fact which makes it right to answer '125' rather than '5' be no more than this: the fact that I meant *plus* rather than *quus*? Why can't we resist the sceptic by pointing to facts about *meaning*, just as such?[17]

Someone who makes this suggestion is likely to claim that there's a hidden and unjustified assumption in the sceptic's challenge. The assumption is that we must offer a *reduction* of the notion of meaning. A *reduction* of a concept is an *explanatory definition* of it. It's not the kind of definition which we might offer to someone who had never heard of

---

[16] The dispute is between the kind of approach found in R. Millikan, *Language, Thought, and Other Biological Categories* (Cambridge, MA: MIT Press, 1984), and the view of the significance of evolution found, for example, in J. Fodor, 'A Theory of Content I', in his *A Theory of Content* (Cambridge, MA: MIT Press, 1990), p. 79. Millikan has applied her general approach specifically to KW's scepticism in 'Truth Rules, Hoverflies, and the Kripke-Wittgenstein Paradox', *The Philosophical Review*, 99, 3. (1990), pp. 323–53.

[17] This kind of approach is suggested by C. McGinn, *Wittgenstein on Meaning* (Oxford: Blackwell, 1984), pp. 160–1.

meaning before: after all, we're all familiar with the word 'meaning', and use it entirely competently in everyday life. Nor is it like a definition of a special scientific use of a familiar word – the kind of definition a physicist might give of the word 'mass', for example. A reduction of the notion of meaning is supposed to be a definition of the concept in the use which we are already familiar with. A reduction is a definition which is supposed to help us understand something of the *point* of the concept of meaning; it's supposed to show us what's at stake when we make claims about meaning, what kinds of consideration are relevant to meaning, what it is that matters enough about meaning to lead us to distinguish meaning from other features of people and things.

To be a definition which is explanatory in this kind of way, a reduction has to do two things. First, it must offer a formula which is, in a sense, equivalent to phrases involving the notion of meaning in the following sense: it must be true of *all* those things which can be said to have the relevant kind of meaning, and it must be true of *only* those things. And, secondly, it must use terms which don't simply exploit the notion of meaning, and can therefore be said to be explanatory of the notion in whatever way philosophical explanations require.

The anti-reductionist will say that this demand is unreasonable. After all, she'll say, we cannot expect to offer a reduction of *every* concept. A reduction has to define a concept in terms which are more basic, from an explanatory point of view. But this means that at some point we have to reach concepts which are fundamental, concepts which are basic to all other concepts. Why should we suppose that the concept of meaning is not basic?

Kripke does consider this response, but regards it as a desperate last resort.[18] I think his reaction can be pressed further. It's not obvious that there must be some concepts for which no explanatory definition can be given. The anti-reductionist tends to imagine that our concepts have a simple structure, with some depending on others, these others depending on others again, and so on, until we reach a base of concepts which are in some sense, self-standing. But this picture seems to depend on a particular conception of the kind of explanation offered by reductions. In fact, it

---

[18] Kripke, *Wittgenstein*, p. 51.

seems to depend on supposing that the explanation is like that which is offered when we introduce a *new* term, or specify a *new* technical sense for a familiar term. If we're doing either of those things, clearly we must offer a definition in terms which are intelligible already. But the whole point of the explanatoriness of reductions is that it's *unlike* that. So it's not at all clear that there will be terms which are basic, and have to be taken for granted in all reductions.

It seems to me that a bald anti-reductionism is not in itself a plausible way of responding to KW's sceptic. But there's a further response available to us, which has some affinities with anti-reductionism. We should look again at the assumptions which the sceptic makes at the very outset. If we do, we'll notice something curious. The sceptic doesn't just challenge me to admit that there are no facts about meaning. The sceptic tries to make the case plausible by undermining my confidence that I mean anything. And he does this by discerning two separate issues in my meaning what I do now. First there's the question of what I meant in the past. Then there's the question of whether I'm keeping faith with my past usage. Why does he separate these issues like this? Why doesn't he just raise questions about what I mean now?

The reason is that, according to KW, I can rationally doubt my past use, but not (or not directly) my present use. The point seems to be that the scepticism can only be raised by treating my own past use as something like the use of a foreign language. That means that KW's sceptic is, in effect, challenging us to find some fact which is available from the perspective of a foreigner, which could be used to justify one way of understanding that past use rather than another.

If that's right, it seems that at the heart of KW's scepticism is something like this familiar assumption:

(RT) Every fact about the meaning of any words in any language, which can be known at all, is available in principle to someone to whom those words are initially radically alien, who proceeds by means of the methods of radical interpretation.

That is to say, it looks as if KW's sceptic gets his scepticism off the ground by assuming just what Quine and Davidson assume, when they insist on the centrality of radical interpretation to our understanding of the nature of language.[19] And this seems to be the real point of that epistemic condition I noted earlier:

> (ME) If there is a fact of the matter about what I meant by 'plus' in the past, it can be used to justify my use of 'plus' now.

There's only space for the *justification* of my present use which the sceptic demands if my past use is treated as something like a foreign language; and that past use will only justify my present use if all the facts about the meaning of a language can be reached from the perspective of radical interpretation.

If this is right, then KW's scepticism can be resisted by denying (RT). Unfortunately, that's no easy thing to do, and to do it thoroughly would be beyond the scope of this chapter (or even this book). A thorough denial of (RT) would involve a whole alternative conception of language. We might expect to begin by supposing that learning a language is a matter, in the first instance, of acquiring certain fundamental habits and casts of mind whose point cannot be understood from the perspective of someone who does not yet have them.[20] But this in itself is not an easy idea to understand. Ironically, it's quite plausible that something like this is involved in Wittgenstein's own view, which was the inspiration for KW's scepticism.

Further reading

Kripke's exposition of the sceptical paradox he found in Wittgenstein provoked an extraordinary flurry of responses. A whole issue of the journal *Synthèse* (58 (1984)) was devoted to it. Among the significant papers in that issue are S. Blackburn, 'The Individual Strikes Back', pp. 281–301, and J. McDowell, 'Wittgenstein on Following a Rule', pp. 325–63. A good survey is P. Boghossian, 'The Rule-Following Considerations', *Mind*, 98 (1989),

---

[19] See chapter 10, § 10.6, above. It is perhaps significant that Kripke himself connects KW's scepticism with Quine's thesis of the indeterminacy of translation (the topic of ch. 11 above): see *Wittgenstein on Rules and Private Language*, pp. 55–7.

[20] This might be taken to be in line with John McDowell's insistence that, on Wittgenstein's view, a KW-type scepticism only arises if we think that following a rule is always a matter of 'interpretation' (which is what Wittgenstein himself denied): see J. McDowell, 'Wittgenstein on Following a Rule', *Synthèse*, 58 (1984) pp. 325–63.

pp. 507–49. These three papers are included, with many others, in a useful collection edited by A. Miller and C. Wright, *Rule-Following and Meaning* (Chesham: Acumen, 2002). Miller himself offers a good introduction to the literature on this topic in his *Philosophy of Language* (London: UCL Press, 1998), chs. 5 and 6. Ruth Garrett Millikan applies a version of evolutionary naturalism to the resolution of the problem in 'Truth Rules, Hoverflies, and the Kripke-Wittgenstein Paradox', *The Philosophical Review*, 99, 3 (1990), pp. 323–53. The background, of course, is in L. Wittgenstein, *Philosophical Investigations*, 3rd edn (Oxford : Blackwell, 2001), I. §§ 137–242. For an attack on Kripke's interpretation of Wittgenstein, see G. Baker and P. Hacker, *Scepticism, Rules, and Language* (Oxford: Blackwell, 1984). An important figure behind Kripke's use of the notion of assertibility, and the community-based 'straight' solution considered here, is M. Dummett. His work is generally too difficult to be considered directly in an introductory book like this, but those interested should read his reflections on the Davidsonian conception of theories of meaning, 'What is a Theory of Meaning? I' and 'What is a Theory of Meaning? II', which are both to be found in his *The Seas of Language* (Oxford: Oxford University Press, 1993).

15   Wittgenstein on the Augustinian picture

Key text

Ludwig Wittgenstein, *Philosophical Investigations*, trans. G. E. M. Anscombe, 3rd edn (Oxford: Blackwell, 2001), part I, §§ 1–32.

15.1   Introduction

This last chapter is devoted to a small extract from a work by one of the most puzzling and awkward figures in the analytic tradition of philosophy of language. Ludwig Wittgenstein met and corresponded with Frege, and was taught by Russell. His first work, the *Tractatus Logico-Philosophicus*, adapted and refined many of their ideas on logic and language. It inspired the scientifically minded philosophers who made up the Vienna Circle, and who in turn had a profound influence on analytic philosophy, particularly in America.

Wittgenstein's later work, of which the *Philosophical Investigations* is the principal text, divides the English-speaking philosophical community. He is often dismissed by those who have a broadly scientific approach to philosophy, though he's read keenly by many of those who don't. This is partly to do with the style of his writing (though, of course, the style embodies something of his philosophy). The *Philosophical Investigations* is not organized systematically: it has no chapters and no simple sequence of thought; it is even disputed whether it contains arguments. Much of it has the form of a probing conversation of the author with himself: Wittgenstein raises a worry – often on behalf of a more traditional approach to philosophy – responds to it, responds to the response, and so on. It's often not clear which of the things which are said represent Wittgenstein's own view, and which represent views which Wittgenstein thinks need to be undermined. In this respect, the text asks to be read more like a literary work than a scientific treatise.

This makes Wittgenstein's later work difficult to deal with in an introductory way. In this chapter, I'll address that difficulty in two ways. First, I'll focus principally on just a short stretch of text. The *Philosophical Investigations* begins with a quotation from Augustine, which presents what seems to be a commonsense view of language. I'll look just at Wittgenstein's initial response to that quotation, up to the point where he seems to offer a simple explicit criticism of it, in § 32. And secondly, I'll look at two different kinds of interpretation of what Wittgenstein is doing here, neither of which can be squared with everything in the text. These two kinds of interpretation are not the only ones possible, and I'll present them in a simplified – even caricature – form. I choose them here because they both present Wittgenstein as standing in fundamental opposition to the mainstream of analytic philosophy of language. Why present Wittgenstein as opposed to the analytic mainstream? There are certainly interpretations of Wittgenstein which find no such clear-cut opposition.[1] I'll focus on a more antagonistic approach for two reasons. First, this is how he is often regarded by those who are quick to dismiss him (naturally, they think that his opposition is not significant). Secondly, it provides us with a way of raising questions about some of the most fundamental assumptions which are common to most of the analytic tradition.[2]

15.2 The Augustinian picture

In § 1 of the *Philosophical Investigations* Wittgenstein presents for considera-tion what purports to be a single view of language. The difficulty is that he

---

[1] John McDowell, for example, seems to see no tension between Wittgenstein and the core of Davidson's philosophy of language: see his two collections, *Mind, Value, and Reality* and *Meaning, Knowledge, and Reality* (both Cambridge, MA: Harvard University Press, 1998). And Crispin Wright seems to see Wittgenstein as a certain *kind* of analytic philosopher, offering positive theories of an analytic sort: see his *Rails to Infinity: Essays on Themes from Wittgenstein's* Philosophical Investigations (Cambridge, MA: Harvard University Press, 2001).

[2] I might add as a third reason that I think this opposition gets Wittgenstein right. Some think that many central analytic assumptions (made by Davidson, for example) are Wittgensteinian in spirit. In my view they can almost all be traced back to Frege, and don't really relate to what's new about Wittgenstein's later work.

presents it twice – once in the quoted words of Augustine, and once in his own gloss on that quotation. It's hard to see exactly what it is about the view attributed to Augustine which Wittgenstein thinks needs questioning.

In the passage Wittgenstein quotes, Augustine outlines a theory about the learning of language. He presents it as something remembered, but it can really be nothing more than a reconstruction of how he thinks he must have learned language – a reconstruction made in the light of some general theory. The theory seems to involve something like the following claims:

(A1) Before undertaking the task of learning language, the learner can:

(i)   Recognize as names the names which those around her use;
(ii) Identify objects in the environment as things fit to be named;
(iii) Tell what she herself thinks and feels.

(A2) The task of learning language consists in two stages:

(i) Discovering which objects are signified by which names;
(ii) Learning to make the right noises in order to be able to express what she thinks and feels.

Wittgenstein himself, however, finds something slightly different here. What he concentrates on initially is not a theory about the *learning* of language, but a theory of the nature of the meanings of words. What he says is this:

(B) These words, it seems to me, give us a particular picture of the essence of human language. It is this: the individual words in language name objects – sentences are combinations of such names. – In this picture of language we find the roots of the following idea: Every word has a meaning. This meaning is correlated with the word. It is the object for which the word stands.[3]

What is it, exactly, that Wittgenstein wants to question about all of this? The two kinds of interpretation I want to consider give different answers.

---

[3] *Philosophical Investigations*, § 1.

I'll call one the *Anti-Metaphysical* interpretation.[4] On this view, Wittgenstein's aim is to remove the temptation to offer metaphysical claims or theories – philosophical claims and theories about the way the world must be. This temptation can be seen in the very idea of finding an *essence* of language at all, so it is (B) which makes the problem really clear. One of the principal faults of the Augustinian picture, according to the anti-metaphysical interpretation, is that it's led by the temptation to look for essences into an unnecessary simplification of language. It's not that Augustine's view is altogether *false*: it's just a simplification.

I'll call the other kind of interpretation I'll consider the *Quasi-Kantian* interpretation.[5] On this view, Wittgenstein is concerned to reject, not *all* metaphysical claims or theories, but a particular kind of metaphysical theory. According to this interpretation, what is wrong with the Augustinian picture is that it presents a *false* metaphysical view – specifically a false view of the relation between language and reality. On this interpretation, what's wrong with Augustine's view can readily be found in the quotation from Augustine, or in (A1) and (A2). It can also be found in (B), of course, but on this view, the problematic feature of the view presented in (B) is the idea that the meaning of words is something *correlated* with them, like objects for which the words stand.

15.3 The Anti-Metaphysical interpretation

If Wittgenstein is right, the Augustinian view holds that all words really function as names. He supposes that the Augustinian view becomes

---

[4] What I call the 'Anti-Metaphysical' interpretation is, in some ways, a caricature of positions to be found in the literature. This is because this is the interpretation which is taken for granted by many of those who dismiss Wittgenstein rather quickly. Nevertheless, there are significant continuities between this caricature and the views of some real people who give pre-eminent emphasis to Wittgenstein's suggestion that traditional philosophy needs therapy (see *Philosophical Investigations*, § 133). P.M.S. Hacker comes close to endorsing this view in his chapter 'Philosophy', in H-J. Glock, ed., *Wittgenstein: A Critical Reader* (Oxford: Blackwell, 2001), pp. 322–47.

[5] An affinity between the later Wittgenstein and Kant is suggested (for example) by A.W. Moore, *Points of View* (Oxford: Oxford University Press, 1997), ch. 6; and more specifically in connection with grammar by Michael Forster, *Wittgenstein on the Arbitrariness of Grammar* (Princeton: Princeton University Press, 2004).

tempting if we think primarily of certain common nouns and proper names, with other words being largely forgotten. According to the Anti-Metaphysical view, what's wrong with this is that many words function in a quite different way. In the last paragraph of § 1, Wittgenstein imagines a rather meticulous use of a bit of language. Someone is sent shopping with a slip marked 'five red apples'. The shopkeeper finds a drawer marked 'apples', and a sample on a colour chart marked 'red', and then he counts his way through the positive whole numbers, putting something from the drawer which matches the colour sample for each number he calls, until he reaches five. The crucial word for the example is 'five'. We might be able to treat 'apple' and 'red' as names – they appear as labels, of a drawer and a colour sample, respectively – but it doesn't seem as if 'five' is here functioning like a name; and yet we can see from the explanation of the example that it is meaningful.

According to the Anti-Metaphysical view, the mistake made by the Augustinian is to try to understand language in abstraction from real life. Words have meaning, it seems, only in the context of the complex activities of our everyday experience. What Wittgenstein aims to do, on this interpretation, is to remind us of the everyday activities which give life to our words. For this he introduces a special term: *language-game*. As he defines the term initially, in § 7, a language-game is a game-like routine in which various procedures are simplified, with some features emphasized, by means of which children can be taught to use words. The term comes to have a larger application in Wittgenstein's text, however. Every kind of activity which provides a context for a word to have meaning, or in which a word has a particular kind of sense, comes to be regarded as a language-game. According to the Anti-Metaphysical view, the principal advice given by Wittgenstein to people tempted to offer metaphysical theories is to look carefully at the language-games in which words are used in real life. What we are interested in is the way in which words are actually used in these language-games.

This leads to the slogan often attributed to Wittgenstein: *meaning is use*. In fact, what Wittgenstein actually says is much more cautious than this (as, indeed, the Anti-Metaphysical interpretation would have predicted). What he says is this:

> For a *large* class of cases – though not for *all* – in which we employ the word 'meaning' it can be defined thus: the meaning of a word is its use in the language.[6]

This picks up precisely what Wittgenstein says about the word 'five' in the context of the shopping example at the end of § 1:

> But what is the meaning of the word 'five'? – No such thing was in question here, only how the word 'five' is used.

The suggestion seems to be that there doesn't need to be an *object* to be the meaning of the word: all that we need is for there to be a proper use of the word in the context of the kind of activity in which all language has its home.

In just the same way, on the Anti-Metaphysical view, we should not insist that there must be some unifying essence which fixes how a word should be used. To explain the point, Wittgenstein focuses on the very word which the idea of 'language-games' brings into focus for us: the word 'game'. What does the word 'game' mean? According to Wittgenstein, we should not expect to be able to define the word; there needn't be anything which all games have in common. After all, there are 'board-games, card-games, ball-games, Olympic games, and so on'.[7] These are called games, according to Wittgenstein, not because they all have some single feature in common, but because there are resemblances between them which are rather like the resemblances between different members of the same family.[8]

The general moral of Wittgenstein's work, according to the Anti-Metaphysical view, is that philosophical problems arise only when we forget about the real-life activities or language-games in which words are used.[9] If we paid more attention to these, we would not expect to find a unifying essence corresponding to every meaningful term, nor would we offer simplifying comprehensive accounts of language in general. This is the chief fault of the Augustinian view, according to the Anti-Metaphysical view. It is not that it's altogether wrong: it's just absurdly simplified. One

---

[6] § 43. I have restored the emphasis on 'all', which is present in the German, but missing in the published translation.

[7] § 66.   [8] § 67.

[9] Compare: 'For philosophical problems arise when language *goes on holiday*' (§ 38).

obvious case is generalized beyond what the actual facts can sustain, simply in order to provide some kind of unifying essence which might provide a metaphysical explanation of how language works.

If this is what's wrong with the Augustinian picture, we might expect there to be some situation for which the Augustinian picture is appropriate. § 2 seems to offer just such a situation: a primitive language-game involving two builders (imaginatively called 'A' and 'B'). One calls out a word – 'slab', 'block', or 'pillar' – and the other brings the appropriate bit of stone. This example is produced precisely as an example of 'a language for which the description given by Augustine is right'.[10] The mistake of the Augustinian seems to be like that of someone who offers the following definition of the notion of a game:

> A game consists in moving objects about on a surface according to certain rules …

To which the response seems to be:

> You seem to be thinking of board games, but there are others. You can make your definition correct by expressly restricting it to those games.[11]

The Anti-Metaphysical view makes Wittgenstein very much a precursor of Austin, whose work on speech acts we've already looked at (in chapter 12). There is, it seems, the same insistence on looking at language actually in operation in everyday life – in Austin's case, looking at the illocutionary acts which are performed when we use words. And there is an at least similar eye for detail and resistance to theory: recall how Austin began with an intuitive-seeming distinction between performative and constative utterances, and ended up being unable to define the difference. And, indeed, we can see a similar distinction in Wittgenstein between words and sentences, on the one hand, and particular uses of them, on the other. Wittgenstein is keen to insist that there are 'countless' different kinds of use of linguistic expressions.[12]

This doesn't make Wittgenstein just like Austin, however. Austin was surely aiming for something much more systematic than Wittgenstein was. When faced with the difficulty of defining the distinction between performative and constative utterances, Austin's reaction was to abandon

---

[10] § 2.   [11] § 3.   [12] § 23.

the distinction and to retreat to a general theory of speech acts. And Austin remained conservative about the meaning of words: he assumed it would be a matter of Sense and reference, in more or less orthodox Fregean style.

The reaction of many philosophers to Wittgenstein is one of irritation: this is likely to be a reaction to the Wittgenstein presented by the Anti-Metaphysical view. According to the Wittgenstein presented by the Anti-Metaphysical view, the kinds of systematic theories of language presented by most of the major philosophers in the analytic tradition are open to the charge of oversimplification. Frege, Russell, Quine, and Davidson all face this charge; and Kripke seems to be trying to avoid it, when he offers a 'picture', instead of a theory, of the way names work.[13]

One of the causes of this irritation is that the Anti-Metaphysical view seems to make philosophical criticism too *easy*. All we need to do, when someone attempts to provide some substantial theory of language, is to point to some oversimplification, or unrealistic abstraction, which is involved in it. And this, at least, surely gets Wittgenstein wrong. The *Philosophical Investigations* is not a record of a series of quick dismissals of too hastily systematic opponents. It offers a series of patient, imaginative, and probing diagnoses of the tendency to go astray philosophically – whatever, precisely, that might involve. Indeed, § 1 shows us an example of that itself. The account of the Augustinian view's conception of the meaning of words which appears in the second paragraph is one which is not just obvious from what is said in the first paragraph.

15.4 The Quasi-Kantian interpretation

A way of approaching the other kind of interpretation I want to consider – the Quasi-Kantian view – is to focus on the fact that Wittgenstein does not merely complain that the Augustinian view offers *some* account of 'the essence' of language: he seems to think that it's wrong in its particular choice of account. Specifically, it's wrong in thinking that all words function like *names*.

What is it that Wittgenstein is worried about here? What is involved in treating all words as names? Clearly it's not just a matter of grammar, in

---

[13] Kripke, *Naming and Necessity*, p. 93.

the ordinary sense. Here's what Wittgenstein thinks such a person will have in mind:

> If you describe the learning of language in this way you are, I believe, thinking primarily of nouns like 'table', 'chair', 'loaf', and of people's names, and only secondarily of the names of certain actions and properties; and of the remaining kinds of word as something that will take care of itself.[14]

This is a grammatically variegated list. Common nouns of concrete objects and proper names are themselves grammatically dissimilar. And Wittgenstein acknowledges that 'names' of actions and properties will seem to fit the model: these look as if they will be nominalizations of adjectives ('redness', 'kindness') and verbs ('action', 'walk', 'smile').

Moreover, in the shopping example which concludes § 1, it seems clear that the adjective 'red' is being treated as a name. In the first place, Wittgenstein's principal worry is not with fitting the word 'red', as it's used in this example, into the Augustinian model (although he is not entirely happy with it): his chief worry is over the word 'five'. And, secondly, the use of 'red' in § 1 seems to fit the conception of names which Wittgenstein suggests in § 15:

> Suppose that the tools A uses in building bear certain marks. When A shews his assistant such a mark, he brings the tool that has that mark on it.
> It is in this and more or less similar ways that a name means and is given to a thing. – It will often prove useful in philosophy to say to ourselves: naming something is like attaching a label to a thing.

What Wittgenstein imagines here seems not unlike the shopkeeper's use of the colour chart with the word 'red' in § 1. If that's right, then it seems that words of a wide variety of grammatical types can be treated as names, without ignoring the grammatical differences between them. And that's just as well, since Augustine himself was well aware (of course) of the differences between different grammatical categories.[15]

---

[14] § 1.

[15] For a generally positive view of Augustine on Language, see M. Burnyeat, 'Wittgenstein and Augustine *De Magistro*', *Proceedings of the Aristotelian Society*, Supplementary Volume, 61 (1987), pp. 1–24.

What is the important thing about names, then? What is the philosophical significance of the suggestion that it helps to think of naming as like attaching a label to a thing? Here's one suggestion: names can only be introduced when it is assumed that it's clear what *kind* of thing is being named. To use the label simile: we can only label something if we can take for granted what we are labelling. This kind of point seems to be made by Wittgenstein himself.[16] And that seems linked with the explicit criticism Wittgenstein makes of Augustine in § 32:

> And now, I think, we can say: Augustine describes the learning of human language as if the child came into a strange country and did not understand the language of the country; that is, as if it already had a language, only not this one.

This looks like a direct attack on a crucial assumption of the Augustinian picture:

(A1)(ii) Before undertaking the task of learning language, the learner can identify objects in the environment as things fit to be named.

This now looks as if it's the same as the assumption that all words work like names, or that the meaning of a word is an object which is correlated with the word.

If Wittgenstein thinks (A1)(ii) is false, as he seems to, it seems that he must hold something like the following view:

(W1) It is only possible to identify an object as something fit to be named from the point of view of the speaker of a language.

That is to say, it's only as a speaker of a language that someone can see something as being fit to be named. Now why should Wittgenstein accept (W1)? A natural suggestion is that he holds (W1) because he holds something like this:

(W2) The world itself does not come already divided into objects fit to be named.

---

[16] See, e.g., §§ 30 and 31.

The interpretation which I'm calling the Quasi-Kantian interpretation takes Wittgenstein to hold something like both (W1) and (W2).[17] (W1) and (W2) seem evidently to be metaphysical theses – claims of just the kind which the Anti-Metaphysical interpretation has him avoiding.

If this is what he thinks, then the notion of a language-game looks as if it will have a rather larger role to play than the one it is given on the Anti-Metaphysical interpretation. Very roughly, it seems that it will only be in the context of particular language-games that objects come to be defined as such. We might call on the analogy with chess which Wittgenstein makes in § 31 to help us here. It's only in the context of the rules of chess that there is such a thing as a king at all. In the same way, we might suggest, it's only in the context of the appropriate language-games that there are objects to be referred to at all. It will be the relevant language-games which generate the concepts which define the kinds of thing we can name.

If this is to be applied strictly, it will have to be applied even to those concepts for which the Augustinian model seems initially plausible: concepts of such things as tables, chairs, and loaves. We will have to say, for example, that what it is for something to be a table is determined by a whole series of activities in which the word 'table' is involved. These will be the language-games which give the word 'table' its meaning (or meanings). In this context, there will be a special point in calling language-games *games*. There will be two features of games which will be important. First, games involve rules. Language-games will provide, and be defined by, rules for using words in particular circumstances. What is involved in something being a table, for example, will then be fixed by the rules for using the word 'table' in the various circumstances in which that word can be used. Secondly, the rules of games are fluid and changeable; they are also, in a sense, arbitrary. The rules of chess define what it is to play chess; but there could have been a game with quite different rules, or whose rules included variations which might seem quite bizarre to us.

The rules for using words – the rules which are produced in the language-games involving those words – are called *grammar* by

---

[17] This interpretation counts as 'Quasi-Kantian' in virtue of a parallel with Kant's distinction between the way the world is as it is in itself – non-spatial, non-temporal, non-causal, containing neither objects nor properties – and the way the world is for a creature with a sensory faculty combined with a faculty of judgement.

Wittgenstein. This looks like an extension of the ordinary notion of grammar, but Wittgenstein means it to coincide with the ordinary notion in at least this respect: a violation of the rules for using a word produces something which is nonsense rather than false. The crucial point for our present purposes is that it seems that Wittgenstein held that grammar, in his sense, is arbitrary.[18] What this means is that the world itself doesn't justify grammar, in Wittgenstein's sense: that is, the world itself doesn't fix some particular range of concepts as the right ones.[19] Any number of different ranges of concepts can properly be deployed in dealing with the world.

This seems to allow the possibility, in principle, of there being ranges of concepts which are equally good at dealing with the world, but which are so radically different from one another that the concepts of one range cannot be translated in terms of the concepts of another range. It may be that this possibility is never realized in fact: it may be that everyone in fact speaks a language whose terms can be translated in the terms of every other language. Moreover, it may be that there are very broadly biological reasons why all human beings speak languages between which translation is possible. It may be that all human beings tend to see the same similarities, to have similar basic interests, and to be inclined to play similar language-games in similar circumstances. But this would not stop it being possible, in principle, for some creatures to speak a language which was perfectly good for dealing with their lives, but which could not be translated into any human language.

This view is at odds with the mainstream of analytic philosophy of language in a different way from that in which the view outlined in the Anti-Metaphysical interpretation is. In chapter 10, we found the following view at the heart of Quine's and Davidson's view of the importance of radical interpretation for the understanding of language:

(RT) Every fact about the meaning of any words in any language, which can be known at all, is available in principle to someone to whom those

---

[18] This idea occurs quite early in Wittgenstein's development. See, e.g., D. Lee, ed., *Wittgenstein's Lectures: Cambridge 1930–1932* (Oxford: Blackwell, 1980), p. 86. It is picked up in a remark put down for consideration in *Philosophical Investigations*, § 372.

[19] This is something which Wittgenstein emphasizes in something which appears in the so-called 'Part II' of the *Philosophical Investigations* (really later material intended to be incorporated into the main body of the work): see *Philosophical Investigations*, p. 195.

words are initially radically alien, who proceeds by means of the
methods of radical interpretation.

The fundamental idea here was that only two things could be needed to
get at the meaning of the words in any language: first, evidence which is in
principle available to anyone; and, secondly, rationality, in working from
that evidence in the construction of a theory. If the view attributed to
Wittgenstein by the Quasi-Kantian interpretation is correct, (RT) is false.
According to the view found by the Quasi-Kantian interpretation, the
meanings of words of two languages might be too different from one
another for interpretation of one in terms of the other to be possible.

How, then, could languages be learned? If the Quasi-Kantian interpretation is correct, there is a special significance to this remark from § 5 of the
Philosophical Investigations:

A child uses such primitive forms of language [as the shopping example in
§ 1] when it learns to talk. Here the teaching of language is not explanation,
but training.

If the Quasi-Kantian interpretation is right, this training must be of a
special kind. It cannot, for example, be a matter of making routine what
could, in principle, be discovered theoretically. It must be a matter of
engendering certain kinds of habit, rather as one might train a dog. It must
be something which looks, from the perspective of radical interpretation,
like a form of conditioning. On this view, the child, in learning language,
must be got to *do* certain things, as if instinctively, without question. It
must acquire certain dispositions and habits. Once it has the dispositions
and habits, the child can begin to reason about and question certain
features of the kinds of language it has learned to use, but it can only do
that once the basic framework provided by these new habits is in place.

There's another respect in which the view found by the Quasi-Kantian
interpretation seems bound to be at odds with the analytic tradition. This
is in down-playing the importance of semantics in general, and of
reference in particular. A semantic theory aims to explain how the
meaning of words contributes to the meaning of sentences. Since
Davidson, this has been done by trying to show how explicit *statements*
of the meaning of sentences can be derived from explicit statements of the
meaning of words. If what the Quasi-Kantian interpretation finds in

Wittgenstein is right, this is bound to have less significance than it initially seemed to. The orthodox view has been that language is meaningful in virtue of some correlation between language and something extra-linguistic. A statement of the meaning of a sentence, or of a word, might then be expected to be a statement of that correlation. Consider, for example, the following Davidsonian statement of the meaning of a predicate:

(sh*) The predicate 'x is a horse' is true of something if and only if that thing is a horse.

This is naturally thought to be an account of how the predicate 'x is a horse' relates to reality, and so to form part of a general account of how language relates to the world. Indeed, it is the assumption that the clauses of a semantic theory characterize, in part, the relation between language and the world which gives semantic theories much of their general significance. The same applies to the philosophical interest in theories of reference, which are standardly taken to be important precisely because of their role in explaining how language relates to the world. A Davidsonian statement of the reference of a name might look like this:

(sb*) The thing referred to by the name 'Bucephalus' = Bucephalus.

A full *theory* of reference would be an explanatory account of what has to be true for such a statement to be true. It would, in effect, provide something explanatory which could be inserted in place of the words 'referred to by' in statements of the same general form as (sb*).

The difficulty is that if what the Quasi-Kantian interpretation ascribes to Wittgenstein is correct, such statements of meaning and reference must fail to get to the heart of the relation between language and the world. An explicit *statement* of meaning or reference needs to use words to give the meaning or reference of the words it is aiming to explain. Thus, for example, the word 'horse' appears as the last word in (sh*) in order to characterize the meaning of the word 'horse' as it appears on the left of that statement. And 'Bucephalus' appears as the last word in (sb*) in order to characterize the reference of the name 'Bucephalus' as it appears before the identity sign. It doesn't matter that the *same* word is used on both the left and the right of such statements of meaning. Evidently *some* word will have to be used, if the meaning is to be stated explicitly, and that will be enough to create the difficulty. The difficulty is that statements of this kind can only help in explaining the relation between language and the world if the use of the words on the *right* of these statements – in giving the meaning and reference which our target words are being said to have – can be regarded as being related quite unproblematically to the world. If (Sh*) is to be regarded as an explanation of how the predicate '*x* is a horse' relates to the world, the relation between the *final* occurrence of 'horse' and the world must be regarded as unproblematic. Similarly, (sb*) can only be regarded as an explanation of how the name 'Bucephalus' relates to the world if relation between the *final* occurrence of the name in (sb*) is regarded as unproblematic. The relation between the words on the *right* in these statements of meaning, on the one hand, and the world, on the other, must be so unproblematic that it can be regarded as a mere correlation.

But that seems to assume exactly what (W2) denies – that the world itself comes divided up into objects fit to be referred to. In that case, if we accept (W2), we have to accept that the general philosophical significance of semantic theories is limited.

This point can be put together with the earlier point about the incompatibility of the view which the Quasi-Kantian interpretation finds in Wittgenstein with (RT). It looks as if the relation between language and the world is something which cannot be explained, according to this view. The formal reason is the one we've just been looking at. An explanation must be in words: explanations are linguistic. In that case the words of the explanation will have to be taken for granted. But this also relates directly to the reasoning which is involved in the Quasi-Kantian interpretation's rejection of (RT). If it were possible to *explain* how the words of a particular language relate to the world, it would be possible to use that explanation to characterize the meaning of those words, from the point of view of another language. This rejection of the possibility of explaining something as fundamental as the relation between words and the world is in itself likely to put the Wittgensteinian at odds with the mainstream of the analytic tradition. Indeed, it looks like a rejection of theoretical philosophy.

This is linked with the way in which the Quasi-Kantian interpretation explains Wittgenstein's apparent hostility to system: for example, his insistence that there need be nothing in common to all the things described by the same word. This need not be a general resistance to system. Instead it can be understood as an opposition to a particular *reason* for expecting that the use of words must be systematic: thinking that the shape of our concepts is justified or demanded by the nature of the world itself. On Wittgenstein's view (as the Quasi-Kantian interpretation has it), we possess the concepts we do as a result of a certain kind of training. That training will look like mere conditioning from the perspective of an outsider: that is to say, it will not be possible, from the outsider's point of view, to see the rationale behind the language-games which the trainee is initiated into. Since trying to find some unifying essence underlying a concept looks like an attempt to find just such a rationale, it's hardly surprising that Wittgenstein is hostile to the search for essences, even on the Quasi-Kantian interpretation.

It's less easy, however, for the Quasi-Kantian interpretation to explain Wittgenstein's first response to Augustine. What he says is that Augustine's error is to suppose that what holds only for a limited range of expressions applies to the whole of language. This in itself is consistent with the Quasi-Kantian interpretation: the mistake would be to suppose that naming could be the fundamental thing in language, since naming presupposes a framework of language-games which would define the kinds of thing to be named. But Wittgenstein goes further than that. He seems to suggest that there might be a complete language – the builders' language of § 2 – for which Augustine's account would be *correct*. And this is very hard to understand if the Quasi-Kantian interpretation is right.

It's also not easy for the Quasi-Kantian interpretation to make sense of some of the things which Wittgenstein says a little after the passages we're looking at, where he seems to show hostility to the idea of saying anything true or false in philosophy. The Quasi-Kantian interpretation represents Wittgenstein as holding a number of significant and disputable philosophical views – (W1) and (W2), in particular. How, then, are we to make sense of this remark? –

> If one tried to advance *theses* in philosophy, it would never be possible to debate them, because everyone would agree to them.[20]

---

[20] § 128.

Perhaps Wittgenstein is here imagining a future philosophy in which everything is clear. Or perhaps he is simply talking about a certain *level* of philosophy: the level at which one might say that something is demanded by, or incompatible with, the rules for using a certain word. It is certainly not obvious that the Quasi-Kantian interpretation can make sense of everything in the text.

15.5   Worries about these Wittgensteinian views

The principal worry about the views presented by the Anti-Metaphysical interpretation is simple: it's hard to make sense of doing any philosophy without holding some metaphysical views. Advocates of the kind of view ascribed to Wittgenstein on this interpretation may be tempted at this point to give an enriched meaning to the word 'metaphysical' – making it mean something like *supernatural*, for example. But metaphysics is both more modest and more pervasive than that: a metaphysical claim is just a claim about how the world must be. It remains a persistent challenge to an advocate of these views to motivate her position without adopting any metaphysical positions herself. Having made that point, I won't pursue the challenge here. Instead, I'll focus on two worries that naturally arise about the view attributed to Wittgenstein by the Quasi-Kantian interpretation.

The first worry is that Wittgenstein might seem to be a *relativist* of an objectionable kind. A relativist is someone who supposes that what is true or false is not true or false *absolutely*, but only relative to a particular culture or framework of concepts. The issue arises most clearly in connection with (W2), which the Quasi-Kantian interpretation attributes to Wittgenstein. (W2) seems to amount, in the end, to the claim that the concepts expressed by our words are not justified by the way the world is. In that case, as we have seen, it seems that there could be two ranges of concepts between which there could be no translation, even though both were equally good at dealing with the world. The worry is that certain views seem to become objectionably immune to criticism.

This worry is most obvious in the areas in which natural science is able to offer explanations, where previously appeal was made to some divinity. Thus, we are told, the ancient Greeks believed that lightning was thrown by Zeus, the father of the gods. Zeus, like the other gods, was portrayed in broadly human terms: eating and drinking, being happy and sad, angry and cheerful – and, notoriously, having affairs. Flashes of lightning were said to be thunderbolts thrown by his strong right arm, most notably when he was angry with people. Now we know, as we suppose, that lightning is an electrical discharge. It's a physical effect of physical causes. It can be explained by natural science. There is no need to appeal to the motives of some superhuman figure. It seems obvious that neither Zeus nor any of the other Olympian gods exists. It seems equally clear that the concepts deployed by contemporary natural science are better at dealing with the natural world than the concepts of ancient Greek religion.

Wittgenstein is famous – some would say notorious – for defending traditional religions against this kind of attack.[21] The defence can be summarized as follows. To think that the ancient Greek religion is disproved by modern natural science is to misunderstand the language-games involved in the practice of Greek religion. The idea that a human-like being produces lightning is not supposed to be anything like a hypothesis of natural science. It is therefore not a rival to the natural-scientific explanation, and cannot be refuted by it.

Is this kind of response convincing? It certainly seems fair to say that the idea that a human-like being produces lightning for recognizably human kinds of reasons is altogether different in kind from natural-scientific explanations. But for all that, many will feel that there is some kind of incompatibility between this ancient Greek religion and modern science. It seems hard to imagine someone engaging seriously with modern science and still believing in the ancient Greek religion. And if that's right, we might want to say that the two practices are not equally good. Someone engaged in modern science seems bound to think that there are no such beings as the ancient Greek gods, while there really is such a thing as electrical discharge.

A possible Wittgensteinian response might begin by acknowledging that anyone who held that the Greek gods and electrical discharge both existed would seem to have a belief in Greek religion rather different from that of the ancient Greeks themselves. To see Greek religion as unthreatened by natural science would require a revision of Greek

---

[21] See, e.g., his 'Remarks on Frazer's Golden Bough', in L. Wittgenstein, *Philosophical Occasions 1912-1951*, eds. J. Klagge and A. Nordmann (Indianapolis: Hackett, 1993), pp. 118-55, and L. Wittgenstein, *Lectures and Conversations on Aesthetics, Psychology and Religious Belief*, ed. C. Barrett (Oxford: Blackwell, 1966), pp. 53-72.

religion – understanding it differently from the way the Greeks themselves did. But this revision – a correction of the practice of the Greeks themselves – might be defended on Wittgensteinian grounds. It might be claimed, for example, that the ancient Greeks themselves misunderstood the language-games which constituted the practice of their own religion (for example, by thinking of their own religion as if it were – as we would put it – a kind of science).

The other natural worry about the view attributed to Wittgenstein by the Quasi-Kantian interpretation is that it is in some way *idealist*. An idealist holds that the nature of the world is somehow dependent on ways of thinking about or representing it. It contrasts with a *realist* view, which holds that the nature of the world is wholly independent of anything to do with thought or representation. As I have presented it, the Quasi-Kantian interpretation takes Wittgenstein to hold that the kinds of things we can name with our words are defined by the rules of the language-games involving those words. So there being such things as tables seems to depend upon aspects of the way we use words, and this looks idealist.

This position will attract objections of two sorts. First, it will seem objectionable to many just because it seems not to be realist. Realism strikes us as the natural view: it seems integral to the very notion of the world that the world is just *out there*, quite independent of anything to do with us or our practices. And, secondly, there will seem to be some internal tension within the kind of idealism which Wittgenstein is here taken to be endorsing. Remember (W2) again. (W2) seems to be saying something about how the world is *independently* of the way it might be thought of, or dealt with in various kinds of language-game. But that seems to presuppose a form of *realism*. How, then, can Wittgenstein coherently endorse a form of idealism?

There are two kinds of response which could be made to such objections. First, a Wittgensteinian might accept the charge of idealism and try to make the idealism palatable. It's not quite clear how this approach would deal with the fact that (W2) seems to undermine itself, on this interpretation: perhaps (W2) would be seen as something which one might initially be inclined to say, but which has to be abandoned once it is seen to be incompatible with the idealism which it encourages. The other response – which I myself prefer – would be to accept (W2), and agree that it's realist, and then argue that, despite first appearances, there is nothing really idealist about the conclusions which the Quasi-Kantian interpretation's Wittgenstein draws from them. The basic shape of this kind of response is clear: if the concepts which define the kinds of thing we name are created by the rules of the language-games which involve the relevant names, those concepts cannot be said simply to correspond to, or reflect, the way the world is in itself. If that's right, saying that these concepts, and the kinds defined by them, are dependent on something to do with the way we represent things is quite different from saying that the way the world is in itself is dependent on the way we represent things. Nevertheless, although the general shape of the view is clear enough, it's not yet clear that a convincing and consistent realist position can really be developed from it.

Further reading

There is a huge literature on Wittgenstein. There are two useful introductory books on the *Philosophical Investigations*: M. McGinn, *Wittgenstein and the Philosophical Investigations* (London: Routledge, 1997) and D. Stern, *Wittgenstein's Philosophical Investigations: An Introduction* (Cambridge: Cambridge University Press, 2004). A useful introduction to Wittgenstein's work as a whole is A. Kenny, *Wittgenstein*, 2nd edn (Oxford: Blackwell, 2005). A detailed commentary on the part of the *Philosophical Investigations* discussed in this chapter can be found in G. Baker and P. Hacker, *An Analytical Commentary on Wittgenstein's Philosophical Investigations* (Oxford: Blackwell, 1983). For a discussion of the opening pages of the *Philosophical Investigations*, see S. Mulhall, *Philosophical Myths of the Fall* (Princeton: Princeton University Press, 2005), ch. 3. B. Williams, 'Wittgenstein and Idealism', in his *Moral Luck* (Cambridge: Cambridge University Press, 1981), pp. 144–63, considers the question whether Wittgenstein was an idealist, in relation to both his early and his later work. P. Winch, *The Idea of a Social Science* (London: Routledge and Kegan Paul, 1958), presents a Wittgensteinian approach to (what we think of as) social sciences which has seemed to many to be relativist.

Glossary

a priori* / *a posteriori A truth is *a priori* if it can be known without recourse to experience, and *a posteriori* if it cannot. (Note that it's an epistemic distinction.)

concept Normally a component of thought; Frege uses the term to describe the functions which (in his system) predicates refer to.

constative A use or utterance whose business is to state something.

de re* / *de dicto Used initially in connection with necessity. *De re* (literally, about a thing) necessity is necessity concerning the nature of a thing itself, and is associated with essentialism (the view that things have essences or essential qualities). *De dicto* (literally, about a way of speaking) necessity is necessity which is really due to a way of describing or thinking of things. We might say, for example, that human beings are essentially mortal: this looks like a *de re* claim – that's how these beings are. But if we say that bachelors are necessarily unmarried, this seems to be a remark about the meaning of the word 'bachelor', rather than a statement about the people who happen to be bachelors (who could, in principle, get married); so it seems to be *de dicto* necessity. This distinction is carried over (largely because of Quine's treatment of a theoretical problem of his own) to the realm of psychology. There is a contrast between having a particular individual in mind and merely thinking general thoughts. In the former case, we might speak of *de re* thoughts; the latter case is then sometimes described as involving *de dicto* thought – simply, it seems, to preserve the traditional terms of a different distinction. The terms are also used to describe different kinds of linguistic *construction* in the areas of both necessity and thought – a relational construction in the case of *de re*, and a non-relational one in the case of *de dicto* – though this, again, seems to derive from a particular feature of Quine's philosophy.

declarative A *declarative* sentence is one which fits grammatically into such contexts as 'Simon says that ...' These are the sentences which are suitable, as far as grammar goes, for saying something true or false.

definite description A singular noun phrase which applies to exactly one person, often beginning with the definite article: e.g., 'the funniest woman in Britain', 'the present King of France'.

demonstrative A linguistic expression whose reference is fixed by some non-linguistic gesture of demonstration (such as pointing): e.g., 'this poodle', 'that drunkard'.

epistemic/epistemological 'Epistemic' means: to do with knowledge. The distinction between the *a priori* and the *a posteriori*, for example, is an epistemic distinction, whereas that between the necessary and the contingent is not. Epistemology is the study of the nature of knowledge, but sometimes 'epistemological' is used to mean *epistemic*.

essential/essence In a common modern usage, a quality is *essential* to something if the thing could not exist without that quality, and a thing's *essence* consists of its essential qualities. In a longer-standing use, still reflected in modern work (e.g., Kripke and Putnam on natural-kind terms), a thing's essence is not just what is essential to it in the modern sense; it is what makes that thing what it is.

extensional/intensional A context in which a sentence can be placed counts as *extensional* if any two sentences with the same truth-value, or any two singular terms which refer to the same object, or any two predicates which are true of the same things, can be swapped within it without affecting the truth-value of the whole. A context is *intensional* if it is not extensional.

indexical A linguistic expression whose reference depends upon the context of its utterance. The class is usually taken to include demonstratives, but will also include personal pronouns, such as 'I', 'you', 'we', and 'she', and other terms such as 'here' and 'now'. The tenses of verbs also display some indexicality.

metaphysical/ontological Metaphysics is the study of how the world must be, and ontology is the study of what there is, but there is a use of the terms 'metaphysical' and 'ontological' which makes them equivalent, and takes them to describe something which concerns how things are or must be *as opposed to* how they might be known.

modal To do with necessity and contingency.

natural-kind term A term which refers to a kind of thing or stuff, when the essence of the kind is determined by nature, rather than (for example) by human interests.

necessary/contingent What is *contingent* could have been otherwise (I could have got up later), but what is *necessary* could not (two plus two could not have been other than four).

object What a singular term refers to.

opaque/transparent As Quine uses the terms, a context is *referentially transparent* if singular terms which occur within it refer to objects and do nothing else, and is *referentially opaque* if singular terms which occur within it do not refer to the usual objects at all. In referentially transparent contexts, normally co-referring terms can be intersubstituted. There is a common use of the terms since Quine which takes 'transparent' to be equivalent to 'extensional' and 'opaque' to 'intensional'.

performative A performative utterance or use is one in which something is done (an act is performed).

possible world A way the whole universe might have been. A possible world has a complete history, from the beginning to the end of time. The notion of possible worlds is used to explain the logic of necessity and possibility in terms of quantification ('all' and 'some', etc.). What is necessary is true in *every* possible world; what is possible is true in *at least one* possible world; what is contingent is true in the actual world, but not in every possible world.

predicate What's left when one or more singular terms are knocked out of a sentence. I mark the gaps with variables. 'x is an idiot' is a one-place, or *monadic*, predicate (one gap where a singular term can go); 'x is stupider than y' is a two-place, or *dyadic*, predicate. There are also, of course, *triadic* (three-place) and, more generally, *polyadic* (many-place) predicates.

proposition A term of complicated history and use. Early in the analytic tradition it's often just the English translation of a use of the German word 'Satz', and means *declarative sentence*: this is the use generally involved in talk of the problem of the unity of the *proposition*. Otherwise (including at some points early in the analytic tradition) it is usually used to mean *what is said by a declarative sentence*, or else *the meaning of a declarative sentence*. In this later use, a proposition is equivalent to a Fregean Thought (if a Fregean theory is accepted) or to a combination of objects and qualities (if a Russellian theory is adopted).

propositional attitude A psychological state which can be described by means of a 'that'-clause ('She hopes that he will drown', 'He thinks that his horse will win', etc.). The term derives from a particular theory of what these states involve, namely: an *attitude* (expressed by a psychological verb like 'hope', 'think', 'wish', 'fear', etc.) towards a *proposition* (what is meant by a declarative sentence – expressed by a 'that'-clause).

propositional function Russell's term for a predicate (with the gaps marked by variables).

quality/property Etymologically, 'quality' means *what-it's-like-ness*; what corresponds to a one-place predicate (*stupidity* is the quality which corresponds to the predicate 'x is stupid'). In modern usage, 'property' is often equivalent to 'quality' (though in an older, originally Aristotelian, tradition, properties are qualities of a special kind, perhaps those which are distinctive of their objects).

reference/referent Originally and still paradigmatically, the relation between a singular term and the object it is correlated with: the singular term *refers* to the object. The term is used to translate the German term 'Bedeutung', which Frege widens to include also the relation between a predicate and the function it corresponds to, and the relation between a sentence and one of the truth-values. The *referent* of a term is the thing the term refers to.

relation What corresponds to a many-placed predicate (*being-to-the-left-of* corresponds to the predicate 'x is to the left of y').

rigid designator A term which designates the same object in every possible world (or, perhaps, more cautiously: in every possible world in which that object exists).

semantics The theoretical explanation of the way in which the meaning of sentences depends on the meaning of their parts. The term is sometimes also used to describe the study of the relation between language and the world. The term 'semantic' is used to describe anything relevant to meaning.

Sense Frege's technical term for a cognitive aspect of linguistic meaning, defined as what enables one to understand two linguistic expressions and not realize they have the same reference.

singular term An expression whose business is to refer to an individual thing; singular terms are naturally thought to include proper names ('Vincent', 'Paris'), some demonstrative expressions ('that ship', 'this water-pistol'), and some other indexical expressions ('I', 'you', 'she').

thought Frege uses this term to describe *what is thought* when someone thinks, rather than the thinking of it. On his theory a Thought is the Sense of a sentence.

truth-function/truth-functional A *truth-function* is a sentence connective of modern (Fregean) sentence logic, the formal counterpart to such English expressions as 'and', 'or', 'if ..., then –', 'it's not the case that', etc. They're called truth-functions because their meaning is defined in terms of the truth and falsity of the result of combining them with sentences, given just the truth and falsity of those sentences. A context in which a sentence may be placed counts as truth-functional if two sentences which have the same truth-value can be swapped within that context without affecting the truth-value of the whole.

truth-value There are classically two truth-values: *true* and *false*. In Frege's mature system, these are treated as objects: the True and the False.

Works cited

Alston, W., *Illocutionary Acts and Sentence Meaning* (Ithaca: Cornell University Press, 2000)

Aristotle, *De Interpretatione, in Categories and De Interpretatione*, trans. J. L. Ackrill (Oxford: Oxford University Press, 1963)

Ashworth, E. J., 'Locke on Language', *Canadian Journal of Philosophy*, 14 (1984), pp. 45–73

Austin, J. L., 'Truth', *Aristotelian Society Supplementary Volume*, 24 (1950), pp. 111–29

    How to do Things with Words, 2nd edn, J. O. Urmson and M. Sbisà, eds. (Oxford: Oxford University Press, 1975)

Avramides, A., 'Intention and Convention', in B. Hale and C. Wright, eds., *A Companion to the Philosophy of Language* (Oxford: Blackwell, 1997), pp. 60–86

    Meaning and Mind (Cambridge, MA: MIT Press, 1989)

Ayer, A. J., *Language, Truth and Logic* (London: Gollancz, 1936)

Ayers, M., *Locke: Epistemology and Ontology* (London: Routledge, 1991)

Bach, K., *Thought and Reference* (Oxford: Oxford University Press, 1987)

Bach, K., and Harnish, R. M., *Linguistic Communication and Speech Acts* (Cambridge, MA: MIT Press, 1979)

Baker, G. P., and Hacker, P. M. S., *An Analytical Commentary on Wittgenstein's Philosophical Investigations* (Oxford: Blackwell, 1983)

    Scepticism, Rules, and Language (Oxford: Blackwell, 1984)

Barker, S., *Renewing Meaning: A Speech-Act Theoretic Approach* (Oxford: Oxford University Press, 2004)

Barwise, J., and Perry, J., *Situations and Attitudes* (Cambridge, MA: MIT Press, 1983)

Beaney, M., ed., *The Frege Reader* (Oxford: Blackwell, 1997)

Bell, D., 'How "Russellian" was Frege?', *Mind*, 99 (1990), pp. 267–77

Blackburn, S., 'The Individual Strikes Back', *Synthèse*, 58 (1984), pp. 281–301

Boghossian, P., 'The Rule-Following Considerations', *Mind*, 98 (1989), pp. 507–49

Bradley, F. H., *Appearance and Reality* (Oxford: Oxford University Press, 1930)

Brown, J., 'Natural Kind Terms and Recognitional Capacities', *Mind*, 107 (1998), pp. 275–304

Burge, T., 'Belief *De Re*', *Journal of Philosophy*, 74 (1977), pp. 338–62

'Sinning Against Frege', *The Philosophical Review*, 88 (1979), pp. 398–432

'On Davidson's "Saying That"', in E. Lepore, ed., *Truth and Interpretation: Perspectives on the Philosophy of Donald Davidson*, pp. 190–208

Burnyeat, M., 'Wittgenstein and Augustine *De Magistro*', *Proceedings of the Aristotelian Society*, Supplementary Volume, 61 (1987), pp. 1–24

Carnap, R., *The Logical Structure of the World and Pseudoproblems in Philosophy*, trans. R. George (Berkeley: University of California Press, 1967)

'The Elimination of Metaphysics Through Logical Analysis of Language', in A. J. Ayer, ed., *Logical Positivism* (Glencoe, IL.: The Free Press), pp. 60–81

Chomsky, N., *Aspects of the Theory of Syntax* (Cambridge, MA: MIT Press, 1965)

'Language and Problems of Knowledge', in A. P., Martinich, ed., *Philosophy of Language*, 4th edn (Oxford: Oxford University Press, 2001), pp. 581–99

Church, A., 'On Carnap's Analysis of Statements of Assertion and Belief', *Analysis*, 10 (1950), pp. 97–9

Davidson, D., 'Theories of Meaning and Learnable Languages', in his *Inquiries into Truth and Interpretation*, pp. 3–16

'Truth and Meaning', in his *Inquiries into Truth and Interpretation* (Oxford: Oxford University Press, 1984), pp. 17–36

'On Saying That', in his *Inquiries into Truth and Interpretation*, pp. 93–108

'Radical Interpretation', in his *Inquiries into Truth and Interpretation* (Oxford: Oxford University Press, 1984), pp. 125–40

'Belief and the Basis of Meaning', in his *Inquiries into Truth and Interpretation*, pp. 141–54

'Thought and Talk', in his *Inquiries into Truth and Interpretation*, pp. 155–70

'On the Very Idea of a Conceptual Scheme', in his *Inquiries into Truth and Interpretation*, pp. 183–98

'Reply to Foster', in his *Inquiries into Truth and Interpretation*, pp. 171–80

'Reality without Reference', in his *Inquiries into Truth and Interpretation*, pp. 215–25

'The Inscrutability of Reference', in his *Inquiries into Truth and Interpretation*, pp. 227–41

'Moods and Performances', in his *Inquiries into Truth and Interpretation*, pp. 109–21

Inquiries into Truth and Interpretation (Oxford: Oxford University Press, 1984)

'A Nice Derangement of Epitaphs', in E. Lepore, ed., *Truth and Interpretation: Perspectives on the Philosophy of Donald Davidson*, pp. 433–46

Davidson, D., and Harman, G., eds., *Semantics of Natural Language* (Dordrecht: Reidel, 1972), pp. 253–355

Donnellan, K., 'Reference and Definite Descriptions', *Philosophical Review*, 75 (1966), pp. 281–304

Duhem, P., *The Aim and Structure of Physical Theory*, trans. P. Wiener (Princeton: Princeton University Press, 1954)

Dummett, M., *Frege: Philosophy of Language* (London: Duckworth, 1973);

'What is a Theory of Meaning? (I)', in his *The Seas of Language*, pp. 1–33

'What is a Theory of Meaning? (II)', in his *The Seas of Language*, pp. 34–93

The Seas of Language (Oxford: Clarendon Press, 1993)

Evans, G., 'The Causal Theory of Names', *Aristotelian Society Supplementary Volume*, 47 (1973), pp. 187–208; reprinted in his *Collected Papers*

'Understanding Demonstratives', in H. Parret and J. Bouveresse, eds., *Meaning and Understanding* (Berlin: de Gruyter, 1981), pp. 280–303; reprinted in his *Collected Papers*, pp. 291–321

The Varieties of Reference (Oxford: Oxford University Press, 1982)

Collected Papers (Oxford: Oxford University Press, 1985)

Evans, G., and McDowell, J., eds., *Truth and Meaning* (Oxford: Oxford University Press, 1976)

Evnine, S., *Donald Davidson* (Cambridge: Polity Press, 1991)

Fodor, J., *A Theory of Content* (Cambridge, MA: MIT Press, 1990)

Fogelin, R., *Wittgenstein*, 2nd edn (London: Routledge, 1987)

Føllesdal, D., 'Quine on Modality', in R. Gibson, ed., *The Cambridge Companion to Quine* (Cambridge: Cambridge University Press, 2004)

Forster, M., *Wittgenstein on the Arbitrariness of Grammar* (Princeton: Princeton University Press, 2004)

Frege, G., *Begriffsschrift, eine der arithmetischen nachgebildete Formalsprache des reinen Denkens* (Halle, 1879); trans. in full in J. van Heijenoort, ed., *From Frege to Gödel: A Source Book in Mathematical Logic, 1879–1931* (Cambridge, MA.: Harvard University Press, 1967)

The Foundations of Arithmetic, trans. J. L. Austin (Oxford: Blackwell, 1980)

'Über Sinn und Bedeutung', *Zeitung für Philosophie und philosophische Kritik*, 100 (1892), pp. 25–50; trans. as 'On Sense and Meaning' in G. Frege, *Collected Papers on Mathematics, Logic, and Philosophy*

'Function and Concept', in G. Frege, *Collected Papers on Mathematics, Logic, and Philosophy*

'On Concept and Object', in G. Frege, *Collected Papers on Mathematics, Logic, and Philosophy*

'Thoughts', in G. Frege *Collected Papers on Mathematics, Logic, and Philosophy*, ed. B. McGuinness (Oxford: Blackwell, 1984)

Philosophical and Mathematical Correspondence, eds. G. Gabriel, H. Hermes, F. Kambartel, C. Thiel, and A. Veraart, abridged for the English edn by B. McGunness (Oxford: Blackwell, 1980)

Posthumous Writings, eds. J. Hermes, F. Kambartel, and F. Kaulbach (Oxford: Blackwell, 1979)

Furth, M., 'Two Types of Denotation', in N. Rescher, ed., *Studies in Logical Theory* (Oxford: Blackwell, 1968), pp. 9–45

George, A., 'Whose Language is it Anyway? Some Notes on Idiolects', *Philosophical Quarterly*, 40 (1990), pp. 275–98

Gibson, M., *From Naming to Saying: The Unity of the Proposition* (Oxford: Blackwell, 2004)

Grice, H. P., 'Meaning', *The Philosophical Review*, 66 (1957), pp. 377–88; reprinted in his *Studies in the Ways of Words*

'Utterer's Meaning, Sentence-Meaning, and Word-Meaning', *Foundations of Language*, 4 (1968), pp. 225–42; reprinted in his *Studies in the Ways of Words*

'Utterer's Meaning and Intentions', *The Philosophical Review*, 78 (1969), pp. 147–77; reprinted in his *Studies in the Ways of Words*

'Meaning Revisited', in N.V. Smith, ed., *Mutual Knowledge* (New York: Academic Press, 1982), pp. 223–43; reprinted in his *Studies in the Ways of Words*

Studies in the Ways of Words (Cambridge, MA: Harvard University Press, 1989)

Grice, H.P., and Strawson, P.F., 'In Defense of a Dogma', *Philosophical Review*, 65 (1956), pp. 141–58

Hacker, P.M.S., 'Philosophy', in H-J. Glock, ed., *Wittgenstein: A Critical Reader* (Oxford: Blackwell, 2001), pp. 322–47

Hacking, I., *Why Does Language Matter to Philosophy?* (Cambridge: Cambridge University Press, 1975)

Harman, G., *Review of 'Meaning'*, by Stephen Schiffer, *Journal of Philosophy*, 71 (1974), pp. 224–9

Hobbes, T., *Leviathan*, ed. J. Plamenatz (Glasgow: Collins, 1962)

Hookway, C., *Quine* (Cambridge: Polity Press, 1988)

Hume, D., *A Treatise of Human Nature*, eds. D. and M. Norton (Oxford: Oxford University Press, 2000)

Enquiry concerning Human Understanding, in his *Enquiries concerning Human Understanding and concerning the Principles of Morals*, L.A. Selby-Bigge, ed., 3rd edn, P.H. Nidditch, ed. (Oxford: Oxford University Press, 1975)

Husserl, E., *Logical Investigations*, trans. J.N. Findlay (London: Routledge, 2001)

Kaplan, D.,'Afterthoughts', in J. Almog, J. Perry, and H. Wettstein, eds., *Themes from Kaplan* (Oxford: Oxford University Press, 1989), pp. 569–71

'Bob and Carol and Ted and Alice', in J. Hintikka, J. Moravcsik and P. Suppes, eds., *Approaches to Natural Language* (Dordrecht: Reidel, 1973), appendix x

Kenny, A., *Frege* (London: Penguin, 1995)

Wittgenstein, 2nd edn (Oxford: Blackwell, 2005)

Kirk, R., *Translation Determined* (Oxford: Oxford University Press, 1986)

Kretzmann, N., 'The Main Thesis of Locke's Semantic Theory', *Philosophical Review*, 77 (1968), pp. 175–96

Kripke, S., *Naming and Necessity*, 2nd edn (Oxford: Blackwell, 1980)

'Speaker's Reference and Semantic Reference', in P. French, T. Uehling, and H. Wettstein, eds., *Contemporary Perspectives in the Philosophy of Language* (Minneapolis: University of Minnesota Press, 1977), pp. 6–27

'A Puzzle about Belief', in A. Margalit, ed., *Meaning and Use* (Dordrecht: Reidel, 1979), pp. 239–83

Wittgenstein on Rules and Private Language (Oxford: Blackwell, 1982)

Larson, R., and Segal, G., *Knowledge of Meaning* (Cambridge, MA: MIT Press, 1995), pp. 56–62

Lepore, E., ed., *Truth and Interpretation: Perspectives on the Philosophy of Donald Davidson* (Oxford: Blackwell, 1986)

Lewis, D., *Convention* (Cambridge, MA: Harvard University Press, 1969)

'Radical Interpretation', *Synthèse*, 23 (1974), pp. 331–44

'Languages and Language', in K. Gunderson, ed., *Language, Mind and Knowledge* (Minneapolis: University of Minnesota Press, 1975), pp. 3–35

Loar, B., 'Two Theories of Meaning', in G. Evans and J. McDowell, eds., *Truth and Meaning*, pp. 138–61

Locke, J., *An Essay concerning Human Understanding*, ed. P. Nidditch (Oxford: Oxford University Press, 1975)

Lowe, E. J., *Locke on Human Understanding* (London: Routledge, 1995)

Lycan, W. *Philosophy of Language* (London: Routledge, 2000)

McCulloch, G., *The Game of the Name* (Oxford: Oxford University Press, 1989)

McDowell, J., 'De Re Senses', *Philosophical Quarterly*, 34 (1984), pp. 283–94; reprinted in his *Mind, Knowledge, and Reality*

'Wittgenstein on Following a Rule', *Synthèse*, 58 (1984), pp. 325–63

'Singular Thought and the Extent of Inner Space', in P. Pettit and J. McDowell, eds., *Subject, Thought, and Context* (Oxford: Oxford University Press, 1986), pp. 137–68; reprinted in his *Mind, Knowledge, and Reality*

Meaning, Knowledge, and Reality (Cambridge, MA: Harvard University Press, 1998)

Mind, Value, and Reality (Cambridge, MA: Harvard University Press, 1998)

McFetridge, I., 'Propositions and Davidson's Account of Indirect Discourse', *Proceedings of the Aristotelian Society*, 76 (1975), pp. 131–45

McGinn, C., *Wittgenstein on Meaning* (Oxford: Blackwell, 1984)

McGinn, M., *Wittgenstein and the Philosophical Investigations* (London: Routledge, 1997)

Mellor, D. H., 'Natural Kinds', *British Journal for the Philosophy of Science*, 28 (1977), pp. 299–312

Meinong, A., "On the Theory of Objects", in R. Chisholm, ed., *Realism and the Background of Phenomenology* (Glencoe, IL: Free Press, 1960), pp. 76–117

Mill, J. S., *A System of Logic* (London: Longmans, Green, Reader, and Dyer, 1875)

Miller, A., *Philosophy of Language* (London: UCL Press, 1998)

Miller, A., and Wright, C., eds., *Rule-Following and Meaning* (Chesham: Acumen, 2002)

Millikan, R. G., *Language, Thought, and Other Biological Categories* (Cambridge, MA: MIT Press, 1984)

'Truth Rules, Hoverflies, and the Kripke–Wittgenstein Paradox', *The Philosophical Review*, 99, 3. (1990), pp. 323–53

Moore, A. W., *Points of View* (Oxford: Oxford University Press, 1997)

Mulhall, S., *Philosophical Myths of the Fall* (Princeton: Princeton University Press, 2005)

Neale, S., *Descriptions* (Cambridge, MA: MIT Press, 1990)

Facing Facts (Oxford: Oxford University Press, 2001)

Noonan, H., *Frege: A Critical Introduction* (Cambridge: Polity Press, 2000)

Orenstein, A., *W. V. Quine* (Chesham: Acumen, 2002)

Perry, J., 'Frege on Demonstratives', *Philosophical Review*, 86 (1977), pp. 474–97

'The Problem of the Essential Indexical', *Noûs*, 13 (1979), pp. 3–21

Plantinga, A., *The Nature of Necessity* (Oxford: Oxford University Press, 1978)

Platts, M., *Ways of Meaning* (London: Routledge and Kegan Paul, 1979)

Putnam, H., 'Meaning and Reference', *Journal of Philosophy*, 70 (1973), pp. 699–711

'The Meaning of "Meaning"', in his *Mind, Language and Reality: Philosophical Papers Volume 2* (Cambridge: Cambridge University Press, 1975), pp. 215–71

Quine, W.V.O., 'Two Dogmas of Empiricism', in his *From a Logical Point of View*, pp. 20–46

'Reference and Modality', in his *From a Logical Point of View*

From a Logical Point of View, 2nd edn (New York: Harper and Row, 1961)

'Three Grades of Modal Involvement', reprinted in Quine's *The Ways of Paradox and Other Essays*, 2nd edn (Cambridge, MA: Harvard University Press, 1976)

'Quantifiers and Propositional Attitudes', *Journal of Philosophy*, 53 (1956), pp. 177–87

Word and Object (Cambridge, MA: MIT Press, 1960)

'Ontological Relativity', in his *Ontological Relativity and Other Essays* (New York: Columbia University Press, 1969), pp. 26–68

'On the Reasons for Indeterminacy of Translation', *Journal of Philosophy*, 67 (1970), pp. 178–83

Ramachandran, M., 'A Strawsonian Objection to Russell's Theory of Descriptions', *Analysis*, 53 (1993), pp. 209–12

Ramberg, B., *Donald Davidson's Philosophy of Language: An Introduction* (Oxford: Blackwell, 1989)

Recanati, F., *Meaning and Force: The Pragmatics of Performative Utterances* (Cambridge: Cambridge University Press, 1981)

Rumfitt, I., 'Content and Context: The Paratactic Theory Revisited and Revised', *Mind*, 102 (1993), pp. 429–54

Russell, B., *Principles of Mathematics*, 2nd edn (London: George Allen and Unwin, 1937)

'On Denoting', *Mind*, 14 (1905), pp. 479–93

Introduction to Mathematical Philosophy, 2nd edn (London: George Allen and Unwin, 1920)

'The Philosophy of Logical Atomism', *Monist*, 28 (1918) and 29 (1919), reprinted in B. Russell, *Logic and Knowledge*, ed. R. Marsh (London: George Allen and Unwin, 1956), pp. 177–281

'Mr Strawson on Referring', *Mind*, 66 (1957), pp. 387–8

Sainsbury, M., *Russell* (London: Routledge and Kegan Paul, 1979)

Salmon, N., *Frege's Puzzle* (Cambridge, MA: MIT Press, 1986)

Salmon, N., and Soames, S., eds., *Propositions and Attitudes* (Oxford: Oxford University Press, 1988)

Schiffer, S., *Meaning* (Oxford: Oxford University Press, 1972)

Remnants of Meaning (Cambridge, MA: MIT Press, 1987)

Searle, J., 'Proper Names', *Mind*, 67 (1958), pp. 166–73

Speech Acts (Cambridge: Cambridge University Press, 1969)

Sheridan, R.B., *The Rivals* (Oxford: Oxford University Press, 1968)

Smith, A. D., 'Rigidity and Scope', *Mind*, 93 (1984), pp. 177–93

'Natural Kind Terms: A Neo-Lockean Theory', *European Journal of Philosophy*, 13 (2005), pp. 70–88

Soames, S., *Beyond Rigidity: The Unfinished Semantic Agenda of Naming and Necessity* (Oxford: Oxford University Press, 2002)

Stern, D., *Wittgenstein's Philosophical Investigations: an Introduction* (Cambridge: Cambridge University Press, 2004)

Strawson, P. F., 'On Referring', *Mind*, 59 (1950), pp. 320–44; reprinted in his *Logico-Linguistic Papers*

'Intention and Convention in Speech Acts', *Philosophical Review*, 73 (1964), pp. 439–60; reprinted in his *Logico-Linguistic Papers*

'Meaning and Truth', in his *Logico-Linguistic Papers*, pp. 170–189

Logico-Linguistic Papers (London: Methuen, 1971), pp. 149–69

Tarski, A., 'The Concept of Truth in Formalized Languages', in his *Logic, Semantics, Metamathematics* (Oxford: Oxford University Press, 1956), pp. 152–278

'The Semantic Conception of Truth and the Foundations of Semantics', *Philosophy and Phenomenological Research*, 4 (1944), pp. 341–75

Wiggins, D., *Sameness and Substance Renewed* (Cambridge: Cambridge University Press, 2001)

'Languages as Social Objects', *Philosophy*, 72 (1997), pp. 499–524

Williams, B., 'Wittgenstein and Idealism', in his *Moral Luck* (Cambridge: Cambridge University Press, 1981), pp. 144–63

Winch, P., *The Idea of a Social Science* (London: Routledge and Kegan Paul, 1958)

'Understanding a Primitive Society', *American Philosophical Quarterly*, 1 (1964), 307–24

Wittgenstein, L., *Tractatus Logico-Philosophicus* (London: Routledge and Kegan Paul, 1922)

Wittgenstein's Lectures: Cambridge 1930–1932, ed. D. Lee (Oxford: Blackwell, 1980)

Philosophical Investigations, 3rd edn (Oxford: Blackwell, 2001)

On Certainty (Oxford: Blackwell, 1977)

'Remarks on Frazer's *Golden Bough*', in L. Wittgenstein, *Philosophical Occasions 1912–1951*, eds. J. Klagge and A. Nordmann (Indianapolis: Hackett, 1993), pp. 118–55

Lectures and Conversations on Aesthetics, Psychology and Religious Belief, ed. C. Barrett (Oxford: Blackwell, 1966), pp. 53–72

Wright, C., *Rails to Infinity: Essays on Themes from Wittgenstein's Philosophical Investigations* (Cambridge, MA: Harvard University Press, 2001)

Zalabardo, J., 'Kripke's Normativity Argument', *Canadian Journal of Philosophy*, 27 (1997), pp. 467–88

Zemach, E., 'Putnam's Theory on the Reference of Substance Terms', *Journal of Philosophy*, 73 (1976), pp. 116–27

Index